The

DEATH

of

CHARACTER

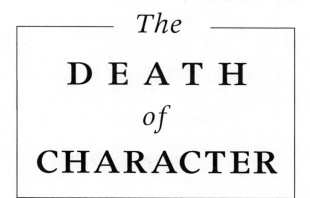

The
DEATH
of
CHARACTER

*Moral Education in an Age
Without Good or Evil*

JAMES DAVISON HUNTER

BASIC
BOOKS

A Member of the Perseus Books Group

Copyright ©2000 by James Davison Hunter

Published by Basic Books,
A Member of the Perseus Books Group

All rights reserved. Printed in the United States of America. No part of this book may be reproduced in any manner whatsoever without written permission except in the case of brief quotations embodied in critical articles and reviews. For information, address Basic Books, 387 Park Avenue South, New York, NY 10016-8810.

Library of Congress Cataloging-in-Publication Data
  The death of character : moral education in an age without good or evil / James Davison Hunter.
    p. cm.
  Includes bibliographical references and index.
  ISBN 0-465-04730-0 (cloth); ISBN 0-465-03177-3 (pbk.)
    1. Moral education—United States.   2. Character.   3. Education—Social Aspects—United States.   I. Title.
LC311 .H86 2000
370.11'4—dc21   00-027937

FIRST PAPERBACK EDITION

Designed by Jeff Williams

For
Stan Gaede
Robert Wuthnow
and
Peter L. Berger

"The issue is what sources can support our far-reaching moral commitments to benevolence and justice."

—*Charles Taylor,* Sources of the Self

CONTENTS

Part Four: Moral Education
After the Death of God

ACKNOWLEDGMENTS

As Alasdair MacIntyre once put it, every moral philosophy has a corresponding sociology. It is with this in mind that this book offers a sociological interpretation of the moral ideals and strategies we as Americans embrace and, in turn, seek to pass on to children. As it will become clear, the tragic nature of this endeavor is impossible to conceal. Though there are favorable things to say about our present circumstances and hopeful indications as well, overall the story that unfolds here is rather foreboding. This essay finds a context in Daniel Bell's discussion of the cultural contradictions of capitalism and elaborated by Friedrich Nietzsche, Philip Rieff, Christopher Lasch, Alasdair MacIntyre, and Charles Taylor. Is it any surprise that the cultural dynamics they describe play out in the moral culture we have created and are passing on to children? Understanding the ways this occurs may be useful for imagining truly creative responses to the dilemma we face.

In completing this undertaking I want to acknowledge with gratitude the assistance I received from Leslie Gunning, Beth Eck, Jeff Mullis, David Mills, Peter Ahn, Corey Widmer, Peter Becker, Brook Whitfield, Kimon Sargeant, Carol Sargeant, Josh Yates, Glenn Lucke, and the other graduate fellows of the Institute for Advanced Studies in Culture. I am very grateful for the careful research provided by Jim Nolan, my research assistant in the earliest years of this project, who, among many other essential tasks, helped with a preliminary draft of Chapter 3, and Daniel Johnson, whose statistical work was indispensable to the second Excursus. Joe Davis, Richard Horner, Steve Neumeister, Jenny Geddes, and Charles Mathewes have provided very helpful discussion and criticism of the matters I wrestled with in this text. I want to express special appreciation to Robert Loftin and Kristen Deede who, in successive turns, provided the most competent research assistance one could ever hope for. Their friendship, geniality, and goodwill have buoyed me far more than they know. In all of this, I want to acknowledge the support of the Institute for Advanced Studies in Culture, a research organization that provided the context and setting for much of the help I just mentioned. I also want to thank Jerry and Deana Parker, who generously provided special resources at a very crucial time to help me complete this project. At Basic Books I have benefited greatly by the patience and encouragement of John Donatich and the editorial insight and advice of Bill Frucht. I cannot thank them enough for hanging in there with me. I am grateful too for the moral support that a number of people have provided over the years—Tom Gilliam, David Turner, Bill and Helen Stehlin, and, most significantly, my parents, Robert and Rue Hunter. I want to thank my extraordinary children, Kirsten, Colin, and Whitney, for lovingly putting up with their distracted father over countless evenings, weekends, and summers. Finally, I want to thank my wife, partner, and best friend, Honey. With her, the span of forever just doesn't seem long enough.

Postmortem

Character is dead. Attempts to revive it will yield little. Its time has passed.

The irony is sharp. The death of character comes at a time when the call to "renew values" and to "restore character" is especially loud, persistent, universal—not to mention urgent. There is much more to this than political posturing. The summons to restore character is felt ardently and, as such, has translated into a myriad of well-intended efforts to revive it: in America, the reservoirs of hope for a renewal of public and private virtue are deep and full.

And one cannot deny it: character will be displayed from time to time in individual cases and within particular communities, exemplary manifestations among ordinary people, more often than not hidden from public attention. Even so, a restoration of character as a common feature within American society and a common trait of its people will not likely occur any time soon. The social and cultural conditions that make character possible are no longer present and no amount of political rhetoric, legal maneuvering, educational policy making, or money can change that reality. Its time has passed.

Character is formed in relation to convictions and is manifested in the capacity to abide by those convictions even in, *especially in*, the face of temptation. This being so, the demise of character begins with the destruction of creeds, the convictions, and the "god-terms" that made those creeds sacred to us and inviolable within us.

This destruction occurs simultaneously with the rise of "values." Values are truths that have been deprived of their commanding character. They are substitutes for revelation, imperatives that have dissolved into a range of possibilities. The very word "value" signifies the reduction of truth to utility, taboo to fashion, conviction to mere preference; all provisional, all exchangeable. Both values and "lifestyle"—a way of living that reflects the accumulation of one's values— bespeak a world in which nothing is sacred. Neither word carries the weight of conviction; the commitment to truths made sacred. Indeed, sacredness is conspicuous in its absence. There is nothing there that one need believe, commanding and demanding its due, for "truth" is but a matter of taste and temperament. Formed against a symbolic order made up of "values" and differing "lifestyles" is the Self—malleable, endlessly developing, consuming, realizing, actualizing, perfecting—but again, something less than character.[1]

The implications are simultaneously liberating and disturbing. There is unprecedented individual freedom that few would be willing to relinquish. But there is also a license that disparages self-restraint and responsibility toward others. This ambivalence is an inescapable feature of our time. They are fused inextricably.

Whatever benefits such a fluid and temporary moral universe may offer, they fail to lessen our dismay when we witness random and senseless violence; our outrage when we see open displays of corruption; our indignation when we observe a flouting of basic standards of decency; and our sadness as we watch callousness when compassion and mercy cry out. But why should we be surprised? When the self is stripped of moral anchoring, there is nothing to which the will is bound to submit, nothing innate to keep it in check. There is no compelling reason to be burdened by guilt. Dostoyevsky had it about right: everything becomes possible—every violence, every deed of corruption, every mockery of justice, every act of indifference—because there are no inhibiting truths. What is more, the indigenous moral institutions of our society that have long sustained those truths are fragile at best, irreparable at worst.

It is in the evacuation of depth, stability, and substance of culture where we witness the death of character.

NOT A NATURAL DEATH

The causes of our dilemma have little to do with individual moral failure. This is an important point. There are, in fact, larger historical forces at work. The demands of multinational capitalism, for example, have created conditions that make a coherent self that unites history, community, and subjectivity all but impossible. Pluralism and social mobility undermine the plausibility and coherence of personal beliefs and their capacity to provide a stable sense of meaning. A steady diet of the contemporary communications media and popular culture undermines our very sense of what is real. The list of factors contributing to this dilemma is formidable; against any of them, individuals have little control.

At the same time, character in America has not died a natural death. There has been an ironic and unintended complicity among the very people who have taken on the task of being its guardians and promoters. Some are clearly hucksters, hawking techniques of moral improvement for profit in the swarming and ever-changing values market. Most, however, are deeply earnest, motivated by a belief that if we just try hard enough and work together, we can somehow fill the values deficit that has occurred in our culture in recent decades. All offer quick bromides on how to raise a moral child, how to give your child great self-esteem, how to raise decent kids, and how to prepare kids for adolescence. But whether sincere or cynical, this mixed array of moral guardians in itself demonstrates our incapacity to cultivate the character for which they call. The end is the reduction of moral exhortation into a peddling of sterile abstractions, weary platitudes, and empty maxims: "Be cool, follow the rules," "Just say no," "Just say yes," "Just don't do it," "Do the right thing."

More ironic still is the complicity of the moral education establishment, those who have given their professional life to the task of moral education. Their mission, of course, is to bring about moral improvement in children and in society, to change the world for the better through moral instruction. As it is currently institutionalized, moral education does just the opposite of what it intends. In its present forms, it *undermines* the capacity to form the convictions upon which character must be based if it is to exist at all.

We say we want a renewal of character in our day but we don't really know what we ask for. To have a renewal of character is to have a renewal of a creedal order that constrains, limits, binds, obligates, and compels. This price is too high for us to pay. We want character but without unyielding conviction; we want strong morality but without the emotional burden of guilt or shame; we want virtue but without particular moral justifications that invariably offend; we want good without having to name evil; we want decency without the authority to insist upon it; we want moral community without any limitations to personal freedom. In short, we want what we cannot possibly have on the terms that we want it.

—— *Part 1* ——

INTRODUCTION

1

The Moral Lives
of Children and the
Moral Life of the Nation

There is much talk these days about the character of America and its people. A great deal of it is laced with anxiety.

Children, inevitably, are the centerpiece of these discussions. It is not just that children figure so prominently in the various measures of social decline—violent crime, drug use, illegitimacy, and so on. The reason most often given is the overused cliché that "children are the future."

This explanation is certainly true, but it is also banal and incomplete.

Children are indeed a symbol of the nation's uncertain future, but we should not imagine that altruism on their behalf, or even concern for society's future, animates this discussion. One need not listen very long to realize that children have become a code for speaking about ourselves; a linguistic device through which we talk about our own desires, commitments, and ideals, and the world we wish to create. Young people thus get caught in a tug of war between adults who have contending ideas about "what is really in their best interest." When this happens, they become one more ideological weapon used on behalf of competing visions of America's future direction; a tool with which competing parties and interest groups leverage political power. In claiming to put children first, we often place them last—or at least subordinate to ideology.

Still, we all share an awareness that profound change is taking place in our society and that children reflect, promote, and bear the consequences of that change. And so it is no surprise that nearly everyone in America acknowledges the need for "values education." Polls show that about 85 percent of all public school parents want moral values taught in school; about 70 percent want education to develop strict standards of "right and wrong." It is understandable, then, that the call for moral education finds a large and receptive audience. Yet the massive billion-dollar "values industry" that has emerged in response is not just a sign of the demand that exists, it is also a measure of the intensity of our fear.

Most of this industry is oriented toward children. Its premise is simple enough: if a tide of moral decadence is overtaking American society, then we must stem that tide by cultivating virtue and character among its people, especially among young people. To this end, we have invested much money and an extraordinary expenditure of human energy—in books, articles, journals, professional associations, congressional committees, legislative action, and so on. Though conservatives tend to be more vocal about the problem, the enterprise is by no means their exclusive domain. Moderates and liberals have claimed an equal stake in the effort. And this values industry is merely one part of a conglomerate of interests, activities, and institutions given to the moral development of children and the strengthening of the moral character of citizens more broadly.

CHARACTER MATTERS

Does character really matter?

The collective wisdom of the ages would say it matters a great deal. In both classical and biblical cultures—civilizations that have been so deeply formative to our own—people well understood there to be a direct association between the character of individuals and the well-being of the society as a whole. Individual character was essential to decency, order, and justice within public life. Without it, hardship was not far off.

The matter of character and social welfare was especially consequential in the case of rulers in both biblical and classical civilizations. As the wisdom writer wrote, "when the righteous are in power, the people rejoice, but they groan when the wicked hold office."[1] Indeed, much of the history of the ancient Hebrews can be told as a story of blessing for faithfulness to God—abiding by God's standard of holiness—and punishment for abandoning those standards. "See, I am setting before you today a blessing and a curse—the blessing if you obey the commands of the Lord your God that I am giving you today; the curse if you disobey the commands of the Lord your God and turn from the way that I command you today by following other gods, which you have not known."[2] Due to the intervention of such faithful witnesses as Moses and Joshua, God brought the children of Israel into the promised land, driving out or destroying their enemies. Yet when they were disobedient, as when they created and worshipped the golden calf, God punished. Under the righteous leadership of the Judges—Othniel, Ehud, Deborah, Gideon, Tola, and Samson—Israel would enjoy long stretches of peace and prosperity. At the death of each of the Judges, however, Israel reverted to idolatry and immorality and the nation suffered for it—until a new Judge was chosen. Under such kings as David, Solomon, Asa, Jehoshaphat, and Josiah, Israel enjoyed good fortune. Yet due to the defiance of Jeroboam, Reheboam, Baasha, Elah, Zimri, Ahab, Jehoram, and Ahaziah, the ancient Jews suffered. The same story is told through the witness of the prophets Isaiah, Jeremiah, Ezekiel, Joel, Amos, Jonah, Nahum, and Zechariah. When Israel reflected the justice and holiness of God's character in its collective life, it was blessed; when it rebelled, the nation was disciplined.

The association between individual character and collective well-being was equally clear to the ancient Greek philosophers. In the *Republic,* Plato held up character as *the* defining qualification of the ruling class. This was for the simple reason that rulers with character were "most likely to devote their lives to doing what they judged to be in the interest of the community." Social disintegration was inevitable if rulers failed in this regard. As Plato put it, "the community suffers nothing very terrible if its cobblers are bad and become degenerate and pretentious; but if the Guardians of the laws and state, who alone have the opportunity to bring it good government and prosperity become a mere sham, then clearly it is completely ruined."[3]

This varied but powerful legacy framed the sensibilities of the Enlightenment intellectuals so influential to the political radicals intent on overthrowing the *ancien régime.* The French philosopher Montesquieu, for example, reiterated the case to his generation and those that followed when he observed that "the corruption of each government almost always begins with that of its principles."[4] Nowhere was this more true than in a democratic regime. In his monumental *L'Esprit des Lois* in 1748, Montesquieu reasoned that "there need not be much integrity for a monarch or despotic government to maintain or sustain itself." In these cases, the power of the prince through the laws he imposed was sufficient to maintain social order. However, in a popular state, power as raw as this was not enough. Rather, the essential ingredient for true justice and order was virtue. Its absence in such regimes, he believed, would be catastrophic. "When that virtue ceases," he wrote, "ambition enters those hearts that can admit it and avarice enters them all."[5]

The American revolutionaries, locating sovereignty not in a monarch or a government but in the people, found the need for character residing there too. They saw strength of character as essential to the vitality of their experiment in democracy. "The steady character of our countrymen," Thomas Jefferson wrote in 1801, "is a rock to which we may safely moor."[6] The significance he gave to people's character was an echo of all he knew from the lessons of history. In his own words, "it is the manners and spirit of a people which preserve a republic in vigor. A degeneracy in these is a canker which soon eats to the heart of its laws and constitution."[7] James Madison was of a similar conviction. "Is there no virtue among us?" he asked. "If there be not, we are in a wretched situation. No theoretical checks—no form of Government, can render us secure. To suppose that any form of Government will secure liberty or happiness without any form of virtue in the people, is a chimerical idea."[8] For Jefferson and Madison, this was a basic article of democratic faith. Citizens should "be encouraged in habits of virtue and deterred from those of vice by the dread of punishments, proportioned indeed, but irremissible." Such were "the inculcations necessary to render the people a sure basis for the structure of order and good government."[9] Two generations later, Alexis de Tocqueville toured the American countryside and discovered that the hopes of the American founders had been provisionally realized—virtue was, in fact, central to the vitality of American democratic life. "These habits of restraint," he said, "are found again in political society and singularly favor the tranquillity of the people as well as the durability of the institutions they have adopted."[10] Yet he too understood the precarious constitution of embodied virtue: "How could society escape destruction if, when political ties are relaxed, moral ties are not tightened?"[11]

It is not surprising that we trace the problems we see today to a weakening of moral commitment so central to character. History and philosophy both suggest to us that the flourishing of character rooted in elevated virtues is essential to justice in human affairs; its absence, a measure of corruption and a portent of social and political collapse, especially in a democracy. The importance of character is a part of the moral imagination we Americans have inherited, a sensibility reinforced by the lessons of history. It is this sensibility that continues to frame our understanding of character today. Commentators abound who catalog the wide range of public problems in the contemporary world "as arising out of a defect of character formation."[12] Character matters, we believe, because without it, trust, justice, freedom, community, and stability are probably impossible.

CHARACTER AND THE GOOD SOCIETY

However one may view the present state of America, the point on which nearly everyone agrees is that American culture *is* changing in profound and often unsettling ways and that morality and character have something to do with it. How, then, are we to understand these changes? How does character fit in?

This question is as old as social science itself and it remains central to its mission. The great French social philosopher of the late nineteenth century, Emile Durkheim, was one of many who made this his life's passion. What, he asked, are the terms by which life—individual and collective, public and private—will be ordered and sustained in a world changing so rapidly? Particularly under the conditions of the modern and now "postmodern" world, is a society that is merely decent, not to mention just, even possible? If so, how and on what terms?

In our time, Durkheim's passion has become everyone's passion. We are restless because the questions are not merely academic. The stakes are tangible, immediate, and consequential.

This book stands in this tradition of inquiry: what are the terms by which American society will be ordered and sustained? After all our effort to make a good society, what are the consequences of our actions—intended or unintended—for individuals and communities alike?

The Demise of Character Within the Larger Dynamics of Society and History

At one level, the passing of character in our day is a consequence of larger, impersonal forces of history within our particular society, in which any one individual is mostly a passive participant. The term "character," as Warren Sussman has argued, achieved its greatest currency in America in the nineteenth century.[13] It was frequently associated with words like "honor," "reputation," "integrity," "manners," "golden deeds," "duty," "citizenship," and, not least, "manhood." Character was always related to an explicitly moral standard of conduct, oriented toward work, building, expanding, achieving, and sacrifice on behalf of a larger good—all those "producer values" embraced within Max Weber's famous phrase, "the Protestant ethic."

But as the American economy began to shift from a focus on industrial production to one of mass consumption in the early decades of the twentieth century, the psychological and ethical requirements placed upon an individual began to change as well. With growing abundance, more emphasis could be placed upon accumulation, leisure, and the cultivation of personal preferences. While the word "character" did not disappear, an alternative vision of the self emerged. This vision was captured by the word "personality"—a word that first appeared in the late eighteenth century but only gained wide currency in the early twentieth. The concept of personality reflected a self no longer defined by austerity but by emancipation for the purposes of expression, fulfillment, and gratification. Here too the social role reflected in the word "personality" shifted from achievement to performance. The advice manuals so popular among the middle classes emphasized poise, charm, appearance, even voice control—all given to the task of impressing and influencing others. In a culture of character, Sussman argued, the public demanded a correlation between achievement and fame; in the emerging culture of personality, that requirement was absent.

In sum, changing ideas of the self reflect changing social structures, structures that impose different requirements upon the role and presentation of the self. The older ideas of the self surrounding the character ideal suited the personal and social needs of an older political economy; the newer ideas reflected in the concept of personality emerged because they better fit the demands of a developing consumer society.

Character and Moral Imagination

But there is much more to be said about all of this. A discussion of character is not only about the kind of self produced in a particular kind of society but about the kind of moral understandings and moral commitments that are possible. Under present historical circumstances, what are the frameworks of our moral imagination? What are the vistas of our moral horizon, and how have they changed? To seek a good society is first a matter of what can be morally envisioned. Only then is it a matter of what can be realized within social institutions and in the lives of real people. To address this matter, then, we must go beyond a discussion of political economy and its modal types of selves to an examination of the changing nature of the moral culture—to the content of moral understanding in contemporary American society, the way it is produced and passed on to succeeding generations.

THE ELEMENTARY FORMS OF THE MORAL LIFE: THE ARGUMENT IN BRIEF

On the face of it, these questions are rather vague; too vague, I think, to elicit a constructive answer. So for analytical purposes, I will focus on a particular element of the question that is especially amenable to practical investigation, namely, an examination of the moral instruction of children. I concentrate on children and the lessons they are taught for reasons suggested by Durkheim himself. In brief, he argued that by examining a phenomenon at its incipient stages of development, one has the opportunity to learn about the phenomenon as a more complex reality. So it is, I would contend, with moral development and moral instruction—the entire endeavor to cultivate character and its attending virtues within succeeding generations. By looking carefully at the ways in which we mediate moral understanding to children, we may learn much about the kind of society we live in and will pass on to future generations. The point bears emphasis. My concern with moral education is not because of any relationship it may have on the development of morality in young people. In fact, as we will see, most moral education programs are astonishingly ineffective at this level. Rather, the significance of moral education is found in its articulation of the moral culture we adults idealize. It is a mirror of the moral culture we prize and thus seek to pass on to succeeding generations.

The Paradox of Inclusion

The heart of our inquiry is *character, its attending virtues, and their cultivation.* We say to ourselves, if we only reach our children while they are young, establish character early on, we can meet the present challenge; we only need to educate our children better. This reasoning is not exceptional. The institutions that educate, schools not least among them, have self-consciously taken on this responsibility for generations.

The problem is that schools—and not just schools, but other institutions that mediate moral understanding to children—have become part of the problem. Indeed, the argument of this book is that for all of our genuine and abiding concern with the moral life of children and the moral life of the nation, the strategies we have devised aggravate rather than ameliorate the problem. Rather than restore character and its attending moral ideals, they are complicit in destroying them.

How can this be?

Consider the circumstances in which we find ourselves. We Americans see all around us the fragmentation of our public life, our increasing inability to speak to each other through a common moral vocabulary, the emptying loss of an *unum* holding together a complex plurality of people and cultures. Against this we feel a powerful urge to establish some manner of cohesiveness in the morality we pass on to children and a stability in the character we seek to build within them. Yet this is not just a private affair. It is a social task that takes place in public. It requires cooperation. Thus we strive *to be inclusive*, taking great pains not to offend anyone by imposing beliefs and commitments that might make people "uncomfortable." This requirement of inclusiveness and civility is reinforced by the dominant educational establishment and the state through their policies of nondiscrimination.

This tension between accommodating diversity in public life and establishing a working agreement in our moral life is a defining feature of our national life; indeed, our collective history. *The problem is where our long-standing aspiration to sustain some inclusive moral order now leads us.* Three broad strategies have evolved in response to this conundrum.

The Psychological Strategy

The first strategy is a pedagogy based upon *shared method*, namely, the ethical neutrality of secular psychology. Its working assumption is that all of us possess an innate capacity for moral goodness; character resides within each of us, largely independent of the relationships we have or the communities into which we are born. These endowments only need to be coaxed out and developed within the personality. Importantly, within the psychological strategy, the tools for understanding moral development have become the means by which morality is to be imparted. Because it grounds much of its perspective in the insights of developmental and educational psychology, it operates with the pretension of scientific objectivity. Its appeal is the fantasy of political and religious neutrality. Its conceit is that it benefits everyone and it offends no one.

The Neoclassical Strategy

The neoclassical strategy advocates a pedagogy based upon *shared virtues*, namely the classic virtues of Western civilization. Both biblical and humanistic in origin, the neoclassical strategy articulates moral ideals that have been distilled through the generations: honesty, integrity, perseverance, tolerance, and so on. Its claim to universality is based upon the observation that these virtues represent the most esteemed attributes of our civilization, agreed upon and firmly established through the ages. It is their endurance over time that makes these virtues exemplary. Here, though, apart from the recognition of the potential for virtuous behavior, no assumption is made about the native capacity for individuals to exemplify these qualities. Quite the opposite. Rather, the virtues must be explicitly cultivated.

The Communitarian Strategy

A third strategy for responding to the need for an inclusive moral vocabulary is a pedagogy based on *shared experiences*, namely experiences that come from life together. The communitarian strategy is distinct in its recognition that the practical routines in social life influence the formation of moral understanding. The most pragmatic of the three, this strategy emphasizes the formative character of strong civic institutions, such as schools, local government, and philanthropic activity in generating an ethic of cooperation. It grounds its claims to inclusivity and universality in the ideals of democratic life and social consensus.

*   *   *

These strategies are not always at odds with each other. Indeed, in practice many of the distinctions between them disappear altogether. Even so, at points they define approaches to the moral life that are mutually exclusive.

Of the three approaches, the psychological strategy is especially noteworthy because it is the dominant strategy within the educational establishment. The other two strategies represent, in part, a backlash to the dominant psychological model. Though they all claim to represent ideals of democratic society, each strategy has partisan political ramifications—the psychological typically appeals to liberals; the neoclassical to conservatives and neoconservatives; the communitarian to neoliberals and social democrats.

The partisan temperament of these strategies is not, in itself, problematic. What is problematic is that *none* of these strategies in theory or in practice is adequate to the task they set for themselves. Why? Morality is *always* situated—historically situated in the narrative flow of collective memory and aspiration, socially situated within distinct communities, and culturally situated within particular structures of moral reasoning and practice. Character is similarly situated. It develops in relation to moral convictions defined by specific moral, philosophical, or religious truths. Far from being free-floating abstractions, these traditions of moral reasoning are fixed in social habit and routine within social groups and communities. Grounded in this way, ethical ideals carry moral authority. Thus, *it is the concrete circumstances situating moral understanding that finally animate character and make it resilient.*

The problem?

In different ways, *all* of these strategies deny or downplay the particularity that is central to moral reflection and engagement and decisive to character development. I will explain more fully later in the book, but for now let me summarize the basic argument. Given its emphasis on therapeutic processes, the psychological strategy tends to dismiss (often with ridicule) the idea that there is any content-filled moral agenda we should pass on to succeeding generations. The task, rather, is to give children the wherewithal to sort out the vast number of competing moral claims that confront them. At the same time, the psychological strategy discounts the importance of binding social relationships and historically embedded obligations in reinforcing moral commitments within the individual. Not least, it provides no place for philosophical, ethical, or religious justification in shaping moral understanding or character itself. Within the psychological strategy, the moral individual envisioned is one who somehow transcends time, space, relationships, and culture altogether but serves some thin notions of the common good when he or she freely chooses.

The communitarian strategy does emphasize the way in which concrete social experience frames our moral understanding, but no place is given for the encumbrances of shared ideals, sacred obligations, and collective memories. Here too the moral content of specific traditions tends to be downplayed, ignored, rejected in favor of an ideal of community that, more often than not, resembles the welfare state.

The neoclassical strategy, by contrast, does insist upon moral content—often referred to as "traditional values" or "family values." Moreover, it gives homage to the Judeo-Christian tradition as a source of that moral reflection. The problem is that in the rhetoric of most of the advocates of this strategy, the terms and phrases like "traditional values," "family values," or "Judeo-Christian tradition" are political slogans more than they are creeds, a partisan rallying cry more than a set of convictions. Indeed, there is no one set of beliefs one can call "Judeo-Christian"; what is called "the Judeo-Christian tradition" consists of numerous and often opposing creeds whose differences the neoclassicists gloss over. In this strategy as well there is a denial of the concrete and complex particularity in the way morality and character are situated.

The problem is this: culturally speaking, *particularity is inherently exclusive.* It is socially awkward, potentially volatile, offensive to our cosmopolitan sensibilities. By its very nature it cuts against the grain of our dominant code of inclusivity and civility. In our quest to be inclusive and tolerant of particularity, we naturally undermine it. When the particular cultures of conviction are undermined and the structures they inhabit are weakened, the possibility of character itself becomes dubious. By now, the moral vocabularies available to us are so inclusive that nearly all particularity has been evacuated.

What is more, this all takes place in a context in which the most durable normative assumptions embedded within our civilization—what scholars call "habitus"—have sustained a pervasive dissolution. In other words, the social and normative environment that makes our inherited moral vocabularies intelligible and inspiring has weakened, far more than we care to admit.

In this setting, all three strategies to cultivate moral understanding and character leave us with little more than vacuous platitudes, lacking any morally compelling logic and emptied of binding moral authority.

Consider the problem in the terms Charles Taylor provides in this book's epigraph. *What, he asked, are the sources that can support our far-reaching moral commitments to benevolence and justice?* It is not that these strategies are totally and equally problematic in response to this question. Rather, it is that all of them—the best of them—are limited from the outset. Whatever other advantages they may have, they all reject or downplay the concrete and particular moral communites that define the parameters of benevolence and justice, that make benevolence and justice common features of the social order.

This, alas, is the bind we are in: we want the flower of moral seriousness to blossom, but we have pulled the plant up by its roots.

* * *

The problem, then, is not psychological. The issue is not some mental or emotional inability to mature morally. Children today are innately as capable of developing character as they ever were in the past. The problem, rather, is sociological and historical. To talk about character is inevitably to talk about the cultural and institutional conditions that allow for its cultivation in children and its maintenance in adults. The death of character, therefore, is finally about the disintegration of these cultural and institutional conditions.

Under the present historical circumstances, the death of character would seem inevitable. Character is a relic of another age; it becomes increasingly curious, even odd, as the moral distinctiveness of particular communities and particular traditions fades into memory.

Yet even against the tendencies of fragmentation in our public discourse and toward homogenization in our moral communities, the residue of moral particularity still makes something of a difference. Evidence from recent research suggests that, even now, the sanctions rooted in specific creeds and specific moral communities (or the lack thereof) remain somewhat consequential for the moral lives of children.

Even here, though, one sees how the workings of the culture flatten out the distinctives that make a difference.

2

Character and Culture

The first task is to rescue the concept of character—indeed the entire lexicon of moral understanding—from the psychologists who presently frame popular discussion of the topic and whose guild jealously guards it.[1]

Character is not, as the psychologist would have it, solitary, autonomous, unconstrained; merely a set of traits within a unique and unencumbered personality. Character is very much social in its constitution. It is inseparable from the culture within which it is found and formed. In significant ways, character reflects, even incarnates, the moral culture. This is not to deny a psychological dimension to character and its formation, of course, but one must go further. Character is at least as much a function of the social order as it is a manifestation of the individual person. For this reason, it is impossible to speak of character—or its death—without also speaking of the larger moral culture in which it is found.

The same is true for morality. Here again we tend to think of morality today in individualistic terms as, for example, the kinds of ethical judgments a person makes or the particular mental and emotional processes engaged in formulating decisions about right and wrong. Either way, we have the psychologist to thank. Whatever psychological dimensions it may have, morality, like character, is also very much social in its constitution. Whatever else it may be, it is, at the least, a complex body of prohibitions and warrants through which social life is ordered and sustained.[2] But it is much more than this. Most of what constitutes morality refers to basic attitudes toward life and an underlying and implicit vision of reality. These not only provide a foundation for our moral life, they also frame the horizon of our moral imagination.[3] Ritualized in habit, routinized in institutions, these codes of interdiction and permission—and more fundamentally, these attitudes, ideals, sensibilities, and dispositions—provide the terms by which individual life is made predictable and social life is made stable.

But morality does not just exist outside of us as an impersonal set of rules and regulations or abstract ideals. It is *received* by the individual, internalized into subjective consciousness, and thus experienced as the basic ordering categories of life. This is to say that morality is not typically experienced as an abstruse set of shoulds and shouldn'ts, nor a list of "values" codified in cheerful axioms. Rather, morality is a *nomos*, a normative universe that constrains us within the boundaries of what is permissible. It is the *doxa* of social life—unalterable, non-negotiable; commanding, demanding in its very constitution. At the same time, morality includes the *explanations* that give these codes coherence and authority for the individual and the community. It is in this way that culture becomes authoritative. Morality demands, requires, expects of people, but in a way that makes sense. It prompts, prods, and encourages people, but in a way that seems natural and logical to them.

ON CHARACTER

What, then, can be said about this thing we call character? The most basic element of character is *moral discipline*.[4] Its most essential feature is the inner capacity for restraint—an ability to inhibit oneself in one's passions, desires, and habits within the boundaries of a moral order. Moral discipline, in many respects, is the capacity to say "no"; its function, to inhibit and constrain personal appetites on behalf of a greater good. This idea of a greater good points to a second element, *moral attachment*. Character, in short, is defined not just negatively but positively as well. It reflects the affirmation of our commitments to a larger community, the embrace of an ideal that attracts us, draws us, animates us, inspires us.[5] Affirmation and interdiction, the "yes" and the "no"—what Henri Bergson called the morality of aspiration and the morality of obligation—are merely two aspects of the same single reality. In the latter instance, it is an affirmation of commitments we have to the larger community. Finally, character implies the *moral autonomy* of the individual in his or her capacity to freely make ethical decisions. The reason, very simply, is that controlled behavior cannot be moral behavior for it removes the element of discretion and judgment. Thus, character enacts moral judgment and does so freely.

Character, then, is defined by the coming together of these moral properties. It is a reflection of creeds that have become convictions and is manifested in choices to abide by those convictions even in, *especially in*, the face of temptation or adversity. Character is, in explicit ways, the embodiment of the ideals of a moral order—it is formed in relation to the imperatives of that moral order that are embedded in the life of a community of moral discourse.[6] "Character," as

Ralph Waldo Emerson put it in his classic essay of this title, is "this moral order seen through the medium of individual nature." It is for this reason that he viewed "men of character [as] the conscience of the society to which they belong."[7]

*   *   *

All of these elements were present in Plato's discussion of society's ideal leaders, the "guardians" of the Republic. Guardians were to be chosen from among those "who appear . . . on observation to be most likely to devote their lives to doing what they judge to be in the interest of the community, and who are never prepared to act against it." They were to be watched closely for their "conviction," their ability to "stick" to the principle "that they must always do what is best for the community." With this end in view, they would be tested from childhood to see that they never abandoned this imperative, even against "hard work and pain and competitive trials." Their conviction must be proven "far more rigorously than we prove gold in the furnace." "If they bear themselves well and are not easily bewitched, if they show themselves able to maintain in all circumstances both their own integrity and the principles of balance and harmony they learned in their education, then they may be expected to be of the greatest service to the community as well as to themselves."[8] Character, in a classic sense, manifests itself as the autonomy to make ethical decisions always on behalf of the common good and the discipline to abide by that principle.

The sacred quality of these moral imperatives cannot be overstated. Character is formed through the slow reception of "god-terms" deep within us—god-terms, as Philip Rieff put it, that exist as "presiding presences." As such, character is shaped not by a cowering acquiescence to rules imposed externally but as conscious, directed obedience to truths authoritatively received and affirmed. In this way the imperatives of social life—both positive in obligation or negative in prohibition and repression—possess a moral power that we recognize as transcending ourselves. By virtue of the authority invested in it, morality is inwardly compelling; it exerts a leverage upon our will. When it speaks to us, we conform to it—not because the required conduct is necessarily attractive to us, nor because we are so inclined by some innate predisposition, but because there is some compelling influence in the authority dictating it.[9]

History reveals instances where yielding to the creed existing within becomes more precious than life itself. Surely this was the test placed upon Sir Thomas More in the sixteenth century. Consider the dialogue from Robert Oxton Bolt's play *A Man for All Seasons* between More and his daughter, Margaret, just moments before his sentencing. Knowing that her father would be released for uttering just a few words, Margaret pleaded with him to give in:

MORE: You want me to swear to the Act of Succession?

MARGARET: "God more regards the thoughts of the heart than the words of the mouth." Or so you've always taught me.

MORE: Yes.

MARGARET: Then say the words of the oath and in your heart think otherwise.

MORE: What is an oath then but words we say to God?

MARGARET: That's very neat.

MORE: Do you mean it isn't true?

MARGARET: No, it's true.

MORE: Then it's a poor argument to call it "neat," Meg. When a man takes an oath, Meg, he's holding his own self in his own hands. Like water. *(He cups his hands)* And if he opens his fingers then—he needn't hope to find himself again. Some men aren't capable of this, but I'd be loathe to think your father one of them.[10]

To deny the conviction of truth in his heart might save his life but it would cost More all that he held sacred. This was much too high a cost to pay. But hadn't he made his point already? To our ears his was a commitment that bordered on irrationality and fanaticism. Margaret herself pushed him on just this point. As she put it, "But in reason! Haven't you done as much as God can reasonably want?" To which More replied, "Well . . . Finally . . . it isn't a matter of reason; finally it's a matter of love."[11] Not only did the Church frame the boundaries of conscience, but his devotion to the Church and its truths provided the source of his capacity to resist the temptation to violate his conscience.

At his trial before the Diet of Worms, in the presence of Charles, the Holy Roman Emperor, Martin Luther offered the same lesson:

Since then Your Majesty and your lordships desire a simple reply, I will answer without horns and without teeth. Unless I am convicted by Scripture and plain reason—I do not accept the authority of popes and councils, for they have contradicted each other—my conscience is captive to the Word of God. I cannot and I will not recant anything, for to go against conscience is neither right nor safe. God help me. Amen.[12]

Surely the compunctions of ideals-held-sacred account for the end of that philosophical innovator Socrates, at his trial in Athens. As he said in the *Apology,*

For I go around and do nothing but persuade you, both younger and older, not to care for bodies and money before, nor as vehemently as, how your soul will be the best possible. I say: 'Not from money does virtue come, but from virtue comes money and all of the other good things for human be-ings both privately and publicly.' If, then, I corrupt the young by saying these things, they may be harmful. But if someone asserts what I say is other than this, he speaks nonsense. With a view to these things, men of Athens, . . . either let me go or not, since I would not do otherwise, not even if I were going to die many times. [13]

The same was true for the churchmen Cranmer and Ridley on High Street, Ox-ford; for the maid-warrior, Jeanne d'Arc at the stake in Rouen. Theirs were ideals so sacred that they were more important than life itself.

Does this mean that character requires religious faith?

No.

This point bears repeating: character does not require religious faith. But it does require the conviction of truth made sacred, abiding as an authoritative presence within consciousness and life, reinforced by habits institutionalized within a moral community.

Character, therefore, resists expedience; it defies hasty acquisition. This is un-doubtedly why Søren Kierkegaard spoke of character as "engraved," deeply etched, graven, "changeable rarely and least of all in extreme situations." In this he was simply following the Greek etymology—"a distinctive mark impressed, engraved, or otherwise formed."[14] In ethical terms a person of good character would be steadfast in wisdom and dependable in commitment. The very idea of character in this historic sense ridicules the "ethical fitness seminar" or the "ten steps to character" now hustled by the merchants of direct-mail morality.[15]

What does the deep-rooted and commanding nature of character say about the individual's autonomy to make moral judgments? Clearly the choice implied here is of a fundamentally different genus than the selections made from a restaurant menu or a clothes catalog. People shaped in relation to commanding truths as presiding presences can neither expunge nor cross certain boundaries, and if they were to try, they would do so in the face of serious consequences. In times past, such occasions were marked by words that are, in our own time, ob-solete: apostasy, heresy, infidelity, sin, transgression—in actions punishable, at the extreme, by death or its social equivalent.[16] This is why the Bible records so many cases of trespass and transgression, faithfulness and obedience. This is also why biographical works, like Plutarch's *Lives of the Noble Grecians and Romans* record much the same lessons.[17] Together these recountings mark the boundaries of moral character.[18] They serve as lessons to generations that follow.

The Sources of Good Character: Forcing the Question

At first blush this way of understanding character and morality might be off-putting to some. On the face of it, it would seem to be contentless, even relativistic. By this definition, not only are the Schweitzers, the Ghandis, the Mother Theresas, and so on people of character but so might all sorts of monstrous people who might make the case to be included as having "character" as well: Goebbels comes to mind, as does Jack Kevorkian and assorted Klansmen too. These too, they would argue, had or have passionately held convictions linked to certain ideals of the common good for which each was or is willing to endure sacrifice.

This observation pushes an important point. Let's face it: just as moralities vary from society to society and epoch to epoch, so do the range of character types that they produce. Some we clearly admire and others we just as clearly loathe.

The point I want to make is that character is comprised of both form and content. By emphasizing the formal properties of character, we also bring into relief the question of content. It forces us to confront the *sources* by which we define the "moral" life and, by extension, "good" character. In turn, it forces us to define exactly what we mean when we use these words.

My premise here is that it is no longer possible to take an understanding of "the moral" and "the good" for granted; neither can one take for granted the content of character—so too the ideals of freedom, fairness, and justice. All of these terms are contested in our day. But while contested and sometimes fiercely, they are not openly and substantively contested. If, therefore, our commitments to benevolence and justice are to have any substance and meaning, if they are not to be merely slogans, it is essential to open a discussion of the means by which we support these commitments.

The Importance of Particularity

But here I move too quickly. Recognizing the diversity of moral traditions and the communities that embody them is not only politically important, but analytically essential.

As I have said, character is defined by the coming together of certain properties—moral discipline, moral attachment, and moral autonomy. But these properties do not exist in human experience without particular content. The substance of moral imperatives differs in real life, as do the moral ideals that inspire them and the moral explanations that make them seem just and right.[19] So too, these moral properties are rooted in specific situations, grounded in concrete circumstances, situated in distinct systems of social relationship. They exist, then, not in the abstract but in rich cultural variety in the context of complex historical reality. Character may possess a common form but is, by definition, diverse in manifestation and practice.

How do we see this in our own circumstances?

The Greek and Hebrew traditions are only the most obvious sources of diversity influential in the West. In the ancient world, character (or "excellence" of character) was defined as a consistency of virtue and moral purpose in guiding one toward a good life. Though developed through habit, character (*éthos*) was manifested through reasoned choices (*prohairesis*) in accordance with prescriptive principles oriented toward the common good.[20] Thus, as I noted before, the guardians in Plato's *Republic* were the ones "most likely to devote their lives to doing what they judge to be in the interest of the community, and who are never prepared to act against it." Their convictions must "stand up to hard work and pain and competitive trials" and must never yield even "under the influence of force or witchcraft."[21] Goodness of character, then, was deeply linked to clear and consistent moral purpose.[22]

In biblical cultures, character was defined in relation to God's distinctive property, His holiness. The expectation was as clear as it was demanding: as God said to Moses, "You must be holy, for I am holy."[23] This was not a matter of outward appearances but rather a holiness that penetrated to the core of one's inner life. Speaking to the prophet Samuel about the boy chosen to be king of Israel, God said, "The Lord does not look at the things man looks at. Man looks at the outward appearance, but the Lord looks at the heart."[24] Jesus reiterated this view when remarking that "the good man brings good things out of the good stored up in him, and the evil man brings evil things out of the evil stored up in him."[25] In the stories of Noah, Lot, Gideon, David, and others, it was the consistency of their inner being before God—defined by intimacy with and obedience to their Creator—that counted them favored.

Clearly these major streams of influence are varied in content as well. Spartan and Athenian cultures prescribed different content for character, not least because they had different ideas of the common good. Within their common biblical heritage, Jewish and Christian traditions offered variations that cannot be dismissed casually. The authoritative and institutional character of Catholicism has historically contrasted with the individualistic and prophetic propensities of Protestantism, while the ritualistic and communitarian spirit of Judaism has long set it apart from either Catholic or Protestant Christianity. Needless to say, the fragmentation within each of these great traditions over the centuries—various Orthodox, Conservative, Reform movements in Judaism; Eastern Orthodox, Catholic, and literally hundreds of Protestant denominations within Christianity—presents still further variation in moral influence.

Added to these particularities of moral content is the wide range of places and circumstances where moral traditions have been embraced and lived. Each of these settings roots individuals not only within a distinct moral community but within a distinct social structure as well. Historically, to be born into such a community was to belong to that community and to be obligated to it in specific ways. These communities framed the horizons of people's identity and aspiration and located them within a collective narrative. The wide and rich range of possibility represented by this social, historical, and cultural particularity is overwhelming.

Particularity and the Matter of Moral Authority

The particular manifestations of moral culture mean that each community will embody different social expectations and place different demands upon the individuals living within it. In other words, moral cultures and the communities in which they are established provide the reasons, restraints, and incentives for conducting life in one way rather than another. Particular moral cultures provide the standards and ideals by which individuals and communities judge themselves good or corrupt, admirable or contemptible. They define commitments within a framework of significance. Not least, they provide the explanations for why things are as they are.

In a very practical way, moral cultures, in their particularity, provide specific explanations for the "whys" of moral behavior: why should one show mercy and compassion? Why should one not cheat or steal or lie or be violent? Why should one persevere in good works when it is not in one's personal interest? Why should one be willing to sacrifice on behalf of others? Why should one care when no one else does? It is only in their particularity that moral cultures provide mechanisms of accountability for those who live within them. They not only tell us to whom we are answerable but the consequences—both good and bad—of our decisions.

The particularity of moral culture certainly operates in a way that all of us are conscious or aware of. Even more powerful, however, are the ways in which it frames deeper, unconscious attitudes and attachments. Indeed, the power of culture is always measured by its power to bind us, to compel us, to oblige us in ways we are not fully aware of. In this, particular moral cultures define the horizons of our moral imagination in ways that we are not fully conscious. They set out the possibilities that we can envision in specific circumstances.

Moral culture, then, becomes authoritative in social life and binding on individual conscience only in the particularity of moral traditions and the communities that embody them. It is in the mystifying complexity of these concrete circumstances that moral authority exists at all.[26] Social scientists often minimize these differences as part of their stock and trade. So be it. In the context of lived experience, however, these differences are constitutive of life and identity.

ON THE DEVELOPMENT OF CHARACTER

If the concepts of character and morality have to be rescued from the tyranny of popular psychology, so too does the idea of the moral development of children. Here too, the tendency is to downplay or ignore altogether the influence of culture in the shaping of character and the development of moral instruction. Most streams of academic and popular psychology view the sequence of moral development in terms that are highly individualistic and psychological as though the process is simply a dynamic of the isolated personality alone. The assumption often made today is that moral sensibilities are innate to every child; they need only be animated and refined.

Whatever individual psychological processes are involved in the development of moral understanding and character, it is fair to say that a person's moral development does *not* occur in a cultural vacuum. Neither does moral instruction. Both occur in a powerfully influential normative context.

Consider the matter this way. Humans are not born with a well-developed moral sensibility, much less "character." Whatever predispositions we may have due to our genetic wiring, we are still mostly "unfinished" at birth.[27] In contrast to other species that have a well-developed apparatus of instincts, we are "instinctually deprived." We don't innately know what is socially acceptable to eat or when to sleep, what clothes are appropriate in what circumstances, or how to act toward others. Our sexual instincts are not reliable guides to how, when, where, or with whom sexual intimacy might be appropriate. We have no sense of what our obligations are toward the environment or toward other species, much less how to treat strangers, how to express empathy with those in need, or even that empathy toward the needy might be a good worth pursuing. We are not born with moral obligations to stabilize life, a worldview to give coherence to life, or ideals to guide our lives.

Thankfully, we do not have to invent appropriate responses to every new situation into which we are thrown. We do not have to construct rules at the moment of action by deducing them from general principles; they already exist, they operate around us by virtue of the communities of which we are a part.[28]

This being the case, we must *acquire* a moral sensibility—we learn what is right and wrong, good and bad, what is to be taken seriously, ignored, or rejected as abhorrent—and we learn, in moments of uncertainty, how to apply our moral imaginations to different circumstances. Over time, we acquire a sense of obligation and the disciplines to follow them.

Much of our moral sensibility, of course, is acquired in our early socialization, through the acquisition of language, and in our natural participation in everyday life. Language itself provides horizons for our moral imaginations. Yet primary socialization is also that stage of life when moral instruction is articulated. Not only are children told explicitly what is right and wrong or good or bad, they are often offered reasons why—why, for example, it is inappropriate to defecate in public; why it is important to show others respect; why it is wrong to cheat, lie and steal; why it is good to show compassion to the suffering. The whats and whys of moral instruction, then, are made explicit for the young in ways that eventually become taken for granted when adults.

I take it as a given that learning (as well as life itself) is dialectical or reciprocal in nature. The individual acts in the world, to be sure, but the world also acts back on the individual. Indeed, a defining moment in this dialectic is the internalization of that *nomos* as the very structure of our worldview and, as we have seen, as the organizing categories of our very identity in all its fluidity and complexity. The moral culture, in other words, is not merely the environment within which identity plays out. It is, even more, a reality that frames the categories of identity, structures the identity, and even indelibly stamps identity. Without the authoritative presence of moral culture, internalized into subjective consciousness, there can be no character or "character development."

Relating to Moral Culture(s)

Character development, then, is formed in relation to a normative order or moral culture. Yet against the "culture and personality" perspective popular in the 1950s, there is no one-to-one correlation between the content of a culture and the content of a personality. Just as there is no unitary culture, there is also no single and unitary personality type. Against uniformity, there is really great diversity. This is especially, if not obviously, true in contemporary America, as we shall see.

Thus, except in more traditional settings, moral culture is rarely, if ever, monolithic. Rather, moral cultures (especially in our own time) are multiple, overlapping, sometimes complimentary; often competing in their influence. Public versus private; dominant culture versus various subcultures; official and approved cultures versus minority, even deviant cultures, and so on. At times, character is formed by the ideals of the dominant culture—as with Thomas More mentioned earlier. Other times, character is formed *against* the dominant culture by the more powerfully internalized codes of an alternative culture—as it was with Socrates, Martin Luther, and Italian reformer Girolamo Savonarola. And while for most people character is formed in the private spaces of family, consider those who inhabit the symbolic space of public life and on whom no other normative demands are placed. With some nausea we reflect upon those politicians, for example, whose positions are driven less by convictions than by focus groups, whose identity is guided less by ideals than by political interests, whose public purpose is defined less by a moral compass than by expediency, and whose legacy is based not upon substantive accomplishment but upon the calculus of image production. The Gingriches and Clintons of our day merely reflect in their person much of the culture they inhabit.

*   *   *

If character cannot be understood independent of the culture in which it is formed, how do children—how do *we*—relate to the complex moral cultures in which we live? Needless to say, children and adults alike rarely relate to moral cultures as full-blown ethical systems. Who has time to master the intricacies of philosophical traditions and their evolution? Most people are too busy, pressed by the practical realities of daily life, to reflect much on how their personal opinions are shaped by larger cultural influences. Yet moral culture still frames their lives. More often than not these moral cultures exist for people as perhaps crudely formed assumptions about what is true and false; what is right and wrong; what is honest and corrupt and so on. Yet, however crudely formed in our minds, however inarticulate we may be about them, our personal grasp of these assumptions relate back to larger moral traditions or styles of moral reasoning in the culture.

Thus, even when we are inarticulate about the moral cultures we live in or operate by, when their principles, maxims, and habits are internalized deep in our consciousness, they act as *moral compasses*, providing the bearings by which we navigate the challenges of life. Far from a philosophical abstraction, moral culture guides our behavior, thinking, and expectations of others. Consciously or not, we refer to these compasses constantly, not only when we are confronted by moral dilemmas but in the rhythms of everyday life.

Here, though, I repeat the essential caveat. Human beings are anything but automatons. We reflect, ponder, act in the world around us in ways that have consequences. Thus while culture is powerful in its shaping influence, it is not all powerful. Rather, we engage the culture of which we are a part and make it

our own. Internalizing culture, then, is an ongoing process that requires us to
adapt to different circumstances.[29]

MORAL EDUCATION AND
THE CULTIVATION OF CHARACTER

Whether it is provided formally or informally, deliberately or unwittingly, moral
instruction, then, is an exercise in the transmission of culture. It is a mechanism
by which character is etched into a person's identity and existence.

In our own time the burden of moral education and character formation falls
especially to the schools. The chorus of voices affirming this comes from every
part of the political and policy spectrum. From the educational establishment:

> There is undeniably a moral vacuum in society today, and educators have
> an urgent obligation to help fill it.[30]

As well as:

> I am absolutely convinced that—given the decline of the family—schools
> can and must play a critical role . . . a more assertive role, a more organized
> role . . . in inculcating basic, core moral values in America's young people.
> This should be a cardinal function of our public schools.[31]

From the political right:

> If . . . the schools were to make the formation of good character a primary
> goal, many other things would fall into place. Hitherto unsolvable prob-
> lems such as violence, vandalism, drug use, teen pregnancies, unruly class-
> rooms, and academic deterioration would prove to be less intractable than
> presently imagined. Moreover, the moral reform of schools is not some-
> thing that has to wait until other conditions are met. It doesn't depend on
> the rest of society reforming itself. Schools are, or can be, one of the main
> engines of social change. They can set the tone of society in ways that no
> other institution can match.[32]

From the communitarian center:

> If the moral infrastructure of our communities is to be restored, schools will
> have to step in where the family, neighborhoods, and religious institutions
> have been failing.[33]

More is better:

> Schools will be better able to develop character if they are in session for more hours during school days, more days a week, and more months a year.[34]

And from the left:

> This vision—still in its nascent form—seeks to use education . . . to enable each student to resist and overcome social and cultural repression, and hence to authorize his or her own moral voice. . . . Where the function of education is to remake or reform society, because the principles and directives of society are, by and large, unreasonable.[35]

Schools are not alone—there are youth organizations, churches and synagogues, and families as well. And yet the burden schools bear is especially heavy.

Nevertheless, because it is an exercise in the transmission of culture, moral education—however it is institutionalized—*is always more a reflection of the social order than a mechanism by which the social order is transformed.* As much as we want to think of moral education as having potential to shape society, the stronger direction of influence is the way in which society shapes, even dictates, the content of education. As Philip Rieff has said, "It is a pathetic, and historic, error to treat the school as GHQ for any movement toward the new society."[36] Like it or not, moral education functions largely as instruction into the normative ideals of the prevailing social order. Sociologically and historically, moral education has always been more about conformity than about transformation.

The question we face is, of course, conformity to what?

Part 2

THE TRANSFORMATION
OF MORAL EDUCATION

3

The Early Modern Regime and Its Transformation

(James L. Nolan, Jr., coauthor)

Concern over character development is anything but new. The project of moral education has long been infused with urgency and gravity even as it has been almost completely transformed over generations.

If we understand moral education as instruction in the normative order, the project of character development involves the articulation of normative ideals as well as the language and logic that make those ideals coherent and authoritative. Needless to say, there is no person or community that fully embodies those ideals; few even come close. But hypocrisy and moral failure in no way diminish their significance and the task of communicating them. On the contrary, these ideals exist as a reality, sui generis. When institutionalized in law, policy, and, not least, the moral instruction of the young, they establish the standards by which individuals and communities alike order their lives and judge themselves as good or bad, worthy or unworthy. Together they point to, and even comprise, the moral designs of the larger social order. It is, then, a history of this evolving project of articulating moral ideals and the mechanisms by which they are transmitted to younger generations that I undertake in this chapter.

The task is made easier, in some ways, because American society has been in flux from its beginning. The reason this is significant is that societies experiencing change tend to be especially self-conscious about their moral ideals and particularly careful to explain the logic that makes those ideals intelligible. The task of elucidating a moral logic is a way of dealing with the uncertainties and the competing alternatives that inevitably arise during such times. Thus in times of social change and transformation—basically all of American history—moral education has constituted an explicit project for the standard-bearers and guardians of the social order.

Though the historical overview I offer here is more illustrative than systematic, the dynamic described is clear. The story is both about the changing content of moral education and the changing institutional carriers of this pedagogy. Only by understanding past generations' social and cultural adaptations can we grasp the nature and significance of our present moment.

MORAL EDUCATION IN THE NEW REPUBLIC

Like so much of American culture, moral education leading up to the founding of the new republic was thoroughly Calvinist and carried principally by the family and local church. The educational mandate placed upon parents during the colonial period was typified by Cotton Mather's exhortation that children should be taught to "remember four words . . . and attempt all that is comprised in them: obedience, honesty, industry and piety."[1] Mather's simple advice was nothing out of the ordinary, even outside the Puritan community. Though anything but a Puritan, John Locke a few decades before advised much the same in his essay *Some Thoughts Concerning Education,* published in 1693. This was a highly influential book—a seventeenth-century equivalent, in some respects, of Benjamin Spock's *Baby and Child Care.*[2] Locke insisted that the child's habits be shaped in accordance with the virtues of piety, loyalty, industry, and temperance.

Why these virtues? The answer makes sense only when we understand the deeply Christian character of the culture into which children were socialized.

Faith, of course, was essential. As Benjamin Wadsworth put it in his popular essay "The Well-Ordered Family," published in 1712,

> Tis absolutely necessary for your Children to be truly Religious. They're Children of wrath by Nature; they can't escape Hell, without true Faith and Repentance. . . . Twould be barbarous, inhumane, worse than brutish, if you should neglect the Bodies of your Children; and thro' sloth and carelessness suffer them to starve and die: how much greater then is your barbarity and wickedness, if you take no care to prevent the everlasting ruine of their Souls?[3]

Needless to say, the social and spiritual pressure upon parents was great. "Amazingly great will your guilt and danger be," Wadsworth argued, "if you neglect the Religious Education of your Children."[4] To this end, parents were to "see to it that [they] instruct everyone of [their] children in the things of God," to "take [their] children with [them] to God's publick worship," and to "indevour that [their] children may rightly understand the great truths and duties of religion."[5]

It is difficult today to imagine why religion was so central to parents and other moral guardians. John Locke himself articulated the reason: to the seventeenth century mind there could be *no* morality without God; virtue could not exist without reverence for God. Locke put it this way:

> *As to the Foundation of* [*virtue*], there ought very clearly to be imprinted on his [the child's] Mind a true Notion of *God*, as of the independent Supreme Being, Author and Maker of all Things, from whom we receive all our Good, who loves us, and gives us all things. And consequent to this, instill into him a Love and Reverence of this Supreme Being. [Emphasis added]

This was not empty rhetoric. Like others, Locke encouraged levels of spiritual discipline unimaginable today, advising parents and masters to keep "Children constantly Morning and Evening to Acts of Devotion to God, as to their Maker, Preserver and Benefactor, in some plain and short Form of Prayer, suitable to the Age and Capacity" as well as to teach children "to *pray* to Him, and *praise* Him as the Author of his Being, and of all the God he does or can enjoy."[6] To this end, it was "necessary he should learn perfectly by heart" the Lord's Prayer, the Creeds, and the Ten Commandments.[7] This advice too was not out of the ordinary. It was echoed by the moralist Eleazar Moody in his widely read pamphlet "The School of Good Manners," which encouraged children to memorize a "short, plain and Scriptural catechism" as well as their baptismal Covenant.[8]

The defining importance of a formal hierarchy of authority in this understanding cannot be overstated. The moral life is defined by and emanates from the authority of God, which in turn is mediated by the authority possessed and exercised by parents. The loving yet stern authority parents exercised would be the means by which children would come to understand God's sovereign love and judgment. Obedience and respect of one's parents was thus an expression of obedience and reverence for God.

Consider, on this count, the advice given by Locke. "Tis true," he said, "Parents and Governors ought to settle and establish their Authority by an Awe over the Minds of those under their Tuition; and to rule them by that."[9] Reverence, maintained by fear and love, was "the great Principle whereby you will always have Hold upon him, to turn his Mind to the Ways of Virtue and Honour."[10] "If the *Reverence* he owes you be establish'd early, it will always be sacred to him, and will be as hard for him to resist as the Principles of his Nature."[11] Consider, too, Wadsworth's instruction to children to "love their parents," to "fear their parents," to "reverence and honor their parents," to "be faithful and obedient to

their parents," and to "patiently bear, and grow better by, the needful chastisement and corrections their parents give them."[12]

The proper relation of children to parents was the heart of moral education.
Children, said Wadsworth,

> should love their parents . . . fear to offend, grieve, disobey, or displease ei-
> ther of them. . . . Children should fear their parents . . . Children should
> Reverence and Honor their Parents . . . Oh it's a very great and dangerous
> crime, for Children to despise or disrespect their Parents . . . Children
> should give diligent heed, to the wholesome Instructions and Counsels of
> their parents . . . Children should patiently bear, and grow better by the
> needful Chastisements and Corrections their Parents give them . . . Oh
> Child, if thou art not bettered by the Correction of Parents, thou art in dan-
> ger of being terribly destroyed . . . Children should be faithful and obedient
> to their Parents [for] when you disobey the lawful commands of Parents,
> you disobey God himself.[13]

Moody's advice to children was even more specific:

> If thou passeth by thy Parents, at any Place where thou seeth them, when ei-
> ther by themselves or with Company, Bow towards them . . . Never speak to
> thy Parents without some Title of Respect, viz. Sir, Madam, Etc. according
> to their Quality . . . Approach near thy Parents at no time without a Bow . . .
> Dispute not, nor delay to Obey thy Parents Commands . . . Bear with Meek-
> ness and Patience, and without Murmuring or Sullenness thy Parents Re-
> proofs or Corrections: Nay, tho' it should so happen that they be causeless
> or undeserved . . . Walking with thy superior in the House or Garden, give
> him the Right (or Upper) Hand, and Walk not even with him, Cheek-by-
> jowl; but a little behind him, yet not to distant as that it shall be trouble-
> some to him to speak to thee, or hard for thee to hear. . . . Among Superiors
> speak not till thou art spoken to, and bid to speak. . . . Strive not with Supe-
> riors in Argument or Discourse; but easily submit thine Opinion to their
> Assertions . . . If thy Superior speak any thing wherein thou knowest he is
> mistaken, correct him not nor contradict him, nor grin at the hearing of it;
> but pass over the Error without notice or interruption . . . Affront none, es-
> pecially thy Elders, by word or deed.[14]

A sovereign God was at the foundation of virtue, and respect for His authority
mediated by the authority of parents was the foundation of godly character. The
premise of moral education, however, was the view that children were born with

sin and their hearts thus inclined toward evil. The parents' central task, a task shared by the community, was to curb and even break the child's instinctive willfulness as soon as it began to appear.[15] All of the Puritan writings about childrearing share this central theme in varying degrees of severity.

The practical question was "how?" If the flesh is at war with the spirit, how does one bring flesh into conformity with the spirit? Perhaps the chief mechanism in this effort was the use of shame; a device encouraged by all of the guardians of the moral order at that time. The connection between shame, virtue, and will formation was elementary.

"Whatever you do," the Reverend John Ward explained, "be sure to maintain shame in them; *for if that be once gone, there is no hope that they'll ever come to good*."[16] Cotton Mather explained to his contemporaries how he caused his own children "to understand, that it is an *hurtful* and a *shameful* thing to do amiss. I aggravate this, on all occasions; and lett them see how *amiable* they will render themselves by well doing. The *first chastisement*, which I inflict for an ordinary fault is, to lett the child see and hear me in an astonishment, and hardly able to beleeve that the child could do so *base* a thing, but beleeving that they will never do it again."[17]

Again, it was not just the Puritans who saw the connection between shame and virtue. As Locke explained: "Shame of doing amiss, and deserving Chastisement, is the only true Restraint belonging to Virtue. The Smart of the Rod, if Shame accompanies it not, soon ceases, and is forgotten, and will quickly by Use lose its Terror."[18] The goal was that children would so internalize the moral order that they would not require external control to ensure social conformity; rather the child himself learns to avoid shame and guilt through self-restraint. Thus for all Locke's emphasis on children's rational capacities, shame became a mechanism by which moral reasoning would be clarified. Nor were the ends of moral development that Locke advocated substantially different from those of his contemporaries. "The great Principle and Foundation of all Virtue and Worth," he contended, "is plac'd in this: That a Man is able to deny himself his own Desires, cross his own Inclinations, and purely follow what Reason directs as Best, tho' the Appetite lean the other Way."[19] Again, "It seems plain to me, that the Principle of all Virtue and Excellency lies in a Power of denying our own Desires, where Reason does not authorize them."[20] Despite his emphasis on the individuality of children, rational conformity with a larger moral order established in Nature by the authority of Reason (a reflection of the mind of God) was still the bottom line. Such conformity, he acknowledged, could be accomplished only through the sublimation of individual desires and expression.

Until the child's will and character were formed, parents and schoolmasters were to leave little to chance. In the seventeenth century mind, one of the most dangerous sins (because of its capacity to breed other sin) was idleness. The religious reasons were explicit. As Benjamin Wadsworth explained: "Christians are bid to be, not Slothful in Business, Rom. 12:11. The Slothful, is called Wicked, Mat. 25:26. If any would not work, neither should they eat, Thes. 3:10 . . . Christians are required, to work with their own hands, I Thes. 4:11. . . . Would you have your Sons and Daughters, live as lazy, idle drones, as useless, nay pernicious persons when grown up? If not, then don't bring them up in idleness. Bring them up to business, some lawful Imployment or another; though you have never so much Estate to give them."[21] Not only idle behavior, but "Vain, Idle and Naughty Words— This is another Sin that Children are addicted to and are to be warned against."[22] The aversion to idleness was so great that colonial governments officially discouraged it. As the Massachusetts Bay Government stated in 1641: "it is desired and will be expected that all masters of families should see that their children and servants should be industriously implied [employed] so as the mornings and evenings and other seasons may not bee lost as formerly they have bene."[23] The often severe circumstances of life in the colonies required hard labor anyway—the whole family, even children of five or six, had to work to ensure the family's survival. So it was that the moral culture of reformed Protestantism made a virtue out of necessity.[24]

*   *   *

The central institution for the moral education of children was the family. As Wadsworth explained, it was the family, and parents in particular, that had "the opportunity, the advantage (and tis a great one) early to teach them; before they can learn of any one else."[25] Though borne by the family and local faith community, this responsibility was reinforced by the governing authorities. Church and state played complementary roles in compelling parents to rear children according to religious requirements.[26] So important was proper childrearing to Massachusetts Puritans, for example, that local governments, through the church, kept an eye on every household. In Boston, a tithing-man checked up regularly on the behavior of ten families assigned to him.[27] The state often went further by mandating Christian education in the larger villages. In 1671, the General Court of Massachusetts passed the following statute:

> It being one chief project of Satan to keep men from the knowledge of the Scripture . . . to the end that learning may not be buried in the graves of our forefathers, in church and commonwealth, the Lord assisting our endeavors; it is therefore ordered by this court and authority thereof, that every township within this jurisdiction, after the Lord hath increased them to the number of fifty householders, shall then forthwith appoint one within their towns to teach all such children as shall resort to him to write and read.[28]

Similarly, the General Assembly of Maryland passed an act in 1723 to make provision for "the liberal and pious education of the youth of this province."[29] All over the colonies, where schools existed, the object was the promotion of Christian virtue in and through the provision of academic skills. For instance, South Carolina's prescription for who could teach in a Charleston school was based on concerns about the advancement of the Christian religion. Enacted in 1712, the statute provided that,

> the person to be master of the said school shall be of the religion of the Church of England, and conform to the same, and shall be capable to teach the learned languages, that is to say, Latin and Greek tongues, and to catechise and instruct the youth in the principles of the Christian religion, as professed in the Church of England.[30]

Thus, where community schools existed, there was no sharp distinction between education into the creeds of faith and moral education.[31] As Carl Kaestle writes of this era, "almost no one could think of morals as separate from God and the Bible."[32] So it was that texts like the *New England Primer*, first published by Benjamin Harris in Boston around 1690 and *the* schoolbook for Protestants for a century to follow, provided, along with the alphabet and the syllabarium, explicit biblical instruction. It offered theologically informed stories along with selections from Proverbs, the Lord's Prayer, and the Apostles' Creed. Children were admonished with maxims like, "He who ne'er learns his ABC, forever will a blockhead be." The ABC's, in turn, were provided through such rhythmic couplets as, "In Adam's fall, We sinned all," "Heaven to find, The Bible mind," "Christ crucify'd For Sinners dy'd," and "The Idle Fool is Whipt at School."[33] Children were also to memorize verses like "The Dutiful Child's Promises":

> I will fear GOD and honour the King.
> I will honour my Father & Mother.
> I will obey my Superiors.
> I will Submit to my Elders . . .
> I will Reverence God's Sanctuary
> for our GOD is a consuming Fire.

Such a curriculum corresponded with community expectations as well as statutory declarations regarding the purpose of education.

*   *   *

The burden of the Puritans especially, and reformational Christianity more generally, defined the framework of moral education through the early decades of the new republic. Clearly the family was the primary institution for moral instruction. As Enos Weed wrote in his *Educational Directory*, "Good principles of morality breeding and a becoming gracefulness, is not generally to be learned by children at school, among a disorderly herd of boys, . . . but may be learned with more ease at home, under the immediate care of their parents or tutor."[34] Yet the church and community school helped the family instill these "good principles" both by reinforcing the authority of parents and by helping to educate children within the institutions of religious faith. In the late eighteenth century, a new vehicle for the moral education of the young emerged—the Sunday School.

The Rise of the Sunday School

As an innovation of the late eighteenth century, the Sunday school movement came about largely in response to the expanding social problems spawned by industrialization. Reform-oriented British and American Evangelicals observed that large numbers of working-class children banded together unsupervised on their one day off from work and raised more than their share of bedlam, "spending their sacred day in noise and riot." The task was to do something constructive with these children in a way that addressed the problem posed by their Sunday behavior.[35]

The first such initiative occurred in 1780, when the British newspaper publisher Robert Raikes decided to instruct the poor children of Gloucester, England, "in the elements both of knowledge and of religion." Raikes and his associates collected children off the city streets, cleaned them up, and kept them in school for two long Sunday sessions each week.[36] The results were striking. As one observer put it, the change in the children "could not have been more extraordinary had they been transformed from the shape of wolves and tigers to that of men."[37] Three years later, he announced the effort in the *Arminian Magazine*. Raikes's work earned the endorsement of John and Charles Wesley, who enthusiastically called it "one of the best institutions which have been seen in Europe for some centuries."[38] As John Wesley wrote in 1784: "So many children in one parish are restrained from open sin and taught a little good manners at least, as well as to read the Bible. I find these schools springing up wherever I go. Perhaps God may have a deeper end therein than men are aware of. Who knows but some of these schools may become nurseries for Christians?"[39] Word spread quickly, and the movement soon caught on throughout England and other English-speaking countries. In America, the first Sunday school was established in Accomack County, Virginia, in 1785, and another soon after in Hanover County, Virginia. These too followed Raikes's model closely in motive and design.

At this stage, the movement in Britain and America was primarily a missionary and philanthropic agency. Sunday schools were charity schools for the children of the lower classes who did not have the advantage of day school. These children spent Sunday "employed in the worst of purposes, to the depravation of morals and manners."[40] Though religious in motive and character, the schools were established by lay people and had only occasional affiliation with the institutional church. They offered instruction in such subjects as mathematics, reading, and writing.[41]

The movement first became institutionalized in America in 1791, in a group called the First Day Society. Located in Philadelphia, its leaders were drawn from the city's elite, all enlightened republicans committed to practical and progressive change. The physician and statesman Benjamin Rush was among its founders.[42] While the First Day schools quickly lost steam, the movement continued to evolve.

The chief impetus for change was the spiritual fervor generated by the Second Great Awakening in the opening years of the nineteenth century. The Sunday school movement grew dramatically, especially along the Atlantic seaboard.[43] Many of the teachers, having only recently experienced religious conversion themselves as a result of the revivals of the Second Great Awakening, were eager to share their faith.[44] Not surprisingly, the schools placed greater emphasis on evangelism and religious instruction than on such subjects as reading and writing. The ultimate aim was not just the evangelization of the unchurched but the renewal of the social order. Sunday schools thus became a key part of the broader reform efforts being advanced by Evangelicals and a mechanism by which to order people's lives in an increasingly disordered society. Along with temperance, tract societies, orphanages, missions for sailors, soup kitchens, and poorhouses, the Sunday school would provide a means by which America would triumph over the impediments to a true Christian civilization.[45]

Like the schools of the colonial period, the early Sunday schools embraced a "catechetical" approach to instruction, in which the truths and duties of the Christian faith were taught through the back and forth of questions answered by verbatim recitation.[46] Moral and religious instruction focused primarily upon rote memorization of long passages from the Scripture and catechism. It was common, one observer notes, for pupils to learn three hundred or more verses a week.[47] The principal objective of this pedagogy was salvation—to get the child right with God through the study and acceptance of correct doctrine and contact with the Scriptures. Later, the catechism was used less in deference to direct material from the Bible.[48]

As the movement grew, Sunday schools began to draw children from the expanding church-going middle classes. The great nineteenth-century churchman

Lyman Beecher was instrumental in encouraging a more inclusive orientation. He did so first by taking his own children to Sunday school in the late 1820s and by inducing his neighbors to follow his example.[49] His efforts gave great impetus to the evangelical Sunday school.[50]

By then the organization reflected its more evangelical mission. The defunct First Day Society was replaced in 1824 by the American Sunday School Union. The Sunday school movement began as an ecumenical parachurch agency run by lay people and concerned with the provision of both secular and religious instruction to the poor. By 1830, however, these first American Sunday schools had all but disappeared, replaced by denominational schools taught by volunteers and an increasing number of ministers and offering a specifically Evangelical Protestant curriculum.[51]

The Rise of the Common School

A major reason for the growing specialization of the Sunday school in the early nineteenth century was the emergence of the "common school." In the more heavily populated Northeast, the inspiration of the common-school movement was the urgency of finding new ways to sustain the moral order in an increasingly dense, complicated, and diverse society.[52] Providing a common education for children of all class and ethnic backgrounds would serve to Americanize and homogenize the population. In the less populated regions, especially in the westward frontier, the common school was born out of the necessity of interdenominational cooperation. The number of Baptists, Methodists, Presbyterians, or Episcopalians in new small towns and cities was insufficient for any group to form its own school. Without "common schools" built upon a Protestant consensus, the children would have no schools at all.[53]

As the idea of the common school took hold, it became clear that a distinct school on Sundays would be redundant, except for training children in religious matters. Yet rather than becoming a competitor to the common schools, the Sunday school came to regard itself as an essential complement and counterpart. The common school would teach the secular subjects and the parish-rooted Sunday schools would concentrate on religious and moral education.

It is a mistake, however, to regard the content of common schooling as "secular" or nonreligious. These schools were permeated with religious, and specifically nondenominational, Protestant content. It was not just the Evangelicals who advocated this. It was widely accepted, even among progressives, that religion was essential to the educational task. As Benjamin Rush insisted in his own plan for education in Pennsylvania in 1786, "religion is the foundation of virtue; virtue is the foundation of liberty; liberty is the object of all republican governments; therefore, a republican education should promote religion as well as virtue and liberty."[54] It was only natural, then, that religion and education would be considered inseparable. Such a position was reinforced by statutes within various state constitutions. Massachusetts's constitution, ratified in 1789, called for the "support and maintenance of public Protestant teachers of piety, religion, and morality"; this was reaffirmed by the state legislature in 1827.[55] The New Hampshire constitution, framed in 1784, provided state support for "public protestant teachers of piety, religion, and morality" on the ground that "morality and piety, rightly grounded on evangelical principles, will give the best and greatest security to government."[56] The Northwest Ordinance of 1787 likewise declared that "religion, morality, and knowledge, being necessary to good government and the happiness of mankind, schools and the means of education, shall forever be encouraged."[57] In all schools everywhere, piety and good character remained the requirements for teachers.[58] And religious orthodoxy defined the terms of piety and good character, even if religious ideals were expressed in a decidedly less sectarian fashion.

Through the early decades of the nineteenth century, schools were locally organized and funded. Churches and families remained the centers of moral instruction; the schools were to assist parents in the socialization of the young, not supplant them.[59] Thus the content of instruction, though technically non-sectarian, was clearly and firmly Protestant and resembled the same type of materials used in non-state-sponsored schools. Neither parents nor church authorities would have it any other way. Consider, for example, the Public School Society, established in New York City in 1805 to provide schools for poor children who could not attend the city's private, usually denominational schools. Consistent with state mandates, New York justified its support for the Society with its promise to implant in children's minds "the principles of religion and morality," and assist them in cultivating the "habits of industry and virtue."[60] Though the Society was nonsectarian, the content of instruction was in keeping with the religious sentiments of the time. Here is an excerpt from a teacher's manual used in the primary grades of the Public School Society schools:

> *Teacher.* My dear children, the intention of this school is to teach you to be good and useful in this world, that you may be happy in the world to come. What is the intention of this school?
>
> *T.* We therefore first teach you to 'remember your Creator in the days of your youth.' What do we first teach you?
>
> *T.* It is our duty to teach you this, because we find it written in the Holy Bible. Why is it our duty to teach you this?

T. The Holy Bible directs us to 'train you up in the way you should go.' What
good book directs us to train you up in the way you should go?

T. Therefore, my children, you must obey your parents.

Scholar: I must obey my parents . . .

T: You must obey your teachers.

S. I must obey my teachers . . .

T: God always sees you. (*Slowly, and in soft tone.*)

S: God always sees me.

T: God hears all you say.

S: God hears all I say.

T: God knows all you do.

S: God knows all I do.[61]

The evangelical character of the common school is illustrated again and again.
The Public School Society suspended classes on Tuesday afternoons to allow
children to be catechized according to the religious preferences of their parents.
It also required students to assemble at the school on Sunday morning, then to
proceed with chaperone to the church specified by their parents.

Needless to say, the evangelical tendencies within the common school movement only gained energy and direction from the Second Great Awakening. In the
expanding Midwest and West the conviction was that schoolteachers would be
"the best missionaries in the world."[62] As one educational entrepreneur wrote in
1835, "We wish to see the school house and Church go up side by side and the
land filled with Christian teachers as well as preachers. [It is] vital to the highest
interests of these states . . . that universal education . . . be taken up as a great
Christian enterprise."[63]

PAN-PROTESTANTISM AND THE BUILDING
OF A CHRISTIAN CIVILIZATION

The middle decades of the nineteenth century brought expansion on the Western frontier, industrialization in the Northeast, immigration on a massive scale,
growth in the size and complexity of the cities, and, of course, civil war. These
decades also brought problems on a new scale—juvenile delinquency, drunken-
ness, prostitution, vagrancy, and brawling. There were hardships—poverty, poor
sanitation, destruction from war—as well as tensions: rioting among the "labor-
ing classes," religious and ethnic hostility, and ongoing racial animus. And yet
there was also great optimism born of the widespread conviction that a Christian civilization was in the making. In this, America was broadly believed to hold

a privileged position and role. Its destiny was to be a "righteous empire," whose mores, manners, and law would reflect true biblical religion. America would be a bellwether in the establishment of the kingdom of God on Earth.

Church and Family

The Sunday school had a privileged position in this "empire" as a primary agent of church growth and of moral reform in society.[64] To accommodate this vision, both the mission (and audience) and the methods of church-based schooling were redefined. From evangelism, the Sunday school shifted its mission to nurturing. The targets of these efforts were no longer the unchurched but rather the middle-class children of the already churched.

Pedagogy changed as well. In this age of empire building, the Rockefellers, H. J. Heinz, and John Wanamaker all made efforts to employ the techniques of their businesses within the Sunday school. Wanamaker, for example, believed that both his Philadelphia mercantile business and the Bethany Sunday school he supervised could profit from the principles of efficiency, mass production, and advertisement. His idea was to make an enterprise known and make it attractive and serviceable.[65] Bethany Sunday school became a sign of progress in that it attracted, handled, and taught literally thousands of youngsters.[66] Indeed, it became the largest Sunday school in North America. A comparable experiment, called the "Akron design," featured a large auditorium divided up in small cubicles. A superintendent administered the weekly lesson plan from his desk at the front of the auditorium. With measured efficiency, "the superintendent could conduct opening exercises, keep an eye on classes and then review the lesson at the close, all from the splendor of his desk."[67] This too met with great success.

A key moment in this period was the establishment of the "International Sunday School Convention," a triennial forum whose purpose was to provide systematic training for teachers and unifying direction for the broader Sunday-school movement. Its goal was to contribute to the development of national unity and empire through a "uniformity of thought and action."[68] At the 1872 Chicago convention the group established the "International Uniform Lessons," a systematic set of Sunday school lessons centered on the Bible that could be studied each Sunday by every person—"from infants to infirms—in every Sunday school."[69] Seven years' worth of lessons took participants through the entire Bible. For the next forty years, the *International Uniform Lessons* constituted the major curriculum material of the Sunday-school world, holding a dominant place until about 1910.[70] The lessons were enthusiastically received and utilized by Methodists, Presbyterians, Baptists, Episcopalians, Congregationalists, Lutherans, Moravians, Friends, members of the Reformed Churches, Adventists—"a mighty host," said Warren Randolph, "to be enumerated only by millions."[71] By 1900 more than 3 million English students and teachers were using them. Additionally, the lessons were translated into over forty different languages. Though the plan, at the outset, was an effort to revive and remedy what was viewed as inefficiency in the Sunday school movement, eventually it took on a life of its own.

*   *   *

In the family as well, the nineteenth century marked a transitional period in the nature of moral instruction. Industrialization precipitated a demographic shift from the country to the cities. Its effect on the family was profound. In the working classes, father and mother as well as older siblings were absent from the home for long hours each day, and in the middle classes, there was an increasing role differentiation with father as provider and mother as child caretaker.[72]

One of the consequences was the development of a literature directed primarily at young men who had left the safety of the rural homestead for the adventures of either the frontier or the city. Often written by Evangelical ministers, books such as *Lectures to Young Men* (1832), *The Young Man's Friend* (1838), *The Young Lady's Companion* (1839), *A Young Man's Guide* (1840), *A Voice to Youth* (1847), celebrated the idealism of youth but warned of the dangers of rash judgment and fast living.

Even more significant was the development of a huge literature on childrearing aimed especially at middle-class mothers. In 1830, a mother looking for a book on child care would have found that the few that were available gave far more attention to physical care, manners, and salvation than to everyday problems of managing children. But a few years later she would scarcely have found time to read all the advice available.[73] *Essay on the State of Infants* (1830), *The Young Mother* (1836), *Letters to Mothers* (1838), *The Mother's Book* (1844), *Uncle Jerry's Letters to Young Mothers* (1857), and *Hints for the Nursery* (1863) were just some of the books available to parents.

By and large, the advice reflected the moral ethos of a rather muscular Calvinism. In John Abbot's *Mother at Home* (1833), for example, mothers were told in no uncertain terms that their own happiness was dependent upon their child's character and that establishing parental authority was the key to the development of good character. "Obedience," Abbot wrote,

> is absolutely essential to proper family government. Without this, all other efforts will be in vain. You may pray with, and for your children; you may strive to instruct them in religious truth; you may be unwearied in your efforts to make them happy, and to gain their affection. But if they are in

habits of disobedience, your instructions will be lost, and your toil will be in vain. And by obedience, I do not mean languid and dilatory yielding to repeated threats, but prompt and cheerful acquiescence in parental commands. Neither is it enough that a child should yield to your arguments and persuasions. It is essential that he should submit to your authority.[74]

Abbot's insistence on "perfect subjection" to the parent's authority is interesting in light of his view of the child's reasoning.

It is certainly the duty of parents to convince their children of the reasonableness and propriety of their requirements. This should be done to instruct them, and to make them acquainted with moral obligation. But there should always be *authority* sufficient to enforce prompt obedience, whether the child can see the reason of the requirement or not. Indeed, it is impossible to govern a child by mere argument. Many cases must occur, in which it will be incapable of seeing the reasonableness of the command; and often its wishes will be so strongly opposed to duty, that all the efforts to convince will be in vain. The first thing therefore to be aimed at, is to bring your child under perfect subjection. Teach him that he must obey you. Sometimes give him your reasons; again withhold them. But let him perfectly understand that he is to do as he is bid. Accustom him to immediate and cheerful acquiescence to your will. This is obedience. And this is absolutely essential to good family government.[75]

How was the habit of obedience established within a child? Abbot offered this principle: "Never give a command which you do not intend shall be obeyed. . . . When you do give a command, invariably enforce its obedience . . . if it disobeys you, all you have to do is to cut off its sources of enjoyment, or inflict bodily pain, so steadily and so invariably that disobedience and suffering shall be indissolubly connected in the mind of the child."[76] This, he said, was a "duty" and "sacred trust that God has committed to your care."

Yet this advice was also tempered by a measure of tenderness absent from the colonial writings on childrearing. Abbot was aware of some of the emerging theories of child psychology and recognized that "there [was] a very great diversity in the natural disposition of children; [that] some are very tender in their feelings, and easily governed by affection; [that] others are naturally independent and self-willed."[77] Depending on the child, parents must establish their authority in different ways. In all situations, he instructed mothers to "guard against too much severity"; to be "ever affectionate and mild with her children"; to "let her gain their confidence by her assiduous efforts to make them happy."[78] "In all cases in which it can be done, children should thus be governed by kindness."[79]

The same effort to balance a traditional Protestant orthodoxy with a new sensitivity to the individual needs and personality of the child is found in Theodore Dwight's *The Father's Book* (1834). Dwight's austere Calvinism is seemingly relentless, first and foremost in his view of original sin. The father, he writes,

> must remember that no child has ever been known since the earliest period of the world, destitute of an evil disposition; and that his infant, however sweet it may appear, has the same propensities within him, and will inevitably betray them. Whatever may be the prejudices, or the theories, of the father on the subject, if he lays out a plan of education on any principles which are not founded on this presumption, he will find that it will not suit the case. If he calculates on leading his child to choose the good by only presenting duty to his view, he will be most grievously disappointed. If he supposes that he has to deal with a being as much inclined to right as wrong, his whole practice in educating it will be full of painful facts to convince him of the contrary.[80]

Dwight's clearly asserted orthodoxy is self-consciously defensive, as though he knew the culture was in a process of forgetting. Indeed, he acknowledges that his views are a bit out of step with the leading edge of public opinion. Against "the lax discipline, and lax views of duty, fashionable with many fathers of the present day," he argues, the father "must sustain his authority and control over his son, or will expose himself and his family to a thousand evils. No trial, no self-denial, no exertion or sacrifice need be thought great, which will reclaim a youth in the early stage of disobedience and inclination to vice." To this end, "Habits of truth and honesty, of reverence for parents, the aged, and especially the Almighty, should be most sedulously cultivated, and insisted upon. Any plain violation of such rules should be noticed and dwelt upon as a thing of great moment—an offense not to be overlooked or slighted. The child should understand, by the earnestness and serious displeasure of the parent, that such practices are not to be tolerated, but perseveringly rooted out, under a solemn sense of duty to God." As if there were any doubt, he states most emphatically that "children should be obedient—must be obedient, habitually and cheerfully so, or they cannot be well educated in any respect."[81]

The resonance of American Puritanism is not noticeably diminished and yet there is a certain change of tone. Dwight cautions, for example, that "[a] young child should not be punished for every fretful expression." Corporal punishments should be but "seldom inflicted." "Soothing words, an embrace, a new and pleasant object of attention, will often suppress rising irritability."[82] Defensive though he may have been about the orthodoxy he admonished, Dwight could not avoid counseling a strong measure of gentleness, forbearance, and sensitivity. The spirit of the age demanded no less.

This liberal, modernist perspective became even more pronounced as the century wore on. Within a decade of Abbot's and Dwight's books, the great orator and preacher Horace Bushnell published *Christian Nurture* (1842). This work provided something of a bridge in the evolution of childrearing expertise, from a view rooted in religion to one resting on psychological foundations. To start with, Bushnell challenged the notion that children were "conceived in sin." Children, he argued, are not tainted with original sin but are "formless lumps" at birth, capable of both good and evil.[83] Bushnell was also perhaps the only writer of his day to suggest that children pass through developmental stages that required parents to maintain different expectations as the children grew up.[84] Parents' disciplinary techniques changed accordingly, as mothers "were encouraged to shield their children from the hazards of the 'outside' world and protect their innocence."[85] These themes were reiterated by Lyman Beecher's daughter Catherine in her books *Common Sense Applied to Religion* (1857) and *Religious Training of Children in the School, the Family, and the Church* (1864).[86]

In the latter part of the nineteenth century the themes of innocence and permissiveness were taken still further. Mattie W. Trippe's *Home Treatment for Children* (1881), for example, tells parents to "abolish law or the appearance of law" and "let [the child] revel in an absolute sense of freedom, feeling only the restraints of affection."[87] Similarly, Hannah Witall Smith writes in *The Science of Motherhood* (1894) that the "will is one of the most sacred parts of our nature and should no more be broken than the main shaft of a steam-engine."[88] Mothers should win their children to goodness by giving reasons behind right behavior, so that the child would learn to choose the right and moral path.

The advice parents received over the course of the nineteenth century was becoming distinctly less strident.[89]

The Transformation of the School

In the early decades of the nineteenth century, the evangelical consensus of faith and ethic had so come to dominate the national culture that most Protestants were willing to entrust the state with the task of educating children, confident that education would remain "religious." The sects identified their common beliefs with those of the nation, their mission with America's mission.[90] And yet the expansion of the common schools also signifies the beginning of an important transition both in the substance of moral instruction and the institutional locus of moral education—away from the family and churches to state-sponsored public schools.

The transformation in the content of moral education can be seen in the popular *McGuffey Readers*. A curricular staple of the nineteenth century—with more than 120 million copies sold between 1836 and 1920—the *Readers* at first followed the more sectarian orientation of the colonial period.[91] Their editor, William McGuffey, taught at Miami University of Ohio from 1826 to 1836 and at the University of Virginia from 1846 to 1873, and was himself trained under three Presbyterian ministers. Not surprisingly, then, he fully integrated a sectarian Protestant worldview with academic instruction.[92]

McGuffey's orthodox Calvinism is captured, for instance, in Lesson XXXVII of the *First Eclectic Reader* (1836):

> At the close of the day, before you go to sleep, you should not fail to pray to God to keep you from sin and harm. You ask your friends for food, and drink, and books, and clothes; and when they give you these things, you thank them, and love them for the good they do you. So you should ask your God for those things which he can give you, and which no one else can give you. You should ask him for life, and health, and strength; and you should pray for him to keep your feet from the ways of sin and shame. You should thank him for all his good gifts; and learn, while young, to put your trust in him; and the kind care of God will be with you, both in your youth and in your old age.[93]

In many respects the early readers read more like lay theology books than children's textbooks. The natural world was discussed and depicted as that which could only be properly understood in relation to God. Children were instructed in moral living from lessons from the Bible. Much emphasis was placed on the afterlife, sin, and salvation through Christ.

This emphasis changed in the later editions. By the third (1879) edition, now edited by Henry Vail, the theistic Calvinist worldview so dominant in the first editions had disappeared, and the prominent values of salvation, righteousness, and piety were entirely missing. Instead, the lessons affirmed the morality and lifestyle of the emerging middle class and those cultural beliefs, attitudes, and values that undergirded American civil religion.[94] Where the 1836 edition contained numerous selections from the Bible, by 1879 the only biblical passages were the Lord's Prayer and the Sermon on the Mount. The Protestant emphasis on piety, righteous living, and salvation gave way to the values of industry, hard work, loyalty, thrift, self-reliance, and individualism. In the 1836 edition the effect of a life of virtue would be realized in the afterlife; in the later editions, the virtue would reap material reward in the present world.

So different were the first and third editions of the *McGuffey Readers* that McGuffey, who compiled only the first edition and who died in 1873, would probably not have approved of the changes. This evolution represents an important shift away from the religious and sectarian emphasis of the colonial period toward the more inclusive content of the common school era. As John Wester-hoff notes, "the history of the Readers' various editions is best understood as a mirror of changes occurring in the history of American public education."[95] As such the early *Readers* are more representative of an era's end than a prototype of nineteenth-century education.[96]

With the changing cultural climate, use of the traditional readers became a matter of controversy. In California, as part of a larger battle with local authorities over control of education, the state board of education stopped using the *McGuffey Readers* in 1875, replacing them with the more progressive *Pacific Coast Readers,* published out of San Francisco. The conflict between the courts, the legislature, and the board of education over use of the *Readers* continued for another four years. Finally, an amendment to the California constitution effectively removed the *McGuffey Readers* as the state-mandated textbook for use in common schools.[97]

The removal of the *Readers* from California's common schools, the usurpation of control of the Public School Society schools in New York, and the introduction of antisectarian laws are signs of the weakening of the Protestant establishment's hold on the expanding educational system. Moral education began to draw more explicitly from a mixture of moral reference points, most identifiably the ideals of liberal individualism and the virtues of classical republicanism.

Horace Mann and Other Reformers

One individual stands out at this defining moment—Horace Mann, without question the most powerful figure in American education at the midpoint of the nineteenth century. A lawyer and educator from Massachusetts, Mann had rejected his New England Congregationalism in favor of progressive Unitarianism. The innovations he later championed reflected his own personal religiosity as much as they did the requirements of the age. Like many educational innovators and reformers, Mann was concerned with the "social ills" created by large numbers of poor children in the urban areas. Along with other important figures in the common school movement, including John Pierce of Michigan, Calvin Stowe of Ohio, and Henry Barnard of Connecticut, he saw the need to impart moral values to help these children become good citizens. "The naked capacity to read and write," he said, "is no more education than a tool is a workman . . . Moral education is a primal necessity."[98] His crusade for public education was at bottom a crusade for moral renewal; the public school would assume a large responsibility for the moral and religious training of children. The problem was that the Calvinist orthodoxy firmly established in the common schools was becoming disruptive in an increasingly diverse population. In the urban centers of the Northeast especially, the increasing numbers of immigrant Catholics and Jews were increasingly unwilling to accept Protestant hegemony in the schools.

For Mann, moral education had to be grounded in a religious conception of the world, but he rejected the methods of previous generations. He wanted the sectarian elements of Protestant faith eliminated from the school. The great common truths of Christianity, he felt, should be taught in such a way that no particular branch of faith or denomination would be favored. While it was still important, for instance, that the Bible be read in the classrooms, Mann insisted that it be read without comment or interpretation.[99] In this way he promoted what he regarded as the basic religious principles common to all creeds and the great, universal ethical principles which govern man's ideal relation to his fellows.

Consider, for example, the following statement written by Mann and issued by the Massachusetts Board of Education in 1847.

> I believe in the existence of a great, immutable principle of natural law, or natural ethics,—a principle antecedent to all human institutions and incapable of being abrogated by any ordinances of man,—a principle of divine origin, clearly legible in the ways of Providence as those ways are manifested in the order of nature and in the history of the race,—which proves the absolute right of every human being that comes into the world to an education; and which, of course, proves the correlative duty of every government to see that the means of that education are provided for all. . . . The will of God, as conspicuously manifested in the order of nature, and in the relations which he has established among men, places the right of every child that is born into the world to such a degree of education as will enable him, and, as far as possible will predispose him, to perform all domestic, social, civil and moral duties, upon the same clear ground of natural law and equity, as it places a child's right, upon his first coming into the world, to distend his lungs with a portion of the common air.[100]

In short, Mann and his colleagues promoted a form of moral instruction that carried much of the moral absolutism of an earlier Calvinism and yet without sectarian dogma, to the end that it would be more universal in its appeal. In effect, it laid greater emphasis on the training of citizens than on the training of Christian disciples.[101] This, surely, was a development consistent with themes evident in the later editions of the *McGuffey Readers*.

This reformist spirit had concrete effects. In 1842, the New York legislature removed control of the schools from the Public School Society, which had overseen them for more than thirty years, and placed it under the auspices of a newly created board of education. By the end of the nineteenth century, forty-one of the forty-six states had passed statutes forbidding sectarian influence within the common or public schools.[102] The legislative directives were aimed not only at sectarian control of schools but also at the use of sectarian instructional materials. An 1875 Arkansas statute held, for example, that "No teacher employed in any of the common schools shall permit sectarian books to be used as a reading or textbook in the school under his care."[103] Similarly, an 1895 New Hampshire statute held that "No books shall be introduced into the public schools calculated to favor any particular religious sect or political party."[104]

State government directives emphasized the republican and industrial-era virtues like moderation, truthfulness, frugality, patriotism, industry, temperance, and promptness. A late nineteenth century statute passed by the Massachusetts legislature, for instance, encouraged teachers to "impress on the minds of the children . . . the principles of morality and justice, and a sacred regard for truth; love of country, humanity and universal benevolence; sobriety, industry and frugality; chastity, moderation and temperance; and all other virtues which ornament human society."[105] Similarly, an 1897 statute in the state of Washington held,

It shall be the duty of all teachers to endeavor to impress on the minds of their pupils the principles of morality, truth, justice, temperance, humanity and patriotism; to teach them to avoid idleness, profanity and falsehood; to instruct them in the principles of free government; and to train them up to the true comprehension of the rights, duties and dignity of American citizenship.[106]

Yet the results were not always consistent. In 1869, the National Teacher's Association resolved that the Bible should be "devotionally read, and its precepts inculcated in all the common schools of the land." In 1884, the Iowa Supreme Court upheld a statute that forbade the exclusion of the Bible from schools. In 1885, the Massachusetts Legislature passed a constitutional amendment forbidding the use of public funds for sectarian schools but at the same time requiring that the Bible be read in the common schools of the state. And at the federal level, Senator Henry Blair of New Hampshire proposed a constitutional amendment in 1888 which would require every state to establish and maintain a public school system for all children in which knowledge, "virtue, morality, and the principles of the Christian religion" would be taught.[107] All of these initiatives illustrate how the American schools lumbered slowly away from a strictly Protestant basis of education to a more complex fusion of nonsectarian Protestant piety to republican idealism and enlightenment liberalism.

Other educational reformers pushed the argument even further. William Harris, for example, recognized the importance of moral instruction but advo-

cated a clear and total separation between church and state, and specifically between religious instruction and public-school moral education. Thus, while
Mann "actually promoted the teaching of 'general' Christianity in the school,
leaving the home and the Church to fill in what he called sectarian doctrines,"
Harris "opposed on principle the teaching of any kind of revealed religion in the
common school."[108] It is not that he rejected the importance of religious faith in
character education. Rather he believed that each institution is responsible for
character education *in its own way*. Religious teaching, and Bible reading in particular, should be left to the churches because their authoritative methods and
sacred surroundings were most conducive to proper communication of religious
principles and faith. The school, by contrast, should attend exclusively to secular
learning. Because of its atmosphere of discipline, Harris argued, the school
would be the most effective agent for moral training.

*   *   *

Not surprisingly, this transformation of moral education met resistance. A Con-
gregational minister in Boston, for example, charged that the purpose of the new
policies "had been to get the Bible out of the school and abolish religious instruction." He protested against the new ideas for building a school library, arguing that it "excludes books as sectarian that inculcate truths, which nine tenths of
professed Christians of all names believe, while it accepts others that inculcate
the most deadly heresy—even universal salvation."[109] A defining moment in this
transformation occurred in an exchange of letters between Frederick Packard,
corresponding secretary of the American Sunday School Union, and Horace
Mann. Speaking for traditional evangelical faith, Packard argued that one could
not teach morality through intellectual training alone. Such an approach artifi-
cially separated the "faculties" through which children learn, whereas true moral
education engaged both "the intellect" and "the affections." Children would behave morally only when they understood, both intellectually and emotionally,
the particular doctrines of Christianity. In Packard's view, true morality could
not be taught through "the beggarly elements of ethics and natural philosophy."
Mann, by contrast, countered that the particular doctrines of evangelicalism—
human depravity, atonement, heaven and hell—had no place in a common
school because they belonged to "the creeds of men" and so "divide[d] one set of
Christians from another." The books of the Sunday School Union, he felt, inspired fear instead of admiration. For evangelicals, this was tantamount to excis-
ing "all religious teaching" from the schools. One of Packard's supporters urged
Mann "to restore the kernel, not the shell—the substance, not the shadow" of
Christianity.[110]

Mann's critics were concerned not just with the emptying of religious content from moral education but with the changing structure of moral authority. One group of Boston schoolmasters, critical of Mann's more flexible and gentle approach to discipline in the classroom, insisted that the "first step which a teacher must take" before he is prepared to offer any moral instruction is

> to obtain the entire, unqualified submission of his school to his *authority*. We often err when designing to exert a moral influence, by substituting . . . persuasion for power; but we soon find that the gentle winning influence of moral suasion, however beautiful in theory, will often fall powerless upon the hearer, and we then must have authority to fall back upon or all is lost. . . . Neither school nor family can be preserved . . . by eloquence and argument alone. There must be authority. The pupils may not often feel it. But they *must know that it is always at hand*, and the pupils must be taught to submit to it as simple *authority*. The subjection of the governed to the will of one man . . . is the only government that will answer in school or in family. A government not of persuasion, not of reasons assigned, not of the will of the majority, but of the will of the one who presides.[111]

Through the last half of the nineteenth century, proponents of competing cultural traditions fought over the authoritative core of moral education in the schools. The outcome was perhaps inevitable. In the effort to accommodate greater religious diversity, educational gatekeepers introduced ever more abstract and universal content into moral pedagogy.[112] Moral instruction became increasingly detached from the substantive traditions, beliefs, and ritual practices of particular faith communities. With the rise of the progressives at the turn of the century, these developments became even more pronounced.

4

The Progressive Turn in Moral Education

The concept of character achieved new levels of public awareness in the late nineteenth century, reflecting the diversity of both secular and religious humanistic opinion. In the minds of many was the view that, "At no former period . . . has strength of character been so indispensable as it is at the present time."[1] But even this forthright affirmation of the importance of character contained an undercurrent of alarm that the ground beneath it was eroding.

Ralph Waldo Emerson's essay "Character," written in 1876, emerged as something of a classic statement of the time.[2] With wistful romanticism, Emerson regarded character as "an undemonstrable force . . . by whose impulse the man is guided but whose counsels he cannot impart." It is an act of nature—indeed, "nature in its highest form." For people who possess it, "the event is ancillary; it must follow him." In Emerson's view, "nature" was not void of substance but rather laden with meaning and purpose. Truth and justice were the highest expressions of the natural order. Character was simply the embodiment of these ideals.

Where Emerson saw character as a given of nature, a special charisma with which one was either endowed or not, by the end of the nineteenth century character was regarded as something one could explicitly develop. Even more, one had a responsibility to do so. James Russell Miller, a minister from Philadelphia, presented the Christian case in his 1894 book *The Building of Character*.[3] "The building of character," he argued, "is the most important business of life." One "cannot dream oneself into a character; you must hammer and forge yourself one." "Then each one must build his own character. No one can do it for him. No one but yourself can make your life beautiful. No one can be true, pure, honorable, and loving for you. . . . But we are ourselves the real builders." Miller regards character as the reflection of core "eternal principles"—truth, purity, and love. These are "the immutable principles which must be built into the foundation of the temple of character."

By the turn of the century, popular literature on character was reflecting the scientific progressivism of the period. Character, for many, was now a matter of "mental efficiency," a product of scientific will and discipline.[4] Writers spoke disdainfully of the "weak" and "feeble-minded" who were "slaves to their passions." Their numbers, "alas, are legion." "A person without character is so much less than man," one professor wrote.[5] Said another, their "principal defect consists in giving the preponderance to emotion over reason." "They pretend that they are not able to change the character of the motives which are the foundation of volition in what concerns their habitual faults, and with this erroneous premise they allow themselves to go ahead, with a *deplorable lack of all resistance*."[6] Against the life and ethic of the milksop are those with "strength of character;" those who possess "power over [their] instincts and passions." As one writer put it, "strength of character is not a simple thing: it is the resultant of a complex effort to exert the will directed upon a single point—the mastery of self."

> Self-mastery is a quality of the will that permits us to choose with reflection the act that we wish to accomplish. It is the power of directing its proper actions to their rightful aim, while at the same time freeing them from all foreign preoccupations. . . . It is above all that which gives us the power to rid ourselves of foreign suggestions . . . [those] motives opposed to the resolution we have fixt upon.[7]

As if to shore up the cultural conventions surrounding character, the Character Education Institute, in 1916, sponsored a National Morality Code Competition for the best children's code of morality. William J. Hutchins won with *The Children's Morality Code* and was awarded $5,000 for "expressing intelligent public opinion as to the moral ideas which ought to be inculcated into the hearts and minds of American children."[8] In some respects it was an unexceptional document. The code included loyalty, truth, self-control, good health, kindness, sportsmanship, self-reliance, duty, reliability, good workmanship, and teamwork. Much more significant was the way the code was framed. In keeping with the spirit of the times, it invoked no religious dimension or authority but rather was "verified by the popular vote of state character education committees, the expert opinion of social scientists," academic literature on moral education, and multiple lists of "desirable human characteristics" and morality codes. It contextualized the codes as "laws of right living which the best Americans have always obeyed." The larger moral appeal and inspiration was patriotic—to "welfare of our country," to what makes the country "great and good," and what constitutes "the good American."

The Character Factory

These ideas simultaneously took institutional form in the youth organizations that deluged middle-class society at the turn of the century. Their public mission was simply to develop strong moral character among the nation's young.

The earliest of the character-building institutions was the Young Men's Christian Association (YMCA), founded in London in 1844. Its roots were clearly in evangelical Christianity: the purpose of the association was "to influence young men to spread the Redeemer's Kingdom amongst those by whom they are surrounded"; its aim, "the winning of young men to Jesus Christ, and the building in them of Christian character."[9] The same impetus gave rise to the YWCA, an institution for women founded on the belief that "the principles of Christianity, understood and consistently applied, offer the solution to modern problems, economic and international, as well as the problems of personal life."[10]

By the beginning of the twentieth century, the cause of public Christianity had become indistinguishable from the advance of civilization itself. And yet the structure of the Anglo-Saxon and Christian empire was also beginning to falter, especially in Britain. Character-building agencies arose in large part as an effort to shore up the insecurities of a middle class whose values permeated national life. The gaps in socialization between home and school would be filled with character-building activities and relationships; thus these institutions would salvage the idle hours of adolescents and so remedy what was perceived as a moral and physical weakness in national life.[11]

The pressures of a faltering empire were especially evident in the emergence of Scouting. Scouting began in 1908 as a quintessential British movement arising out of the social and historical circumstances of Edwardian England, whose needs it addressed and whose values permeated it.[12] The aim of character formation was much more ambitious than simply giving middle-class boys something constructive to do. As H. S. Pelham wrote,

> He is going to be a man one day. In his hands lie the future of the city, the country, and the church to which he belongs. His own future, therefore, is one of paramount importance to Church and State . . . . Surely men of education and wealth should learn that perhaps the greatest service they can render to the State is to train the future citizen by bringing to bear upon him when he is young and unsettled the influence of a strong and healthy character.[13]

Thus, when Boy Scouts pledged—on their honor—to do their "duty to God and country" and to keep themselves "physically strong, mentally awake, and morally straight," they served their own best interest and those of the nation.[14] The founder of the Boy Scouts, Robert Baden-Powell, was explicit about this in 1908: "Our business is not merely to keep up smart 'show' troops, but to pass as many boys through our *character factory* as we possibly can: at the same time, the longer the grind that we can give them the better men they will be in the end."[15]

The ideals of the Girls Scouts were complementary. "If character training and learning citizenship are necessary for boys, how much more important it is that these principles should be instilled into the minds of girls who are destined to be the mothers and guides of the next generation."[16] Thus Juliette Low, founder of the Girl Scouts, wrote in 1919 that the explicit purpose of the Girl Scouts was "to promote the virtues of womanhood by training girls to recognize their obligations to God and country, to prepare for duties devolving upon women in the home, in society and the State, and to guide them in ways conducive to personal honor and the public good."[17] These duties, while distinct from those of boys, were no less demanding of austerity, discipline, and fortitude. In the first Girl Scouts handbook, published in 1913, the first duty discussed under "how girls can help their country" is "Be Womanly."

> No one wants women to be soldiers. None of us like women who ape men. An imitation diamond is not as good as a real diamond. An imitation fur coat is not as good as real fur. Girls will do no good by trying to imitate boys. You will only be a poor imitation. It is better to be a real girl such as no boy can possibly be. Everybody loves a girl who is sweet and tender and who can gently soothe those who are weary or in pain. . . . For the boys [Scouting] teaches MANLINESS, but for the girls it all tends to WOMANLINESS and enables girls the better to help in the great battle of life.[18]

Toward this end, girls are told that "to carry out all the duties and work of a Scout properly a girl must be strong and healthy" by "sleep[ing] with the windows open summer and winter" so that they "will never catch cold," not to sleep in "too soft a bed" for it "tends to make people dream which is unhealthy and weakening," not to "lay abed in the morning thinking how awful it is to have to get up." Rather, girls should "rouse out at once and take a smart turn of some quick exercise." They should also "[k]now how to do many useful things" and to "do them in the best way, the shortest way, and in the most economical manner." The payoff is when they "are grown up and have children of [their] own to bring up" then they will "know what food to give them, how to look after their health, how to make them strong, and how to teach them to be good, hard-working, honorable citizens in our big growing country." In the lines that immediately follow, the manual states the end of the matter: "Almost every man you read of in history, who has risen to a high position, has been helped by his mother. We have had many great and good men and they were made great and good by their mothers."[19]

Here too, as one would expect, the character the Girl Scouts and other character organizations sought to build was, more often than not, explicitly Christian.[20] As Richardson and Loomis wrote in 1915, the Boy Scout organization "recognizes religion as a *most necessary* and *vital force* in the development of a boy's character."[21] Indeed, more than half of the early troops were church-sponsored, and nearly a third of all Scoutmasters were ministers.[22] Girl Scout instructors were told that "the Sabbath is too often a day of loafing, and, morally, the worst day in the whole week." Therefore girls "should without fail, attend Church or Chapel, or a Church Parade or Prayers of their own, on Sunday mornings"; Sunday should be "a day of rest" and of "practic[ing] good turns."[23] This spiritual basis also underlay the development of the Camp Fire Girls. Luther Gulick, the founder of the Camp Fire Girls, explained in 1912: "If ever woman was needed, it is today. The very riot of our material riches is the peril of our souls. Woman is already taking hold of the present material world, giving to it and bringing into it the love and service and spiritual relations which in the old days created the home . . . The Camp Fire Girls is an organization which aims to bring the power of organization and the charm of romance again into the humble acts and needs of daily life."[24]

Though Protestant in foundation and Victorian and Edwardian in mission, these institutions were soon to feel the winds of change, change that came primarily from innovations in educational theory and practice.

Schools

During the progressive era—in educational history, roughly the first half of the twentieth century—educators placed a great emphasis upon the themes of personal freedom and individual rights in curricula, themes that were present but only just detectable at the end of the nineteenth century. By this point schools had become the dominant institution in the lives of children, not least because education had now become compulsory. Massachusetts was the first to pass a compulsory attendance law in 1852. In a few decades, all but a few Southern states had passed similar laws.

The commitment to moral education in the schools did not waver at all in the early years of the twentieth century. At the beginning of this period, ambitious new programs for "character education" and "citizenship training" became nearly ubiquitous in classrooms across the nation. Educators continued to believe that religion had a role to play, but they insisted that the institutions of democracy and capitalism carried important moral influence too. The ideals of personal faith, politics, and economy were viewed as overlapping and mutually reinforcing in ways that provided a cluster of ethical lessons essential to life in contemporary America. Justice, individual liberty and the consent of the governed, personal character (including such qualities as promptness, truthfulness, courtesy, and obedience and industry), social propriety in public and private life, and the superiority of Protestant civilization all occupied an uncontested, quasi-sacred place in mainstream public discourse and social life. The inculcation of these ideals among the young and among the immigrant was a high priority.[25] To this end, schools—often mandated by state legislatures or local boards of education—revised history and literature curricula to more fully reflect these ideals, strengthened discipline standards for pupils, instituted daily flag salutes and citizenship-oriented assemblies.

Yet Progressive school reformers began to promote even further reaching changes in the content of moral pedagogy as well as its methods. At the center of these efforts were the ideas of the philosopher and educational theorist John Dewey.

The heart of Dewey's innovations was a rejection of revealed religion as the foundation of educational practice. The progressives' goal was not so much to secularize the public schools but rather to redefine "religion" and "faith" so as to delete any supernatural and sectarian elements. For Dewey, faith in a divine and fixed authority, and ideas of the soul and its eternal destiny, were no longer possible as the foundation of Western civilization, of stable institutions, or of social progress.[26] It was therefore necessary to reject the supernaturalism, fixed dogma, and rigid institutionalism with which Christianity had been historically associated. As Dewey stated in his "Credo" on religion, "faith in its newer sense signifies that *experience itself is the sole ultimate authority*."[27] And yet Dewey was not a subjectivist either; he had faith that the collective effort of science and the scientific method could address most human problems. The point of connection between science, faith, and education was his belief in the mutability of life. The outstanding fact in all branches of natural science, he observed, is that to exist is to be in process. What is self-evident in the natural world must also be applicable to religion, morality, and politics. In applying these to education, Dewey was in agreement with Mann in opposing sectarian religion in the public school, and in agreement with Harris against any form of supernatural religion in the classrooms. He placed his faith in values verifiable in social experience.

In practice, Dewey's methodology implied a shift away from "morality" as something to be imposed upon the child. Rather, children were to be regarded as having the capacity to determine their own moral standards. He believed that the natural tendency toward justice and goodness resided within the intellectual and moral faculties of the child. Dewey and his colleagues agreed that the definition of moral behavior depended more upon the circumstances in which the individual existed than upon a code of a priori rules. Thus, "Chastity, kindness, honesty, patriotism, modesty, toleration, bravery, etc., cannot be given a fixed meaning, because each expresses an interest in objects and institutions which are changing."[28] Dewey's methodology was reflected in his concept of character. Early in his career, perhaps in deference to the popularity of the concept, Dewey did speak of character as something to be cultivated, yet he was also critical of the transcendent mystique it carried in the popular literature. Later, though, Dewey devalued the concept. Character was not so much living according to certain moral principles, but rather simply the "interpenetration of habits" in a person's life.[29] These habits predispose people to act in certain predictable ways. So it is that a person's habits define their character. – personality

It is important to emphasize that though Dewey rejected objective and fixed standards as a foundation of moral understanding and character development in favor of deliberative and contextual criteria, he did not embrace a facile relativism. Like many social philosophers during the progressive era, Dewey had great confidence in the power of reason and scientific inquiry to guide behavior. Correct moral behavior merely required the individual to think rationally about his particular life experience and then to act accordingly.

It is also important to emphasize that Dewey did not entrust his faith to isolated reason or isolated experience. Morality, for Dewey, originated in society; all ethical and moral understanding, therefore, was social. Identity too was social. As he once noted, "What one is as a person is what one is as associated with others in a free give-and-take of intercourse."[30] So too, Dewey believed that ethics itself could be understood only in the context of complex social relationships whose meaning could be determined only in actual experience.[31] The new *summum bonum* of social life in the modern world was democracy itself—a social order that could not allow for values superior to those of the shared experience of democratic living. Democracy, for Dewey, was inherently moral; its institutions authoritative; its practices exemplary for personal conduct. In his naturalist frame of reference, moral values were nothing more than civic values; moral virtue was democratic virtue. It is not difficult to see, then, that for Dewey, democracy was less a form of government than a way of life—a spiritual community.[32]

In this light, schools would not only be the handmaiden of democracy, they would themselves be a mode of democratic life. They would model democratic experience in embryonic form and in so doing, "teach morals . . . every moment in the day, five days in the week."[33] The object, he argued, was not to get children to quarrel endlessly about which moral rules should prevail in this or that hypothetical situation, but rather to help "the formation of a sympathetic imagination for human relations in action; this is the ideal which is substituted for training in moral rules."[34]

Children, then, were capable of arriving at socially intelligent decisions through informed observations of complex realities. Thus, if one merely presented to them the realities of their world, they could make informed social decisions. To this end, Dewey and his supporters called upon the schools to teach a mode of reasoning about moral decisions, provide students with sufficient information about society, and encourage habits that would foster personal growth and a commitment to a liberal democratic community.[35] If the schools rewarded this behavior it would continue into adulthood. Teachers needed only to improve students' social understanding to ensure that everyone would act properly.[36]

Needless to say, Dewey's project had revolutionary implications. As a matter of pedagogic principle he regarded the typical school's heavy emphasis upon rigid conformity (in the classroom and on the playground) more as an impediment to the development of children than as an aid. The entire system of traditional pedagogy was simply flawed. The progressive conception of moral education sought change first through championing individual freedom through practical, experiential, and scientific engagement. As Dewey put it, moral education should be centered in "reflective thought, not in character training or heart warming."[37] The locus of moral authority shifted from external, objective criteria to subjective experience mediated by social relationships.

Not only did progressive education emerge as a powerful rival to the Puritan and romantic formulations, it undermined the very possibility of sustaining traditional cultural systems in education. Progressive educational ideas foreshadowed the continuing transformation of moral education and public education generally.

The evolution toward subjectivity was more evident in theory than in practice. In the early years of the twentieth century, Dewey was frustrated by the slow incorporation of his ideas into educational practice. Yet change eventually came. By 1919, schools reflecting his educational philosophy were "rapidly coming into being in large numbers all over the country."[38] Its main influence was in the application of scientific method to the curriculum for the purposes of making education a direct preparation for life. Equally influential was the new-found emphasis on the independence of the child for the purposes of liberating children to develop socially, intellectually, and morally.[39] In its general contours, this formal shift in educational philosophy remains intact today.

The extent to which Dewey's ideas spread through the landscape of public education is evident in the 1951 publication *Moral and Spiritual Values in the Pub-*

lic Schools, a report of the National Education Association's Educational Policies Commission.[40] The commissioners asserted anew that "an unremitting concern for moral and spiritual values continues to be a top priority for education." The challenge in the rapidly changing postwar environment was to define those values and their relation to the legacy of powerful religious traditions. The strategy, in short, was to reject the particularity of moral and religious tradition in favor of the essence common to all. In slightly different terms, they explicitly encouraged the adoption of the "consensus" moral and spiritual values held by people in America—the values "shared by the members of all religious faiths." "However we may disagree on religious creeds," they explained, "we can agree on moral and spiritual values. The fact that we can agree to judge behavior in terms of common values and at the same time agree to differ with respect to the religious interpretation of the source of these values is an asset and achievement of no mean importance." The policy of the public schools must be "hospitable to all religious opinions and partial to none of them."

A range of moral and spiritual values was listed for the reader, including moral responsibility, common consent, brotherhood, moral equality, the pursuit of happiness, spiritual enrichment, and the like, but at the top of the list, "fundamental to all that follow," was "the supreme importance of the individual personality."[41]

> This value requires a school system which, by making freely available the common heritage of human association and human culture, opens to every child the opportunity to grow to his full stature. It favors those plans of school organization and instruction which recognize and meet the varying needs and aspirations of individuals. By exploring and acknowledging the capacities of each child, education seeks to develop all his creative powers, to encourage him to feel that he can do things of value, that he belongs, and that he is wanted. It discourages every tendency toward despotism.[42]

To their credit, the commissioners recognized that it was not sufficient to assert values without moral explanations. As they explained, "*from the point of view of educational policy and program*, sanctions [or moral explanations] are of primary importance. Children and young people typically, and sometimes annoyingly, want to know *why*. They do not readily believe, or trust, or act upon, the instruction of those who tell them that this is no reason at all for preferring one kind of conduct over another, or that any reason at all will do equally well. . . . On neither pedagogical nor on ideological grounds can the schools ignore the problem of sanctions"—the problem posed by the question *why*.[43] To this end, they offered an illustration in which a young boy was given the wrong change by a store clerk, to the boy's advantage. Seven explanations were invoked as possible reasons why the boy should return the money, including the appeal to fair play, punishment, property rights, guilt feelings, group approval/disapproval, authority, and empathy. Any of these explanations might work, they declared, but they stressed that the choice of sanctions "should involve the largest possible freedom for the child's reason. Other things being equal, the more responsible self-determination and judgment that can be brought to bear on a moral situation the better. It follows that the sanctions used should be adapted to the maturity of the child."[44] Though the authors recognized that explanations rooted in religious doctrine "may play a powerful role in the moral and spiritual instruction of home and church," they were deliberately excluded for the simple legal reason that they "may not be explicitly invoked in the public school classroom."

In line with Dewey's pedagogy, all of these values are "dictated by reason" and "subject to reinterpretation in the light of new experience[s]." The values can and should "be reappraised from time to time." Moreover, the particularities of religious faith, whether Protestant, Catholic, Jewish, or Muslim, are not discounted so much as safely privatized. Finally, at the very center of this moral universe is the individual—supreme, autonomous, rational, evolving, and basically good.

The Broader Influence of Progressivism

Dewey, of course, was not alone. Indeed, as it is often said, if Dewey didn't exist he would have had to be invented: for the ideas of the inherent goodness and teachability of the child, so hostile to the Calvinism of earlier generations, were becoming widely popular as early as the 1890s. Consider, for example, Kate Wiggins's *Children's Rights*, published in 1892. "Parental authority," she observed, "never used to be called into question; neither was the catechism, nor the Bible, nor the minister." But now they were—all of them. "It seems likely that the rod of reason will have to replace the rod of birch."[45] Needless to say, the rod of reason was embodied in the authority of science. For Wiggins, the change was long overdue.

Her book further illustrates the shift away from the biblical dogma, catechism, and hierarchy of a "God-centered" view of moral development to an approach that was more child-centered, egalitarian, and secular. Wiggins barely restrains her contempt for the old methods of training and discipline, calling them "all equally dull, blind, and vicious," and "positively degrading." She states that "blind obedience to authority is not in itself moral." "The child who obeys you merely because he fears punishment is a slave who cowers under the lash of a despot." So too the "endeavor to secure goodness in a child by means of bribery, to promise him a reward in case he obeys you, is manifestly an absurdity. You are destroying the very traits in his character you are presumably endeavoring to build up."[46] Her impatience naturally extended to the traditional sources of moral authority. Where previously parents were sovereign and unquestioned, she angrily contends that "in too many cases parents interfere . . . mischievously and unnecessarily."[47]

Against the traditional ways, Wiggins gave voice to the view that a child has "inalienable rights" including "the right to his childhood," the "right to a place of his own, to things of his own, to surroundings which have some relation to his size, his desires, and his capabilities," as well as "the right to more justice in his discipline than we are generally wise and patient enough to give him."[48] All were rights to be respected. Moreover, most children, "have a tolerably clear sense of right and wrong needing only gentle guidance to choose the right when it is put before them" as well as "a natural sense of what is true and good." All that was necessary was to "surround the child in his earlier years with such an atmosphere of goodness, beauty, wisdom, none can doubt that he would unconsciously grow into harmony and union with the All-Good, the All-Beautiful, and the All-Wise." Thus it was no longer wise to use "an arbitrary and a threatening manner in our commands to children, when a calm, gentle request, in a tone of expectant confidence, would gain obedience far more quickly and pleasantly." The parents' task, she concluded, *"is to train responsible, self-directing agents, not to make soldiers."*[49] As she explained, "With every free, conscious choice of right, a human being's moral power and strength of character increase; and the converse of this is equally true."[50]

Scholarly reinforcement for this approach came from the ideas of G. Stanley Hall, perhaps the most influential of the early child-centered educators and an early mentor of Dewey's at Johns Hopkins. Hall's paradigm was a rationalist and evolutionary one, in which the individual, through the succeeding stages of childhood, recapitulates the epochs of history. In this model the concept of "adolescence"—which he described as a kind of second birth, marked by a sudden rise of moral idealism, chivalry, and religious enthusiasm—acquired a central place in the lexicon of moral theory.[51] Instead of a time to build character, childhood was understood as an "easygoing, cavorting stage which youngsters must pass through peaceably if they were eventually to become mature, self-controlled adults."[52] Hall counseled parents "to be indulgent with young children; to treat them as young animals who simply have to behave as they do."[53] "The guardians of the young," he said,

> should strive first of all to keep out of nature's way, and to prevent harm, and should merit the proud title of defenders of the happiness and rights of children. They should feel profoundly that childhood, as it comes fresh

from the hands of God, is not corrupt, but illustrates the survival of the most consummate thing in the world; they should be convinced that there is nothing else so worthy of love, reverence, and service as the body and soul of the growing child.[54]

In all, the transformation in the formal ideas about the development of children and the role of teachers and parents in assisting in the process was Copernican. At the center of this transformation were children, who were no longer regarded as degenerate but rather as innocent, vulnerable, and malleable. From this point on, the emphasis of moral instruction was upon protecting and molding children to the responsible and rational living out of their personal freedom.[55]

*   *   *

Indeed, the innovations of the expert quickly became the fashion within other areas of social life. In the realm of religious faith, a division had opened between fundamentalists and modernists in theology, ecclesiology, and, not least, the moral pedagogy of the Sunday school. On one side, evangelicals wanted to keep Sunday school pretty much as it had always been—evangelistic, biblical, systematic. On the other side were a new order of church professionals, committed to reforming Sunday school in accordance with changing fashions of American culture. These professionals were drawn to the progressive educational theory represented by Dewey's experimental philosophy and to the theological innovations embodied in the social gospel of Walter Rauschenbusch.

Under the auspices of the Religious Educational Association, founded in 1903, progressives determined to break out of the routinized and antiquated methods of the Uniform Lessons era. Religious educators first pushed beyond the Akron design (see Chapter 3) in the organization of church-school facilities. They often persuaded congregations that learning was enhanced by settings more comfortable and functional than auditoriums with partitioned cubbyholes.[56] At the same time, a new class of professionals supplanted the established leadership of the Sunday school movement; the clergy of the old moral order gave way to the psychologists and educators of the progressivist movement. Volunteers were treated, perhaps unconsciously, as potential trainees and beneficiaries of the experts' guidance.[57] A corresponding shift took place in the moral pedagogy of the Sunday schools. Children were less and less regarded as sinners in need of conversion and more as individuals whose unique personalities and needs would require individual attention.

At the forefront of this movement was George Albert Coe, a senior statesman in the Religious Education Association (REA) and in every way a philosophical compatriot of John Dewey. As a religious liberal he reworked the language of faith into terms compatible with the pragmatism advocated by Dewey and James. Faith was not a body of doctrine or an acceptance of authority but rather "an ambition to create a moral universe."[58] Likewise, truth was comprised of values that would influence human conduct to the good—"a priori truths existing in static rigidity from all eternity are ruled out."[59] The Sunday school was to provide "an experiential model of American society at its best—a foretaste of the Kingdom of God," understood as the ideal social order.[60]

It was not only the fundamentalists who resisted these innovations. Even in the mainline churches one could find voices of wariness. Figures such as H. Shelton Smith at Duke, Walter Athearn at Boston University, E. G. Homrighausen of Princeton, and Walter Horton of Oberlin all took issue with the secular and psychological reductionism of their colleagues. They all acknowledged the important insights of contemporary philosophy and psychology but held their ground on eternal transcendent truths of their faith. As Athearn put it, "The world cannot be saved by pedagogy alone. . . . Christianity implies the truth of certain metaphysical and ethical theories and the untruth of others."[61]

Notwithstanding these sorts of tensions, it was progressives who had their way in the mainline churches. By the early 1940s, the Presbyterians, Methodists, Lutherans, and Episcopalians had largely accepted a psychologically based pragmatism as the framework for the religious education of the youth. Of course, educational psychology and experienced-based instruction were a bit slower working into the actual pedagogy offered in parish Sunday schools, yet the terms were set. Transcendent moral truths and the authority of Christian traditions were moving inexorably to the margins.

*   *   *

Within the middle-class family as well, the new science of psychology was becoming a more authoritative source of moral instruction than religion. Not only did the Deity disappear from books and articles on child care, but the role of family legacy and the church in shaping popular ideas of parenting weakened as well. The world of children became the property of professional child-trainers—kindergarten teachers, social workers, pediatricians, psychologists—people convinced they knew what they were doing.[62] The new science of psychology did not always lead to uniform ideas, but its influence in framing public discussion was undeniable.[63] In the early decades of the twentieth century, the institutional authority of psychology had become foundational.

By the late 1940s and early 1950s, the early years of the baby boom, parents were eager for new advice. Popular magazines were filled with the advice of psychologists, psychiatrists, and other experts happy to impart their wisdom. In

Children Have Their Reasons (1942), for example, parents are asked "Why go it alone?" The response: parents and child psychologists form a partnership. "The day is at hand when going to see someone interested in mental health will be included in every child's annual list of events."[64]

Writing in *Parents Magazine*, one consulting psychologist contrasted the old ways of disciplining children with the new. In brief, her argument went this way: Rewards? They send the wrong message. Praise? Children know when it is superficial. Punishment? One only adds insult to injury. Isolation? It does just the opposite of what the parent intends. Reasoning? It tends to take the problem away from the child. The new and better way to deal with discipline problems is to give the child

> the opportunity to tell us and show us how [they] are thinking and feeling so that we may help [them] work these things through. . . . When we fail to help a child release his feelings, when we handle him so that he denies them and pushes them into his unconscious mind they move out of his control. . . . Self-control . . . lies in keeping the 'bad' feelings in the open until they work themselves out.[65]

The bad child, in other words, is merely misunderstood. Therefore, it is necessary "to find out *why* he feels so unsure of himself." Writing in *Better Homes and Gardens* on the question "If Your Youngster Lies, Cheats, and Steals," another psychologist explained that "cheating . . . often represents a youngster's attempt to compensate for feelings of insecurity or inferiority"; and that dishonesty is often children's way of "showing their need for approval." Whatever the case, it is essential for parents to make the youngster "feel strong and secure enough to face life without fear or confusion."[66] As still another expert put it, "If we can keep 'punishing' to a minimum, and instead put the emphasis on leading him cheerfully and affectionately, we hope he will stand securely on his own feet much more quickly."[67] Not only do the old methods of moral education in the home not work but, as the new guardians of the moral order pointed out, "the person most apt to suffer from emotional disorders later in life is the one who is an overgood child, the child who conforms to too great a degree."[68]

As progressive psychological understandings of the relationship between children and the moral order became popularized, so too did the progressivist assumptions about moral character. "The actual building of character is an individual, personal thing," wrote Rhoda Bacmeister (sounding much like Dewey), and any moral prescriptions "must be adapted to meet the needs of the particular child."[69] Explaining how "old ideas of character building have given place to new ones" another expert concluded that "we should not worry so much about neatness, perseverance, obedience and other isolated traits, but we should be very much concerned with feelings and attitudes which the child is developing toward life and toward other people. These are the things which count in life and build real character."[70]

Hierarchical notions of family government were likewise quickly becoming passé, replaced by a more egalitarian and democratic structure. Parents, said one, "belong beside the child, the two working honestly together to become better disciplined individuals."[71] The child's behavior was in this way remarkably improved. As one psychiatrist put it, "If you want your child to do what you want him to do when you want him to do it, then you must first learn to do for your child what he wants you to do when he wants you to do it. If you conform to the child's wishes, he will conform to yours."[72] The "healthy child-parent relationship," a family psychologist explained, is marked by a "spontaneous exchange of feeling . . . on both sides."[73] One mother, describing her experience with a "flexible form of democratic government" involving her children's help to establish the family rules, found that it had "strengthened our children's self-reliance, self-discipline, and self-respect."[74]

Discrediting the Character Ideal

By the end of the progressive period the concept of character had largely been discredited. The starting point was, in many respects, the legendary Dewey himself. His devaluation of character from a force of nature to a mere set of habits that pattern a person's everyday life was a decisive step in this direction. Thus weakened, the word lost its moral cachet and its distinctive rhetorical power. It is not surprising that even Dewey eventually retreated from the concept.[75]

The flourishing of scientific psychology was another key factor, especially in the use of new educational testing techniques.[76] For instance, the most famous of these, the Hartshorne and May studies conducted in the mid-1920s,[77] found little or no relationship between character-education techniques and various forms of good and bad behavior. *In nuce*, they found that "good character" was not a unified trait and thus could not be cultivated by any single educational technique. Good conduct was mostly situation-specific. Though later reevaluation of the data has since called into question some of the conclusions, the effect at the time was to undermine the idea that character has any bearing on the actual conduct of a person's life. Character might be an inspirational metaphor in moral ideology but as a concept it lacked any empirical validity. For the psychologist of the period, the term lost its technical significance and therefore its scientific value. Thus it was logical for Harvard's Gordon Allport to state, in the 1930s, that character was merely "personality evaluated and personality is character devalued." We "must frankly admit that [character] is an ethical concept" and, as such, "the psychologist does not need the term at all; personality alone will serve."[78]

Clearly the progressive period marks the early ascendance of the science of psychology and the simultaneous retreat of moral theology. The fate of the concept of character is an indication of this transformation. Not only was the concept of character discredited, but the very idea of moral excellence was displaced by the ideal of personal effectiveness. Accordingly, the classic and religious virtues associated with strong moral character (such as courage, loyalty, truthfulness, integrity) had now given way to the grammar of psychological well-being (self-confidence, integration, and social adjustment).

Psychological Humanism
in the Postwar Era

Schools continued to practice rather conventional programs of moral education through the 1930s, 1940s, and 1950s. These programs relied upon a diffuse civil religious faith and accordingly reflected a traditional collection of moral standards roughly equivalent to the Scout's pledge. By midcentury, however, the framework of change within moral education had been fully established.

Within academic discussion—through the work of such people as Erik Erikson, Benjamin Spock, Carl Rodgers, B. F. Skinner, Haim Ginott, and Rudolf Driekurs—psychology had no rival as the way to think about moral life and understanding. With this dominance came the ongoing reinterpretation of traditional methods of moral education and their underlying religious ideals. Religious tradition was not so much attacked and debunked as it was explained, rationalized, and thus trivialized. For G. Stanley Hall, for example, who had put the concept of adolescence on the map fifty years earlier, religious conversion could now be understood merely as a developmental stage—"a natural, normal, universal, and necessary process at the stage when life pivots over from an auto-centric to an heterocentric basis."[79] The foundation of psychological reductionism Hall had helped lay down became commonplace, making traditional methods of moral education seem anachronistic if not inhumane. In Erik Erikson's *Identity and the Life Cycle*, for example, the emphasis one finds on "shame, doubt, guilt and fear" in traditional forms of authority tends to have the effect of depriving a child of an enduring sense of independence. For Erikson, traditionalists excel in the "negative" side of the second stage of development, encouraging shame and doubt within children as opposed to a healthy ego identity marked by a lasting sense of autonomy and self-reliance rooted in self-esteem.[80]

* * *

Expert opinion reflected this attitude in the parenting literature. In books like *Baby and Child Care* (1946), *Don't Be Afraid of Your Child* (1952), *Have Fun with Your Children* (1954), *Democracy in the Home* (1954), *The Happy Child* (1955), *Between Parent and Child* (1955), *Your Child's Self-Esteem* (1970), *How to Parent* (1971), and *Raising a Responsible Child: Practical Steps to Successful Family Relationships* (1973), traditional religious faith is dealt with sparingly or not at all. Rudolf Driekurs's *Children: The Challenge* (1964), for example, regarded traditional methods of moral instruction as potential detriments to "true growth and development."[81] Driekurs discouraged parents from discussing the consequences of life after death with a child because it "cramps [the child's] style, denies him freedom of growth and the strength to assume responsibility."[82] In a four-page chapter revealingly entitled "Use Religion Wisely" (and saved for second to last), Dreikurs described a scenario in which a mother denounces her daughter's "bold-faced lie" as something displeasing to God. In Dreikurs's view, this only "adds to [the daughter's] discouragement." He writes, "It is so much easier for a child to be good that he has no need to be bad unless he has met obstacles in his environment that have caused him to become discouraged and turn to misbehavior as a way out of his difficulty. Since the child has a purpose in his misbehavior, moralizing does not change it nor remove the obstacle. . . . Far from needing the condemnation implied in 'moralizing,' the child needs encouragement and help out of his difficulty."[83]

The turn in this literature was decidedly lenient. Words like "training" disappeared from the child-care vocabulary. Concern for character development largely disappeared as well. In its place emerged a concern for developing the child's happiness and self-regard.

* * *

The historical premises of youth organizations were challenged as well. The emphasis on character development through the inculcation of classic and Christian virtues gave way to more psychologically sophisticated ways of imparting values. Likewise, the founders' educational aims gave way to recreational and therapeutic purposes.[84]

The evolution was clearly uneven—the Boy Scouts, for instance, remained stoutly traditional in its mission. Yet nowhere was this tendency more evident than in the Girl Scouts, particularly as its leadership reconceptualized ideas of obligation toward others and the social world. Juliette Low, the founder of the Girl Scouts, regularly preached the theme of denial of self and service to others.

Consider, for example, changes in the organization's second law: a Girl Scout is "loyal."[85] Of this, Robert Baden-Powell had said, "A Guide is loyal to God, and the King, to her parents and Guides, to her friends and fellow-workers and to those over and under her at school or at work. She must stand by them through thick and thin. She will never speak ill of them herself, and will stick up for them if she hears other people doing so." The 1929 *Girl Scout Handbook* explained:

> That she is true to her Country, to the city or village where she is a citizen, to her family, her friends, her church, her school, and to those for whom she may work, or who may work for her. Her belief in them may be the very thing they need most, and they must feel that whoever else may fail them, a Girl Scout never will. And she is not only loyal to people but also to the highest ideals which she knows.

By 1948, the Handbook explained that loyalty means that "she is true to the things *she thinks are right and good.*"[86] By 1972, the Girl Scouts had deleted this law completely, replacing it with "I will do my best to be fair." Their justification for the change was that "many younger girls did not understand the word [loyal]; older girls and adults asked 'loyal to what?'" Acknowledging the "dangers of uncritical loyalty" the Girl Scouts felt this new law better focused girls on the "need to learn to make unbiased judgments and to work for equity and justice."[87]

Likewise, according to the tenth law, a Girl Scout was to be "clean in thought, word, and deed." In 1920 and again in 1929, the handbook summarized this law as "good breeding." "Good breeding means first of all thoughtfulness of others, and nothing shows lack of breeding so quickly as a lack of such politeness to those who happen to be serving us in hotels, at home, in shops, or when traveling or anywhere else."[88] Moreover, "a good housekeeper cannot endure dust and dirt; a well cared for body cannot endure grime or soil; a pure mind cannot endure doubtful thoughts that cannot be freely aired and ventilated." Finally, "It is a pretty safe rule for a Girl Scout not to read things nor discuss things nor do things that could not be read nor discussed nor done by a Patrol all together." The 1948 edition added that the Girl Scout should "not stoop to words or deeds that would bring shame upon her or upon others."[89] A decade later, in 1958, the law remained the same, though their explanations change. Being clean in thought, word, and deed, now meant that

> just as she stands for a clean, healthy community and a clean, healthy home, so every Girl Scout knows the deep and vital need for clean and healthy bodies in the mothers of the next generation. This not only means keeping her skin fresh and sweet and her system free from every impurity, but it

goes far deeper than this, and requires every Girl Scout to respect her body and mind so much that she forces everyone else to respect them and keep them free from the slightest familiarity or doubtful stain.

By 1972, the law was changed to "I will do my best to show respect for myself and others through my words and actions." As explained in the National Council Meeting workbook, "'Clean in thought, word, and deed,' and its implications, were grounds for humorous or even contemptuous dismissal of the tenth law by girls."[90]

The catalyst for these and other changes in 1972 was a survey of about 4,000 troops nationwide, representing more than 80,000 girls. Reflecting some of the same emphasis experts were now placing upon personal experience and reflection as well as individual autonomy, the Girl Scout leadership specifically sought wording that would "encourage girls to examine and clarify ethical concepts for themselves."[91]

Back to Schools: Toward Values Clarification

The popularity and influence of psychology were most clearly established in public education. To be sure, the influence of progressive educational philosophy came upon hard times—at least in theory—after the Russians launched Sputnik 1. In the late 1950s, for example, President Eisenhower advised educators "to abandon the educational path that, rather blindly, they have been following as a result of John Dewey's teaching."[92] Indeed for a time, educational theory focused more upon academic achievement in science, math, and foreign languages than upon moral education.[93] But conservative criticism had waned by the early 1960s.[94] In retrospect, the backlash was more an aberration than a sea change in moral education. Progressive theory reemerged in new forms in the 1960s as the public search for what constituted the proper nature and substance of moral education continued.

It is not insignificant, in this regard, that about the same time (1962–63) the Supreme Court ruled prayer and Bible reading in public schools to be unconstitutional.[95] On the face of it, these decisions revoked the patronage of the state from traditional religious authority at the same time that they marginalized religious sanction from the structure of formal education. These events were not isolated either but surrounded by a series of similar changes codified at the state level.[96] For example, the Idaho law regarding the "duties of teachers," first instituted in 1893, had mandated teacher duties according to the ideals of the republican and industrial era: "Every teacher shall . . . keep himself or herself without reproach, and endeavor to impress upon the minds of the pupils the principles of truth, justice, morality, patriotism and refinement, and to avoid idleness, falsehood, profanity, vulgarity and intemperance; give attention during every school term to the cultivation of manner."[97] In 1963 this law was repealed and replaced with the following: "In the absence of any statute or rule or regulation of the board of trustees, any teacher employed by a school district shall have the right to direct how and when each pupil shall attend to his appropriate duties, and the manner in which a pupil shall demean himself while in attendance at the school."[98] Absent in the 1963 law were instructions regarding the promotion of character through the inculcation of the republican virtues of patriotism, temperance, and the like. Its accomplishment was to evacuate moral content from the law.

*   *   *

With this legal transformation, any remaining threat to progressive ideals in moral instruction from traditional religion was formally eliminated. The educational establishment received this change with enthusiasm. In the early 1970s, for example, the dean of the Harvard School of Education wrote in a book on moral education that the traditional morality rooted in religious faith—the morality of "the Christian gentleman"—had done its damage. There was no doubt that "the 'old morality' can and should be scrapped."[99] On its heels came a more fully developed articulation of ideas introduced during the progressive era. By now the models of the developmental psychologists—Jean Piaget and Lawrence Kohlberg most notably—had become the theoretical centerpieces for understanding the moral growth of children. Yet their efforts had little practical effect in the schools. Though not at all incompatible with the theories of the developmentalists, the pedagogy of "values clarification" became the method of choice for instructing children at the curricular level.[100]

The values clarification approach was first developed by Louis Raths, Merrill Harmin, and Sidney Simon in *Values and Teaching*, published in 1966.[101] Spread by teacher workshops and paid for in part by state and federal tax dollars, Values Clarification quickly became the reigning fashion in moral education. The initiative clearly represented a refinement of earlier trends in moral education. Dewey's experiential theory of moral growth in a democratic setting and Carl Rodgers's client-centered model of therapeutic intervention were especially influential.[102]

The premise of values clarification was no different from earlier efforts. Raths et al. recognized the need to provide moral education to young people. As Merrill Harmin put it,

Too often schools supply only a knowledge of facts, concepts, or cognitive skills. Yet this knowledge is not enough to equip young people for coping with problems in today's pluralistic and complex society. Young people have become aware that their schools are failing them, and an increasing number of students are no longer willing to tolerate a curriculum that does not acknowledge their needs, interests, and concerns. Schools, as well as homes, must offer young people a way to develop a set of values upon which they can act and base their lives.[103]

The problem now was one of contemporary circumstances. Young people, the authors argued, exist in a new and complicated world of competing and confusing value *perspectives*—political, religious, and ideological—each of which tries to impose itself on the young. The plurality of ideologies and their attempted imposition constitute the crisis of moral education that demands a new approach. As Raths and his colleagues put it, "The theory recognizes that many people today have difficulty 'pulling themselves together.' Decisions seem too complicated, pressures seem too varied, changes seem too unsettling. As a consequence, some people flounder in confusion, apathy, or inconsistency. They cannot get clear on their values. They cannot find life patterns for themselves that are purposeful and satisfying."[104]

Values clarification was not so much a theory of moral education as it was a technique by which young people would develop their own values. As the authors put it, "It does not teach a particular set of values. There is no sermonizing or moralizing."[105] Indeed, "the teacher who instructs at the values level is accepting and nonjudgmental. He may correct students on the facts level, but he understands that there are no right and wrong answers to questions at the values level."[106] "The goal is to involve students in practical experiences, making them aware of *their own* feelings, *their own* ideas, *their own* beliefs, so that the choices and decisions they make are conscious and deliberate, based on *their own* value system."[107] The point is "to help people learn the valuing process and apply it to value-rich areas in their own lives."[108]

In *Values and Teaching*, teachers are encouraged to work with their students to implement these seven steps: 1. Choose their values freely; 2. Choose their values from alternatives; 3. Choose their values after weighing the consequences of each alternative; 4. Prize and cherish their values; 5. Share and publicly affirm their values; 6. Act upon their values; 7. Act upon their values repeatedly and consistently. These steps have been reduced to the three stages of 1. Choosing–steps 1–3, 2. Prizing–steps 4–5, and 3. Acting–steps 6–7.[109] In the "choosing" stage, students are helped to "choose values that are appropriate for them."[110] This stage teaches them "decision making skills."[111] It is essential not to neglect one's feelings, for they help "determine what we think is worthy and important."[112] In the prizing stage, "techniques are used that stimulate discussion centering on accurate identification and understanding of what a person believes is important or satisfying to him. The insight gained here will be used to help people make more realistic and potentially rewarding choices among the many conflicting values of our society."[113] Finally, in the acting stage, values are translated into appropriately consistent behaviors. The beauty of it all is that "the responsibility for what a person prizes, chooses, and acts on rests completely with the individual."[114]

This form of values education is not about the transmission of specific value contents but rather about *the development of the valuing process* in children. As Maury Smith explained, "Most of us still feel the effects of the Puritan and Victorian eras, when values were defined primarily in terms of moralistic 'shoulds' and 'should nots.' Values clarification as a methodology considers this moralistic stance to be an imposition upon the individual of predetermined values, and it seeks instead a method whereby individuals can discover their own values."[115] The program opposes any notion of morality as conformity to some external code or set of values, or as morally conventional behavior that is exclusively determined by a social agency or institution. It rejects a broad range of outside forces that come to "impose values": religion, social institutions, science, reason, and tradition. It is not that these institutions are decadent or worthless; but they should not be the determinants of value decisions. The problem with "traditional approaches to values" (such as teaching through example, persuasion, or the presentation of cultural or religious dogma) is that "they have not led and cannot lead to values . . . that represent the free and thoughtful choice of intelligent humans interacting with complex and changing environments. . . . Those methods do not seem to have resulted in deep commitments of any sort."[116] By following the values clarification method, students "have been helped to become more purposeful, more enthusiastic, more positive, and more aware of what is worth striving for."[117] Not least because of the harm they are alleged to have done, advocates ridicule the "moralizing, preaching, indoctrinating, inculcating, or dogmatizing" of all those traditional teaching methods that seek to impose values externally.[118]

So what are values? Values are personal preferences, inclinations, and choice; they are "not so much hard and fast verities as they are the results of hammering out a style of life in a certain set of surroundings. After a sufficient amount of hammering, certain patterns of evaluating and behaving tend to develop. Certain things are treated as right, desirable, or worthy. These become our values."[119] True to the connotation, the concept cannot and does not distinguish between "moral" and "nonmoral" issues. Indeed, advocates consistently used the phrase "values education" rather than "moral education" when speaking of the process. The difference is both vast and intended.

The advantages of this technique, according to its advocates, are numerous. It "encourages people to give more time and energy to value-related thought . . . , to reflect more deliberately and comprehensively about their own values and about the value questions of society as a whole."[120] It allows people to focus attention on aspects of their lives that may indicate things they value; it helps them to accept others' positions nonjudgmentally; it invites more comprehensive reflection on values, encouraging more informed choices, more awareness of what a person prizes and cherishes, and better integration of choices and prizings into day-to-day behavior; and it nourishes a sense of the possibility for thoughtful self-direction. Precisely because values are in flux, values clarification can help children "have more values, be more aware of the values that they have, have values that are more consistent with one another, and especially, be ready to use the valuing process as they continue to grow and learn."[121]

Historical Change and Abiding Paradox

The concern for moral education has never really diminished through the course of American history. It was as urgent in the seventeenth century as it is today. Constant through the ages is the sense of "moral crisis" that attends the young. Panic, outrage, passionate admonishments from the moral gatekeepers of society—so it has been in each succeeding generation.

While the sense of urgency has not diminished, the task of moral education has changed dramatically. The institutional location, the sources of moral authority, the content of moral instruction, and the purposes of moral education have all been fundamentally transformed.

The Paradox of Inclusion

However interesting and significant this transformation is on its own terms, the history of moral instruction in America also contains an important subtext, one that accounts in large part for the direction of its overall transformation. The subtext of this historical narrative is defined by the attempt to answer the question: how is it possible to provide moral education for the young in an increasingly diverse society, one that protects dissent?

Every generation has sought to make moral education inclusive and universal. Yet without fail, any consensus that is achieved is soon attacked (and legitimately) as narrow, sectarian, not inclusive. In turn, a more inclusive solution is then offered, and the process repeats itself. Thus when colonial ministers demanded a moral education rooted in religion, in fact they meant the particular, though dominant, doctrines of Puritanism. Recognizing the limitations of Puritanism in the new republic, early nineteenth-century reformers sought to expand the foundation of moral education to the universal truths of Christianity. Yet universal Christianity more often than not took shape as the particular doctrines of a nondenominational Evangelical Protestantism—much to the chagrin of the new and expanding Catholic population. In response, Horace Mann sought a more cosmopolitan solution in a "nonsectarian" liberal Christianity, one that had the markings of rationalism, Unitarianism, and transcendentalism. It was not long before he too was accused—and rightly—of a sectarianism of his own. As his critics argued,

> Everything is sectarianism with him, except what squares exactly with the notions of Universalists and those who have been absurdly called 'pious deists' and theophilanthropists. Teach one jot of truth more and you are sectarian, and shall lose your school, or your school shall lose its proportion of the public fund for education. What is this, but to establish by law, that Universalism . . . shall be the State religion, taught by public authority, to the exclusion of the views of evangelical dissenters of every name?[122]

As another of his chief critics put it, "it is proper to keep dogmatic theology out of school. Let it be kept out on both sides—the dogmatism of unbelief, as well as the dogmatism of belief."[123]

Dewey's reforms were yet another attempt at a more inclusive and cosmopolitan solution. For him, moral education would reflect a "common faith"—a naturalist moral philosophy that would emerge from the workings of the democratic community—from life together, not from a transcendent entity or a historic tradition.[124] This model and the character education of his day have also been battered by the accusation of ethnocentrism—another word for sectarianism. In turn, Dewey's model evolved further toward a more refined blend of secular rationalism, psychological pragmatism, and liberal individualism—all reflected in various theories ranging from Kohlberg's "developmentalism" to Rath's "values clarification."

The paradox has remained.

Against the urgent demand made in every generation for a common moral education, is the question: how can it be conducted in a way that satisfies everyone? What are the moral parameters of its pedagogy? Who defines its principles? How shall these principles be taught, and by whom? By what authority and reasonings shall they be grounded? Every effort to find a solution that is both effective and inoffensive has eventually fallen apart by revealing its own particularity.

Of course the story is not yet complete.

How do these issues play out in our own generation? What has the paradox of moral education wrought in our own time? And what are the consequences? These questions occupy us in the next chapters.

The Crisis of
Character . . . That Isn't

Is there a "crisis of character" in our day? I am agnostic on this question, if only for the historical reason that every generation for the past two centuries has seen its youth as being in such a crisis. Hearing these claims generation after generation tends to make one numb to this particular cry of distress.

Consider the word "crisis" itself. In Western usage, the word derived from the field of pathology in which it was understood as "a critical point in the development of a disease." Linked to its etymology in the Greek (krisis, from krinein), meaning "decision," the word comes to us as "the decisive moment."

Leave aside the rhetorical trope of speaking of cultural history as somehow "diseased"; the question this phrase invites is, Is our own time the decisive moment or perhaps a decisive moment for the standing of character? Here again, I am doubtful. My hunch is that if a "crisis" in character has occurred, it was probably in the late nineteenth century, precisely when people became self-conscious of the importance of character and initiated the myriad of programs and organizations to sustain it in the young.

Consider yet another aspect of the word "crisis." The word implies that there are decisions to be made, that human agency can make an important difference. Can human agency make a difference with regard to a crisis of character? Surely it could make some difference—if the nature of the "crisis" is well understood and the right actions are taken. Yet one cannot help but recognize already that there is something about the historical unfolding of our moral culture that resists all of those efforts to change it or finesse it or oppose it.

Perhaps it is best to do away with the word "crisis" in this instance. It does not illuminate our circumstances very well.

What one can say with certainty is that America in the twentieth century witnessed a profound transformation in its moral culture and this transformation has significant consequences for the moral socialization of the young. What follows from here is a description of this ongoing transformation and an interpretation of its consequences.

5

The Psychological Regime

The observation is unavoidable.

When it comes to the moral life of children, the vocabulary of the psychologist frames virtually all public discussion. For decades now, contributions from philosophers and theologians have been muted or nonexistent.[1] Anthropologists and sociologists are likewise absent from the discussion. Historians have been busy documenting the major developments in this realm of social life, but their influence has been limited mainly to their guild. Rather it is the psychologists, and in particular the developmental and educational psychologists, who have owned this field—in theory and in practice. All of the major players in the last half of the twentieth century have been psychologists. Erik Erikson, B. F. Skinner, Benjamin Spock, Robert Havighurst, Carl Rodgers, Jean Piaget, Abraham Maslow, Rudolf Dreikurs, William Glasser, Lawrence Kohlberg, Louis Rath, Sidney Simon, Jane Loevinger, Daniel Levinson, Robert Selman, Maurice Elias—their assumptions, concepts, and paradigms have largely determined how all of us think about the moral lives of children, and indeed about moral life generally.

Why Psychology?

Why has psychology become so dominant? The discipline itself has maintained over the years that, as the science of human motive and behavior, it comes closest to a rational understanding of that difficult and elusive phenomenon, human nature. As such, psychology is in a position to specify the conditions that permit or impede the full realization of a person's natural creativity, productivity, and well-being. Understanding the range and expression of moral sensibilities is central to this task insofar as it helps to specify what are, in fact, the constituting elements of "the good life."

There are sociological reasons why psychology has emerged as *the* framework for understanding the moral life as well. With theology in all its forms discredited as a public language, psychology has offered a seemingly neutral way to understand and cultivate the best qualities of the human personality. It is "science" after all, and science, we are inclined to believe, is "objective." In the wake of the diffused Christian consensus dominant through the first half of the twentieth century, the psychological approaches to moral education seem so much more inclusive—more inclusive, less offensive, less problematic on legal grounds. Indeed, its most vocal proponents have maintained that the framework psychology offers in understanding the moral life is, in fact, objective, and its application to education is universal.

Psychology and Morality

From the beginning, the centerpiece of the psychological strategy has been the concept of "development." For some theorists the concept of development is a fundamental axiom made explicit in carefully worded theoretical propositions. For others it is just part of the accepted wisdom that forms a background of their thinking.

The basic idea is simple. For centuries it was thought that children were merely small-sized adults who, over time, grow large in a quantitative sense.[2] Against this, the modern concept of development suggests that children grow up by moving through a hierarchy of qualitatively distinct stages of evolution and maturation, much like the development of an egg to a caterpillar to a butterfly. Each stage is unique in that it represents a new way for children to order their experience and perceptions of the world. The process is not reversible—each stage depends upon and presupposes the prior stage. Unlike a butterfly, however, children do not automatically move to higher stages of development. Rather the shift from lower to higher stages requires some sort of catalyst, typically provided by certain experiences with other human beings, experiences which propel a shift from lower to higher stages.

Though a few philosophers from the classical age held similar notions about the advancement and improvement of mind and character, it was John Dewey who brought a "developmental perspective" to bear on the problem of mass education in a modern democracy. As we have seen, Dewey contended that the purpose of education should not be a mere acquisition of knowledge and skills for industrial workers but the intellectual and ethical development of the citizen. It would be the school in particular that would be the catalyst for moral development among the citizenry. Dewey's educational vision inspired succeeding generations of psychologists to translate a developmental ideal into empirical and scientific scholarship. The literature is now voluminous.

Needless to say, these scholars differ on many of the conceptual and analytical issues of human development and on what they believe is most important. Jung, for example, focused on the development from fantasy to reality. Piaget focused on the stages by which children apprehend time, space, and causality—thence to a capacity for increasingly rational moral judgments. Erik Erikson focused on emotional growth as children grow capable of increasing ethical awareness. Kohlberg studied growing children's increasingly sophisticated moral reasoning, whether under ordinary circumstances or in situations of tension and conflict. Jane Loevinger added insights into the process of ego development—how children function with increasing skill and competence as they get older. Robert Selman contributed to our understanding of interpersonal development—from self-preoccupation to "intersubjective understanding" or willingness to take others into consideration in one's everyday behavior. James Fowler has described the stages of "faith development" as they lead individuals toward a "realistic" and "universalistic" faith. And so on.

This broad-ranging field has generally seen morality as a consequence of an interplay of intellect and emotions. Earlier theorists saw morality primarily as a category of knowledge and moral judgment as a *rational* capability. Indeed, from Dewey to Kohlberg, no distinction was made between intellectual and moral development. Piaget, for example, declared that "the essence of all morality is to be sought for in the respect which the individual acquires for [society's] rules."[3] His chief task as a psychologist was therefore to understand how the mind comes to respect those rules. Cognitive development for children represents the evolution of a child's understanding of rules—from believing that rules are to be obeyed because adults have imposed them, to believing that rules are the outcome of a free decision and worthy of respect because they are based upon mutual consent.

Though now fading in popularity, the work of Lawrence Kohlberg has been especially influential, at least among theorists. For Kohlberg, the distinctive feature of "the moral" is not found in the old Boy Scout (or Aristotelian) "bag of virtues" (truthfulness, temperance, kindness toward others, and the like) or, as in Piaget's case, an attitude toward rules. ("Virtue is knowledge of the good. He who knows the good chooses the good."[4]) Kohlberg insisted that virtue was "always the same ideal form regardless of climate or culture."[5] The essence of morality for Kohlberg was found in *the kinds of reasoning* brought to bear on situations of tension and conflict—the ways a person decides what to do when confronted by a moral dilemma.[6] He found that as children get older their reasons for doing the right thing become more complex: they tend to evolve from staying out of trouble, to acting out of self-interest, to wanting social approval, to wanting to be responsible in society, to living up to an implied contract, to acting out of principles of social justice. Thus, it is not *what* we decide that determines how morally developed we are, but *how* we reason about our choices.[7]

While morality, in this perspective, is mainly defined in terms of a rational competence that gets expressed in increasingly sophisticated principles of moral reasoning, many psychologists would insist, too, that a person's emotions are inextricably linked to moral judgment. How can there be cognition without affect (or feeling) or, for that matter, feeling without reflection? Hence the emphasis many theorists place on empathy—the ability to imagine oneself in the place of others. In the higher stages of moral development, empathy is essential. It is implicit in Erikson's concept of "mutuality" (that one will not do to others what is hateful to oneself), in Piaget's notion of "decentering" (maturing beyond egocentrism by learning to take the viewpoint of someone else), in Kohlberg's concepts of benevolence and justice (involving equality, respect for the dignity of others, and trust).

Since the 1960s much of the research has given even greater prominence to the role of emotions in the development of moral understanding. It is our empathy with the plight of another that prompts ethical demands for justice; it is our uncertainty in the face of confusing events that prompts the effort of self-understanding; it is fear in the face of danger that invites the ideal of courage; it is our natural worry about threats to our livelihood or our well-being that prompts the virtue of caution; and it is out of the experience of exhaustion or boredom that we learn to seek moderation.[8] This research has had a much greater influence on the curriculum than the more rationalist approaches.

This observation bears repeating: in the translation from theory to practical pedagogy, the dominant thrust of psychology has been *affective*. In the field, the centerpiece of this orientation has been the emotions surrounding one's own self-concept and well-being captured in the concept of "self-esteem." We are told that children who feel good about themselves tend to do well in school, are less likely to take drugs, will be sexually responsible, and will be more tolerant of others. Indeed, in recent times self-esteem has become virtually unassailable as a general prescription in child rearing. Since the 1970s, the idea of mental and emotional well-being has become established as the foundation for positive social behavior and moral conduct. As one advocate put it, "the level of a student's self-esteem is central to school reform, change agency, foreign competition, and just making sure kids turn out as we know they should."[9] Another wrote, "self-esteem is central to what we make of our lives. . . . It is intricately tied to what we will achieve in the course of a lifetime. Perhaps nothing affects one's health and energy quite so much as the health of our self-esteem. . . . We must not underestimate the role of self-esteem and its contribution to student achievement and performance."[10] In brief, "positive self-esteem is essential for all youngsters if they are to develop in healthy ways."[11]

Though "self-esteem" as a concept lost some currency in the 1990s, other terms have arisen to take its place. One prominent repackaging of this affective approach to moral education has come in the term "emotional intelligence," or what its theorists call the EQ or "emotional quotient." After it was popularized by Daniel Goleman's 1995 bestseller *Emotional Intelligence: Why It Can Matter More than IQ*, hundreds of schools instituted programs based upon the idea. The enthusiasm for EQ is as high as it ever was for self-esteem programs. Says one advocate, "We believe it needs to be comprehensive, just like science and math. . . . Every child, every school, every year."[12]

The Psychological Strategy As Regime

The debates and discussion within this larger field are complex, to be sure. The research that forms the core of this general strategy is serious academic scholarship that has offered important insight into the psychology of moral understanding. *Yet as these theories find their way into curricula and other forms of practical pedagogy, the theoretical diversity rapidly disappears. Indeed, the real significance of this scholarship is found less in its details than in the way it diffuses into the larger culture as a guiding wisdom for thinking about moral life.*

Such a diffusion is not at all surprising. The study of moral development was never intended to be a merely academic one, but was intended to have a broader impact. The urgency of Dewey's educational vision—and those of Piaget and Kohlberg and their successors—was based on a straightforward logic: if we know what moral development is, then we will know what moral education ought to be. We can then proceed to devise programs that stimulate moral sensibility among children. It is in this way that the assumptions, concepts, and paradigms of secular psychology have largely shaped the way we all think about the moral lives of children.

And not only children . . .

The influence of psychology on our understanding of moral life has, in turn, had an impact on American culture. To whom do school systems turn when they need counseling for their students, or lawyers when they need "an expert" in court to explain the behavior of criminals, or journalists seeking opinions for a story on juvenile delinquency? We summon the psychologist, the child psychiatrist, the psychiatric social worker. The specialized knowledge of such individuals has become the common sense and working wisdom of parents, educators, and policymakers alike.

*   *   *

It is in the structure of this diffusion that we see this collective endeavor as a *regime.*

By regime I simply mean the complex network of institutions, ideas, ideals, and interests whose collective purpose is to propagate a general strategy of moral understanding and learning. Culturally, the regime goes far beyond whatever academic ideas are currently fashionable. Clearly, particular ideas and programs are packaged and presented in ever-changing ways. But the framing ideas, the mechanisms of diffusion, the institutional structures that support them, and the disparate group of elites that derive their livelihoods from them share common assumptions and interests. These ideas, mechanisms, structures, and elites do not change so quickly. It is in this way that I speak of the prevailing moral education establishment as a regime.

Dominated as it is by perspectives diffused and diluted from professional psychology, this regime is overwhelmingly therapeutic and self-referencing; in character, its defining feature is a moral framework whose center point is the autonomous self. This regime's strategy of moral education now pervades *all* of the mainstream institutions that mediate moral understanding to children.

The point of this chapter, then, is not to comprehensively review the programmatic ways moral understanding is mediated to children today, but rather to illustrate the distillation and diffusion of psychological models of moral understanding in the main contemporary institutions of moral education.

SCHOOLS

Public education has remained the dominant institution for the formal moral education of children. Though not exclusive to these settings, it has been health classes, sex-education programs, drug education training, and conflict resolution exercises that have provided the main contexts within which moral instruction is offered.

What lessons are taught?

By the late 1980s, many curriculum publishers and practitioners were going out of their way to distance themselves and their agendas from the very idea of values clarification. Yet it is also clear that the dominant strategy of moral education in the public schools has continued to frame its pedagogy in the same psychologistic terms: the importance of feelings as a guide to one's values, an emphasis on individual choice, the centrality of self-regard or self-esteem to the student's moral maturation. Accordingly, the programs available to schools typically have continued to employ the techniques of a general therapeutic peda-gogy—positive imagining, role-playing, the sharing of feelings and values in small groups, and so on.

Consider a few examples of curricula in use—not a comprehensive review, but typical. One program of moral education for elementary school children, produced by American Guidance Service, is called DUSO—Developing Under-standing of Self and Others.[13] Through the early 1990s this program, which em-ploys puppets to enact situations of moral conflict, was used by over 150,000 teachers. The premise of the curriculum is the relationship between self-esteem and achievement. "Learning," its developers contend, "is fostered by an environ-ment that builds a child's positive self-concept and feelings of acceptance and belonging.[14] Its agenda is to [help] children recognize their own worth."[15]

The first component focuses upon "Development of Self," with sections on "Knowing Oneself," "Understanding and Expressing Feelings," "Exploring One's World," "Becoming Self-Reliant and Independent," and "Solving Problems." Among its goals are "To accept and value oneself as worthwhile," "To recognize one's capabilities and achievements," "To initiate independent, self-reliant ac-tion," and "To recognize one's likes and dislikes."[16]

Central to the cultivation of self-regard is the child's awareness of his or her own feelings. So it is that the curriculum features opportunities for children "to express their own feelings and opinions."[17] By talking with others about feelings, goals, and behavior, children can learn that these things are dynamically related. In the author's rationale,

> Children are at once thinking, acting, and feeling beings. Their thoughts and actions always involve feelings. . . . The feelings that accompany learn-ing have a significant effect on how well children learn. If they have posi-tive feelings, children tend to participate with a high degree of motivation and involvement and are more likely to derive permanent gains from their efforts. If children's feelings are negative, they are poorly motivated, partic-ipate on a minimal basis, and are less likely to derive permanent gains.[18]

To this end children are taught to "be conscious of feelings"; to "be able to cope with rejection"; to "clearly express [their] feelings"; and to "act on one's feelings with courage."[19] In another section of the curriculum, entitled "Understanding Feelings," the goals are to help children "to see how feelings influence choices"; "to discriminate between real and imagined fears"; and to "select appropriate ways to express feelings."[20]

One of the activities DUSO uses to cultivate these skills is the "Feeling Word Activity," forty-one exercises that introduce words for different feelings. The teacher introduces the DUSO puppets and presents a brief dialogue between the characters. Then children are asked to identify how one of the characters feels. Any words that accurately describe the feeling are acceptable. If the word that is the focus of the activity is not mentioned by the children, the teacher introduces the word. The feeling-word activity "sad" offers a dialogue between two puppets, Mr. Schneider and Theresa.

MR. SCHNEIDER: I see you and your family are moving, Theresa.

THERESA: We're going to Oklahoma. You've been a nice neighbor, Mr. Schneider. I'll miss you. I'm going to miss my school and my friends, too. I was just sitting here looking at our house. It makes me feel, oh, kind of funny inside.

MR. SCHNEIDER: It's hard to leave people and things that you love.

THERESA: Yes, it is. I cry about it when I think about never coming back to this town again.

How was Theresa feeling? (Any words that accurately describe the feeling are acceptable. If no one says sad, say, 'She seems to be feeling sad.' What was Theresa sad about? What are some other things that people feel sad about? When are some times that you feel sad? (Children might like to role-play or use puppets to enact the situations.)[21]

DUSO stories or activities are "followed by a discussion in which children identify feelings and practice applying their own values when problem-solving a particular situation."[22]

*   *   *

Skills for Adolescence and *Skills for Growing* (K–5), offered by Quest International of Granville, Ohio,[23] are other curricula in widespread use—by 1998, over 150,000 teachers in the United States alone had been trained to use them; roughly 27,000 schools, in every state and in thirty other countries, had adopted them. Each year approximately 2 million students go through these programs.[24]

Like many other programs, Quest distances itself from values clarification. "Quest's programs are values-based curricula. The core values which are consistently reinforced are the positive behaviors of self-discipline, good judgment, responsibility, honesty, and the positive commitment to family, school, peers, and community. . . . Quest in no way supports or promotes 'values clarification,' a term which refers to the technique of leading participants to think about their values without judgment, discussion or definition about right or wrong. Quest's programs promote values and clear messages about right and wrong, such as, 'Stealing is wrong,' and 'Drug use is wrong.'"[25] Yet *Skills for Adolescence* shares the basic orienting assumption of values clarification: the defining importance of emotional well-being in the moral life. Students are told, for instance, that "we can understand ourselves only when we know how we're really feeling."[26]

A key part of the curriculum is "to understand that young adolescents experience a wide range of common feelings and that these feelings are normal"; "to explore appropriate ways to communicate feelings"; "to examine the range of emotions and learn positive responses to outside influences"; "to learn how to perceive troubling emotions such as anger and frustration as positive challenges"; and "to learn how positive emotions promote good feelings about oneself and others."[27] Among the activities that young people are given to do are: to develop a "feelings" vocabulary; to construct a "rainbow of feelings" display (to illustrate the range of emotions that are experienced by individuals) to create a "feelings continuum" (and identify where they are on it at a given time); an "Emotion Clock" worksheet (to remember the day's feelings as well as they can); and a "Scrapbook of Emotions." The objectives of the exercises are to help students "define [their] 'feelings'"; "recognize the range of feelings experienced by classmates"; "state reasons why having a range of feelings is normal"; and "begin to develop a vocabulary that accurately describes a variety of feelings."[28]

Not surprisingly, *Skills for Adolescence* also frames positive self-regard in the vocabulary of subjective emotion. Self-confidence, for example, is defined for teachers as "feeling good about who and what you are"; its constituent parts are feeling skillful, feeling appreciated, and taking responsibility.[29] The educational mission is for everyone to "learn to feel better about ourselves and help others feel better about themselves."[30]

The emphasis on emotion does not stop with individual self-understanding but becomes a mechanism of shared discourse on matters of collective concern. With the issue of cultural diversity, for example, the curriculum contends that "the topic of emotions provides a good opportunity for students to develop cross-cultural understanding." "Some cultures favor being emotionally demonstrative, while others teach that emotions should be 'felt inside' without any outward expression. Cultures also differ in regard to when, how, and to whom certain emotions can be expressed. During Unit Three the students should be encouraged to share ways of handling emotions that may be unique to their backgrounds."[31]

*   *   *

The incorporation of psychological ideals and assumptions into the mainstream of culture and policy is also marked by their embrace by government agencies.

As James Nolan has documented in great detail, twenty-one states have written into their educational mandates the provision of moral instruction and services committed to self-exploration and self-esteem.[32] At the federal level as well, psychologistic models of self-development have been sanctioned through the Head Start program; through various Health and Human Services programs for troubled, poor, or minority children; and through the Department of Education substance-abuse programs.

In July 1987, for instance, the Washington, D.C., Board of Education convened the Commission of Values-centered Goals for the District of Columbia Public Schools.[33] Its tasks were to examine existing values-centered educational programs, develop goals for values-centered curricula, recommend curriculum guidelines, and report its findings and recommendations to the Board of Education. The Commission proceeded with a particular sense of urgency because the problems of the District were (and remain) so serious. For one, the commission recognized that young people increasingly perceive "that the pursuit of material wealth is more valuable than honesty, integrity or commitment." It also noted that "60 percent of all District babies are born out of wedlock each year, 20 percent of [which] were to teenagers," "nearly 40 percent of all District children are [living] in families headed by a single mother who is likely to be raising her children in poverty," and that the District's drop-out rate was more than 15 percentage points over the national rate.[34] The moral life of its young residents was of paramount importance; the District badly needed to find a way to "encourage students to develop a sense of self that goes beyond a preoccupation with instant self-gratification."

The Commission rejected relativism on its face. As a baseline to its policy recommendations, the Commission affirmed five character traits or values that students should be encouraged to develop: *self-esteem*—to help students develop a strong sense of their own worth; *self-discipline*—to help students understand that responsible, creative work is the key to self-reliance; *family, kinship, and belonging*—to help students nurture and value supportive family relationships at home and at school; *moral and intellectual maturity*—to help students learn their history, understanding their roles in contributing to the continuum of human history, and pursue moral and intellectual growth; and *responsibility to self and others*—to help students revere the gift of healthy bodies and minds, appreciate the interdependence of all things, behave compassionately toward others, and learn by example and experience that unselfish service is a key component of self-gratification.[35]

Among the Commission's policy recommendations was that the District's schools emphasize the "build[ing] of students' self-esteem as a central ingredient of the curriculum at all instructional levels and in all subject matter areas where applicable." The rationale for this was the view that "self-esteem is the key to academic learning. Without a positive sense of self . . . it is impossible for a child to learn academic subjects." How would self-esteem be developed? "The commission recommends that the D.C. Public Schools' educational curriculum encourage students to develop a positive self-image by examining their own value structures and behavior, as well as giving them an opportunity to translate abstract values of compassion and generosity into direct service that will enrich others' lives as well as their own."[36]

Sex Education

Historically almost all moral education has been, at some implicit level, sex education as well. But sex education as such was the brainchild of progressive-era reformers in the early twentieth century. Even then, "scientific" sex education was part of an effort to teach restraint. According to one authority in 1912, instruction "should aim to keep sex consciousness and sex emotions at the minimum."[37] Yet it was not until the 1960s, against widespread fears of overpopulation, that the call came for a more energetic and far-reaching approach to sex education. The logic was simple enough: information about sexuality could be an effective means of controlling fertility, especially among minorities.[38] Momentum for such policy only increased in the two decades that followed, spurred on in part by the Guttmacher Institute's report *Teenage Pregnancy: The Problem That Hasn't Gone Away* (1981), and later by calls for comprehensive sex education to stem the spread of AIDS. It was only in 1990 that the Sex Information and Education Counsel of the U.S. (or SIECUS) published its controversial set of national guidelines for "comprehensive (or K–12) sex education."[39]

The premises of comprehensive sex education (known more recently as "family life education") lie not only in various social fears but in a reading of adolescent biology and psychology. Advocates begin by assuming that children are inherently sexual, even when they are not conscious of it or when they seem to have no interest in it. Their sexuality is constantly unfolding from birth to young adulthood, and their sexual understandings are continually challenged as their bodies develop and their social experience broadens. It is inevitable that adolescents will explore their sexuality and, in our day, at younger and younger ages. It is unrealistic for parents, teachers, or other adults to imagine otherwise.

The threats to sexual responsibility are not temptations against moral resolve but ignorance (through widespread misinformation) and shame (through repressed and inappropriate feelings). The challenge, then, is to offer young people an education that informs and liberates, that instructs them in the basic facts of sexual relations and that frees them from the guilt, embarrassment, and prejudices that derive from the perception that sexual pleasure is neither normal nor desirable. Unless sex education of this kind is presented to children early in life, what they learn is likely to be, in the words of a *New York Times* editorial, "too little, too late."[40] Sexually transmitted diseases, teenage pregnancy, abortion, and other social problems are the natural outcomes.

It comes as no surprise that the dominant models of sex education since the 1970s have all operated with a moral logic framed by the assumptions and imperatives of developmental psychology. At all ages young people are particularly instructed in the nurturing of emotional self-awareness as the means by which they will come to terms with their sexuality. From elementary school through high school, the vocabulary of sentiment is central.

Of the myriad available sex education programs, Virginia's *Family Life Education: Curriculum Guidelines* is fairly typical.[41] These guidelines are meant to provide schools with tools to influence their students' attitudes toward family living, personal relationships, sexual development, and other aspects of human sexuality. To this end, the guidelines were designed to help young people develop a positive self-concept, grow in understanding of self and others; develop a scientific vocabulary, understand and develop a wholesome attitude towards human sexuality as a basic factor throughout life, and acquire insights and values regarding human sexuality.[42]

In the earliest years (K–3rd grade) the students learn to understand themselves, develop a feeling of belonging, talk about their feelings and emotions, and understand positive ways of dealing with them.[43] In the late elementary years they begin more detailed study of sexuality and human development. Beyond the scientific nomenclature surrounding the body and sexual relations, students in these grades gain a "deeper understanding of emotional growth and how it relates to everyday life."[44] A central part of these specifications, then, deals with factors that encourage or inhibit the acquiring of "emotional maturity," including a positive self-concept, the development of respect for others, and a facility for open, interpersonal communication.[45]

Middle school and high school students receive much the same instruction, but in an age-appropriate package. Central here is the effort to encourage more sophisticated moral reasoning. For example, students are encouraged "to write or tell of situations in which someone had to make a judgment as to what is right or wrong." Teachers then unpack the decision, discussing, in part, "how valid the choice was."[46] In this they are assisted by an approach to moral reasoning framed by a cost-benefit calculation. Adolescent sexuality, they are told, "may produce psychological . . . problems they may not be able to cope with at this age"— "guilt feelings," and "feelings of depression." If pregnancy results, "the girl may have to give up the child for adoption which may affect her emotionally." Besides the psychological costs, the young person may contract a venereal disease, drop out of school, and lose friends.[47]

The warnings are much the same everywhere. "Sexual activity outside of marriage," another program instructs,

> can make you feel anxious and worried about getting caught, about becoming pregnant. It can also create a sense of disappointment by not living up to the standards you and/or your parents set for you. You could also feel dishonest knowing that you don't really feel what you know intercourse is saying to your partner. If pregnancy does result, the emotional trauma of abortion, adoption, or raising a child at this time in your life would be truly painful and long-lasting.[48]

Complementing the psychological assumptions are therapeutic techniques—such as role-playing, small-group sharing and discussion, assertiveness training, gender-reversal exercises, and self-affirmation—all geared toward enlightening and empowering young people to make rational, sensible, independent decisions about their own sexual behavior and identity. At the end of the day, the moral imperative guiding all such pedagogy is not some antiquated notion of rectitude or even a clear conscience but, rather, basic survival with one's emotional and mental health intact.

Drug Education

Moral education aimed at curbing drug use among young people has also been prominent. Again, there are a variety of curricula from which to choose. *Here's Looking at You 2000*, offered by the Comprehensive Health Education Foundation (or CHEF), contains three major components: information (on such topics as gateway drugs, chemical dependency, fetal alcohol syndrome, and driving and using drugs), social skills (how to be assertive, make friends, say no to trouble, and deal with pressure), and bonding (discovering personal strengths, learning in cooperative teams, and identifying ways to have healthy fun without drugs).[49] *Natural Helpers* centers its program around peer counselors, who receive thirty hours of training in a retreat setting to "prepare them to prevent some of the problems of adolescence, intervene effectively with troubled friends, choose positive ways of taking care of themselves, and improve their school and community." One of its goals is "trying to help their friends clarify their feelings."[50]

DARE, or Drug Abuse Resistance Education, is especially notable because it is the largest school-based drug education program in America. By 1998, 26 million students from all fifty states had been instructed by the program. Seventy percent of school districts and 10,000 communities in the United States use it. With expenditures nationally reaching $750 million, DARE has become a major moral education industry.[51] The DARE program extends from kindergarten through senior high school, and there is a parent program as well. Though primarily concerned with drug usage, in the later years it has also addressed interpersonal conflict, violence, and gangs.

The substance of the program is fairly straightforward. First, the *judgment* to say no to drug use is rooted in a utilitarian logic that focuses on personal consequences. The problem is that drugs are "unsafe" and "harmful." Though the word is underplayed, the "immorality" of drug use is strictly tied to its negative repercussions; a point reinforced by armed, uniformed police officers who help teach the program. The *courage* to "dare" is rooted in one's sense of well-being. If you feel good about yourself, you will not need drugs; if ever tempted, you will have the moral wherewithal to resist. To this end, the program helps young people explore and understand their emotions, particularly as they bear on the needs that drugs appear to satisfy. The building of self-esteem is a core part of the curriculum through the elementary and middle-school years. Beyond this, the program helps young people identify and manage the stresses of late adolescence. Finally, the *discipline* to deal with temptations centers on various techniques that students might use to rebuff those enticements. Learning to "just say no" is one of the primary techniques. In short, the moral logic of DARE is a logic of cost-benefit analysis grounded in physical and emotional health.

In drug education, as in so many other moral education programs, specific techniques and strategies may differ but the framework of moral understanding is very much the same.

THE FAMILY

Needless to say, by midcentury psychology had become authoritative in popular parenting literature as well. Following the warm and optimistic counseling of Benjamin Spock, the psychoanalytic perspective of Haim Ginott and Thomas Gordon dominated the parenting literature of the late 1960s and early 1970s. Ginott, the creator of "play therapy," and Gordon, the designer of "parent effectiveness training," advised parents to become, in effect, therapists to their children.[52] In the manner of William Glasser's approach to moral education in the schools, they presupposed the natural inclination of young people to be good and stressed the development of communication skills as the means to self-understanding, personal esteem, and interpersonal intimacy and cooperation. Only by responding to their emotional and psychological needs would parents help children realize their moral potential.

Against mounting evidence of increasing sexual promiscuity, teenage pregnancy, delinquency, violence, and drug abuse among the young, however, the permissive model of parenting drew broad criticism. A backlash of sorts formed, with some parenting experts and educators calling for a return to parental authority and discipline in the home.[53] For writers such as Lee Canter, "happy, motivated, and responsible learners" would develop in a context defined by reliable and consistent limits established through techniques of positive reinforcement and negative consequences (such as the withdrawal of affection and removal of privileges). Though conservative on its face, this "assertive-discipline" school was not exactly traditionalist in its underpinnings. The basic authority parents wielded over children was framed in contractual rather than essentialist terms; it would be negotiated rather than expressed as the natural legitimate influence wielded by the parent. The therapeutic framework for understanding misbehavior also remained intact. Young people who were difficult were said to be unhappy rather than bad. For this reason it was counterproductive for parents to moralize, demand obedience, or punish by spanking. The emphasis, rather, was on offering problem-solving skills to enable the young to develop and maintain positive relationships with parents and others along with warm and positive support to empower children to overcome their challenges.[54] While some advocates of assertive discipline continue to advocate this model, it is not exactly a fundamental challenge to the psychological model of parenting.

The most interesting contribution to understanding the role of parents to their children since the early 1980s comes from the Swiss psychoanalyst Alice Miller. Her books, *For Your Own Good: Hidden Cruelty in Child-rearing and the Roots of Violence* and *Thou Shalt Not Be Aware: Society's Betrayal of the Child*, were powerful indictments of conventional views of the role and purpose of parenting. Different in tone from so much of the emotivist therapeutic reasoning prominent in the earlier parenting advice, her framework nevertheless offered a radicalization of the assumptions that prevailed among the psychological gatekeepers of parental guidance.

The heart of her inquiry was a fascination for the origins of the holocaust.[55] Her answer was straightforward: "I have not been able to find a single [perpetrator] who did not have a strict and rigid upbringing."[56] The horrendous accomplishments of these individuals could all be traced back to the mistreatment they experienced at the hands of their own parents. Hitler himself grew up in a typically authoritarian family environment: the father established himself as the sole and undisputed ruler of the family; the mother and children were subservient to his will, obediently accepting humiliation as a mode of life. Not only was Hitler physically abused by his father, but his grandfather had abused his father in a predictable cycle of intergenerational mistreatment. Likewise, Adolf

Eichman and Rudolf Höss "were trained to be obedient so successfully and at such an early age that the training never lost its effectiveness."[57] So it was for an entire generation of Nazi true believers. The Germans, Miller argued, had been

> raised to be obedient, had grown up in an atmosphere of duty and Christian virtues; they had to learn at a very early age to repress their hatred and their needs. And now along came a man who did not question the underpinnings of this bourgeois morality, . . . someone who . . . put the obedience that had been instilled in them to good use, who . . . provided them with a universal means for finally being able to live out in a thoroughly acceptable and legal way the hatred they had been repressing all their lives.[58]

The holocaust, she concluded, would have been "impossible without this kind of upbringing."[59] Indeed, the legacy did not end with World War II. "With these dynamics in mind, we will not be surprised to learn from the statistics that 60 percent of German terrorists in recent years have been the children of Protestant ministers." "When terrorists take innocent women and children hostage in the service of a grand and idealistic cause, are they really doing anything different from what was once done to them?"[60]

Thus the traditional middle-class family may be characterized as "the prototype of a totalitarian regime."[61] All are victims of what she calls a "poisonous pedagogy"—child-rearing practices that suppress all vitality, creativity, and feeling in the child while reinforcing the autocratic position of the parents.[62] The consequence of this pedagogy is nothing less than a "soul murder," an experience that occurs whenever parents insist upon submission to their authority, when they suppress the needs of their children, and when they arbitrarily allocate rewards and punishments as well as praise and humiliation to keep them in line.[63]

Miller's inquiry led her to conclude that the very foundation of middle-class family life was pathological for children and for society at large. The problem was not so much on the surface of family life. The various child-rearing philosophies parents relied upon were mostly irrelevant to the true nature of parenting. Nor would it matter if parents demonstrated consistent kindness, generosity, and forbearance toward their offspring. There was no harmless pedagogy.[64] Rather, the nub of the problem was in the subtext of family life, namely the unconscious struggle for power between adults and children. In this struggle, the children invariably lose, suffering psychological brutality at the hands of their parents. What has long been regarded as the natural, even instinctive, conduct of parents is now seen for what it is: a pathology that destroys the psychological well-being of children. Such child-rearing practices spread violence throughout society, from one generation to the next; for each generation is captive to the violence perpetrated upon it in childhood.

Miller's perspective might well have been lost in academic obscurity, except that it was embraced by the therapist and media celebrity John Bradshaw. In his ten-week PBS series and book entitled *The Family*, Bradshaw repackaged Miller's ideas for popular dissemination. Very prominently, he posed Miller's question, "How could Hitler happen?" His response was a condensed version of Miller's own explanation: "Hitler and Black Nazism are a cruel caricature of what can happen in modern Western society if we do not stop promoting and proliferating family rules that kill the souls of human beings." What rules are these? The rules of "obedience" and "submission" to parental authority. "Soul murder" was not just Germany's problem but America's as well. It occurred, Bradshaw claimed, in 96 percent of all American families. Even progressive parents resort to "authoritarian" parenting in times of stress and in so doing, crushed the souls of their children.[65]

Bradshaw's solution to "soul murder" was a reversal of the process through a "revolutionary method of self-discovery and spiritual renewal." The technique, rooted in a modified twelve-step program, would return adults to the inner child that had been subjugated long before by their parents.

Bradshaw and others built a small industry of self-help literature upon this model. For those either unwilling to seek radical professional therapeutic advice or unable to pay for it, books such as *Soul Survivors* and *Twelve Steps to Self-Parenting* packaged such ideas for wide popular consumption. And yet this is but one stream of popular advice parents have been offered.[66]

*   *   *

Of the less sensationalist programs available to parents, a typical offering is STEP (Systematic Training for Effective Parenting), produced by American Guidance Service in Circle Pines, Minnesota. "People need training to become effective parents," STEP tells us.[67] Not only is social life as confusing as ever, but the old strategies of child-rearing have become obsolete. The authoritarian approach in particular is simply "inappropriate and ineffective." Originally formulated in the early 1970s, STEP sought to "help parents reconsider their present methods of raising children" by offering a new "philosophy of child training" as well as practical "ideas and skills" for becoming "a more effective parent." Initially packaged for a 6th–7th grade reading level, it was later repackaged to a 4th grade level.[68] By the late 1990s, over 3 million parents, some through mandated programs, had used some part of the program.

In many ways, the ideas, skills, and even philosophy presented in this curriculum are little more than a repackaging of Rudolf Driekurs's strategies of the early 1960s and Thomas Gordon's Parent Effectiveness Training of the 1970s. Based upon the view that all behavior has a social purpose, the "cornerstone" of the STEP program is to teach parents that children typically misbehave with specific goals consciously or unconsciously in mind. Whenever people are discouraged or frustrated, misbehavior often emerges as a response. A child may be seeking attention, power, or revenge, or simply withdrawing from social activities due to a sense of inadequacy. The key is to recognize meaning latent within antisocial conduct. How? "STEP teaches parents to identify the goals within three clues: how the parent feels when a misbehavior occurs, what the parent does about the misbehavior, and how the child responds to what the parent does."[69]

The problem is that when parents don't understand the purposes behind misbehavior, they often react in ways that reinforce it. To break this vicious cycle, parents are instructed in a variety of therapeutic techniques. For example, they learn to change their "self-talk" from demanding, complaining, and blaming to self-dialogue that is constructive. In the comforting words of STEP's Parent's Handbook, "You can change your self-talk. To do this, start by looking at your feelings. Ask yourself: 'Am I annoyed? angry? hurt? discouraged? Or am I *committed* to helping my child stop misbehaving?' You don't need to feel angry with your child. You can talk yourself into feeling calm and capable of changing your response."[70] Parents learn to "listen for feelings," a skill that, once mastered, "helps children know they are understood." Parents are told to use "the words 'You feel' before the feeling, and 'because' to tell the reason for the feeling. 'You *feel* jealous *because* Mike got picked and you didn't.'"[71] They are taught to see the importance of self-esteem and learn techniques for improving it. Parents, for instance, are not to praise their children (because praise words "judge") but rather to encourage (because encouragement uses words that call attention to a child's effort). "Children need to learn to cooperate—not to be "better" than others. Children need to feel accepted all the time—not just when they do something right. Children need to learn to think for themselves—not to please somebody else."[72] In the end, "using a lot of praise, or only praise will not help you meet the challenge of parenting."[73] Not least, parents are taught never to punish their children but to discipline them in positive and constructive ways, when necessary, by showing respect, expecting the youngster to cooperate, negotiating choices with them, and applying consequences that, among other things, are "firm and friendly," that "allow choice," and that demonstrate "respect to the parent and the child."[74]

Beyond such programmatic material and the popular co-dependency literature, the largest part of parenting advice in the 1970s, 1980s, and 1990s has focused on the need to build children's self-esteem. In works such as Dorothy Briggs's *Your Child's Self-Esteem* (1970), Donald Dinkmeyer's *Raising a Responsi-*

ble Child (1973, 1996),[75] and Stephanie Marston's *The Magic of Encouragement: Nurturing Your Child's Self-Esteem* (1990), the techniques of client-centered counseling are distilled to anxious parents. Among the "6 Easy Ways to Get Kids to Behave," presented by a popular psychologist in 1987, was the mandate to "let kids express their emotions."

> Teach children to communicate their feelings, both positive and negative, so they won't bottle them up inside. . . . Help them talk about feelings and express needs in a way that doesn't hurt them or others. When children aren't allowed to express their feelings, the emotions don't go away. . . . Try to understand what the child is feeling. Feed back to him, in your words, the feelings you have heard him express.[76]

In a 1987 *Redbook* magazine article, "You Can be a More Sensitive Parent,"[77] the children's television figure Fred Rogers placed affective moral reasoning at the center of his advice. As he put it to parents, "be true to yourself and do what *your* feelings tell you is right."[78] The challenge, as one psychologist noted, is that "men in this culture are handicapped when it comes to dealing with feelings. And it's feelings that matter most in parenting—both your child's and your own. Most men are not attuned to the emotional dimension in human interactions."[79] What was good for the goose was also good for the gander. "I have come to believe," Rogers noted,

> that what children most need to acquire in their early years is a feeling of self-worth and a positive outlook on the world. I believe that children who develop these traits will be most able to learn whatever else they need to learn when the time comes. . . . Letting our children find *their* true selves may mean resisting the desire to impose our own interests on them or suffering disappointment when they do not follow in our footsteps. But this freedom to find themselves is an important step in the development of all children's true potential.[80]

Dinkmeyer counseled parents that "none of the standards, values, and goals we set for the child can be achieved until he himself feels adequate and self-satisfied. The child can only function as an effective human being after he believes in himself."[81] Similarly, Marston instructed parents that "children thrive in an environment where they aren't afraid of being evaluated and judged. Encouragement fosters independence, self-esteem, a willingness to explore and to experiment, as well as an acceptance for oneself and others."[82]

By the end of the 1990s, the advice parents received in the mass market had hardly changed for decades. Consider, for example, Letitia Baldridge's *More than*

Manners: Raising Today's Kids to Have Kind Manners and Good Hearts (1997), a book remarkable if only for the hyperbole with which it was marketed. Ann Landers described Baldridge as "the premier authority on manners in America, whose books are considered gospel." The book's dust jacket promised readers "a road map to raising and guiding kids who succeed in life through decency and honor." Conservative in tone, *More than Manners* posed as a practical follow-up to William Bennett's *The Book of Virtues*. The book, we are told, is what "millions have been waiting for." It offered to show parents and other concerned adults how to teach kids behaviors that would make the world around them a better place and would allow them to be courteous and compassionate with family and friends and out in public while still standing up for themselves, to use conciliation instead of confrontation with peers, authority figures, and others, and to gain respect and become leaders without becoming wimps or bullies.

The most significant section of the book is entitled, "When a Child Asks, 'Why Do I Have to Be Kind?'" Here, Baldridge spells out the moral logic of her very different gospel. "Children," she says, "should understand that: Kind manners and good behavior make you feel really good about yourself," "Kind behavior makes your world function better," "Consideration colors the world in brighter, happier hues" (in that "the space they occupy becomes warmer and more comfortable"), "Civility and kind manners give you a strong sense of self," and "When you practice civility, people are drawn to you and you find yourself with lots of friends."[83] All five of her reasons ground the moral imperative to kindness in a person's subjective well-being. In short, children should cultivate kindness primarily for the emotional benefits it offers the person and secondarily for the practical benefit of making their world "function better." In the final analysis, Baldridge has not strayed an inch from the psychological individualism so prevalent in the child-rearing literature.

Despite the interesting variations one may find, a diffusion of formal psychological and psychoanalytic theory has continued to frame the parameters and the content of moral instruction within the family. The psychological regime, for all of its variations and permutations, remains firmly established in the market of parenting wisdom.

YOUTH ORGANIZATIONS

Youth associations, of course, remain a fixture of the social landscape. They currently number over three hundred and range in size from a few hundred members to several million. These organizations often explicitly share the mission of "transferring parts of the nation's cultural heritage—beliefs, skills, attitudes, values—to young Americans gathered in troops, groups and teams under adult guidance."[84] The old emphasis on the needs and concerns of others remains. There is even an awareness that the present cultural context makes that goal difficult. As a youth leadership magazine put it, the challenge is "to make the *me* generation the *we* generation."[85] Yet here too the moral ideals of responsibility, trust, collective solidarity, and mutual tolerance, among others, are largely framed by the premises and techniques of psychology. Indeed personal autonomy and self-realization occupy the heart of their moral cosmology.

The extent of this psychologization of moral understanding is by no means uniform throughout the range of youth organizations. But the tendency is pervasive.

An interesting case, in light of the historical and cultural changes it reflects, is the YMCA. Originally devoted to "the purpose of developing Christian personality and building a Christian society," the organization has since repudiated its sectarian commitment, in favor of the more inclusive techniques of psychological understanding and improvement. As early as 1963 the National Council of YMCA announced its goal of developing participants' "self-confidence and self-respect and an appreciation of their own worth as individuals." From 1979 to 1984 the National YMCA developed new operating goals which included, among other things, a commitment to "providing leadership in values education that helps individuals and groups examine and apply their own values in today's pluralistic society." As a part of this, the organization would take "leadership in planning and implementing community efforts on behalf of youth that promote positive self images, increase access to meaningful social roles, and change conditions that foster alienation and anti-social behavior."[86] Thus the first objective of the YMCA Youth Sports program would be "to build self-esteem." Sports, the organization explained, provides "an excellent means of learning personal goal setting to develop a healthy self-image and increase self-esteem."[87]

The YWCA, in recent years, has piloted a new program called PACT (Peer Approach Counseling by Teens), in which girls are encouraged to talk with their peers about issues related to sexuality. The program has been applauded for its "enhancement of self-esteem" among participants. Self-esteem is an explicit objective because "one of the critical contributing factors to teenage pregnancy and parenthood in our society is low self-esteem." Even if it does nothing to help alleviate problems associated with teenage sexual behavior, PACT will still be counted a success because communities now "have at hand a new resource for promoting self-esteem for adolescents."[88]

The Girl Scouts provide perhaps the ideal illustration of these tendencies in the mainstream of youth organizations—ideal, in part, because the Girl Scouts have sought to "progress as society progresses."[89] By the 1990s, the organization had 3.5 million members, making it the largest girls' organization in the world. Because it focuses on girls from the ages of five through seventeen, it has a huge potential influence on their moral socialization.

Concern with the self, and particularly the concern with self-betterment is not at all new for the Girl Scouts. As early as 1916, the *Girl Scout Handbook* expressed an explicit interest in the challenge of "self-improvement." This challenge, however, was framed exclusively in the moral language of a duty to others, and especially of women's social obligations toward men. As the handbook put it,

> One of the most fundamental laws of life is that, in the natural course of things, the influence of women over men is vastly greater than that of men over one another.
>
> This is what gives to girls and women a peculiar power and responsibility, for no Girl Scout or other honorable woman—whether old or young—could use her influence as a woman excepting to strengthen the characters and to support the honor of the men and boys with whom she comes in contact.
>
> Kipling, in *Kim*, says that there are two kinds of women,—*one kind that builds men up, and the other that pulls men down*; and there is no doubt as to where a Girl Scout should stand.
>
> . . . To gain and always retain the power to be a true woman friend to the men who belong in her sphere of life is not always an easy matter for a girl, for she cannot do it unless she keeps a watch over her own faults and weaknesses so that the best of her is always in control. . . .
>
> The chief difficulty in acquiring this happy and cheerful dignity comes from the desire to be admired, which is a tendency inborn in the great majority of women. It stands in the way of their greatest strength and usefulness, because it takes away their real independence and keeps them thinking about themselves instead of about others. It is a form of bondage which makes them vain and self-conscious and renders impossible the truest and happiest companionship between men and women friends.
>
> 'Be prepared,' therefore, to do a true woman's full duty to her men by never allowing the desire for admiration to rule your actions, words, or thoughts. Our country needs women who are prepared.
>
> Prepared for what?
>
> To do their duty.[90]

More than a half century later, the ideal of self-improvement had not diminished. "As a Girl Scout," the 1980 *Handbook for Cadette and Senior Girl Scouts* read, "you are challenged to be the best possible person you can be." Yet the task of self-improvement had been entirely reframed by the vocabulary of psychology. "The challenge," the *Handbook* stated, is to "discover more about yourself—

you the person and the Girl Scout."[91] The cultivation of subjectivity is not subtle. Senior scouts are told that "you can pioneer your own 'inner space.'"

> How can you get more in touch with *you*? What are *you* thinking? What are *you* feeling? . . . Every option open to you through Senior Scouting can, in some way, help you toward a better understanding of yourself. Each can help to increase your awareness of your own strengths and needs, to recognize how you relate to others, to discover avenues for self-expression, and to make the most of the unique you. . . . Put yourself in the 'center stage' of your thoughts to gain perspective on your own ways of feeling, thinking, and acting.[92]

This message of self-improvement through introspection was established as an important theme of the Girl Scout program by the mid-1970s and since then has only become more prominent. As of the early 1980s the Girl Scouts had established four program emphases as goals for girls. First among them was "deepening self-awareness" and "developing self-potential."[93] At the heart of this agenda remain the tasks of "foster[ing] feelings of self-acceptance and unique worth," "promot[ing] perception of self as competent, responsible, and open to new experiences and challenges," and "encourag[ing] personal growth."[94] Toward this end, girls are instructed in the techniques of "positive thinking," self-esteem, and understanding emotions through such exercises as "The 'Me' Interview," which instructs the adolescent girl to interview others concerning their views of her strengths, and the "Now I Am" exercise, which instructs her to evaluate her personal development. Another exercise has the girl write positive statements about herself and put them in strategic places that she will regularly see, such as in her purse, locker, or drawer.[95] By the late 1990s, the organization was explicit in promoting itself as "a non-threatening forum for self-discovery as well as for social, emotional, and intellectual growth."[96] In its own view, "the fundamental principles of the Movement" remained the same; they had only been reworked in a "language meaningful both to today's girls and to those who will become members in the decades ahead."[97]

It is interesting how the moral significance of emotion has changed over these years. Early in the century, for example, one of the Laws of Scouting was that a girl be "cheerful." The 1913 handbook explained that the Girl Scout should be cheerful "under all circumstances." "When she gets an order she should obey it cheerily and readily, not in a slow, hang-dog sort of way, and should sing even if she dislikes it. Scouts never grumble at hardships, nor whine at each other, nor frown when put out. A Scout goes about with a smile and singing. It cheers her and cheers other people, especially in time of danger."[98] The 1920 handbook puts it with even greater severity.

This means that no matter how courteous or obedient or helpful you try to be, if you are sad or depressed about it nobody will thank you very much for your efforts. A laughing face is usually a loved face, and nobody likes to work with a gloomy person. . . . It has been scientifically proved that if you deliberately *make* your voice and face cheerful and bright you immediately begin to feel that way; and as cheerfulness is one of the most certain signs of good health, a Scout who appears cheerful is far more likely to keep well than one who lets herself get 'down in the mouth.' There is so much real, unavoidable suffering and sorrow in the world that nobody has any right to add to them unnecessarily, and 'as cheerful as a Girl Scout' ought to become a proverb.[99]

Even as late as 1956, a *Leader* magazine explained, this code was rooted in benevolence: "A girl learns to show a cheerful face to the world then because of concern for others. If she must give way to emotion (and who doesn't at times—it's healthy) she does so in private."[100] But by the closing decades of the twentieth century, emotional restraint in deference to the concerns of others had largely disappeared. Instead, according to the 1987 *Handbook*, "it often helps you and people you deal with to express your feelings openly and honestly." Here the moral significance of feelings resides in their very existence and in the clues they provide to self-discovery. By 1996, the law "to be cheerful" had been eliminated altogether. The national board explained that the word cheerful "was perceived as outdated and unrealistic in the face of adversity."[101]

Today girls are told that "your feelings are part of what makes you special. The way you feel about yourself affects the way you act and the way others act too." This is why they must understand their feelings. To this end, they are encouraged to "talk about what makes people feel happy. How do you act when you feel happy? How do you treat other people? Try sharing your good feelings with people you like. When you tell them about how you feel, they might feel that way, too! . . . Talk about what makes people feel unhappy or angry. . . . Letting your feelings show can help make you feel better."[102] It "can also make it easier for you to get along with others."[103]

The emotions of the autonomous self, then, have emerged at the vortex of moral understanding, particularly in "the development of values"—a second programmatic aim of the organization. It is through the prism of their feelings that girls are to learn what their values are.[104] Values also "grow from life experiences."[105] Coming out of such a base, it is only logical that values are seen as both pliable and relative. "Differences in values do not necessarily mean that certain ones are better or worse than others—they are just different. The ability to understand such differences and to relate them to what you feel and believe in, is a part of becoming aware of yourself and others."[106] It is these values, rooted largely in sentiment, that provide the foundation for moral action. As a 1987 *Handbook* put it, "Thinking and feeling things through before you act will help you make decisions you feel good about making." When it comes to dating, for example, a girl should "not feel pressured into going out with someone." Rather, "consider your own feelings, your values, and your needs." As to narcotics, "If you want to feel good about yourself and in control of your own well-being, say no to drugs." The same applies to staying physically fit. It not only makes one healthier but influences "the way you feel emotionally."[107] This moral equation extends to the other two programmatic aims of the Girl Scouts: "relating to others with increasing understanding, skill, and respect" and "contributing to the improvement of society through the use of her abilities and leadership skills, working in cooperation with others."[108]

Once again, values rooted mainly in an awareness of one's feelings are integrated into a cost-benefit analysis of personal and social consequences. This, in the end, is the logic of moral decisionmaking.[109]

A Faltering Regime?

The fading memory of such theorists of moral development as Piaget, Erikson, Dreikers, and Kohlberg suggests that the psychological regime may now be faltering. Few people openly embrace values clarification any more, and enthusiasm for cognitive development strategies of moral education has certainly declined. The stirrings within evolutionary psychology generate some academic excitement, but they have not been translated into practical methods of moral instruction. In general, the intellectual vitality fueling this broad strategy of moral education has waned.

As I noted before, however, the real significance of academic psychology is its diffusion into popular culture. Despite the varied and still evolving state of theory, the practical programs and techniques of moral education—in schools, family literature, and youth organizations—all embody a remarkably similar message. Life and its ethical challenges are best approached through a kind of utilitarian calculus ordered by the imperatives of emotional well-being. Techniques vary, to be sure, but the framing ideas and assumptions that guide moral instruction have remained fairly constant. If anything, the literature promoting this paradigm of moral understanding has increased in volume. Through Internet booksellers one can find over nine hundred titles that offer techniques for improving personal self-regard—91 percent of them published in the 1990s, 61 percent since 1995.[110] They include *501 Ways to Boost your Child's Self-Esteem* (1994), *365 Ways to Build Your Child's Self-Esteem* (1994), *100 Ways to Enhance*

Self-Concept in the Classroom: A Handbook for Teachers, Counselors, and Group Leaders (1993), *The Adolescent Self: Strategies for Self-Management, Self-Soothing, and Self-Esteem in Adolescents* (1991), *Be Full of Yourself: The Journey from Self-Criticism to Self-Celebration* (1998), *Believe in Yourself* (1996), *Building Dreams: Helping Students Discover their Potential* (1996), *Character Development: Encouraging Self-Esteem and Self-Discipline in Infants, Toddlers, and Two-Year Olds* (1991), *The Confident Child: Raising Children to Believe in Themselves* (1998), *Creating a Positive Self-Image: Simple Techniques to Transform Your Life* (1995), *Developing Positive Self-Image and Discipline in Black Children* (1997), and *Full-Esteem Ahead, Keys to Strong Personal Values and Positive Self-Esteem* (1992)— the titles go on and on. The psychological strategy remains established as a fixed and powerful regime in moral education.

It is not, however, unchallenged.

6

The Neoclassical and Communitarian Backlash

By the late 1980s and early 1990s, discontent with the psychological regime in moral education and character development had grown enough to form a genuine backlash. Yet this backlash has found its sharpest articulation not in educational theory but in political rhetoric. Through their frequent denunciations against the bromides of self-esteem, conservative celebrities such as William Bennett, Gary Bauer, and Lynne Cheney, and conservative academics such as Christina Hoff Sommers and William Kilpatrick, have generated contentious public debate and even a sense of panic over the state of moral education. Though this movement does have educational consequences, the critics' high political visibility creates the impression that the backlash has been far more successful educationally than it has actually been.

The voices of criticism are not only conservative. They are also traditionalist, feminist, classical liberal, and progressive humanist. These varied critics share certain commitments. First they share a conviction that a society that emphasizes individual rights without a concomitant pledge to certain shared public responsibilities is not sustainable over the long haul. There is, in this, a common sensibility that the vitality of civic and political institutions cannot be sustained on its own. Any decent public order cannot be taken for granted but is something for which one must work. Thus a healthy social order requires that citizens be capable of transcending personal interests; of envisioning and committing to a larger, common good. Critics also share the conviction that moral education must articulate and advocate a more robust moral content than the psychological strategy permits. Without abandoning the quest for an inclusive moral education, they have rejected anything like value neutrality.

Christina Hoff Sommers, a key figure within neoclassical circles, spoke to this matter directly.

> Is there really such a thing as moral knowledge? The reply to that is an emphatic "Yes." Have we not learned a thing or two over the past several thousand years of civilization? To pretend we know nothing about basic decency, about human rights, about vice and virtue, is fatuous or disingenuous. Of course we know that gratuitous cruelty and political repression are wrong, that kindness and political freedom are right and good. Why should we be the first society in history that finds itself hamstrung in the vital task of passing along its moral traditions to the next generation?[1]

From this range of criticism, two general approaches have coalesced in reaction to the psychological regime: the neoclassical and the communitarian.

THE NEOCLASSICAL STRATEGY

The neoclassical alternative to the psychological regime has been, in some respects, an attempt to revive the character education system established in the early decades of the twentieth century; in other respects, it attempts to recover the enduring tradition of moral education of the last millennium and more.[2] The general moral cosmology of this strategy operates within what philosophers call "metaphysical realism." In short, the true nature of the universe exists as an objective reality. Its complexity is neither random nor aimless but ordered and purposeful, and its design can be known to us through both revelation and reason. For neoclassicists, morality is distilled from a consensus of the ages. What makes the classical virtues so enduring and inclusive, then, is that they reflect the moral order of the universe that civilizations, in all their diversity, recognize and affirm. C. S. Lewis spoke of it as the "Tao"—a moral law shared universally across competing traditions.[3] Others speak of a "core morality," a "moral canon," and of "timeless truths." Right and wrong are not, in the final analysis, matters of opinion but essential qualities that all civilizations over the ages have discerned. They are also reflected as hard realities against which human experience will confirm: through well-being—by conformity to the moral law; or in ruin—by resisting the moral law. Because humans are so unformed at birth, the only way that the young acquire virtue and learn to live well in everyday life is in the formation of habits through imitation and practice.

In this light it is easy to see why the main focus of the neoclassical strategy is on the development of specific moral behaviors rather than on a general framework of developing moral reflection or reasoning. To the moral injunction to honor one's parents, for example, the emphasis would be upon those behaviors that demonstrate deference and courtesy (such as appropriate dress, speech, and posture). To the moral imperative to show kindness to strangers, the emphasis would be upon acts of friendliness and respect. To the moral ideal of compassion, the emphasis would be upon expressions of sensitivity and generosity. The strategy takes a pessimistic view of human nature: people are prone to act out of self-interest. The neoclassical strategy of moral pedagogy emphasizes the need for the individual to comply with legitimate moral authority, and for individual behavior to operate within acceptable social standards. At a bare minimum, the agenda within schools is simply to "demand good behavior from students."[4] Toward the end of developing moral habits in the young, children would live with a durable and pervasive system of rewards and punishments. They are to be commended when they demonstrate virtuous behavior and criticized and disciplined when they behave badly.

The Importance of Habit

The cornerstone of the neoclassical strategy is the Aristotelian argument that virtue is acquired in much the same way as other skills and abilities—through practice. "We acquire the virtues by first acting just as we do in the case of acquiring crafts," said Aristotle, in a famous passage from his *Nicomachean Ethics.*

> For we learn a craft by making the products which we must make once we have learned the craft, for example, by building, we become builders, by playing the lyre, lyre players. And so too we become just by doing just actions, and temperate by doing temperate actions and brave by brave actions . . . and in a word, states of character are formed out of corresponding acts.[5]

In the spirit of Aristotle, there is among most neoclassical figures a sense that people possess certain natural virtues—an innate tendency to be temperate, just, courageous, loyal, and the like. But without proper habituation, these capacities remain isolated and underdeveloped, leaving the person morally stunted. Thus, it is by repetition that moral actions become second nature to us. All of the proponents of the neoclassical moral pedagogy agree on this point: the first objective in moral education is to develop good "habits of the mind, habits of the heart, and habits of action."[6] Someone like James Q. Wilson merely echoes Aristotle when he argues that good character "is formed not through moral instruction or personal self-discovery but through the regular repetition of right actions."[7] Recognizing that children are not always pliant, William Kilpatrick notes that "sometimes compulsion is what is needed to get a habit started."[8] In principle, this is only the beginning.

Aristotle and his heirs recognize that the formation of habits is an abbreviation of a much more complex process of socialization. More than irrational behavioral conformity, the development of character also involved a cognitive and affective process of understanding and affirming certain moral ends with discernment and judgment in the context of different situations. Habits of moral action merely prepare the ground for true moral conduct, in which moral action is intended, not listlessly conformed to. In this, persistence was never enough; proper instruction from a reliable teacher would be essential. "Just as in the case of the crafts," Aristotle explained, "the same causes and means that produce each virtue also destroy it. For playing the lyre produces both good and bad lyre players. . . . For if this were not so there would be need of no teacher."[9] To this end, proponents of the neoclassical alternative also advocate strong mentoring by adults who are themselves well-practiced in virtuous behavior. As one educator reflected,

> How can I teach civility? I can be civil. I can use good manners with my . . . students. Instead of giving orders, I can say 'please' and 'thank you.' . . . I can model these behaviors myself. . . . How can I teach compassion? I can be compassionate. I can put myself in another's position. I can ask my . . . students, to imagine how another feels in a situation of conflict or hurt feelings. I can be sensitive to another's fear and loneliness and lend a listening ear or a pat on the shoulder. . . . How can I teach courage? I can be courageous. Instead of gossiping about the friend who hurt my feelings, I can speak directly to that friend. This takes courage.[10]

Without this guidance, the argument goes, children are lost. They are at best "an ethical tabula rasa." It is up to "good teachers [to] draw out energy, enthusiasm, verve, and spirit—even courage—as they impart knowledge and model virtue."[11]

Literature and Moral Understanding

Again, for all the emphasis on generating *habits* of good moral conduct, the neoclassical strategy is not a crude behaviorism, as its critics sometimes charge. Especially important to the revival of this pedagogy is the use of great literature from the past—or at least talk about its use. The legends, drama, folk tales, and stories passed down from previous generations, neoclassicists contend, are a robust body of moral instruction capable not only of reinforcing desirable behaviors and stigmatizing improper behavior but of stimulating the moral imagination and intelligence of the young and educating them into the intellectual complexities of competing moral principles.

Though long advocated by scholars such as Robert Coles, the position has become a pedagogical cause célèbre principally among conservatives and neoconservatives. The most well-known, of course, is William J. Bennett, whose *The Book of Virtues* was published in 1993.[12] Neoclassicists' enthusiasm for the potential of literature and history to accomplish what "Values Clarification" and other psychologistic approaches have not is unqualified.

The reasons for using literature and history in moral pedagogy are numerous and mostly uncontroversial. For Bennett the key reason is straightforward. "Many of the clearest moral lessons," he argues, "can be found in classic stories from literature and history."[13] Beyond this, "these stories . . . are interesting to children." The conservative political activist Gary Bauer made the same case as Assistant Secretary of Education in the Reagan administration. "I have great confidence in the power of stories to teach," he declared. "The literary device of showing instead of telling is a very effective way to convey truths to young minds."[14] Beyond this, Sommers noted that "help[ing] children become acquainted with their moral heritage in literature, in religion, and in philosophy"[15] is a universally established way to teach the virtues. Universal and therefore uncontroversial.

Advocates of the neoclassical pedagogies offer more psychologically interesting reasons as well. Psychologists, for example, have suggested that cognitive functioning operates along two tracks, the propositional and the narrative. Both order a person's experience, but they are fundamentally different in kind and consequence, and neither can be reduced to the other. The propositional mode attempts to operate within logical universals and so tends to be separated from an emotional, social, or historical context. The narrative mode, by contrast, requires imagination, an understanding of human intention, and an appreciation of the particulars of time and place. Empathy is virtually impossible to generate, much less sustain, on the basis of abstract rationalistic principles alone, but it is virtually inevitable, however, in a narrative mode of thinking. Only after empathy exists can a child begin to make sense of moral principles. It is for such reasons that William Kilpatrick argued that "morality needs to be set within a storied vision if it is to remain morality."[16] As Sommers put it, "literary figures . . . provide students with the moral paradigms that Aristotle thought were essential to moral education."[17] Here too the argument is hardly contentious.

What are contentious are the social and political uses of literary and historical narrative. Such stories do indeed "give children some specific common reference points," as Bennett put it, by "anchor[ing] our children in their culture, its history, and its traditions. They give children a mooring."[18] They also have the potential of reasserting a common frame of reference in a culture in which commonality is severely strained. As William Honig put it, the essential purpose of the public schools would be "to bind together a diverse and pluralistic society by disseminating the guiding morality that inheres in our best literature and history."[19] The question is, on whose terms will children be anchored? Which stories and whose history will provide the common frame of reference for society? Not long after the publication of Bennett's *The Book of Virtues*, Colin Greer and Herbert Kohl produced a decidedly liberal compendium entitled *A Call to Character: A Family Treasury of Stories, Poems, Plays, Proverbs and Fables to Guide the Development of Values for You and Your Children*. Steven Barboza edited an African-American anthology entitled *The African-American Book of Values: Classic Moral Stories*.[20] Like *The Book of Virtues*, these collections seek to anchor children culturally and morally in a set of common reference points; but the mooring points are entirely different. It is a testimony to the power of narrative in character formation that this is recognized and contested.

THE COMMUNITARIAN STRATEGY

What goes under the name of communitarianism is, in fact, a fairly diverse social movement and philosophy. It varies so widely within itself that it is difficult to speak of it as a coherent movement. One finds within its reach both religious conservatives and old-fashioned welfare-state liberals. What general consensus exists centers mainly around the critique of individualism and the liberal moral philosophy that sustains it. For communitarians, the moral fabric of community has unraveled at the end of the twentieth century. With the weakening of the institutions that traditionally provided moral authority and with nothing to fill the vacuum, Americans have lost control over the social and political forces that govern their lives. To sustain a viable public order, then, it is essential to revitalize civic obligations through the renewal of key mediating institutions such as the family, the school, and the church. These are the natural seedbeds for the creation and support of civic virtues.

In light of this criticism, it is not surprising that the communitarian vision of moral education tends to emphasize the public virtues of citizenship—self-restraint, civility, social responsibility, and the duties of participatory democracy—over the private virtues favored by the neoclassicists. Though their social agenda often has a conservative flavor, communitarians typically articulate a vision of morality by social consensus (as distinct from the inherited moral consensus of the neoconservatives). There are, as Amitai Etzioni points out, "myriad values we all share." Even in the specifics, "there is more consensus than at first seems to be the case."[21] Despite the oft-heard criticism that communitarianism is really nothing more than "Reaganism with a human face" or conversely "socialism with a human face," the communitarians' agenda states emphatically its opposition to any authoritarian control over individuals. Rather, the consensus of which they speak is more "a climate," as Etzioni puts it, "that fosters finding agreed-upon positions that we can favor authoritatively."[22] Moral authority, then, is found in community because the consensus of the community has been internalized within individuals. Only as such does it become authoritative to them.

The emphasis upon social consensus has a rationale: individuals are social creatures inextricably embedded in their communities. As such, their identity, their most meaningful relationships, and their morality can only develop from a healthy connection to the social fabric of which they are a part.

The Importance of Experience

If, for communitarians, morality exists by social consensus, its moral pedagogy operates mainly through social experience. It is through experience that students participate in moral community and practice moral action. The roots of this view are, again, Aristotelian. Experience was always a precursor to the possession of character and practical wisdom, for it schools the individual in the range of circumstances within which the virtues would find expression. "Courage will thus require opportunities for endurance of great danger; temperance will require the more ubiquitous conditions of needing to moderate bodily desires. . . . And while such experience will be acquired piecemeal, it must eventually be integrated to form larger, more interlocking patterns."[23]

Persuasive as Aristotle has been, in more recent times, the importance of experience to moral pedagogy received impetus from studies conducted in the 1970s and 1980s. None was more important in this regard than the work of James Coleman. In Coleman's view young people in the nineteenth century lived lives that were "action-rich" and "education-poor." A century later, the reverse was true: young people were now not only excessively inward-looking but insulated from a range of adult responsibilities. His report, submitted as part of the National Commission on Youth, called for the creation of "new environments" in which young people could perform public service and other important civic roles. He even went so far as to recommend a "National Youth Service" program that would provide all young people the opportunity to serve their community or the nation for at least one year.[24] This was merely the first of a barrage of studies (many sponsored by the Carnegie Foundation) that came to the same conclusion. Each recommended that high school and college students meet their "social and civic obligations" by undertaking volunteer work in the school or community.[25]

The communitarian movement continues to press the importance of experience in moral and civic education. For Amitai Etzioni, the premise is the social science observation that "experiences are more effective teachers than lectures. . . . Thus, the first step toward enhancing the moral educational role of schools is to increase the awareness and analysis of the school as a set of experiences."[26] The pedagogical uses of school experiences are implicit but essential:

> Are [parking lots] places in which wild driving takes place and school authorities are not to be seen, or are they places where one learns respect for others' safety, regulated either by faculty or by fellow students? Are the cafeterias places where students pelt each other with food and the noise is overwhelming, or are they civilized places where students can conduct meaningful conversations over lunch? Are the corridors areas where muscles and stature are required to avoid being pushed aside by bullies, or are they safe conduits patrolled by faculty or students? Does vandalism go unpunished, are drugs sold openly, and are pupils rewarded or punished according to criteria other than achievement . . . ? Or is vandalism held in check and the damage, when vandalism does occur, corrected by the offending students? Are drug sales dealt with swiftly and severely? Are students treated according to reasonable and understandable criteria?[27]

Etzioni further encourages the generation of social bonds in schools through less classroom rotation and more stable contact among students and between students and teachers. Without an encompassing, extensive, and "value-rich" bonding, moral education is not likely to succeed.[28] Beyond this, there is an endorsement of such moral educational initiatives as role-playing, moot courts, peer mentoring, and conflict mediation. In addition, communitarians insist upon an integrated relationship between the school and community service and go so far as to recommend a year of national service as "the capstone of a student's educational experiences."[29] Service learning of this kind has the capacity, as communitarians put it, to engender empathy with those in need, an awareness of social problems, and an awareness of oneself as an integral part of community life. Advocates also point to yet higher political ends that service learning can achieve in a context of social fragmentation. For one, service can be "a vital constituent in the relationship between rights and duties under a strong democratic regime."[30] Even more, as Charles Moskos put it, "because of the relative weakness of other forms of community . . . , our cohesion depends upon a civic ideal rather than on primordial loyalties."[31] In this way, service-learning as a vehicle of civic education can be a means by which communities are drawn together again.

FROM THEORY TO PRACTICAL PEDAGOGY

As one moves from social theory to educational practice, however, the differences between the neoclassical and the communitarian approaches largely wash out. Even at the level of pedagogical prescription, there is a melding of interests and concerns on all sides. Part of the reason for this has been political. The White House Conferences on character-building and civil society, congressional resolutions, and various state mandates have been largely indifferent to subtle differences of pedagogical theory. So too the alliances that emerged in the 1990s to mobilize resources and interests toward this more conservative pedagogy— such as the Character Counts! Coalition, the Character Education Partnership, and the Communitarian Network—also draw eclectically from both neoclassical and communitarian ideas of moral education. All of these initiatives operate under the rubric of "character education," a term that refers not to moral education generally but to a particular kind of moral training committed to the ideals and methods articulated by neoclassical and communitarian educators and polemicists.

Toward Pedagogical Prescription

Perhaps the key advocate of character education in this more old-fashioned sense has been Thomas Lickona. Lickona, author of *Educating for Character: How Our Schools Can Teach Respect and Responsibility* and other works on the topic, argues that there is no single script for effective character education. Indeed, of all the academic proponents of moral education, Lickona has sought to synthesize ideas from a wide range of conceptual and instructional paradigms. Even so, he advocates a set of broad principles that serve as criteria in the development of character-education initiatives. These principles are rooted in natural law. Those, he asserts, are objective. As one might expect at this point, the principles and the initiatives they spawn aim toward moral inclusiveness based upon "widely shared, pivotally important core ethical values" such as "caring, honesty, fairness, responsibility, and respect for self and others."[32] Distilled, he contends, these reduce to "two universal moral values [that] form the core of a public, teachable morality: respect and responsibility."[33] As Lickona puts it, "these basic human values transcend religious and cultural differences and express our common humanity."[34] They are not merely consensual but "rationally-grounded, non-relative objectively worthwhile moral values" that make a claim on our conscience and behavior.[35] The objectivity of these values is established through natural law. As Lickona writes,

There is a natural moral law that inhibits injustice to others and that can be arrived at through the use of human reason. This natural moral law is consistent with revealed religious principles (such as 'love your neighbor' and 'Thou shalt not steal') but has its own independent logic that even children can grasp. The educational implication of this universal natural law is very important: it gives public schools the objective moral content—"Be just and caring toward others"—that they may legitimately teach in a religiously diverse society.[36]

The heart of his synthesis is a conceptual scheme that identifies three decisive components of virtuous character: moral knowing, moral feeling, and moral action. Moral knowing, he argues, involves knowing moral values, perspective taking, moral reasoning, decision making, and self-knowledge. Moral feeling, he says, relates to conscience, self-esteem, empathy, love of the good, self-control, and humility. Finally, moral action is a critical component of a good character, involving competence, will and habit. The goal, then, is to help children understand, care about, and act upon core ethical values.[37] By beginning with a model that includes cognitive, affective, and behavioral dimensions, he is able to invoke with approval the ideas of everyone from Jean Piaget, Louis Raths, and Lawrence Kohlberg to William Bennett and Kevin Ryan; and programs as diverse as values clarification, moral dilemma discussion, role-playing, conflict resolution, and service-learning.

Out of this grab bag of moral education initiatives, Lickona does play up both the neoclassical and communitarian concern for the cultivation of moral habit in everyday life. "To develop good character," he has written, "[students] need many and varied opportunities to apply values such as responsibility and fairness in everyday interactions and discussions." "Through repeated moral experiences students . . . develop and practice the moral skills and behavioral habits that make up the action side of character." Added to this are principles that develop the institutional support for these experiences. The school itself must be "a microcosm of the civil, caring, and just society we seek to create as a nation." "The daily life of classrooms as well as all other parts of the school environment must be imbued with core values." Accordingly, the "school staff must become a learning and moral community in which all share responsibility for character education and attempt to adhere to the same core values that guide the education of students." Teachers and staff must not only model the core moral values but "recruit parents and community members as full partners in the character-building effort."[38] All of this translates into classroom and schoolwide strategies that include teaching conflict resolution, cooperative learning techniques, teacher as caregiver, model, and mentor, teaching values through the curriculum, moral discipline, and maintaining a democratic classroom environment and moral community in the classroom.

Programs of Character Education

From the late 1980s through the 1990s, the pervasive sense of urgency to provide some moral content against the thin gruel of values clarification gave rise to a flurry of character education programs in schools across the country. Many states enacted laws like Act 95–313 in Alabama in 1995.[39]

> NOW, THEREFORE, BE IT RESOLVED, that the members of the Alabama State Board of Education do hereby direct local boards of education to develop and implement, at the beginning of the 1995–96 school year, a comprehensive K–12 program for character education to consist of at least ten minutes of instruction per day; and
>   BE IT FURTHER RESOLVED, that this program of character education will focus on students' development of the following character traits: courage, patriotism, citizenship, honesty, fairness, respect for others, kindness, cooperation, self-respect, self-control, courtesy, compassion, tolerance, diligence, generosity, punctuality, cleanliness, cheerfulness, school pride, respect for the environment, patience, creativity, sportsmanship, loyalty and perseverance.

Needless to say, this remarkable law says more about the cultural and political climate of our time than it does about educational vision. But such are the inducements that guide this genre of moral pedagogy. In the field itself one finds at best a patchwork of approaches that lack either philosophical or pedagogic coherence.

The Character Counts! Coalition represents perhaps the most significant effort to give the character-education movement some coherence. It was initiated by the Josephson Institute of Ethics in 1992 when it brought together a group of politicians and religious and civic leaders in Aspen, Colorado to discuss the problem of moral decline in America and the need to teach values to the young. The "Aspen Declaration," forged at that meeting, affirmed six "core ethical values rooted in democratic society" that "transcend cultural, religious, and socioeconomic differences." These "six pillars of character" were respect, responsibility, trustworthiness, justice and fairness, caring, civic virtue, and citizenship.[40] The Coalition itself formed about a year later and by 1999 it was a national partnership of over three hundred different organizations, including church groups, teachers' and principals' unions, youth organizations, charities, and foundations.[41] Together these organizations claim to reach "more than 40 million young people." As a coalition, they are "united in one overriding mission: strengthening the character of America's youth"[42] by "integrating character education into new and existing educational programs." "The hope is that by using a consistent language with kids, the lessons of good character will be reinforced and better understood."[43] Through its "Six Pillars," coalition members have been able to revamp their values education material to stress these "core values." Toward this end, the national office has produced a range of materials, including posters and charts, videotapes, songs and activities, a "Good Ideas" collection of lesson plans, and an "Exercising Character" curriculum, not to mention ethics and character-development seminars and workshops.

Complementary in its objectives is the Character Education Partnership (CEP), also founded in 1992. As a clearinghouse of character-education resources and information, it too is "dedicated to developing civic virtue and moral character in our nation's youth as one means of creating a more compassionate and responsible society."[44] Not surprisingly, its membership overlaps that of the Character Counts! Coalition.[45] Like all such organizations, the CEP unequivocally "rejects moral relativism." "Some things are right and others wrong."[46] The organization openly embraces "core ethical values such as respect, responsibility, honesty, self-discipline, fairness, and caring."[47] Importantly, the CEP maintains that it "is not affiliated with any party or creed" and is a "nonpartisan, nonsectarian organization."[48] Its values are defined by social consensus. As a clearinghouse, the Partnership collects and distributes information on education and community-based character- and civic-education programs, offers help in implementing such programs, publicizes the progress of character education, and sponsors national and regional conferences on the topic.

In principle, all such efforts seek to establish the teacher as a moral exemplar and the school as a moral community in which the teaching of values is "interwoven throughout the climate of the school district." The school must be a "caring community" that embodies moral ideals. In principle too there is a commitment to involving parents, families, and other civic organizations in the process of character education. But in practice, a comprehensive approach to character education is rare. Fragmentation characterizes both the kind and quality of programs one actually finds in schools. Among them are virtue-of-the-month programs, word-of-the-week programs, citizen-of-the-month programs, conflict resolution training, and cooperative-learning. Consider, by way of illustration, a few representative programs in use.

The Community of Caring, an initiative of the Joseph P. Kennedy foundation in Washington, D.C., seeks to address "destructive attitudes that lead to early sexual involvement, teen pregnancy, substance abuse, delinquent behavior and dropping out of school." As one would expect, it is committed to the proposition that values can and should be taught in schools. Toward this end, the Community of Caring affirms "five core values—caring, respect, trust, responsibility, and family"—"core values that are believed to be universally accepted."[49] These form the basis of a K–12 program designed to "create a caring and respectful school environment in which students begin to understand the relationship between their values, their decisions, and their actions." This initiative is not so much a specific curriculum or set of classroom activities but an attempt to shape an entire school culture. It involves the training of teachers in the nature of values and how they are incorporated in everyday life, student discussions about the relationship between values, decisions, and actions, student forums on issues of practical problems, community service, and the integration and involvement of families with the school.

The Pasadena-based Jefferson Center for Character Education claims its programs have been used in over 60,000 classrooms, serving over 5 million students.[50] Among the more popular program materials the Jefferson Center offers are *Responsibility Skills*[51] for elementary school–age children and *How to Be Successful in Less than Ten Minutes a Day*[52] for middle-school children, the latter chosen as one of the National School Board Association's "100 Best Curriculum Ideas." Each program centers around a dozen or more directives: "be friendly," "be polite," "be responsible," "be a goal setter," "be confident," "be on time," "be here," "be a tough worker," and so on. As Center materials describe them, these are primarily language programs by which children are taught "the words, concepts, and skills of personal responsibility." The logic is simple: because "many children do not possess the basic language of responsible behavior, . . . acquisition of these concepts will lead to appropriate behavior."[53] Integral to these programs is instruction in "the attitudes and skills that can be used by youth to say 'No' to drugs and alcohol [among other problem behaviors such as 'poor attendance, . . . disruptive behavior and apathy'] this year, next year, and beyond."[54]

The Character Education Institute (CEI), based in San Antonio, provides among other things a "Character Education Curriculum" for pre-kindergarten to ninth grade students.[55] By the early 1990s the program had been used in over 45,000 American classrooms in more than 430 cities. Its goal, very simply, is "to develop responsible citizens" by developing within each child both the "inner strength" and critical thinking skills to respond appropriately to peers, the self-discipline to reach their goals, and the recognition of the importance of working together cooperatively. To this end, it affirms such "universal values" as courage, honesty and truthfulness, justice and tolerance, honor, generosity, kindness and helpfulness, freedom of choice, equal opportunity and economic security.[56]

The Teel Institute for the Development of Integrity and Ethical Behavior is a fairly small outfit based in Kansas City, Missouri, that has produced Project ESSENTIAL, a school-based curriculum that reaches from pre-K to 12th grade. Though its use is fairly limited—roughly 58 schools in 21 school districts, representing about 9,000 students and 1,300 teachers—it aspires to teach "principles of character and integrity on a national scale."[57] In particular, it seeks "to develop responsible citizens whose behaviors, attitudes, and values are reflective of four universal principles which are critical to psychologically secure, productive, and ethical living: viewing errors as positive opportunities to learn and grow; understanding the appropriate roles of emotion and rational thought, which leads to self-discipline; fulfilling both personal and social responsibilities; and equally respecting one's own rights and the rights of others." Being universal, they "transcend cultural difference and are inherently moral at their very core."[58] Project ESSENTIAL uses games, songs, group discussions, personal journals, decision making, moral-reasoning exercises, goal-setting, cooperative teamwork, as well as conflict management skills to teach these principles.

The Heartwood Institute, based in Pittsburgh, is also committed to fostering "moral literacy and ethical judgement in children by educating them in universal virtues common to the world's cultures and traditions." Implemented in roughly 350 schools nationwide by 1999, it provides an elementary school level, multicultural ethics curriculum that uses world literature—folk tales, legends, biographies, hero stories—to "introduce a language of ethics, foster literacy, good judgement and moral imagination." In the Heartwood list, the "seven universal attributes" are courage, loyalty, justice, respect, hope, honesty, and love. These provide the common vocabulary about what is valued in each school community. Heartwood acknowledges that success depends upon infusing the life of the school community with values talk of this kind. Its goal is to plant "the seeds of good citizenship in your children . . . [and so to] create a society of worthy role models and true heroes—responsible, caring adults into whose hands we will one day trust the future of the world."[59]

Yet another program is "Learning for Life," a subsidiary of the Boy Scouts of America, whose mission is to "serve others by helping to instill core values in young people and in other ways prepare them to make ethical choices throughout their lives so they can achieve their full potential."[60] The moral educational component focuses primarily on the elementary school–age children, while for middle and high school aged kids the program is oriented more toward the development of a career through the assistance of role models. For the younger children, the program is classroom-based as well and uses the usual techniques of role-playing, small-group discussions, reflective and moral-dilemma exercises, and hands-on activities. When implemented properly, its proponents say, it helps the young enhance their "self-confidence, motivation, self-worth" as well as assisting in the development of character and "positive personal values."

*   *   *

In the realm of sex education, neoclassical and communitarian educators most commonly advocate abstinence programs. This, for example, is the position adopted by the Character Education Partnership.[61] Buttressed by polling evi-

dence that shows roughly two-thirds of the American population favoring abstinence education, the Character Education Partnership argues that premarital
sex "poses a grave threat to young people's physical, emotional, and character
development and [that it] also harms the nation's public health and the moral
character of our society."[62] The "moral principle" involved is that one should
never "take serious, unnecessary risks with one's own or another person's physical, emotional, or spiritual welfare."[63] Sexuality should be supported by self-control, a strong sense of responsibility, prudence, self-discipline, and even courage.

Of actual curricula, one of the more widely used is produced by Teen-Aid,
based in Spokane, Washington.[64] It is significant in part because it dovetails with a
fairly standard character education program for elementary aged children.[65] Its
premise, as one would expect, is that character flaws generally lead to self-destruc-
tive behavior—which may have sexual consequences like unwanted pregnancy
and sexually transmitted disease. With the right tools and incentives, they contend, children and adolescents can exercise the kind of self-control that will protect them from these perils. Its core junior high text is *Me, My World, My Future*[66]
and its message is that abstinence offers freedom from both guilt and worry about
sexually transmitted disease, pregnancy, or loss of reputation; not to mention providing a sounder basis for a healthy self-appreciation and interpersonal trust. Its
strategies are to teach assertiveness and decision making skills "which take into account respect for family values, and the impact of their choices on their present
and future goals," and the basic information about the risks of adolescent sexual
activity. Teen-Aid's promotional materials highlight the distinctions between
comprehensive sex education advocated in the psychological tradition and abstinence sex education. For the former, "the teacher's principal role is as facilitator"
where for the latter, "the teacher is director giving guidelines, standards, and reasons." For the former, "knowledge is aimed at awareness" whereas for the latter,
"knowledge is aimed at prevention." The former advocates strategies where "emotions, opinions, feelings predominate"; for the latter, "truth predominates." With
the former, there is the belief that "most teens will be sexually active, and the best
that adults can hope for is that they will act 'responsibly.'" For the latter, the sense
is that "most teens do abstain while many others respond to 'Secondary Virginity'
and start over again." Not least, with the former, "abstinence is presented as a
choice" but for the latter, "abstinence is presented as the goal."[67]

PSYCHOLOGY AFTER ALL

"There's no doubt," one conservative claimed, "that the pendulum is swinging
back from self-expression to self-discipline."[68] As these representative cases pre-

sent themselves in their own words, the distinctions between the new character education and the dominant therapeutic schools of moral education are fairly pronounced. But with a closer look, the line distinguishing the newly revised character education programs and the affective and psychological strategies of moral education grows indistinct. One always finds, at the very least, deep ambivalence about the role of affective strategies within a stated commitment to "objective" theories of value. But more than this, many of the prevailing assumptions of developmental psychology and client-oriented therapy strongly influence or even frame the very terms by which character education, narrowly defined, is practiced.

The Community of Caring, for example, frames much of its moral argument within the standard affective language of psychology. For instance, the organization claims that its key text, *Growing Up Caring,* helps students "experience heightened self-esteem and self-awareness"[69] and that the way they handle their emotions has a direct effect on their sense of self-worth. "Self-worth," that text contends, "affects every aspect of your life: your performance in school, your creative talents, your energy level, your relationships with others, and your overall satisfaction with life."[70] Toward this end, it is essential that the child learn to "appropriately" express rather than to withhold or "repress" his or her emotions. As *Growing Up Caring* assures readers, "Perhaps you have heard that you shouldn't show your emotions. Your parents may have said 'don't cry.' A teacher may have told you, 'There's nothing to be afraid of.' However, your good mental health depends on your ability to recognize your emotions and to express them appropriately."[71] "If you don't express emotions or if you dump them on others, you feel guilty or down on yourself."[72] By contrast, "persons with a positive self-worth are also able to have good relationships with other people. When you care about yourself you are in a better position to care for others."[73] In one exercise, students are encouraged to write a letter to themselves describing how special they are. "Imagine that you need to be convinced of your worth as a person. Write a letter to yourself. Tell why you are special. Include all your good points. Think of the talents you have that could be developed. Mention your values. End the letter. 'Love,' and sign your name."[74] The point is reinforced in the guidelines for creating a Community of Caring school, in which teachers are encouraged to consult such resources as the book *101 Ways to Develop Student Self-Esteem and Responsibility.*[75] They are also pointed to *Values and Teaching,* by Raths, Harmin, and Simon—the designers of values clarification.

In framing the moral problem of cheating, *Growing Up Caring* shows a picture of a girl looking over the shoulder of another while taking a test. The caption reads, "Cheating, in any form, is bad for your self-esteem."[76] The moral argument is not that cheating is objectively wrong because it violates a universal value or principle, but that it lowers one's self-esteem. Elsewhere, the same text shows a young woman stealing something out of a store. An adjacent picture shows two people watching the robbery via a hidden camera. The caption under the photograph says, "One way to test the impact a decision will have on your feelings of self-worth is to imagine a picture being taken of you implementing your decision and that picture being shown to your parents."[77]

The Character Education Institute, to take another example, makes a point of disavowing values clarification. Instead its literature argues that "traditional family values form a framework for conducting . . . discussions, role playing and other activities that emphasize the consequences of the students' behavior."[78] Even so, its *Character Education Curriculum* features an exercise where teachers are instructed to help students "recognize their need for having standards."

> 1. Recognize our present values. What is important to us? Are our values evident by the physical and mental activities with which we choose to spend our leisure time, the people we choose to admire and emulate, the material goods on which we choose to spend our money, and most important, our willingness and ability to stand by our values?
>
> 2. Examine our present values for any conflicts that might exist. Is what we say what we do? Our credibility with others will be strengthened by the consistency between what we 'say' and what we 'do.'
>
> 3. Observe the differences between our values and the values of others. Our values should be strong enough that we can allow others to hold different values.
>
> 4. Recognize the consequences of our actions. Decision-making and problem-solving require that we recognize our alternatives, gather as much information as possible about each alternative, and make our decision or try to resolve our problems.[79]

Though no reference is made to values clarification, that is in essence what this exercise asks for. It makes no reference to "objective values" that might inform the child about what the substance of his values should be. Values are arrived at through internal reflection and, once recognized, acted upon. Affect is not one of many factors but rather central, if not paramount, to self-understanding and moral engagement. As an instructional manual for teachers explains, "learning to express themselves freely yet being careful to consider the feelings of others, too, may well be the most important social skill developed in students."[80]

Elsewhere, the Character Education Institute does affirm enduring values to the point of encouraging teachers to correct children when they come to the wrong conclusion about what is moral and what is not. In its own words, "The lessons have been designed to logically guide the students to the right answer."[81] But how are these values taught to children? The moral logic they promote encourages children to follow the consequences of their actions. Significantly, this cost-benefit logic is filtered through the child's sentiments. Why should one be good, say by caring for another? Because "it will make you feel better." Why should one not be bad, say through stealing or cheating? The reply: "How would it make you feel if someone did that to you?"

Here too, a child's moral behavior is linked directly to self-esteem. As CEI contends, "The lack of self-esteem is the most common factor found among persons who engage in student alcoholism, drug abuse, crime and even suicide."[82] It also notes that self-esteem is closely related to academic performance.[83] At the same time, constructive virtues such as responsibility derive from positive self-regard.

> Students who are most likely to become responsible citizens are those who have a good self-esteem; hence, those students who accept responsibility, increase their own self-esteem. Have you ever thought less of yourself when you did what you were supposed to do? You may not like having to fulfill your duties and obligations, but when you do, you realize that you are responsible and your respect for yourself increases.[84]

Precisely because "self-concept" is "the most significant factor in a student's personality,"[85] self-esteem "is totally underlying everything [the Institute] does."[86] To encourage the development of positive self-concept, the Institute offers exercises like "The Me Activity."[87]

The Jefferson Center also teaches core values such as politeness, friendliness, punctuality, goal-setting, and the like. Yet its mission includes the mandate to "write, promote and disseminate curriculum and training programs for schools and families to teach . . . self-esteem."[88] The reason is that "feeling good about myself" is one of the ingredients of success,[89] a point reiterated in its *Responsibility Skills: Lessons for Success* curriculum. "Try to stress," the manual advises, "that success is not just having money or possessions, but also knowing one's self, feeling good about what you do and being able to help others. For example, a painter may not sell many paintings, but she may feel happy and fulfilled in her work."[90] Like the Community of Caring and the Character Education Institute, the Jefferson Center provides exercises to help students develop higher levels of self-esteem. An entire unit in the *How to Be Successful* curriculum is devoted to the techniques of "Self-Talk," where students are encouraged, on the one hand, to see how negative statements make a person fail, and on the other, to learn to write affirmations and to use positive statements daily, not least after making mistakes. Students write in their notebooks that it is "my daily responsibility to

TALK POSITIVELY to myself because I want to T—Take care of myself, A —Accept myself, L—Like myself, K—Know myself."[91] The reason for this is that "successful people continue to talk positively to themselves."[92] Other exercises encourage students to "accept their likes and dislikes . . . to accept their strengths and weaknesses . . . to like themselves . . . to take care of themselves" and to "think of ways to reward themselves."[93]

The same ambivalence is found in the Teen-Aid abstinence-based sex education curriculum. Consider, for example, the following advice, offered to help students evaluate the moral decision of engaging in premarital sexual activity.

> Sexual activity outside of marriage can make you feel anxious and worried about getting caught, about becoming pregnant. It can also create a sense of disappointment by not living up to the standards you and/or your parents set for you. You could also feel dishonest knowing that you don't really feel what you know intercourse is saying to your partner. If pregnancy does result, the emotional trauma of abortion, adoption, or raising a child at this time in your life would be truly painful and long-lasting.[94]

The focal point for this moral decision is an emotional calculus defined by one's emotional and subjective well-being. At every level it is the child's feelings that are to be understood and consulted. It is not that engaging in sex outside of marriage is foolish or morally wrong, but that it may make the child "feel anxious and worried." Even the value of honesty is emotionally laden—"you may feel dishonest." And the basis for this feeling of dishonesty is not that the student defrauded, used, or lied to his sexual partner, but that he didn't "really feel" what he knew intercourse to be saying to his partner. This is consistent with the notion of honesty discussed earlier in the curriculum, that is that "real" honesty is being in touch with and expressing one's feelings. Throughout, the student is encouraged to evaluate the risks of premarital sex in terms of the "emotional trauma" that may result.

In the curriculum, students are encouraged to take up activities like sports and camping as alternatives to drug use. The reason for choosing these options is the anticipation of good feelings. Participating in sports and the like "can lead to a discovery of personal talents, skills, and interests. It is that process of discovery that generates excitement and creates a positive, uplifting feeling."[95]

In the chapter "Caring," students are told that "listening to our own feelings and trying to meet our own emotional needs can help us meet the needs of others. Becoming a caring person takes practice, and caring for ourselves can become an ongoing lesson in how to care for others."[96] "Taking good care of ourselves helps keep us healthy, of course, and we can then have the energy to care in some way for others. Caring for ourselves also teaches us how to care for others. If we value and respect ourselves, we are better able to appreciate and respect others."[97]

A sense of personal well-being is also seen as an ingredient for successful living generally. Teen-Aid's material instructs students that "when you talk about ways to feel good about yourself, you are also describing the ingredients for success."[98] To this end, the program encourages students who are feeling down to talk to themselves in order to build themselves up. "When you talk to yourself, say positive things that help you believe you can succeed. 'Negative messages' will only result in self-doubt and a lack of confidence. Positive 'self-messages' could be, 'I know I can do this, I did well on that exam, I have what it takes to succeed!'"[99] Elsewhere students are encouraged to seek affirmation from those around them. If this is not forthcoming they are told to give themselves "positive feedback." They are told, "Concentrate more on building yourself up—or sending yourself frequent positive messages and noting the many good things that you do. Maybe set a weekly goal for yourself and when you achieve that goal 'pat yourself on the back' with a snack, extra TV time, or a phone call to a friend."[100]

The Teel Institute also endorses self-esteem as "one of the most fundamental needs of every human being."[101] Indeed, the four "universal and inviolable principles" on which the Institute bases its curriculum are elsewhere described as "four principles of self-esteem." The Institute does make the explicit caveat that "self-esteem cannot be given; it must be earned. . . . Neither can genuine self-esteem be developed by focusing on unconditional self-affirmation. . . . Rather, self-esteem is based on the knowledge that one is trying one's best to become more capable and more worthy—the best that one can be."[102] Self-esteem must be "an earned outcome of behavior, attitudes, and values held." It is the effect, not the cause, of moral behavior—a point often made by conservative advocates of character education. Yet at the level of practical pedagogy this distinction is often blurred. Self-esteem, after all, is "*based on the knowledge* that one is trying one's best."[103] As Institute literature puts it, "if a student practices the skills and behaviors taught by Project ESSENTIAL, then she/he *cannot help but feel* both capable of achievement and worthy as a person. *Feeling both capable and worthy*, the student will theoretically begin to evaluate himself or herself more positively, resulting in a high self-esteem score on a Self-Report inventory."[104] In this, the student's emotional sensibilities provide the very framework within which competence and worthiness are measured and the means by which self-esteem is defined. In short, whether cause or effect or both, affect defines the moral language and the horizons within which character development is to take place.

Not to be excluded from this review are the Boy Scouts of America. Unlike the Girl Scouts, the Boy Scouts have a reputation as a holdout against certain elements of cultural progressivism. The reputation is certainly justified by its efforts to resist the inclusion of atheists and homosexuals in its ranks. Yet in educational practice, one finds the strong influence of affective psychology. Its Learning for Life curriculum makes the theme of ethics explicit in the sixth grade. Here, the moral logic of "making good decisions" is very simple: "we feel good about ourselves, others feel good about us, and we don't have to worry about negative consequences."[105]

Even in a movement as visible as the Character Counts! Coalition, one finds the same ambivalence. Consider the testimony of Nancy Van Gulick, a trainer in the movement, before the National Commission on Civic Renewal in 1997. On that occasion, she spoke fervently for the objectivity of values and the need to communicate solid moral content to children. "We have to make them conscious of right and wrong," she insisted. In the same breath, however, she declared that "we have to make them committed to doing right, meaning it feels good to do right. Teach them that it feels good to do right. When you help the little old lady across the street, that feels good. You know, when you do the right thing, it feels good. When you do the wrong thing, it feels bad. Teach them to be committed. Make them feel committed to doing the right thing."[106] The founder of the Coalition, Michael Josephson, expresses much the same ambivalence. As a practical ethicist, he is as articulate a person as one can find on the moral foundations of good character. He has knowledge of different and complementary philosophical paradigms which compel one toward ethical living. At the same time he suggests that the question, Why be ethical? is not really important because we already know "the virtue of virtue."[107] That "inherent sense of right and wrong . . . tells us it's better to be a good person. I just know that I feel better when I'm doing the right thing."[108]

CONCLUSION

Through the 1990s the dominant regime of moral education seemed to founder under a formidable backlash of traditionalists and communitarians. These intellectuals' and polemicists' withering contempt for values clarification, self-esteem quick fixes, and other psychological schemes has been severe, and the relentlessness of that scorn has clearly fueled the ongoing search for effective alternatives. The important theoretical differences between the neoclassical and the communitarian strategies have mostly evaporated in the translation into particular programs of instruction. Advocates of the new and improved character-education pedagogies end up with an unequivocal affirmation of moral content in the advocacy of values. They generally agree that young people should be required to engage these values through the habits and challenges of basic life experience, especially when these ideals and practices are integrated in the entire life of the school and in the fabric of the larger community.

The appeal of this newly revived character education has been great. The curricular innovations represented by the character education movement have become popular in many schools across the country, among many educators, and even in the major educational bureaucracies. In this there is a real sense among its advocates that something important has taken place, a sea change in the way children's moral needs are addressed. The old models of moral education have fallen out of favor; a new era in moral education aimed at recovering a more traditional moral pedagogy has dawned, one capable of reversing the moral disintegration of American society. The sense of hope among many advocates is palpable.[109]

Yet while the political visibility and social organization of this backlash have been overwhelming, a closer look at the popular pedagogy of character education raises serious questions about whether there has been any reformation at all. The assumptions, vocabulary, and techniques of secular psychology are ubiquitous.[110] Rather than provide a challenge and an alternative, the new character education simply reworks the psychological strategy within a traditional format of moral education. In this there is an implicit ambivalence that goes beyond a desire merely to include an affective dimension in moral instruction. Traditional moral values are explicitly affirmed but they are taught through programs interwoven with precisely the same therapeutic premises and techniques their political proponents deride. At the end of the day, the dominant strategy of moral education is not challenged as much as it is repackaged. The backlash against therapeutic practices in moral education has been more effective at the level of political discourse than educational practice. By the time the challenge to the dominant psychological strategies of moral education reaches the classroom, it has come to resemble what it was supposed to replace.

7

The Ambivalence
Within Faith Communities

The place that religious faiths and the communities that embrace them now hold in the work and culture of moral education is peculiar and complex. Once the dominant regime of moral education in American society, its cultures are now fragmented[1] and its institutions marginalized.[2] Indeed, faith communities in all their diversity are neither part of the present moral education establishment nor a visible part of the backlash.[3] They are, rather, peripheral to both.

And yet, although peripheral to the larger culture-forming institutions, they retain a prominent role in local communities and in the lives of many numbers of Americans. Feeding these local structures with curricular material, of course, are religious denominations and other para-ecclesiastical organizations. Within these, there is considerable ambivalence in the mix of both traditional biblical teaching and psychological assumptions, concepts, and methods. The cultural packagings are varied, as one might expect. There is also considerable variation in the mixture—some emphasizing scripture and tradition and others emphasizing the psychological. That there is a blending of the two is invariable.

AMONG PROTESTANTS

Numbered among the harshest critics of secular public education in the late twentieth century have been religious conservatives, Evangelicals most prominently. They have also emerged among the greatest champions of an older-fashioned character education. Though often concealed, conservative religious faith has clearly animated much of the traditionalist backlash to the moral education establishment, inspiring virtually the entire movement of abstinence-based sex education.

Conspicuous in this mix is James Dobson. As the head of the Evangelical family ministry Focus on the Family, he has been at the forefront of opposition to nearly every cultural change since the late 1960s. Whether battling the National Education Association, SEICUS, Planned Parenthood, or the liberal wing of the Democratic Party, his opposition to progressive organizations and causes has been consistent, strident, energetic, and fairly effective. At the same time, as a family psychologist he has dispensed advice to literally millions of parents and children. Dobson thus presents an instructive case of the mainstream Evangelical approach.

Dobson's book *Preparing for Adolescence*, perhaps his most significant effort to reach Evangelical adolescents with moral guidance, has sold over one and a half million copies and has had an extraordinary sway within the Evangelical subculture. This short book is "designed to acquaint you with yourself . . . to give you a better grasp of who you are and where you appear to be going."[4] With the first chapter on self-esteem and a later one on emotions, *Preparing for Adolescence* depicts self-understanding and moral action as dependent upon the categories of contemporary psychology. The message is implicit but sustained throughout: growing up requires ongoing introspection—about one's feelings of inferiority, sexual identity, problems, looks, indeed every aspect of a teenager's emotional life.

As one would expect, the book offers a distinctively Christian commentary on these challenges. Dobson speaks of the obligation to obey God's will as revealed in Scripture. He also speaks of God's values as distinct from "man's values," of the example of Christ and his courage, of the need for prayer before making decisions and the need for reading the Bible as a source of guidance. Thus the "appetite for sex"

is something God created within you. I want to make this point very strongly. Sex is not dirty and it is not evil. Nothing that God ever created could be dirty. The desire for sex was God's idea—not ours. He placed this part of our nature into us; He created those chemicals (hormones) that make the opposite sex appealing to us. He did this so we would want to have a family of our own. . . . So sex is not a dirty thing at all; it's a wonderful, beautiful mechanism, no matter what you may have heard about it.

However I must also tell you that God intends for us to control that desire for sexual intercourse. He has stated repeatedly in the Bible that we are to save our body for the person we will eventually marry, and that it is wrong to satisfy our appetite for sex with a boy or girl before we get married.[5]

At the same time, the very first reasons Dobson gives against premarital sex are the risks of venereal disease; against marriage at a young age, the likelihood of divorce and being a parent before one is emotionally prepared. Likewise, the leading reasons for resisting the pressure of peers to smoke cigarettes, drink alcohol, or take drugs are the consequences to health and emotional well-being. With the emphasis on self-esteem, the book enshrines a positive self-concept as the adolescents' most significant category in thinking about the self and what the self should aspire to.

Thus, in the lessons Dobson conveys to young people, the importance of a sustained introspective gaze, self-understanding, and well-being are established as the paramount moral categories. Biblically based moral standards, then, *are framed within* the language and concepts of popular psychology, not the other way around.

The moral horizon Dobson conveys is not uncommon within Evangelicalism. The framework of popular psychology also organizes Kenneth Erickson's *Helping Your Children Feel Good About Themselves: A Guide to Building Self-Esteem in the Christian Family.*[6] This is a sentimental book that expresses earnest concern for developing children. Here too, self-esteem is made the cornerstone of a healthy childhood and even a healthy society. Quoting Dobson, Erickson bases his argument on the consequences of low self-esteem.

> In a real sense, the health of an entire society depends on the ease with which the individual members gain personal acceptance. Thus whenever the keys to self-esteem are seemingly out of reach for a large percentage of the people, as in twentieth-century America, then widespread 'mental illness,' neuroticism, hatred, alcoholism, drug abuse, violence, and social disorder will certainly occur.[7]

As an Evangelical, Erickson grounds the idea of self-esteem in the love of God. "Teaching children the almost-unbelievable truth about God's love," he writes, "is one of the major tasks of parents."[8] Beyond this important theological caveat and occasional Bible verse, there is little to distinguish his advice from that of secular family therapists. On the one hand, he emphasizes the building of self-esteem and self-confidence as ends in themselves, techniques of communication and problem solving, and the "inner child" (or "the stowaway child within"); on the other hand, he criticizes perfectionism and shame-based morality. Although he writes of the importance of forgiveness, the problem of sin is all but absent. In a way that is typical within the Evangelical subculture, Erickson provides parents a range of specific and practical therapeutic techniques for improving their relationships with their children and, ultimately, their children's self-esteem. These include meeting frequently with other parents "to identify and share the major problems experienced in communicating effectively with their children," holding "family inventory sessions" in which parents and children identify and record favorite things to do together, scheduling "family discussion sessions where each member is asked to think of, and share, two special qualities they like in each of the others," recalling the number of times they affirmed or criticized each member of the family, estimating "the amount of one-on-one time they spend with each child per day" and comparing it to the actual amount of time spent with the child, selecting positive traits they would like to pass on to their children and identifying a "trait-for-this-week" that they will incorporate into their parenting practices, and "los[ing] no natural opportunity to serve as a family 'hug therapist' . . . resolv[ing] that when they feel lonely or hurt, they will ask for a healing hug from their spouse or their children."[9]

Much the same theme is found in Charles Gerber's *Christ-Centered Self-Esteem: Seeing Ourselves Through God's Eyes*.[10] Here again, the terminology and presuppositions of secular psychology provide the framework for Christian self-help. In the view of this professional counselor, not only is "correct biblical self-esteem . . . a vital ingredient to being successful . . . it is the main ingredient." Unlike most of the Evangelical books of this genre, Gerber stays very close to biblical texts in his treatment of self-esteem; each point is backed up with verses from the Bible. The author justifies this by arguing that the Bible is "the ultimate source of self-esteem." Gerber's purpose, then, is to "show how important it is that a person build his or her esteem from God's side of the cross at Calvary and not their side of the cross." The key to biblically based self-esteem, he argues, is "Christ's esteem for us." By contrast, "low self-esteem is a doctrine of the devil; a cleverly disguised and disgusting lie taught by the devil for the purpose of killing, stealing and destroying mankind." "Satan is the author of low self-esteem. I believe that for a Christian to have low self-esteem, he or she is believing the low esteem lies that Satan tells, with the help of society and the media." Typical of the formulae found in Evangelicalism, Gerber offers a "prescription to improve your self-esteem" that includes the recommendation that each person "spend time with God, reading the Bible," "remember your successes," "state positives about yourself," "do a weekly inventory of positive traits you see in yourself," "smile and maintain good eye contact," "become your best friend," and "stop wanting to be someone you are never going to be, and probably should not be."[11]

Then there is Nell Mohney's *Don't Put a Period Where God Put a Comma: Self-Esteem for Christians*,[12] a sweet book filled with inspiring stories whose purpose is to instruct Christians in the "abundant life" as mentioned in the gospel of John. For Mohney, the greatest obstacle to abundant life is negative self-image. "Many Christians have low self-esteem because they haven't yet accepted God's grace. Some even believe that because we are sinful and unworthy of God's grace, we should have low self-esteem. . . . As Christians we need to remember that we are made in the image of God . . . , redeemed by Christ, and empowered by the Holy Spirit."[13] The antidote, of course, is a positive self-image. "We no longer have to live with feelings of loneliness, rejection, and unworthiness," Mohney writes. "Instead, as we receive God's love, we are able to perceive ourselves as 'new creations'—persons full of potential and worthy of respect. When we learn to love ourselves, we can be open to others, see them as persons of worth, and be instruments through whom God's love is made visible."[14] Here again, she punctuates her lessons with specific techniques "for developing high self-esteem," "reducing harmful stress," "developing better attitudes," "overcoming negative emotions," "becoming more optimistic," and "building self-confidence."[15] Mastery over the self in this way is important because a positive self-image is central to the "Christian value system."[16]

In these and other books there is a curious blending of cultural ideals and conceptual categories. This is not an unconscious parroting of contemporary moral psychology. Evangelicals seek, rather, to co-opt the psychology for their own purposes, making therapeutic concepts subordinate to biblical wisdom. The premise is that psychology provides tools that are, by themselves, theologically and morally neutral but useful all the same when linked to the truths of Christian faith. Yet insofar as popular psychology provides the framing categories for this literature of popular guidance and admonition, it is the Christian worldview that undergoes a peculiar reworking.

*   *   *

Despite an easy and contemporary coherence in all of these books, the cultural incongruities these advice books represent are, from a historical point of view, breathtaking. In part because the claim to orthodoxy is not so aggressively adhered to, such incongruities are not nearly so obvious or even pronounced among mainline Protestants. But the ambivalences are unmistakable.

The effort to link lay theological education and developmental psychology was already well established in the mainline Protestant churches by the mid-1960s.[17] In a document produced by the Division of Christian Education of the National Council of Churches in 1966, for example, leaders from sixteen Protestant bodies outlined a strategy by which each member denomination could construct its own curriculum of religious education. Beyond better "use of the Bible in curriculum," they sought to better understand "the relationship of theological foundation and psychological insights in Christian nurture." Toward this end, their strategy was meant to integrate "learning theory" and "developments in contemporary education" in a Christian context. As a matter of practical theology they explained that "the person's perception of his whole field of relationships, especially the way others relate to him and accept or reject him, greatly influences his capacity for self-acceptance. The self-acceptance, in turn, becomes a key factor in his capacity to be outgoing in his relationships with others and with God, his Creator." Over the ensuing decades, the various mainline Protestant denominations have negotiated these insights in similar ways.

The United Church of Christ, for example, offers a pamphlet especially for youth in its "Looking Up" series. Entitled "Feeling Good About Yourself: Helping Young People Build Self-Esteem," the booklet argues that self-understanding and self-love ("self-esteem, self-worth, self-acceptance, self-image, or just feeling good about yourself") are the beginning of the moral life and remain forever central to it. "Loving myself is at the heart of living, loving, and growing. Unless I love myself, it is harder for me to love others and to be loved by them. Life's problems are easier to figure out and face up to if I love myself. Growing into healthy maturity and being successful are helped by how much I value myself."[18] The message to young people is clear: the foundation of goodness, and especially altruism, is love of self: "We cannot give love if we don't have the love to give. And the love we have to give has its roots in our love of Self." The booklet even goes on to counsel its readers that to love oneself "is holy." Having made this clear, it then warns young people about the excesses of narcissism—where people are so fixed upon themselves that they give little thought or concern for anyone else. This is love of Self "gone wrong." "Persons who are selfish are so insecure that they need all the attention they can get, not only from others but also from themselves." The problem with these individuals is that they were improperly cared for when they were young. The answer for them, as for all young people, is to learn a proper form of self-love. It is to this end that readers are invited on a journey of self-discovery, a journey that never ends for the simple reason that the "self is always becoming, always growing, whether we're aware of it or not."[19]

The importance of self-understanding and self-regard to both a healthy and a moral life appears in the United Methodist literature as well. Of the many materials the denomination provides, one of the most interesting is *Devo'zine*, the devotional magazine designed to help Methodist teenagers to "develop a lifetime pattern of spending time with God and reflecting on what God is doing in your life." The message is familiar:

> Low self-esteem can keep us from achieving our goals, forming solid friendships, and seeing the good in others. It can even hinder our relationship with God. On the other hand, when we have healthy self-esteem, we realize that we are not perfect and are comfortable with that; are able to laugh at our mistakes rather than punish ourselves; can step out, share who

we are, and try new things; view God as the loving, compassionate, and generous Creator of good things.[20]

Here again, readers are not left alone with self-examination to achieve a positive self-regard but can develop by seeing themselves "through the eyes of God, who believes in you."[21]

In helping them sort out their values, *Devo'zine* encourages readers to apply "critical thinking skills" to the values of television. The cost-benefit calculus is familiar: "Are the characters honest or dishonest? What are the consequences of their honesty? dishonesty? Are the characters especially selfish? Do they routinely show disrespect for one another? What are the results? Are the characters aggressive or violent? What are the results of their aggression?" But embedded within this utilitarian logic is an appeal to transcendence. "What would Jesus think about the program? How would you feel if Jesus were watching it with you?"[22] Moral choices too are framed within a psychology of emotional need. For example, "destructive choices meet a need of some kind. They do so in the wrong way, but they still meet a need. Bad choices may temporarily make us feel good about ourselves." Yet "to deal with sin, just saying no isn't enough. We need to fill our lives with Jesus, who is better and stronger than sin."[23]

Because the reformed tradition in theology is known for its tendencies toward rational elucidation, it is not altogether surprising that the literature mainline Presbyterians offer their youth is far-reaching. Here too, whether on the moral life generally or on sexuality and drug use, the material reflects much the same pattern of ambivalence. The general orientation rejects "handing out absolutes" for these "can sometimes be a disservice to youth." Rather, one "must teach youth how to think, how to make faithful decisions, and how to live with the consequences of their choices."[24] The stories and metaphors of biblical literature are used copiously throughout as a tool of moral instruction.

This church's pedagogy on sexuality, most fully developed in *God's Gift of Sexuality*, is unusual for its thoroughness and the fact that theology frames the discussion in its entirety—for all age groups. It offers, right up front, seven biblical and theological principles to guide an understanding of sexuality: "God created us and gave us the gift of our sexuality; God created us for life in community; our church is a community of love; our church is a community of responsibility; our church is a varied community; our church is a community of forgiveness; and God gives us responsibility for our own decisions."[25] The theology is squarely in the liberal tradition and therefore inclines the denomination toward progressive views of abortion, homosexuality, and premarital sex. It also maintains a critical awareness of sexism, homophobia, and racism. At the same time, the curriculum's authors are biased toward restraint—for example, "young people who are not married should not engage in sexual intercourse."[26] In this framework, "young people . . . learn a method of responsible decision making that can become a model for their lives."[27] The model includes the typical techniques of hypothetical moral dilemmas, self-esteem exercises, and value-clarification activities. Here too, the moral reasoning passed on to the young speaks of the importance to one's moral autonomy of feeling good about oneself. Yet consistent with its theological emphasis, the document states emphatically that one's sense of worth is enhanced by recognizing that God created us as one of his good creations.[28] Indeed, overshadowing all is the view that "in our decision making, we are instructed by God's Word to us."

The Presbyterian drug prevention curriculum, *Together: Growing Up Drug Free*, is thorough as well but more like other mainline Protestant and Evangelical literature in its emphasis on psychological assumptions.[29] Thus, for example, while the manual openly recognizes that affective education focusing on self-esteem would be limited in its effectiveness, one of the fundamental factors in its alternative model (beyond teaching the consequences of drug use and interpersonal skills to resist peer pressure) is the "development of self-concept" which "includes helping children to discover and believe in their own competence, responsibility, and personal worth."[30] Therapeutic assumptions concerned with basic biological, psychological, social, and spiritual needs frame the argument, but the starting point is emotional well-being through self-understanding. Repeated to all age groups, in age-appropriate language, are lessons on the nature of feelings—that (1) "feelings are real," "as real as things we can see or touch"; (2) "feelings are not right or wrong," they "merely are"; (3) "doing good feels good"; and (4) "feelings change."[31] The objective in these lessons is to change feelings through actions. If one is upset but responds in a way that is good, "your upset feeling will change into a good feeling" but "if you feel upset and do something you know is wrong, your resulting feeling may be different, but it will still be an upset feeling."[32] Emotional self-understanding is not only the starting point but is also one of the threads that ties all lessons together, whether it is in dealing with peer pressure, the consequences of drug use itself, or the development of refusal skills. Here too, stories from the Bible provide a point of reference, as do affirmations of God's love and strength, but the moral imagination is framed more by the categories of psychology than either scripture or theology.

CONTRASTING APPROACHES

Within Catholicism and Judaism, the moral education curricula have kept remarkably free of the influence of secular therapeutic strategies—at least the influence is not so obvious. A number of factors may explain this. For one, both Catholicism and Judaism have historically sought to survive as minority faiths in a Protestant-dominated culture. These faiths also possess an identity rooted in ritual and tradition as well as a more deeply embedded historical self-understanding than Protestantism. While not untouched by psychology, their curricula present a striking contrast to the overt synthesis found in Protestantism.

Among Catholics

There are dozens of curricula for Catholic youth. They range widely but most are carefully integrated into Catholic tradition and moral teaching. Needless to say, the advantages of having the Imprimatur of a Bishop and of being declared "Nihil Obstat"—officially free of doctrinal and moral error—are not small.

Typical among these curricula is the Silver Burdett Religion Program, "This Is Our Faith."[33] Aimed for use in the Catholic parish, its emphasis is on the Roman Catholic understanding of the Church's structure, government, and sacraments. Though the material is presented in age-appropriate ways, the focus is upon preparing children for participation in the Sacraments of Eucharist and Reconciliation. In each year, students are taught a three-step process of "Learning About Our Lives," in which young people are presented with a relevant story or experience, are taught particular doctrines, and then learn to apply these truths to their daily lives.

In the fourth grade, attention turns to matters of morality. Young Catholics learn that they "are called to choose between good and evil in [their] daily lives, and to care for others." Building upon knowledge of the Ten Commandments, the Beatitudes of Christ, and the creeds of the Church "as guides for living the way of Jesus," the pedagogy focuses upon stories of moral virtue, particularly on "Jesus as the example of Christian life and love," and "the Holy Spirit as our helper and our guide in times of temptation." In this they learn that "goodness and love come from God and are manifest in creation."[34] Biblical teaching is integrated into all of the lessons of the curriculum. A central part of their moral education is instruction in prayer—the act of contrition, act of Faith, act of Hope, act of Love, and the Our Father.

The curriculum's emphasis on the church as a community is also striking. Children are taught that the Catholic community is a singular one, marked by its creeds and its worship, formed by the actions of individual and corporate prayer, and expressed in its capacity to care and to minister. It is not insignificant that children are instructed in community through the biographies of great Catholic exemplars, such as Father Damien, who cared for the victims of leprosy on the island of Molokai in the late nineteenth century; Dorothy Day, who founded the Catholic worker movement to help the urban poor; and Agnes Boy-axhui, a Romanian émigré who as Sister Theresa founded the Missionaries of Charity to care for the sick and dying in the slums of Calcutta.

Different in the organization of its material but similar in its theological orientation is *Growing with the Catholic Church*, published by Sadlier for younger teenagers. This curriculum provides lessons in Catholic history, faith, and doctrine. Within it is a separate volume of moral instruction entitled *Growing with the Commandments*, designed to "help you know how you are to live for God and for others in faith, hope, and love." Indeed, after two introductory chapters describing the nature of faith, hope, and love, as well as conversion, conscience and sin, the main chapters are organized around the meaning and application of the Ten Commandments. The method here is similar to the Silver Burdett program: at every level, after considering some of the quandaries of daily life, the "story and vision of [the] Catholic faith are presented." The story that unfolds draws "from the Scriptures, Tradition, the teachings of the Church, and the faith life of [the] Catholic community." Moral lessons are drawn from "what God has made known to our ancestors" and point to "the way that rich Tradition calls us to live now." It is in this latter challenge that young Catholics can see themselves as part of this living and unfolding narrative—"as followers of Jesus."[35]

The same thick theological orientation guides "Parent to Parent," a handbook for parents who want to provide their children with "a Catholic vision of human sexuality." Informed by the U.S. Catholic Conference of Bishops' *Education in Human Sexuality for Christians*, the lessons are framed by "seven theologically-based principles that form the foundation for a Christian description of human sexuality."[36] As parents are told, "It is extremely important that we teach Catholic doctrine. Our children need a firm foundation in the fundamental teachings of the Catholic Church at this age, so that they may have a solid base from which to grow."[37] At each age level, these principles are reaffirmed and applied. Along with this are explanations of the Church's prohibitions against masturbation, homosexuality, abortion, and the like. And yet because conscience is central to Catholic ethical teaching, the booklet also provides four principles for those "thinking of making a decision contrary to Church teaching."[38] Except in the recognition that children of different ages are going through physiological and emotional changes, psychological categories are largely absent.

And Among Jews

Many of the curricula used within Jewish communities resemble those found in Catholicism. Theological differences, say between Orthodox and Reform movements, naturally carry different cultural sensitivities on matters such as gender and sexuality. Yet the moral pedagogy of all denominations is deeply rooted in the Jewish tradition, texts, and theology. *Stories From Our Living Past,*[39] for instance, is not unlike *The Book of Virtues* by William Bennett or *The Call to Character* by Colin Greer and Herbert Kohl, except that its moral framework is rooted in a particular theological and historical tradition. To teachers, the curriculum states,

> The source of our identity as Jews goes back four thousand years to our ancestors' conviction that human life has meaning in a world that has purpose; that a single Truth, at once unitive and universal, pervades all of reality. This is the experience of the One God. The vintage of that ancient insight was distilled in our Torah, and the continuing life of the Jewish people is the process of fermentation. Judaism abounds with stories and parables as the vessels to contain the wine of our tradition, and that wine is constantly aging and mellowing, acquiring its unique flavor and bouquet from generation upon generation of interpretive wisdom and understanding. . . . By animating ethical concepts, and by breathing life into cultural values, these stories enable us to see how values and concepts interact.[40]

The moral order within which instruction takes place is emphasized again and again, for instance, in Louis Newman's *A Child's Introduction to Torah:*

> The Bible's stories and laws reflect the Jewish religious faith assumption that the universe is not morally chaotic. Its purpose is given in a number of key Biblical terms defining categories of human behavior. The most crucial are: righteousness, justice, and holiness. . . . They take on meaning through laws observed, contemplation, learning, and instructive ritual. Jewish ritual is a derivative of this faith. It is the deliberate and purposeful self and group-training for the express purpose of facilitating the daily acting-out of key concepts. The laws of Torah, ethical and ritual, promote human harmony and are in accord with God's purpose.[41]

Another illustration of Jewish ethical teaching for young people is an adaptation of the *Pirke Avot,* or *Sayings of the Fathers,* put together in the text, *When a Jew Seeks Wisdom.*[42] Oriented toward the practical moral questions of how we treat others in daily life, the book's purpose is to introduce the moral teachings of the Jewish tradition; to help the young "learn the tradition anew, as if uncovering each idea and custom for the first time." Because people possess both the *Yetzer Tov* (the impulse for good) and the *Yetzer HaRa* (the inclination toward evil), "every one of us inwardly struggles between what is good and what is evil, as well as what is right for the world in which we live [and] this struggle gives meaning to our lives and to the world around us." It is precisely because of the complexities of life that the traditions provide a guide, with "markings of eternal truths." And so, on the value of life, one master taught:

> Every person must have two pockets. In one pocket should be a piece of paper saying, 'I am but dust and ashes.' When a person is feeling too proud, he should reach into the pocket and withdraw the paper to read it. In the other pocket should be a piece of paper saying, 'For my sake, the world was created.' When a person is feeling disheartened and lowly, he should reach into this pocket, withdraw the paper and read it. For each of us is the joining together of two worlds. Of clay we are fashioned, but our spirit is the breath of God. We must seek to balance in our lives what is ordinary and what is holy, what is creaturely and what is sacred.

On the value of labor, "Rabbi Tarphon used to say, It is not up to you to complete the work, yet you are not free to abstain from it." On the value of peace, "Hillel said, Be of the disciples of Aaron, loving peace and pursuing peace, loving your fellow creatures, and drawing them near to the Torah."[43] And so it goes through the values of knowledge, study, courage, patience, love, community, possessions, sensitivity, argument, and Torah, among others, each lesson punctuated with maxims and stories from the tradition. In what seems to be its only nod to contemporary moral thought, the author does emphasize that each individual possesses freedom of choice, but even here that freedom is framed within the responsibility of maintaining the boundaries and solidarity of the Jewish community and seeking peace within and among other groups.

Taking a very different approach is the book, *How Do I Decide?: A Contemporary Jewish Approach to What's Right and What's Wrong*.[44] Here the selection of moral issues is more contemporary: it includes drinking and drugs, eating disorders, abortion, sexuality, gender roles, intermarriage, the care of the elderly, euthanasia, participation in war, and so on, from a Jewish perspective. Though framed in modern format and diction, the text draws heavily on Jewish tradition and literature for "insights, values, and truths that are still uniquely valid."[45] Though illustrated by copious selections from the Torah, Bible, Talmud, folk tales, and rulings from various rabbinic authorities, the text does not offer "conclusive answers" but aims to "stimulate your own thinking" toward ethical action.[46] Here too, psychological categories and language are conspicuous by their absence.

WITHIN LOCAL COMMUNITIES

There remains, within various faith communities, a determined effort to ground the tools of moral education within biblical literature and theological tradition. These efforts vary considerably, as we have seen, in the degree to which they embrace the language and assumptions of contemporary psychology. Because they are among the most self-conscious about the preservation of their orthodoxy it is a bit ironic that Evangelicals are among the least self-conscious about their embrace of therapeutic categories and ideals. Whatever else is lost in this bargain, such syncretism does provide a contemporary diction that is both relevant to the young and easy for them to grasp. The evangelical message is compatible with the other moral messages they are hearing elsewhere in the culture. Catholics and Jews are equally remarkable in the degree to which their curricula are unsusceptible to psychological influence. But their traditional message is at risk of failing to connect with the very ones it is meant to influence.

There is, of course, more to the story. Within particular churches, parishes, and synagogues, such distinctions tend to flatten out to the kind of utilitarian formulae advocated through the dominant regime. For example, when asked how she would deal with a student who stole something from a classmate, the principal of a Catholic school in San Antonio said, "First, I'd ask them why they did it. I'd ask them about how it makes them feel, and how would they like it if somebody did that to them?" But if they felt okay about it? "I'd say, 'You know, you can't get away with it all of your life. It just doesn't work that way.'" Would she ever use the language of the Catholic faith to deal with these matters? After all, the setting was a Catholic school sponsored by the Catholic Church in the very Catholic city of San Antonio, Texas. To this, she answered quite matter-of-factly, "Oh, no, that kind of language would probably not relate to them anyway. When I was growing up I personally might have responded to someone if they said, hey, this is a sin. Today, though, I don't think that young people would respond to that. The most you could say to them is that this is not allowed."[47] A youth minister in a large Presbyterian (PCUSA) church in Chicago made much the same admission. When asked about his work with kids on these kinds of moral issues, "Do you ever invoke the name or the example of Christ?" He too said that he didn't. "No, I don't. Sometimes I think I should, but I find it artificial. For these kids, the symbols [of the faith] don't mean anything."[48] And for a rabbi in charge of religious education in one of New York City's largest Reform synagogues: Do the young people he works with ever hear theological concepts like "sin" used to help make sense of moral good and evil within various ethical issues? "Sin isn't one of our issues. My guess is that in twelve years of religious school our kids will never hear the word. It's not a Jewish concern. It doesn't exist by us, for better or for worse."[49]

As to the moral ideal of well-being, it is ubiquitous in youth ministry. The concept of self-esteem, in particular, is never far from the articulated objectives of such work. And yet this ideal is not embraced without reservation. "Yes," said the Presbyterian youth minister, "self-esteem is touted in youth ministry every-where. It has become our standard. Yet what does self-esteem have to do with Christianity? Jonathan Edwards didn't have a damn thing to do with it. Isn't the denial of self at the heart of Christian faith? To me it can kind of degenerate into solipsism, self-worship, so to me it's somewhat superficial."[50] And yet, in balance, he continues to see it as a worthy aim. "It's true," a Baptist youth minister in Dal-las said, "you wouldn't find Christ talking about self-esteem."[51] The principal of the Catholic school in San Antonio also embraced the ideal but, in the same breath, interpreted it in the language of her faith. "Self-esteem is very much a ba-sic teaching of the Catholic church: You are created good and the Holy Spirit has gifted you and empowered you."[52] The director of education at Central Syna-gogue in Manhattan affirmed it as well but framed it in communal terms. "I do want them to understand what a healthy Jewish identity is," he said, "so we have some very deliberate units that are called 'Proud and Jewish' which unquestion-ably build up their self-esteem as young Jewish people."[53]

Irrespective of theology or tradition, within actual congregations there is a set-ting and a structure for a kind of moral instruction that occurs without curricu-lum at all—or perhaps the instruction that comes with being a participant in a particular interpretive community. Consider the situation of Central Synagogue. Like virtually every congregation, their cornerstone is their religious school. The leadership of the congregation, however, has had to struggle to make community a priority. "If our parents had their way," the director of education noted,

> they would send a car for the finest Hebrew teacher they could find and have that teacher delivered to the child's home for instruction and then have the car return the teacher to wherever he or she lives. That request comes a thousand times a month. 'Can't I import Abraham, Isaac and Jacob to teach my kids? If Moses was available, we'd hire him and his agent.' Well, we won't go for that because we want that sense of community. We want our kids to be in this building.

So the congregation provides the equivalent of the Catholic religious educa-tion—an afternoon supplemental school of Jewish education one day a week. The ideal is for students to participate for the entire twelve-year sequence. Nearly all stay through their bar mitzvah, and a majority stay through the end of twelfth grade. In this particular congregation they have a residency requirement, mandating children to stay with the program through confirmation. Why? "Sometimes you don't give the kids the option to do or not do certain things. One of them is dropping out of a religious institution that is going to teach them, even against their will, what it is that they need to know as functioning

Jews in the world today." The pressure placed on parents to stick with the program is not insignificant and often causes tension.[54]

> Oftentimes a parent will say to us, 'You know, you're not the only show in
> town. There are other synagogues. There are other places our son can have a
> bar mitzvah so we don't need to put up with your rules.' To these we say,
> 'You know what? Go there. We don't want you if that's going to be your atti-
> tude.' Sometimes you have to cut back the leaf of a plant because it's imped-
> ing the growth of the entire organism. Sometimes it's healthy to cut off
> leaves that are withering or are in the process of withering because they will
> infect the rest of the plant. We know that we can't serve the whole Jewish
> community. What we want to serve are those people who are committed to
> it so that we can do the best job we can.

Community has a hard edge. To those young people who actually participate,
the time is congenial. When they arrive in the afternoon for instruction, they
find thirty to forty pizzas stacked up in the lobby, from which they help themselves. Often, the younger kids are served by teenagers. Three hundred young
people sit in the lobby in clusters of three and four. The director knows each one
by name. As he explained,

> It's important to me to know all 350 kids by name, know their brothers and
> sisters, know their parent situation. So I ask every child by name, 'How was
> school today?' Or, 'You look a little tired. Do you want to lie down in my of-
> fice?' Or, 'We missed you last week.' I spend a lot of time knowing who's
> here, who isn't here. It's not for punitive reasons but so I can deliver a mes-
> sage to these kids, 'Gosh, somebody knew I wasn't here. Someone cared.'
> It's the personal touch. It blows them away that somebody cares.

The work of the community goes further in the food program they offer to the
indigent twice a week.

> We want our kids to see their parents serving food to the 400 men and
> women who come for the meal. These parents are here at 4:30 in the morning
> cooking eggs and making hot breakfasts for the homeless, and then buttering
> sandwiches so that afterwards, they can carry a bagged lunch with them. It's
> interesting. Their parents' limousines may be lined up ready to whisk them to
> their corporate headquarters, but they are the same people who got up at
> four in the morning to be here. It happens fifty-two Thursdays a year and
> fifty-two Fridays a year—our volunteers are there and their kids see it.[55]

In a large Baptist church in downtown Dallas, the situation is similar. Sunday school for adolescents and teenagers is a Bible-study hour. It begins with a large group time where all the kids are together for announcements and music. Then they are funneled into smaller classes where they examine scripture and apply it to their lives. The logic is simple. Says the head youth minister, "Our teachers can keep up with a class of ten students much easier than all six hundred who are on our roster." As for himself,

> When I go into a particular Sunday school department or a particular meeting we're having, one of the things I try to do is to speak to every one of the students who's there and when possible use their name and speak to them and be interested in them. Another thing I do is to write a birthday card to each one every year. It's small but it makes them feel like somebody out there cares for them.[56]

On Wednesday nights the church offers a discipleship program where some of the men on youth staff disciple different groups of high school students in an eight- to ten-week program on theology and the spiritual disciplines. Those older students in turn disciple middle school–age kids in those same disciplines. The church also offers an elaborate choir program that takes a mission trip every summer, and it also maintains a 1500-bed mission to the homeless in Dallas where Sunday-school classes regularly visit to help serve lunch or collect clothes and gather different household items people might need. "These are some of the things we do to get them involved in actually putting their faith to work. What they're being taught they are actually able to do."[57]

Precious Blood Catholic Church, on the edge of Chicago's worst housing projects, has few of the resources that they do at the Baptist or Jewish congregations just mentioned. The aspirations of its youth leader, however, are much the same.

> You have to create a society here. That's the only way. It sounds crazy but that's what we have to do. How do we expect them to act normal when they don't have the normal things that kids should have? So we have to have an after-school program, we have to create church for them, and we have to create family for them because none of this has been provided for them in the home. That's the job we have to do.[58]

AN UNEVEN BLENDING

The fate of traditional faiths in the contemporary world is a subject of voluminous research. It would be far too ambitious to try to locate these notes in any coherent way in that discussion. My purpose in this review has been more modest: in short, to illustrate the complex ways in which faith communities relate to the contemporary project of educating children morally. While the story is endlessly complex, a few things are clear. To remain hermetically closed to the encroachments of the modern world would be next to impossible. It is not surprising, therefore, that the main bodies of faith in America have embraced and synthesized a model of individual psychology as a framework within which biblical morality is mediated. It happens in different ways in each broad community of faith, but some operate with structures of communal life that are more resistant to these encroachments than are others. Why Protestantism generally is so much more syncretic with secular psychology than either Catholicism and Judaism is a matter of speculation. Perhaps it is because, as a rule, historic Protestantism has always been a more individualizing faith than either Catholicism or Judaism; its traditions of personal piety are less integrated into collective rituals and associations. The organizing principles of Protestant faith perhaps find a parallel structure with therapeutic cosmology of secular psychology.[59] That Evangelical Protestantism, despite its public posturing to the contrary, is at least as comfortable with a therapeutic understanding of morality and moral development suggests once again that the resistance cultural conservatism offers to the dominant moral trends in America may, in fact, be little resistance at all.

Moral Education and the Triumph of the Therapeutic

To understand the moral education of children is to understand something of the elementary forms of the moral life in a society. In teaching basic moral sensibilities to the young, the rudimentary elements of the moral culture are formally articulated, bringing into relief what in adult life is often unspoken and taken for granted. Thus the history of moral education, while interesting in its own right, also reveals much about the character of normative change in American society. Though there is unevenness, the broad outlines of change over the past two centuries or so are clear enough.

It is important to emphasize that these historical changes are not merely a matter of a change in the ideas imparted to the young. Rather, the transformation is more comprehensive—entailing a basic transmutation in the dominant regime of moral socialization. The *content of moral instruction* changed—from the "objective" moral truths of divine scriptures and the laws of Nature, to the conventions of a democratic society, to the subjective values of the individual person. The *sources of moral authority* shifted—from a transcendent God, to the institutions of the natural order and the scientific paradigms that sustain them, to the choices of subjects. The *sanctions* through which morality is validated changed—from the institutions and codes of the community to the sovereign choices of the autonomous individual. The primary *institutional location* through which moral understanding is mediated changed as well—from the family and local religious congregation and their youth organizations, to the public school and popular culture. So too the *arbiters of moral judgment* changed from the clergyman to the psychologist and counselor. Accordingly, the *character of moral pedagogy* changed—from the cultivation of a sense of good and evil through memorization of sacred texts to a largely emotive deliberation over competing values. In this, the *premise of moral education* changed as well—from the sense that children are, for all their other endearments, sinful and rebellious to a sense that they are good by nature and only need encouragement. Finally, there has been a transformation in the *purpose of moral education* itself—from mastery over the soul in service to God and neighbor, to the training of character to serve the needs of civic life, to the cultivation of personality toward the end of well-being.

Yes, there is a challenge to the dominant psychological regime of moral education in our day. The challenge presented by the neoclassical and communitarian alternatives, however, is more political in nature than educational. As these alternatives are translated into practical pedagogy, they are largely co-opted through a reliance upon existing psychological concepts, techniques, and ideals well institutionalized in the education schools, bureaucracies, and professional associations. At this level, all of the distinctives that set the neoclassical and communitarian strategies apart from the psychological regime mostly dissolve.

The influence of a diffused secular psychology extends as well to the remnants of biblical faiths in America—especially Protestantism. Now on the margins of culture formation, this once dominant regime has itself been reworked by therapeutic assumptions, language, and ends. While there are elements of the religious establishments that evade the psychologization of moral instruction, they do so in pockets of cultural resistance, ones typically removed from the centers of culture formation.

Thus the psychological regime of moral education is challenged, but not decisively so. Alternatives exist, but none that are significantly different or that could make a significant difference. In varying degrees, all of the major strategies of moral instruction operate with a paradigm that is, at root, self-referencing and oriented toward the end of personal well-being. In this, moral education—uneven as it is—roughly mirrors the moral culture of which it is a part.

And this, after all, is really the point: Moral development for the young does not take place in a vacuum but in a normative order, bounded by history and embedded in a network of powerful institutions and complex social relations. In this light, moral education is clearly of a fabric with the larger moral culture. In our own day the conflict within moral education reflects the conflict over the culture broadly. And yet in *this* realm, the conflict turns out not to be so deep. The desire to maximize personal interest and minimize personal cost in all of life's arenas, linked to the imperative to satisfy affective needs, is a moral commitment held unevenly but held by virtually all. This shared cultural orientation demonstrates how thoroughly and how profoundly therapeutic our moral culture has become. It is a moral culture ideally suited for individuation in social life and moral meaning. In a context where a range of language games, identities, and life worlds proliferate, a therapeutic discourse becomes our *lingua franca*.

What does it all mean? What are the unintended consequences?

— *Part 3* —

UNINTENDED
CONSEQUENCES

8

The Impotence of
Contemporary Moral Education

Among parents, educators, and politicians there is a palpable urgency to deal with what one ethicist has called "the hole in the moral ozone" of contemporary American society.[1] That urgency, however, can distract us from a rather basic question: Do any of our strategies actually work? If they do—if some or all accomplish the task they have set for themselves—then the only thing left to do is to refine the programs, improve their techniques, and expand their use and influence.

The growing body of evidence, however, inspires neither confidence that the various programs are effective nor hope that modifying them will make them any more so. There is, of course, some variation in this. Some programs are better than others. But cumulatively, their effectiveness is at best less than impressive, and certainly not adequate to the challenge they are meant to address.

THE IMPOTENCIES OF
THE PSYCHOLOGICAL REGIME

Despite its many guises, the constant feature of the psychological strategy, as we have seen, is an individualism oriented toward liberating the self through autonomous decision making and reforming the self through personal understanding. In practice, this often plays out as the simplistic proposition that personal psychological and emotional well-being is the foundation of positive social behavior and virtuous conduct. And so the logic goes: until young people develop a stable sense of positive self-identity that is reinforced by successful learning experience, it is not possible for them to engage in the type of self-evaluation that can generate the positive feelings, motivations, and behaviors they need to be well-integrated, morally responsible members of society.[2] Thus, it is "from [a] shift in self-concept" as one educator put it, that "lasting behaviors and values" come.[3] Unfortunately, the evidence shows otherwise.

The studies are myriad. Working through all of them would be both tedious to the reader and unnecessary. (Though a general overview can be found in the endnotes of this chapter, summary news reports can be found in forums as prominent as *Time, Newsweek, U.S. News and World Report*, the *New Republic*, the *New York Times, Commentary*, and *American Educator*.) *In nuce*, these studies present conclusions that are as unambiguous and indisputable as any body of social scientific analysis can provide. The nub of it is this: *there is little or no association, causal or otherwise, between psychological well-being and moral conduct, and psychologically oriented moral education programs have little or no positive effect upon moral behavior, achievement, or anything else.*[4] Even analysts who are sympathetic to this overall strategy have come to the same judgment.[5]

The same applies to specific drug- or sex-education programs operating within this broad strategy. The popular DARE program, for example, is remarkably ineffective.[6] In the case of sex education, the majority of such programs increase a student's knowledge, increase a student's tolerance of the sexual practices of others, and modestly increase the use of contraception. Few, however, reduce risk-taking sexual behavior or teenage pregnancy.[7]

Proponents and critics alike offer a range of explanations of why, study after study, the associations between psychological well-being and "positive" moral conduct are invariably weak or nonexistent. The most consistent explanation points to the studies' methodological shortcomings. Phrases like "design flaw" and a "need for further research" are repeated like mantras. The implication is that if researchers had only tweaked the variables in such and such a way, they might have found the results for which they were looking. While there may be some merit to this argument, against the aggregate body of evidence it does not ring true.[8] In the most rigorous of these studies, the cumulative weight of evidence is clear and overwhelming: high levels of psychological well-being, however measured, do not correlate with stronger adherence to moral virtues, a strong sense of social responsibility, improved academic performance, or any of the other laudable goals these programs claim to promote. The cognitive-development programs of Lawrence Kohlberg, though different in design, cannot boast any greater effectiveness.[9] Indeed, fundamental aspects of his "just community" experiment in democratic education in the "Cluster School" proved to be nothing less than a social and moral fiasco.[10] Overall, the promises of the psychological strategy of moral understanding and instruction, however they are packaged and promoted, remain unfulfilled.

The Weakness of the Neoclassical
and Communitarian Alternatives

The alternative strategies of moral instruction—neoclassical and communitarian—build upon a commitment to teaching moral standards that have their origin outside of the self, at least in theory. One such strategy focuses on socializing children into the inherited rules and narratives distilled from ancient traditions. The other tries to integrate children into the normative standards defined by the social group. In both, the development of virtuous habits in the young through reinforcing compliance with external authority (for instance, through rewards and punishments) is central to the educational mission.

This more recent cycle of character-education programs has yet to be studied as thoroughly as those that employ the psychological strategy. From what we know so far, however, their actual effectiveness is also highly dubious.

The earliest effort to evaluate character-education programs of the kind now advocated by neoclassical and communitarian educators was the "Character Education Inquiry" led by Hugh Hartshorne and Mark May between 1924 and 1929. The study focused upon deceit, service, self-control, and the nature of character itself and its implications for "character education with particular reference to religious education."[11] Nearly 11,000 children between the ages of eight and sixteen, from twenty-three communities across the nation, were studied in one way or another, and while the methods were by no means flawless, the conclusions were rather shocking. In the case of deceit (examined through cheating, lying, and stealing) the authors concluded that

> the mere urging of honest behavior by teachers or the discussion of standards and ideals of honesty, no matter how much such general ideas may be 'emotionalized,' has no necessary relation to the control of conduct.[12]

As to service-related morality through acts of charity and cooperation, the authors concluded that

> efforts to train children in forms of charitable and cooperative behavior . . . have very little, if any, effect. Even when presumably specialized efforts are brought to bear on the problem, as in Sunday schools and clubs, the effects, if they be effects, are not great enough to make members stand out as being consistently superior to non-members.[13]

As to a morality of self-control through acts of inhibition and persistence,

the implications of our Studies in Deceit and our Studies in Service . . . are
borne out in this investigation of persistence and inhibition. There is little
evidence that effectively organized moral education has been taking place.[14]

Overall,

This does not imply that the teaching of general ideas, standards, and ideals
is not desirable . . . but only that the prevailing ways of inculcating ideals
probably do little good and may do some harm.[15]

Needless to say, a study this old can only be suggestive of what one may find
from programs today. At the same time, if such programs were ineffective in the
1920s, when the broad moral culture in America was so much more conservative, then similar programs resurrected in our contemporary social and cultural
context are likely to fare no better.

Evidence about the effectiveness of the renewed character-education programs
of the 1990s is scant and, where it does exist, it is mostly anecdotal.[16] But there are a
few serious studies. On the more general character-education programs, the evidence is mixed. Some demonstrated some positive effects in the short term for certain kinds of moral sensibilities; but over the long term, children who went
through these programs showed no substantial or consistent difference from those
who did not.[17] Especially when character education consists of an exhortation in
platitudes (say through "virtue of the week" programs), pledges (such as abstinence contracts), and programs of reward and punishment, the new character-
education programs have almost no effect at all.[18] Abstinence based sex-education
programs, like Teen-Aid or Sex Respect, do seem to influence certain abstinence
values in the short term, but not over the long term. Nor do they delay or reduce
the frequency of intercourse.[19] Community service programs do not fare much
better. These programs can positively affect young people's personal development
(for instance, if they enjoy meeting and working with new people with whom the
program has put them in contact), but do not necessarily enhance their sense of
civic responsibility.[20] In sum, the newly revived character education programs favored by neoclassical and communitarian educators appear no more likely to have
an enduring effect on children than those in the psychological strategy.

UNIMPRESSIVE AT BEST

It goes too far, of course, to conclude that all major programs of moral education are of no account. Still, the very best of them are unimpressive—not only in
their long-term but also in their short-term effects.[21]

Still, where studies evaluating moral education programs reveal their inadequacy, they often signal ways in which they *could* be effective. There is a body of evidence that shows that moral education has its most enduring effects on young people when they inhabit a social world that coherently incarnates a moral culture defined by a clear and intelligible understanding of public and private good.[22] In a milieu where the school, youth organizations, and the larger community share a moral culture that is integrated and mutually reinforcing; where the social networks of adult authority are strong, unified, and consistent in articulating moral ideals and their attending virtues; and where adults maintain a "caring watchfulness" over all aspects of a young person's maturation, moral education can be effective. These are environments where intellectual and moral virtues are not only naturally interwoven in a distinctive moral ethos but embedded within the structure of communities.

Needless to say, communities with this level of social and cultural integration and stability are scarce in America today. Moral education operates against the backdrop of a social life that is intensely fragmented, a shifting polity of abstruse bureaucratic proceduralism, a moral culture framed by a diffuse therapeutic individualism, and an economy of saturated consumerism. Add to this the fact that these programs are typically low-intensity activities conducted over a relatively small number of hours over the course of the school year, and it is no wonder that they are so ineffectual. At the end of the day, these programs may do more for adults than they do for children. At least they salve our conscience that something constructive is being attempted.

Moral Cultures and
Their Consequences

The significance of a diffused psychology that permeates moral pedagogy—not least in its influence over the neoclassical and communitarian alternatives—resides not primarily in its ineffectiveness. Rather much more may be at stake in its unintended consequences. What happens when therapeutic individualism is no longer a mere pedagogy but a worldview? What are the practical effects when an entire generation internalizes the psychological understanding of moral life as the framework of their moral imagination?

To get at this matter, we must compare therapeutic individualism with other worldviews and their effects on the moral understandings, commitments, and decisions of those who embrace them. What one finds is that however fragmented different moral cultures are at the end of the twentieth century, however flattened out they may be by a psychological moralism, differences in moral culture are still discernable and the consequences of these differences are quite remarkable.

MORAL CULTURE AS MORAL COMPASS

To understand better the relationship between world view and practical morality I consider a body of evidence from surveys of opinion conducted with children and young adults where the focus is on the moral judgments these young people make and the factors that go into their decisions. In one particular study I participated in at the end of 1989, over 5,000 children from over 200 schools across the country were questioned about the nature and consequences of their moral commitments.* The diversity within this group was impressive: boys and girls in grades 4 through 12, from wealthy, poor, and middle-class backgrounds; representing white, black, Hispanic, and Asian ethnic composition; from the inner city, the suburbs, and the open country.

These children also divided among themselves in terms of their moral frames of reference—the rudimentary ethical systems they live by that reflect different foundations of moral understanding and commitment.[23] The divisions among moral cultures these children lived within were broadly defined along lines suggested by Robert Bellah and his colleagues in their important work, *Habits of the Heart.*[24] In this study, as shown in Figure 8.1,

- Sixteen percent of the children indicated that they operated within a *theistic* moral culture. The children who live by this moral orientation are not necessarily the same as those who are religious—those, say, who believe in God (82 percent of the total), attend church weekly (56 percent), or even claim to have a life-altering religious experience (34 percent). Rather, these children are those who tend to make moral judgments in accordance with a religious authority such as scripture or the teachings and traditions of a church or synagogue. Children working within a theistic frame of reference, typically members of faith within the once prominent biblical traditions of Christianity and Judaism, try to *base their actions* upon "what God or scripture tells [them] is right."
- Twenty percent operated within a *conventionalist* moral culture. These children defer to the general social practices and conventions of their social world. For these, authority figures, representing the prevailing customs and conventions of their community, are looked to for moral guidance in decision making. A child relying on a conventionalist moral compass would "follow the advice of an authority such as a parent, teacher, or youth leader."
- Twenty-five percent indicated that they operated within the moral culture of *civic humanism*. Children in this moral orientation tend to make moral decisions according to what they perceive to be in the best interests of the community or social group. This orientation has its roots in classical humanism, where an understanding of civic responsibility was based on the principles of the natural order—a *nomos* which was seen to dictate individual deference to the "common good." Though diluted in substance, vestiges of this classic understanding of

---

* For the sake of readability, I simply focus on the highlights of this study and its analysis in the main text. For those interested, technical details can be found in the endnotes.

FIGURE 8.1   The Moral Cultures of Young People

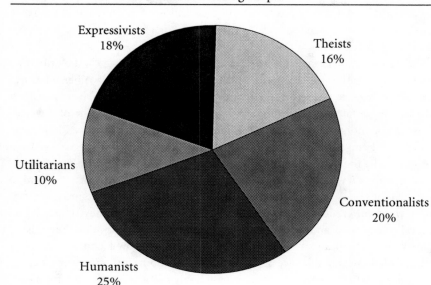

social life can still be seen today. In its contemporary context, children operating with a civic humanist moral culture make decisions in accordance with what they perceive to be the common good of the neighborhood, town, or the nation at large. In this situation, they are willing, in principle, to submit their personal interests to the interests of the larger community.

- Ten percent were committed to a *utilitarian* vision of moral understanding. The utilitarian moral culture regards personal self-interest as the focal point for moral decision making. Judgments are made on the basis of how a particular decision would serve the individual's self-interests. Those relying on this moral compass "do what would improve [their] situation or get [them] ahead."
- Finally, eighteen percent identified themselves within an *expressivist* framework of moral understanding. Like the utilitarian, the expressivist moral culture represents an orientation whose authority stems from the individual. However, unlike the former, the expressivist bases decisions less upon rational choice toward self-serving ends than upon the calibrations of emotional sensibility and felt need. In other words, the young person living within an expressivist moral culture would make moral judgments in accord with the expression of certain subjective states or satisfaction of certain emotional or psychological

need. Faced with difficult moral circumstances, a person operating within this moral frame of reference will tend to do what will make him or her feel good.

As moral compasses rather than formal philosophical systems, the utilitarian and expressivist have a curious, even symbiotic relation to each other. They can almost be regarded as opposite sides of the same coin—utilitarianism reflects the instrumental side and expressivism reflects the emotional side of a world-view whose moral center is the autonomous self and whose moral ends are personal well-being. Together they comport most completely with the orientation promoted by the psychological regime.

There are a few other points to note about this typology. Against the kind of particularity I have argued is essential to understanding character and its formation, these differences are rather rough. To the extent that they reflect actual moral orientations among young people, we need to recognize that they exist as "the fragments of a conceptual scheme, parts which now lack those contexts from which their significance derived."[25] It is also important to recognize that, in everyday practice these moral compasses are only more or less distinct from each other; each moral orientation is influenced to varying degrees by the others. Still, for purposes of general analysis, the distinctions are instructive.

A Few of the Questions Asked

All of the young people in the survey were asked difficult questions about their worries, problems, aspirations, ideals, and commitments. They were also asked to respond to specific hypothetical dilemmas ranging from such basic issues as stealing, lying, cheating, and drinking to the temptations of sexual foreplay and premarital sex, abortion, and homosexuality. There were also problems concerning altruism and civic commitment. Most of these were presented as credible predicaments in which young people might realistically find themselves, but for which they would have to draw upon all of their moral resources in making a judgment. They were asked to imagine themselves in dozens of these situations and to then say what they would most likely do. While not all of the answers could be framed in terms of simple right and wrong, they did reflect different degrees of restraint and personal sacrifice.

Some of the questions posed fairly straightforward situations. On cheating on a test, for instance:

You sit down to take an important test. You know you don't know the answers to most of the questions because you haven't had enough time to study. There is a person sitting next to you who is very smart and well-prepared and you can see her answers. In this situation, you would probably:

Try to copy her answers on your own test.
Once in a while glance at her test for ideas about the right answers.
Answer the test as best you can by yourself, even if you won't do well.

On lying about an act of vandalism:

Some school property has been destroyed. Your best friend brags to you that he did it. The school principal asks you if you know what happened. In this situation, you would probably,

Deny that you know anything about it.
Deny it at first, but later leave the principal an unsigned note telling who did it.
Tell the principal who did it.

On underage drinking:

You go to a party where some of your friends are drinking alcohol. Someone hands you a drink. In this situation, you would probably,

Refuse the drink.
Take the glass but only pretend to drink it.
Drink with them but not feel great about it.
Drink with them without worrying about it.

Other questions dealt with altruism and self-sacrifice:
On helping a classmate:

You already have a regular after-school activity you've said you would do, but you learn that a student in your class had a bad accident and cannot come to school for many months. The teacher asks you if you would be willing to give up your activity for two or three afternoons each week for those months to help that student with schoolwork. In this situation, you would probably,

Go ahead with your own activity but feel badly about not helping.
Give up your activity so that you can help, but only if your activity is not that important to you.

Give up your activity so you can help, but only until you can find someone
   else to take your place.
Help the student no matter what you have to give up.

On helping a homeless person:

You are walking down the street near where you live, and you see a person
you don't know who is very poor and has no home. That person asks you
for some money. In this situation, you would probably,

Tell him he ought to get a job.
Try to avoid him.
Give him a little money.
Stop and talk to him about his problems.

Still other situations dealt with sexual morality:
On "foreplay":

You are on your third date with a person of the opposite sex. You like each
other very much. You would like to go beyond kissing, but you are not sure
of just how far you should go. In this situation, you would probably,

Be willing to go a lot beyond kissing.
Be willing to go a little beyond kissing.
Not be willing to go beyond kissing.

On premarital sex:

You have had a steady relationship for a long time and you feel very much
in love. At this point your girlfriend or boyfriend tells you they want to have
sex with you. In this situation, you would probably,

Have sex.
Try to hold off if you can.
Refuse to have sex for now.
Insist on waiting until you are married.

Advice to a friend about an unplanned pregnancy:

An unmarried friend of yours just found out that she is pregnant. She does-
n't know what to do for sure. She asks you for your opinion about what she
should do. In this situation, you would probably,

Advise her to have an abortion.

Advise her to have the baby but give it up for adoption.

Advise her to have the baby and keep it.

Other moral attitudes and behaviors were examined as well.

Needless to say, morality is far more than the way we handle everyday dilemmas. More significantly, as I have argued, it involves presuppositions about the normative order; the vision of the good (and an understanding of evil) and of the right (and of wrong) that shape our obligations, forge our commitments, and influence our attitudes as we approach the specific and often fuzzy conflicts and dilemmas we inevitably face in life. Even so, these situational decisions can be illuminating of the interaction between a world view and a life lived.

The Consistent Bearing of Moral Compass

As one would expect, opinion divided considerably. Some children thought it was okay to cheat, lie, and steal, others wanted to hedge their answers, and still others emphatically rejected these options altogether. Some children were very altruistic toward strangers and other children were indifferent. Some children were sexually permissive, others less so, and still others, not at all. The array of responses was complicated indeed.

How, though, does one make sense of the complex array of responses? Why would one youngster cheat on a test and another not? Why would one youngster avoid the homeless person and another either help him with money or talk with him about his problems? And why would one teenager advise their friend to have an abortion, another advise her to carry the child and then put it up for adoption, and still another advise her to keep her baby?

Put differently, what accounts for this diversity of moral commitment?[26]

Social scientists typically favor a range of background factors, such as race, class, and gender, to account for such differences. But against this one finds something quite remarkable: *children's underlying attachments to a moral culture were the single most important and consistent factor in explaining the variation in their moral judgments.* It was the children's rudimentary ethical systems, in other words, that provided the most far-reaching and dependable explanation for the decisions they made. *These assumptions act very much like moral compasses, providing the bearings by which they navigate the complex moral terrain of their lives.*[27]

The pattern is a clear and consistent continuum ranging from expressivist and utilitarian at one end to theist at the other. In general, the students least likely to say they would cheat, lie, or steal, and the most likely to show restraint in sexual matters, were those operating within a theistic moral orientation (I would do what God or scripture says is right), followed by those working within a conventionalist moral framework (follow the advice of an authority such as a parent, teacher, or youth leader). Conversely, the students most likely to cheat, lie, steal and least likely to express restraint in sexual matters were the expressivists (I do what makes me happy) and utilitarians (I do what will get me ahead). Humanists (I would do what is best for everyone involved) were in between in every case. In many of these instances, the difference between groups of children was enormous.

The General Pattern
Children with Different Moral Compasses
Their disposition toward:
1.) Longstanding Moral Norms

License	←	→	Restraint

2.) The Needs of Others

	Indifference	←	→	Self-sacrifice		
Expressivist/	←→	Civic	←→	Conventionalist	←→	Theist
Utilitarian		Humanist				

The same pattern is discernible with regard to altruism and civic commitment. The students most likely to demonstrate compassion toward those in need were the theists, followed by the conventionalists; those least likely to show compassion toward others were the expressivists and utilitarians.

Down to Cases

The consistency of these outcomes demonstrates the importance of moral culture in shaping the moral life and understanding of children. Let me give some examples. Though only 12 percent of the children say they would be willing to cheat outright on the exam, those operating from either the expressivist or utilitarian moral compasses were three times more likely to do so than those operating from a theistic position, as shown in Figure 8.2. There is a similar range among those unwilling to cheat at all. Only four out of ten from the utilitarian, expressivist, and civic humanist positions would have been unwilling to cheat, compared to over half of the conventionalists (54 percent) and theists (61 percent). Likewise, one third (36 percent) of the children say they would lie about their knowledge of the vandalism. But by itself this figure disguises the differences in the respective moral compasses that give the children their bearings on the issue. Children who operated from expressivist and utilitarian assumptions were about twice as likely to lie as those who operated from conventionalist as-

FIGURE 8.2   Personal Disposition Toward Cheating and Stealing

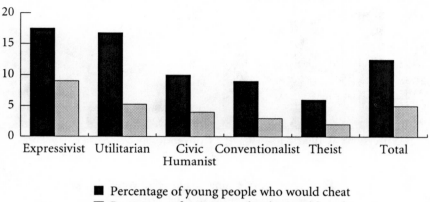

- ■ Percentage of young people who would cheat
- ▨ Percentage of young people who would steal

FIGURE 8.3   Personal Disposition Toward Lying

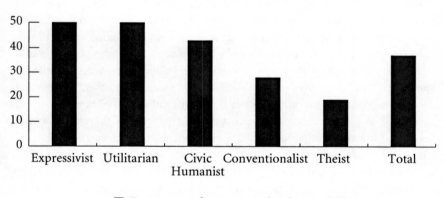

- ■ Percentage of young people who would lie

sumptions, and two-and-a-half times more likely than the theists (see Figure 8.3). Children working from civic humanist assumptions also expressed a greater tendency to lie. Only one-third of the children living by either the expressivist or utilitarian moral compass would refuse a drink at a party. This compared to two-fifths of the civic humanists, more than half of the conventionalists, and over three-fourths (79 percent) of the theists. The same general pattern (but in the reverse) can be found among those who would drink without worrying, as shown in Figure 8.4.

FIGURE 8.4   Attitudes Toward Underage Drinking

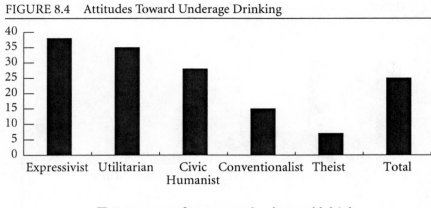

■ Percentage of young people who would drink
   underage without worrying

In a situation where a young couple on their third date are faced with the dilemma of whether to go beyond kissing, the conventionalists and the theists were more prone toward complete restraint than the children relying on expressivist, utilitarian, or civic humanist moral compasses. The same applied to the unmarried couple very much in love who are contemplating sexual intercourse. Indeed, the identical pattern can be observed in the children's response to the statement, "sex before marriage is OK, if a couple loves each other." Twenty percent of the children operating with a theistic moral compass agreed with this compared to 69 percent of the expressivists, 64 percent of the utilitarians, 60 percent of the civic humanists, and 45 percent of the conventionalists. The mirror image of this is seen in response to the statement, "sex before marriage is never right because it is a sin." Just under one-fourth of the children in the expressivist, utilitarian, and civic humanist moral cultures agreed with this compared to 70 percent of the theists.   (See Figures 8.5 and 8.6.)

In the matter of abortion, although most of the teenagers[28] would advise their friend not to have one, they were divided between those who felt she should keep the baby and those who felt she should give it up for adoption. Only about one in eight (12 percent) said they would suggest that she have the abortion. But here again large differences emerge among the different moral compasses. The theists were the least likely to advise the friend to have an abortion and the most likely to encourage the girl to have the baby and keep it. Those living by utilitarian and expressivist principles were the most likely to favor abortion. The impact of moral culture on how an adolescent views this issue was underscored by the way they responded to the statement, "abortion is all right, if having a baby will

FIGURE 8.5 Personal Disposition Toward Premarital Sex

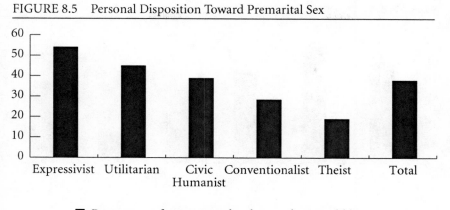

■ Percentage of young people who say they would have premarital sex (junior high and high school students only)

FIGURE 8.6 On the Morality of Premarital Sex

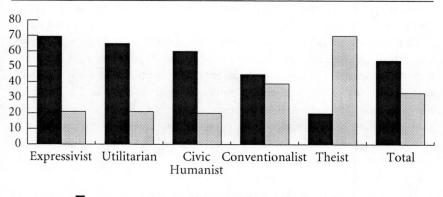

■ Percentage who say it is okay if the couple loves each other
☐ Percentage who say it is not okay; it is a sin

change your life plans in a way you will find hard to live with." About four out of every ten children relying on the expressivist, utilitarian, and civic humanist compasses agreed with this, compared to 27 percent of the conventionalists and 13 percent of the theists.

The influence of moral culture was equally powerful in the children's attitudes toward other issues. About one-third of the children agreed that "homosexual relations are OK if that is the person's choice" but the theists were the

FIGURE 8.7   On the Morality of Suicide

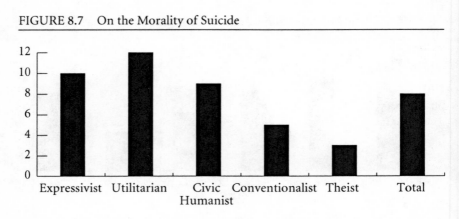

■ Percentage of young people who say suicide is okay because
it is a personal choice

least likely to agree with this. The humanists and the expressivists were the most
likely to agree. So too with suicide, as shown in Figure 8.7. Eight percent of all
children agreed that "suicide is all right, because a person has a right to do whatever he wants to with himself," yet again this masks a range among children relying on different moral compasses. Only 3 percent of the children with theistic
moral compasses agreed with this compared to 10 percent of those relying on an
expressivist moral compass and 12 percent using a utilitarian compass. Moral
culture also had a significant impact on the priorities children had as they faced
the future. Children with utilitarian (especially) and expressivist moral orientations were most likely to make a priority out of making money and becoming famous. The conventionalists, expressivists, and civic humanists were most likely
to make a priority out of getting married and having a good family life. The theists were virtually alone in emphasizing a close relationship to God.

The same pattern emerged when considering the matter of helping others.
The children living by theistic and conventionalist compasses expressed greater
altruism toward the injured classmate. Roughly half (49 percent) of the theists
and two-fifths (40 percent) of the conventionalists said that they would be willing to help the student no matter what they had to give up, compared to roughly
one-fifth (22 percent) of the utilitarians and only about one-third (32 percent)
of the expressivists and civic humanists (34 percent). Likewise, the expressivists
(16 percent) were the most likely to tell the homeless person to "get a job" and
the least likely to stop and talk to him about his problems. Here they contrast
most starkly with those who were guided by theistic and civic humanistic moral
compasses. So too with their attitudes toward charity. Most of the children
wanted to give to charity in the future, but the theists and civic humanists were

the most likely to want this, and the expressivists and utilitarians the least likely. The same pattern extended to the idea of performing a year of volunteer service.

Even when subjected to rigorous statistical analysis, the conclusion is the same: the moral culture children were living within was the most important determinant of their behavioral predispositions.[29] The influence of moral culture cuts across the boundaries of economic circumstances, race and ethnicity, gender, age, and family structure.[30] Thus, for example, a white youngster from the wealthy suburbs of Greenwich, Connecticut, who lived by theistic ideals would tend to make the same decisions as a Hispanic youngster of the same age and moral orientation from the ghettos of south central Los Angeles. And a black teenager who lived by a utilitarian moral compass from the upper-middle-class neighborhoods in Mobile, Alabama, would very likely make the same moral judgments as a white teenager with a similar orientation from the farmlands around Sioux City, Iowa.

The Findings Reconfirmed

The results of this research are not idiosyncratic. Another study, conducted in 1996, explored similar issues among eighteen to twenty-four year olds and found much the same pattern.[31]

On matters of sexual morality, those operating out of a theistic moral culture were the least likely to sanction birth control for teenagers without their parents' knowledge or permission, and the most likely to say that watching pornographic movies, premarital sexual intercourse, and homosexuality were morally wrong. Two-thirds of all theists opposed pornography and premarital sex, and three-fourths opposed homosexuality on moral grounds. By contrast, young adults living by expressivist and utilitarian moral compasses were the most likely to support the distribution of birth control among minors and the least likely to find pornography, premarital sex, or homosexuality at all morally problematic. Less than one-fourth of young people of these moral commitments had any problem with these behaviors. Once again, those working within a humanistic moral framework tend to fall between the two extremes.

The pattern generally played out in view of one's obligations toward others. Eight out of ten young adults operating with a theist and humanist moral orientation embraced the "golden rule," urging one to "do unto others as one would have others do unto you." Those working from an expressivist and utilitarian moral compass were the least likely to embrace this traditional social ethic.[32]

This general social orientation was reinforced by attitudes reflecting what one might argue is the opposite of the golden rule. To the statement, "Realizing your full potential as a person is more important than helping others," seven out of ten (71 percent) of those with an expressivist moral compass and slightly more than half of those with a utilitarian moral compass agreed with this position. About one-third of the humanists (35 percent) and theists (28 percent) endorsed this view. Likewise, the respondents most likely to embrace "looking out for number one" as a philosophy of life were the expressivists and utilitarians, and the theists the least likely.[33]

The pattern is reflected as well in these young adults' sense of responsibility toward others. To the local community those operating with an expressivist and utilitarian moral compass are the least likely to express a strong sense of responsibility. They were also the least likely to express responsibility to their friends or coworkers. Theists were those most likely to express responsibility in these ways.[34]

In this survey individuals were also queried about their attraction to a life of carefree indulgence. To what extent do they embrace the dictum, "live for today"? Is "money," for them, "the key to life's satisfactions"? Does the expression "eat, drink and be merry" describe their personal code? Again the differences among those operating with different moral compasses was fairly dramatic at the extremes and, at this point, fairly predictable. Young adults working with an expressivist or utilitarian moral compass were two to three times more likely than theists to embrace these views. Humanists resembled the theists in their views of money but were almost as likely as expressivists and utilitarians to endorse the code "eat, drink and be merry."[35]

FACTORS BEYOND MORAL CULTURE

The Enduring Effects of Social Class, Race, and Gender

Though the moral culture young people live within is significantly more important than their social background or their physical characteristics in the way they sort out moral issues, it does not mean it is the only influence. When holding all other factors constant—including the moral compass they turn to—several key background features of their lives show themselves to have independent effects on how they negotiate moral decisions.

There are ways, for example, in which the relative wealth of a child's family makes some difference in the child's moral commitments. All other things being equal, the children from the middle and upper middle class were slightly more inclined than their less privileged classmates to be lenient in their views of underage drinking, premarital sex, homosexuality, and abortion.[36] They were also slightly less likely to show compassion toward others in need. On this matter, the most striking differences in the worldviews of children were found between the extremes of economic circumstance. The children from the poorest circumstances stand out because of their underlying despair and futility. It is they who face the most pressure to take drugs, disobey parents and teachers, smoke, join a gang, or engage in sexual relations. They were also dramatically more likely to see suicide as an acceptable option. And it was they who most saw the futility of politics and other kinds of civic activity. By contrast, children of the wealthiest circumstances were distinguished by their greater indecision concerning specific moral dilemmas. While wealth generates options, these options can create uncertainty as well as freedom.

Racial and ethnic characteristics, we would predict, should be another source of difference. Coming disproportionately from the working and lower classes, minorities should face some challenges to growing up that their middle-class white classmates could hardly imagine. But some aspects of growing up are common to all. One of the remarkable findings of the 1989 study was how similar white, black, and Hispanic children were in the way they confronted the problems they face in common. The diversity of moral perspective and opinion one finds among white children can be found just as intensely in the black and Hispanic communities. "Values," such as they are, do not have color. There simply is no African-American take on honesty or an Hispanic approach to civic duty. Nevertheless, the study showed that the racial and ethnic background of children does have independent effects on the way they view the world. But rather than sharp differences, it would be best to call them tendencies. Regardless of their moral compass, minority (particularly Hispanic) children tend to be less libertarian on matters of sexuality[37] and more disposed to show kindness toward others in need.

Gender is also important (see Figure 8.8). This research corroborates the findings of the Harvard psychologist Carol Gilligan: girls do speak "in a different voice." Their approach to moral decision making is different from that of boys.[38] Regardless of the moral culture they drew from, girls were consistently more caring and altruistic than boys, and more service-oriented as well. They were also more inclined to show restraint in sexual matters and more inclined to honesty and fair play. The differences in the ways that boys and girls actually respond to concrete situations are in part based on inclinations toward different moral cultures. Girls tended to draw from the expressivist and humanist moral cultures while boys were slightly more disposed toward the utilitarian. For example, when asked, "What is the most important reason for helping people in your community?", girls were more inclined than boys to say that it was because "It makes you feel good personally." Boys, by contrast, were more inclined to respond that "It might help you get ahead."

FIGURE 8.8   On Helping an Injured Classmate, by Gender

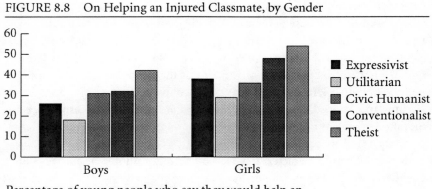

Percentage of young people who say they would help an
injured classmate no matter what they would have to give up

Beyond Moral Compass: The Effects of Family and Faith

Independent effects can also be found in family composition.[39] Young people
who live with both their mother and father were less likely to hold permissive attitudes on lying, drinking, premarital sex, and abortion. Religious background
had important independent effects as well. Far more significant than the *type* of
religious faith, however, was its *intensity*. Protestants and Catholics were not notably distinct from each other in their moral values. Instead, regular attendance
at services and a sense that religious faith was very important were the factors
that set young people apart—sometimes even overriding the dominant moral
compass they claimed to live by. Thus, for example, children who lived by expressivist or utilitarian moral compasses who also attended church regularly
with their families showed considerably more restraint in cheating, lying, stealing, drinking alcohol, and sexual behavior, and were more inclined toward caring for others. Even among children who claimed a theistic moral compass,
those who attended services regularly showed greater restraint and greater altruism than those who did not. The moral community and teaching that religious
institutions provide, then, have a consistent influence on the moral lives of children even when the children are, for all practical purposes, indifferent to what
those institutions stand for.

What Happens When Children Grow Up

As important as moral culture is in orienting young people in the moral decisions they make, something very important happens as young people grow older
that has a tremendous impact upon many moral commitments they previously

FIGURE 8.9   On Helping an Injured Classmate, by Age

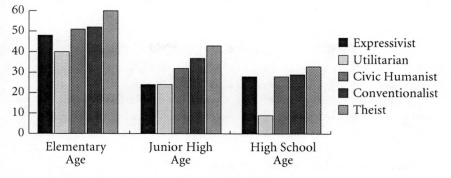

Percentage of children who say they would help an
injured classmate no matter what they would have to give up

held.[40] Needless to say, one can only make inferences about growing up from comparisons across age. Given this qualification, one can draw tentative conclusions. Regardless of the moral culture in which they operate, as children grow older they become more lax in the way they view their likely response to a wide range of moral dilemmas. For example, 65 percent of the senior high school children said they would cheat on a tough exam, compared to 53 percent of the junior high school children and 21 percent of the elementary age children. The older children were also more likely to lie, steal from their parents, and to drink while underage. They show far less restraint in their attitudes toward premarital sex. This tendency, again, cut across differences of moral culture. For example, even among theistically oriented children, the older ones were more likely to say they would cheat on an exam or have premarital sex than their younger counterparts. The pattern is without exception.

As children grow older they also become more self-absorbed and less thoughtful of others. When considering whether they would change their plans to help an injured classmate with his schoolwork, the elementary age children were much more likely than either the junior or senior high school students to help out (see Figure 8.9). Half of the youngest children in the survey said they would help "no matter what" they had to sacrifice, compared to one-third (32 percent) of the junior high schoolers and one-fourth (25 percent) of the senior high school children. So too when confronting a homeless person, the older children were slightly more inclined than the younger to offer the person some spare change but no more likely to stop and converse with him about his problem.

The critical question, again, is why. What is it about growing up that leads to a decline in restraint and personal sacrifice? It is not a stretch to conclude that young people are influenced by the prevailing moral culture and by the institutions that mediate that culture to them.

THE SIGNIFICANCE OF PARTICULAR
MORAL CULTURES, EVEN NOW

Surveys are nearly always crude tools of observation. Subtle differences, special circumstances, particular details that make up social life in all its complexity are nearly always given short shrift. Among other things, distinctions in the particularity of moral cultures—their content and social organization—are overlooked in this analysis, mainly because the instrument was too blunt and unsophisticated to detect them. In the end, surveys are what they are and one is always unwise to expect too much from them. Even so, they do offer clues. In the survey research reviewed here, the clues are about as clear as they ever come. The broad patterns of findings are too consistent to ignore and far too compelling to reject out of hand.

The most significant finding is that though today's moral cultures are only the shards of larger traditions of moral understanding, distinctions exist even in a general population of young people. Children do bring cultural resources—including moral vocabularies—to bear on the circumstances of their lives, and they make moral decisions that show deliberation and consistency. When embraced as a worldview, the different moral cultures into which children are socialized plainly predispose them toward different patterns of moral choice and commitment—patterns so strong that they cut across the boundaries of economic circumstance, race and ethnicity, gender, age, and family life.

But not only are differences in moral culture still discernable, they also remain consequential. Even as shards of larger moral systems, these moral cultures have consequences within the lives of those who embrace them. Though mediated through social factors that have independent effects, different moral compasses do indeed point to consistently different moral outcomes. These differences are most visible at the extremes, and depending on one's vantage point, the moral outcome is mixed. To be sure, those young people with a theistic moral compass tend to be less tolerant of social change and diversity in lifestyle, but they also are most likely to show altruism and restraint against the temptations of license. By contrast, young people living within the moral cultures most sympathetic to the reigning psychological paradigm are much more tolerant of diversity in lifestyle, but their choices consistently demonstrate the least restraint and least likelihood of altruism in the choices they make.

At the same time, the relationship between young people and the moral cultures they inhabit is, by no means, static. Though one can only infer change from historically fixed data, the inference is clear: as children grow older their moral compasses tend to change too. Most significantly, those who hold to either a conventionalist or a theistic moral compass tend to let go of those moral cultures as they grow older.[41] In the same way but with more practical consequences, all children as they grow older—across moral cultures—tend to become less altruistic in their disposition toward those in need and more willing to fudge the boundaries of moral propriety.

Various institutions including the schools, do, in fact, mediate moral understanding to children—both formally or informally. It is impossible to say, of course, whether moral pedagogies generate a larger culture of therapeutic individualism in the young, or only validate it. Perhaps they do both. To the extent that young people come to embrace it as their worldview and it functions as a moral compass, the worldview of therapeutic individualism predisposes them toward certain moral ends that advocates of these pedagogies would all repudiate.

9

Lessons in Subjectivism

Part 1: The Psychological Strategy

Psychology As Cosmology

As a strategy of pedagogic theory and practice the psychological approach to moral education offers many lessons indeed. But on this let us be clear. The *implicit* framework of moral understanding and engagement it conveys is far more influential than any substantive lessons (say, about drugs, sex, or interpersonal conflict) to which it is applied. *Psychology, in brief, presupposes cosmology and it is this cosmology that frames the basic terms of children's moral comprehension—the horizons of their moral imagination.* Whatever the specific influence on children this pedagogy may have, then, the effects of psychology and psychologically oriented moral education on the culture that children inhabit and inherit is much more powerful. In large part this is because the framing categories of this pedagogy mirror a larger therapeutic moral order elucidated nearly everywhere else in the culture—in public discourse, the popular media, television talk shows, family advice, and religious instruction. Psychological pedagogies, then, offer formal socialization into this therapeutic culture. Within this cosmology one finds clues to its impotence as an approach to moral instruction.

The Priority of Process Over Content

At the center of this framework—its primary, weight-bearing beam, if you will—is an advocacy of process over content.

The premise of this position is a rendering of specific and "objective" moral content as secondary to the task of moral instruction and the cultivation of character. In some cases, content-based instruction is deliberately rejected; in other cases, it occurs as the net effect of favoring a particular method of moral teaching. Yet underlying all is a working subordination of metaphysics to method—a subjection of some notion of moral reality, to which one must or ought to conform, to the process whereby morality is acquired.

The original inspiration for this position has been and remains Dewey's philosophical and educational pragmatism. For Dewey, as I noted earlier, the rejection of metaphysics was a matter of principle. Speculation about the nature and content of truth was simply pointless anymore because it could never be established. Moral goods and moral ends, for him, only existed when something needed to be accomplished; that is, say, in the resolution of a concrete problem in real life. To impose a moral principle from outside any particular situation, or to suggest that a dogma or some set of abstract "oughts" be forced upon moral actors would be senseless for it would only produce an artificial outcome. Such efforts were, in his own words, nothing more than "the conning over and drumming in of ethical precepts." Dewey did not reject moral content outright; he acknowledged that "health, wealth, industry, temperance, amiability, courtesy, learning, esthetic capacity, initiative, courage, patience, enterprise, thoroughness and a multitude of other generalized ends are . . . good."[1] But these goods, he believed, should not be pursued as preexisting absolutes. They were simply givens of social life whose specific meaning would be worked out in particular situations. For this reason, he thought the idea untenable that "if you can only teach a child moral rules and distinctions enough, you have somehow furthered his moral being."[2] The task instead was to recognize the need for a particular response for each particular situation. One should seek to discover the good *within* the situation. "A moral law," he wrote, "like in physics, is not something to swear by and stick to at all hazards; it is a formula of the way to respond when specific conditions present themselves. Its soundness and pertinence are tested by what happens when it is acted upon."[3] The tools, in this case, would be the judgments of reason, even science itself. In his pragmatist framework, the true "virtues or moral excellencies" would be redefined as "wide sympathy, keen sensitiveness, persistence in the face of the disagreeable, balance of interest enabling us to undertake the work of analysis and decision intelligently. . . . [These] are the distinctively moral traits."[4] It is for good reason that Dewey spoke of his philosophy and educational theory as "instrumentalism." The very term captured the essence of the priority he placed upon method over content.

A generation later it was the client-oriented therapy of Carl Rodgers that inspired further innovations in pedagogy along these lines. The focus, however, expanded from the moral dilemma to the moral actor himself. As Rodgers put it, one should accept oneself "as a stream of becoming"[5] in a lifelong process of "self-actualization." The fully actualized person would see himself as "a fluid process, not a fixed and static entity; a flowing river of change, not a block of solid material; a continually changing constellation of potentialities, not a fixed quantity of traits."[6] For Rodgers, the techniques of self-actualization were as valid for education as they were for therapy. The decisive connection, in his mind, was the way in which the teacher would become a *facilitator* of these therapeutic ends to his or her students.[7] The teacher becomes a tool in a process that students define for themselves and, in their very person, are. Students may call upon his knowledge, yet the teacher would not want students "to feel that they must use him in this way." "He would want to make himself known as a resource-finder. . . . He would want the quality of his relationship to the group to be such that his feelings could be freely available to them, without being imposed on them or becoming a restrictive influence on them."[8] In the entire endeavor, content recedes in significance; pedagogically speaking, process—through facilitation, the mastery of techniques of empowerment, the acquisition of new ways of seeing oneself—is all.

Rodgers was aware that the implications of his therapeutic approach to education were "startling," even "drastic."[9] At the time, they certainly were. And yet soon, the innovations he advocated would become commonplace among progressive educators.

The basic position has been reaffirmed time and again since his day, often with open contempt for prior methods of moral instruction. In his influential book *Schools Without Failure*, William Glasser denigrated content-based moral education as "preaching and threats."[10] "We teach thoughtless conformity to school rules," he wrote in 1969, "and call the conforming child 'responsible.'"[11] Moral behavior, he insisted, needed to be seen more as "a part of life rather than as dogma."[12] Louis Raths and Sidney Simon, who championed values clarification through the 1970s, dismissed the old-fashioned practices of "sermonizing" and "moralizing," condemning these techniques as the "inculcation of adults' values upon the young."[13] This, they claimed, was nothing less than "indoctrination."[14] The higher goal of values clarification, rather, was to "facilitate the valuing process."[15] So too with the cognitive-development model: for all its differences with the values-clarification model, advocates spoke derisively of the "bag of virtues" school of moral education.[16] For Kohlberg and his disciples, the classical virtues really were not at all universal but historically specific. Worse, they had evolved into cultural standards that were now, at best, "psychologically vague," referring more to social convention than ethical importance. For that reason alone, classical virtues should no longer be taken seriously. Against this, as we have seen, Kohlberg offered a structural interpretation of the moral life that, following Piaget, defined moral life less in terms of the content of moral judgment and more in terms of the structures of judgment—formal characteristics that he believed were truly universal. The purpose of moral education, he insisted, was to increase the individual's capacity to engage in moral reasoning at ever higher levels.

Educators in the tradition of Piaget who call themselves constructivists hold the same commitments. Any content-based curriculum presented as objective morality is by definition problematic—indeed, reality has no ontological status, but rather exists through active, intersubjective experience.[17] Traditional pedagogies are thus derided as "boot camps," and their teachers "drill sergeants." Teaching should consist of drawing out values as the need arises. As one handbook put it, "we are talking about a process, not a product. In this process, children wrestle with questions of what they believe to be good and bad, right and wrong. They form their own opinions, and listen to the opinions of others. They construct their morality out of daily life experiences."[18] The last thing one should do, therefore, is to dictate moral norms to children.[19] Instead, "the teacher's role is to co-operate with children by trying to understand their reasoning and facilitating the constructive process."[20]

On it goes through the world of educational journalism. Popularizers like Hunter Lewis[21] and Alfie Kohn[22] ritually disparage "character-building" rooted in moral content and instead insist on a process in which individuals determine for themselves what values they will live by.

In practical terms, the *modus operandi* of this position is always recognizable: be careful not to impose external standards on children or upon the situations in which they find themselves. Rather, the teacher should "accept the student as he is, . . . understand the feelings he possesses"; and "provide an unconditional positive regard . . . empathiz[ing] with the [student's range of] feelings" to "hold the student as a person of value no matter what his condition, his behavior, or his feelings." In doing so, one forswears "any type of moral or diagnostic evaluation, since all such evaluations are always threatening."[23]

The practical implications of this approach have been teased out in a variety of teaching methods. Consider, for example, the advice William Glasser offered to teachers in 1969:

> If a child misbehaves in class, the teacher must ask, "What are you doing?" If she is warm and personal, if she deals with the present and does not throw the child's past misdeeds in his face, he will almost always reply honestly and tell what he is doing. The teacher must then ask . . . whether his behavior is helping him, her, the class, or the school. If the child says, 'No, what I am doing is not helping,' the teacher must then ask the child what he could do that is different. This is exactly the opposite of what happens in almost all schools and homes when a child misbehaves. . . . This traditional but ineffective approach removes the responsibility for his bad behavior from the

child. The teacher makes the judgment and enforces the punishment; the child has little responsibility for what happens. . . . In Reality Therapy, the child is asked to select a better course of behavior.[24]

This technique was central to the moral pedagogy of values clarification where one was to be "accepting and nonjudgmental";[25] it was central to Kohlberg's "just communities" where teachers could advocate a particular point of view but were to avoid indoctrinating students; it remains central in the moral teaching of multiculturalism, in which the entire point is to refrain from judging "another's culture" but rather to tolerate people whose way of life differs from one's own; and of constructivism, where, say in conflict resolution, the teacher should "acknowledge/accept/validate all children's feelings and perceptions of the conflict." Parents too are encouraged not to use "praise words" mainly because they too imply a judgment that is difficult to live up to. Instead, one should use "the language of encouragement" for encouragement "looks at how the child feels" rather than what they do.[26] For others as well, the dictum is repeated: "suspend judgment," "give up 'you-judgments' of [the] child's person,"[27] "do not take sides," and the like. This conviction was also the basis of various efforts over the years to abandon grading in schools—for the purpose of grading is to measure children against an extrinsic criteria; its net effect is to undermine the sense of self-worth of a majority of students. Thus, the shared ideal is that it is counterproductive to "impose" any values on another and inappropriate to "moralize."

Leveling Social Authority

The effort to relate to children with therapeutic open-mindedness is not just a matter of teacher comportment. It affects the actual role teachers play in the classroom. The psychological regime encourages teachers to abandon their traditional role of lecturer dishing out authoritative instruction, and instead become "a consultant" or "a facilitator" in the classroom.[28] They still, of course, have a special responsibility to organize the classroom community and to challenge it to engage in self-reflection and criticism, but their authority in these duties is less direct. As Jean Piaget put it as early as 1963, the imposition of adult authority is "absurd" and "immoral."[29] For him, any adult should simply be "an elder collaborator and, if he has it in him, a simple comrade to the children."[30] Carl Rodgers, then, was not alone in his advocacy of a new role for teachers. Kohlberg's "just community" employs the same argument. In just communities, students and teachers are to "participate as equals" in the creation and enforcement of rules. Each has one vote, and they are constrained to work within the democratic process. Advocates recognize that "the educators obviously would have special authority by virtue of their positions, but would try to operate as formally equal members of a democratic group."[31] This view is explicit in parental advice as well. "To achieve [the] parental goal" of raising responsible children who grow into responsible men and women, "parent-child relationships need to be based on democratic principles." "Democratic child-rearing methods are based on mutual respect and equality."[32] Others also speak of the essential requirement in moral education for "shared responsibility for deciding what gets learned and how the learning takes place."[33] Authority here does not disappear but it is transformed. What is called "democratic" loses its historic and specific meaning. It refers not to a mode of ordering political life but to a process of social organization *tout court*. Democracy, then, is a code word for participation and choice in any context. As one theorist put it,

> democracy is more than simply a form of political governance or a set of procedures for carrying out such a form. Rather it is a disposition or, more broadly, a way of life in which people define and seek personal and social efficacy through full participation . . . and in which each person sees all others as having the right to self-governance.[34]

The net effect is that established structures of authority recede in social significance; the moral authority of the social order is demystified and deconstructed.

A Wearing Away of Normative Distinctions

As moral education grows less and less committed to propagating some objective moral content, and as the social authority that would reinforce that content weakens, the clarity of normative distinctions between some notion of good and evil necessarily fades. In both theory and practice, the ancient boundary markers have weathered away.

Dewey, who put very little emphasis on the problem of evil or of good, was not troubled by this. Having abandoned metaphysics, he could no longer regard these basic distinctions as theologically or philosophically relevant. The distinctions carried no ontological status. At best they were givens of our culture; their usefulness lay primarily in prompting individuals to respond to particular situations in beneficial ways. Thus where "evil" existed it was as specific deficiencies arising in specific social situations. The problem of evil was simply "the practical problem of reducing, alleviating, as far as may be removing, the evils of [social] life."[35] Real virtue was found in the methods used to solve problems.

The weakening of metaphysical ideals as an operating foundation to psychology and progressive educational philosophy accounts for the same tendency within the range of psychological pedagogies. For the client-centered therapeutic theorists who followed Dewey, categories of good and evil or right and wrong simply were not relevant to either their therapeutic or educational theories. Virtue, if it exists at all, would be considered identical to the actualization of one's nature and predispositions. It is human potency—the productive use of human powers. By the same token, evil is the flawed self, the self that has failed to become fully actualized.[36] In values clarification the teacher was explicitly instructed to "correct students on the facts level, but [to] understand there are no right and wrong answers to questions at the values level."[37] The whole point of Kohlberg's paradigm was to get away from a traditional framework of right and wrong. The "Heinz dilemma" (see Chapter 5, note 6) elucidated a different framework for thinking about moral distinctions. The issue of good and evil did not so much disappear as change form, as the lines of distinction were redefined according to degrees of moral reasoning relative to an ideal of justice. Thus, as one develops, one does become "more moral" but this is not the same as becoming good. Where selfishness exists, it does so as a result of inadequate cognitive functioning. Where exploitation and oppression exist, they do so as a result of developmental failure. Here again, evil is neither natural nor innate and, therefore, not an enduring feature of human existence.

Among constructivists as well, these labels have no intrinsic meaning for they have no ontological status. Good and evil, right and wrong, have no objective character; where they exist, they do so as categories of meaning that individuals create out of their experiences. And so it is that teachers are encouraged to cultivate within their students the attitude that rules of social life can change and that they can actively change them.[38] To this end young people are given opportunities to vote on the rules they will live by in their classroom.

Consider too the neologism, "prosocial," an increasingly popular phrase among moral educators to describe positive social values and behavior, those that benefit others. This new phrase distances the moral educator from the older vocabulary of moral distinction. In this new vocabulary, the categories of "right" and "wrong" are reframed in a way that deemphasizes moral judgment. Normative distinctions are retained in a way but without the emotional edge that the old words carried. It is curious to note in this regard that the word "prosocial" is never contrasted with words like "evil," and not typically contrasted with the word, "antisocial." Rather it is contrasted with the more amorphous word "negative" or merely its "absence"—as in the "absence of prosocial" values.[39]

One also sees this pattern in practical pedagogies. In the DARE curriculum, for example, the entire problem of drug use (and violence) is not framed as "wrong" but rather as *unsafe* and *harmful*. As to emotions, curricula everywhere insist that they "tend to be pleasant or unpleasant rather than good or bad."[40] In STEP too, misbehavior is defined as "actions and words that are disrespectful or ignore others' rights, refusal to cooperate when the child knows how to cooper-

ate, and behavior that is dangerous to the child or others." In this program, misbehavior results from a cost-benefit analysis in which the child learns that misbehavior "pays off more than cooperating."[41]

Within the various psychological pedagogies, the old normative categories
that frame the moral imagination simply are not salient. Where they retain some
significance, they are understood to be historically and culturally contingent—
useful but not, in any enduring sense, real.

The Sovereign Self

At bottom, the psychological pedagogies posit a self that is paramount in ethical
significance. This is illustrated most clearly in the way the self becomes the locus
of moral authority.

Dewey himself would have strenuously objected to this tendency, yet those
who claim his legacy are far less inhibited. From the generation of Carl Rodgers
and Abraham Maslow onward, most have been unabashed in declaring this view
categorically true. Rodgers believed that becoming a true person meant that the
locus of judgment shifts internally to the self. "The individual," he wrote, "increasingly comes to feel that this locus of evaluation lies within himself. Less and
less does he look to others for approval or disapproval; for standards to live by;
for decisions and choices. He recognizes that it rests within himself to choose;
that the only question which matters is: 'Am I living in a way which is deeply satisfying to me, and which truly expresses me?' This I think is perhaps *the* most
important question for the creative individual."[42]

The position has been echoed time and again. In more recent formulations,
learning is a process whereby "meaning, ethical or otherwise, [must] be actively
invented and reinvented, from the inside out."[43] And again: "The individual who
is autonomously moral follows moral rules of the self. Such rules are self-
constructed, self-regulating principles."[44]

Thus the emphasis, in all psychological pedagogies, upon choice or rational decision making. True values "represent the free and thoughtful choice of intelligent
humans interacting with complex and changing environments."[45] But they must
be "freely chosen," "chosen from among alternatives," and "chosen after due reflection." Pedagogically, "teachers should help children . . . make free choices whenever
possible, . . . search for alternatives in choice-making situations [perspective taking, as others put it], . . . and weigh the consequences of each available alternative."[46] As Alfie Kohn put it, "children must be invited to reflect on complex issues,
to recast them in light of their own experiences and questions, to figure out for
themselves—and with one another—what kind of person one ought to be."[47] It is
only through choice that values become one's own; that moral life comes to manifest an "intrinsic commitment." Family-based moral education programs, too, encourage parents to be "democratic" by permitting "their children to make some

decisions alone," and to "ask for their children's ideas about some family decisions." Giving choices is "a way to help children become responsible."[48]

Such a moral pedagogy presupposes a self that is, unconditionally, the locus of authority. In this subjectivism one finds the decisive link to the moral cultures of expressivism and utilitarianism. In one, moral reasoning follows the logic of emotional well-being; in the other, the logic of expediency and advantage. Both elevate the self as the center and sole arbiter of moral deliberation.

Within this frame of reference the moral agent tends to exist as narrow "slivers of will."[49] Thus the most significant moral act is making a choice. Choosing itself, not what one chooses, becomes the heart of morality.

Against Institutions

The sovereignty of the self is only reinforced by an explicit skepticism toward the authority of social institutions. Institutions retain their legitimacy only to the extent that they serve the expressive and utilitarian needs of the individual. The key is that the social environment must not be too restrictive but must encourage self-examination. Under such circumstances, one can develop into a psychologically healthy person.

Mostly, however, institutions are the source of false and oppressive expectations. Thus, if the goal of moral education is to allow the authentic self to manifest its creative potential as a moral agent, it is essential to get beyond the self one is not—the collection of facades rooted in conformity to others' expectations. One of the necessary outcomes of finding and expressing one's true self is to "move away from facades," "away from oughts," "away from meeting expectations," "away from pleasing others." As Rodgers explained, those who are beginning to come to terms with who they really are

> do not wish to be what they 'ought' to be, whether that imperative is set by parents, or by the culture, whether it is defined positively or negatively. They do not wish to mold themselves and their behavior into a form which would be merely pleasing to others. They do not, in other words, choose to be anything which is artificial, anything which is imposed, anything which is defined from without.[50]

Among the cognitive developmentalists, the lowest stages of moral development are almost always described as mere conformity to social prescriptions—efforts to avoid punishment or disapproval, to obtain rewards, or simply to maintain stability. The higher stages, by contrast, are defined first by an inward distancing from the rules of society, which in turn provides the foundation for a morality of *self-chosen* ethical principles. The highest levels of moral growth are described by words such as "autonomy." Yet individual autonomy, the theorists insist, does not mean egoism or selfishness. Quite the contrary, moral maturity, they say, always leads to social responsibility. The lives of Abraham Lincoln, Martin Luther King, Gandhi, Albert Schweitzer, and Mother Theresa are often cited as examples of this high moral faculty. Never mind the strong social and humanitarian concerns implicit in these figures' ethical ideals. The ideals themselves, we are told, blossomed from within.

Constructivists similarly argue that any "conformity to authority is not socialization into a free society. It is more like socialization into a prison atmosphere."[51] Moralities of obedience, it is said, simply encourage conformity from fear of punishment or hope of reward. Schools that take their own institutional authority seriously, then, are part of the problem. The same is true with parents or other authorities who have power to coerce. The code is "to educate children to think for themselves about all ideas, including those of adults." Not to do so leaves them vulnerable as "victims of others' ideas."[52]

In sum, the perspective offered by contemporary developmental psychologies essentially invert the old formula by teaching us that moral maturity is *not adaptation to, but liberation from* the constraints of the social order.[53] This is why shame is so problematic. Shame is the sense that one has done something wrong or inappropriate vis-à-vis others' standards. It points to places in one's life where external demands from the family, the school, the culture more broadly have become oppressive. Shame, in the final analysis, is a sign of the need for liberation.

Pedagogies of Permission

Much more can be said of the cosmology implicit in the psychological strategy of moral education. But even now, certain particulars are becoming clear.

The prevailing moral educational establishment builds its pedagogy on a framework of moral understanding that is distinctive, to say the least. This pedagogy, and the cosmology within which it is embedded, are ahistorical, heedless of the distinct features at play in this moment. With one or two exceptions, the psychological pedagogies are also asociological; that is, they fail to incorporate any sustained reflection about the nature and impact of such important character-forming institutions as the family, youth organizations, churches and synagogues, and even the schools. It is true that some speak of the way the "social atmosphere" of the school provides a "hidden curriculum," but the nature and influence of this "atmosphere" are at best nebulous. The idea sounds right but it proceeds without any robust understanding of the nature, power, and dynamic of institutions. In addition, its theorists are thoroughly inattentive to the independent yet powerful moral influences of the media, the market economy, and the contemporary political culture and how they interact with the consciousness of children and the culture of the schools themselves. Not least, the psychological strategy is utterly oblivious to the moral influence of deeply embedded cultural ideals, motivations, and taboos, except as they inhibit individual self-expression and psychological maturation.

As a consequence, psychological pedagogies, both in theory and in practice, portray the moral life of children in a vacuum—disembodied moral understandings acquired by faceless children who grow up (or in the antiseptic cant of developmental psychology, going through "stages of moral development") for all practical purposes without real families, real schools, real media influences, real peer groups, or real synagogues and churches. The portrait is of children living outside of history, culture, and a complex social world.

Morality and the Unencumbered Self

Grant them their due. The theorists of the psychological strategy do achieve their goal in theory if not in practice. The person envisioned by this moral cosmology is, in fact, autonomous—so much so as to exclude the possibility of commitments that go beyond subjective choices or obligations that are antecedent to personal choice. There simply is no framework for making sense of commitments that come, for example, by being raised as a member of a particular community or being a part of a particular social stratum. If such constitutive attachments exist, they do so as an obstacle to moral development. So too, there is no possibility of a moral actor possessing, in a constitutive sense, moral perceptions that develop simply by virtue of having lived in a particular time and place in history.[54] Likewise, any conception of good or evil bound up in the contours of an individual's or a group's identity in the constitutive sense is ruled out from the start. In this cosmology, the moral agent is alone, unconstrained, unencumbered, and radically self-governing.

The subjectivism of this cosmology seems to imply that these pedagogies are really relativistic. Conservative critics regularly make hay of this. On the face of it, however, the criticism is wrong. The use of such terms as "moral maturity," or Erikson's characterization of the highest level of ethical maturity as a "universal sense of values assented to,"[55] or Fowler's depiction of the final stage of faith development as a "universalizing faith" that leads to the imperatives of "absolute love" and justice.[56] Even the proponents of values clarification argued that certain values inhered within their model. The method, they said, "definitely promotes the values of thinking, feeling, choosing, communicating, and acting." Stung often by accusations of moral relativism, they went further, claiming that their method promoted "rationality, justice, creativity, autonomy and equality."[57] So too moral content was an explicit part of Kohlberg's cognitive development paradigm. Even if one were to observe differences in moral standards across different cultures, he contended, a rational analysis can reconcile them through the concept of *justice*. Accordingly, Kohlberg and his followers explicitly advocated just communities in which students would participate in democratic decision making concerning the common life of the group. And from Dewey onward, there is not a theorist or practitioner operating within this larger strategy who has not spoken in sanctified tones of "democracy" and its moral requirements.

As one moves beyond theory toward principles of pedagogical practice there are frequent endorsements of specific content in moral education. Alfie Kohn, for example, decried the "rampant individualism" and the self-esteem that undermines a communitarian ethic and strongly endorsed collaboration as a key moral objective.[58] Even Abraham Maslow spoke of "valuelessness" as "the ultimate disease of our time."[59]

*   *   *

Proponents of the psychological pedagogies do, in fact, speak of justice, compassion, caring, respect, tolerance, and even the Golden Rule. But where do these ideals come from? How are they to be understood?

The ideals of justice and compassion are rooted neither in the conventions of social life or public discourse, nor in an external or transcendent standard inherited from any particular moral tradition.[60] Rather, these ideals are rooted in the rights (the desires, feelings, needs, and potentialities) of the autonomous individual. The self, in brief, is both the source of all moral sensibility and the final object of moral accountability.

How is this? In the psychological paradigm of moral education, the elementary forms of the moral life are innate and found within sensibilities possessed by all individuals.[61] Benevolence, compassion, and justice reside within each of us and need only to be coaxed out. As Rodgers put it, everyone possesses the capacity "to expand, extend, become autonomous, develop, mature." Moral capacity "exists in every individual, and awaits only the proper conditions to be released and expressed." "Whether one calls it a growth tendency, a drive toward self-actualization, or a forward-moving directional tendency, it is the mainspring of life."[62] "This tendency may become deeply buried under layer after layer of encrusted psychological defenses; it may be hidden behind elaborate facades which deny its existence."[63] In psychotherapeutic circles Abraham Maslow argued much the same. Human beings do have an inner core. "As much as we know of it so far, it is definitely not 'evil,' but is either what we adults in our culture call 'good' or else it is neutral."[64] For him, the tendency toward self-fulfillment in people was "instinctive."

Man demonstrates *in his own nature* a pressure toward fuller and fuller Being, more and more perfect actualization of his humanness in exactly the same naturalistic, scientific sense that an acorn may be said to be 'pressing toward' being an oak tree, or a tiger can be observed to 'push toward' being tigerish, or a horse toward being equine. Man is ultimately not molded or shaped into humanness or taught to be human. The role of the environment is ultimately to permit him or help him to actualize *his own* potentialities, not *its* potentialities.[65]

What are those potentialities? "Creativeness, spontaneity, selfhood, authenticity, caring for others, being able to love, yearning for truth are embryonic potentialities belonging to his species-membership just as much as are his arms and legs and brain and eyes."[66]

One finds these ideas playing out in practical pedagogy as well. "Where do feelings come from?" asks the STEP program. "Feelings come from beliefs," is the reply. But "where do beliefs come from?" "They come from experiences [children] had when they were very young."[67] "Children decide what to do about each family value. One child may accept a value. Another may reject it. Either way, each child decides what is important to him or her in the family." With religion, for example, STEP offers the following illustration.

Jerome and Renée live with their mom and grandpa. Grandpa is religious. He spends much of each day in religious activities. Mom doesn't take part in any kind of religion. She and Grandpa often argue about this. Jerome likes to go to church with Grandpa. He is learning all he can about his grandpa's religion. Renée wants to go to Sunday school with her friend Tuleesha's family. But she's afraid to ask her mom. She doesn't want her mom to feel unhappy about her going to church.

STEP goes on to explain that "the adults in this family don't agree about religion. Clearly religion is important in Jerome and Renée's family. Jerome and Renée don't fully understand all the issues. Still, they are making choices about religion."[68] The point is that there is little if anything in this paradigm that exists prior to personal experiences and the choices one makes about those experiences. As the STEP program tells us, "each of us creates our own feelings. Many people find this surprising. Yet it is true."[69] These ideas translate into a range of practical pedagogies.[70]

These basic assumptions form the very foundation of the developmental perspective—from Dewey to Erikson, Piaget, through Kohlberg and the new constructivists too. The assumption is that the natural direction of cognitive/affective moral development within the person is toward autonomy, in which the autonomous individual naturally manifests strong moral controls that lead toward *social* justice, *social* welfare, *democratic* harmony, and *collective* well-being.

It all begins, however, within the individual. So it is that recent advocates of constructivism describe moral values originating as "feelings of necessity." Moral ideals such as "quality" or "excellence" in schoolwork are rooted in the satisfaction received from a high level of achievement. "Feeling good," William Glasser instructed us, is the basis—"the physiologic incentive"—of the pursuit of such ideals.[71] Moral turpitude is merely a sign that needs are not being met. As Alfie Kohn put it, "if students disappoint us, it is almost always because they are missing something they need."[72] Justice itself, at its heart, is a feeling. Community too is framed individually in terms of "feel[ing] connected to their peers" and having "the experience of the classroom as safe and supportive."[73] In the end, ideals of corporate life are invoked and even celebrated, but they too are conceived as affective and rational extensions of the autonomous self.[74] Caring is another value that is self-generating from the needs it fulfills. Though it is selfless in a certain way, as Milton Meyerhoff puts it, "in caring for the other, in helping it grow, I actualize myself."[75] The theme is again echoed in certain feminist theories of moral education as well. Nel Noddings's moral education alternative, for example, begins with the premise that "to care and be cared for are fundamental human needs."[76] Citing Martin Heidegger, she describes care "as the very Being of human life . . . the ultimate reality of life."[77] "An ethic of caring," Noddings wrote, "locates morality primarily in the pre-act consciousness of the one-caring. Yet it is not a form of agapism. There is no command to love nor, indeed, any God to make the commandment."[78]

In our historical moment, we continue to affirm the importance of benevolence and justice. The question of why one should pursue these moral ends remains open for discussion. Why should I be good? Why should I care? Why should I pursue justice? Within the psychological paradigm of moral education the response is clear: there is a need within all of us to be good, to care, to pursue justice. Ethical reflection and moral pedagogy within this strategy are reluctant to go further than this.

There is, obviously, internal debate among the theorists of this strategy as to whether the origin and character of moral sensibilities is rational, affective, or some combination of the two. But in the end, they all share the conviction that *moral reality is, finally, a subjective reality*; that *moral authority is, finally, a subjective authority*; that *moral norms are the aggregate of rudimentary subjective sensibilities*. Unencumbered by prior obligations, commitments, and relationships, the person is capable of creating, out of no other resources than his or her mind and emotions, the moral ends and moral justification to which he or she is committed.

The psychological strategy of moral education does indeed offer moral content, but its distinctiveness finally resides in what Michael Sandel calls the "deontological" nature of the moral cosmology in which it is embedded: its rejection of any metaphysics rooted outside of the self.[79] Here again the self, as an agent of choice, is constituted and exists prior to any moral ends it may affirm.[80]

The consequences? Practically, the psychological strategy of moral education may be set up to oppose certain behaviors like the use of drugs, violence, sexual promiscuity, cheating, stealing, "rampant individualism," and so on. But there is nothing intrinsic to the strategy itself that leads to these ends. Likewise, the strategy may be set up to promote other behaviors, attitudes and ideals such as achievement, fidelity, compassion, tolerance, community, democracy, and the like, but here again, there is nothing intrinsic to the strategy to lead to the ends. These moral ends are conceived as extensions of an autonomous self yet these ideals are themselves subordinate to self and, often enough, its overriding moral purpose of self-actualization and fulfillment.

As such these moral ends are incapable of acting back upon selves and ordering their passions in any socially or politically coherent way. A moral code that is, at bottom, self-generating and self-referencing undermines the existence of and adherence to a prevailing communal purpose; it precludes the possibility of any compelling collective discipline capable of regulating social life. Simply put, there is nothing to which the self is obligated to submit. In the end the connection between the autonomous and unencumbered self and these moral ends are not only arbitrary but they are also without binding address. Further still, they lack any coherent social purposes. Any agreement one finds in public life is purely fortuitous.

Clearly the proponents of the psychological strategy of moral education—theorists and practitioners alike—are well-meaning. The ideals of justice, compassion, respect, community, and democracy are invoked sincerely and earnestly. Yet their view of the self as moral agent and as the *fons et origo* of moral life simply cannot sustain those ideals.

Pedagogies of Permission

It is precisely because this moral cosmology cannot sustain the moral ends that it attaches itself to that, while neither simply relativistic nor contentless, the psychological pedagogies are finally pedagogies of permission. They offer permission because there is nothing inherent within this broad cosmology to inhibit individual appetite. There is nothing that restrains the will or limits desire.

On the one hand, in its more exclusive emphasis on the individual, these psychological pedagogies ignore, downplay, or dismiss as destructive the social world as a character-forming force. There is no dialectic between the individual and society. There is only—or primarily—the individual. As one proponent put it, "All that we get from the outside world is information. We then choose to act on that information in the way we believe is best for us." In the end, "all human behavior is generated by what goes on inside the behaving person."[81] In such a view, culture is, at most, neutral in content and passive in its relation to human beings.

What are we to make of this? Historically and cross-culturally it is a given that a society's ethical system rested, to one degree or another, upon a code of renunciation. One had to renounce the self and its appetites in order to contribute sacrificially to the common good, to remain faithful to one's spouse, to defend the honor of one's family name, to prepare for battle. In the psychological pedagogies, renunciation is at best an incidental part of the moral imagination. Where it remains possible, it is always provisional; always subject to reevaluation according to the expressive or utilitarian needs of the sovereign self. Its implicit ethic, then, is one of release from the inherited compulsions or controls within the culture. Whereas the past, moral perfection was rooted in some form of deprivation, the therapeutic ethos creates a moral logic of fulfillment rooted in the satisfaction of needs and desires. The dominant psychological strategies of moral education are the means by which this is formally inculcated among children. In this, the moral imagination is shaped not by communal purpose or collective ideals of transcendent good but by a commitment to personal well-being.

Beyond Dewey

It is important to note that Dewey himself would have been alarmed by this propensity in moral education. Even in his own day he was suspicious of the tendency, already apparent in popular psychology, to "emphasize states of consciousness, an inner private life, at the expense of acts which have public meaning and which incorporate and exact social relationships."[82] The year he wrote this was 1939. For Dewey, the very idea of perfecting an "inner" personality was a sign of social disintegration. "What is called inner is simply that which does not connect with others. . . . What one is as a person is what one is as associated with others, in a free give-and-take of intercourse."[83] When Dewey spoke of the release, maturing and fruition of the potentialities of human nature, he was not referring to an individualized and psychologized moral understanding. As he put it as early as 1897, "there is nothing in the make-up of the human being, taken in an isolated way, which furnishes controlling ends and serves to mark out powers. If we leave out the aim supplied from social life we have nothing but the old 'faculty psychology' to fall back upon."[84] Growth, for Dewey, was principally social—"growth in shared experience," "growth in associated living," "growth in the good society."

But we have gone far beyond Dewey; far beyond the complex moral culture in which he operated and took for granted.

PART 2: THE NEOCLASSICAL AND COMMUNITARIAN ALTERNATIVES

We have seen that as one moves from theory to actual curricula, the neoclassical and communitarian alternatives tend to embrace many of the key assumptions, concepts, and ideals of the psychological strategy of moral education. To the extent that these alternatives, in actual practice, embrace the framework of the dominant strategy, the analysis just laid out logically extends to them as well.

But let us put that rather significant problem aside for the time being. Let us imagine that this kind of syncretism has not taken place; where neoclassical and communitarian strategies take form in curricular practices untainted by prevailing psychologisms but are consistent in the transition from theory to practice. In this way these alternative strategies maintain the distinctiveness they intend and thus are genuine alternatives to the psychological regime.

The fundamental problem that the neoclassical and communitarian want to address is the loss of "any sense of objective morality." As Thomas Lickona put it, objective morality has been "washed out of the culture."[85] The pedagogical tactics that he and other character educators offer are designed to redress this deficit. It is for this reason that the first order of business in the alternative strategies is always an explicit affirmation of objective moral content in the advocacy of specific "values" or virtues. As Lickona put it, "Character education reasserts the idea of objective morality. . . . [A] truth . . . independent of the knower. . . . Thus, objective moral truths have a claim on our conscience and behavior."[86] They "demand that we treat as morally wrong any action by any individual, group, or state that violates these basic moral values."[87] As we have seen, nearly every character-education organization and curriculum offers its own list of approved values. Though the values vary, the important thing is that all groups explicitly affirm "values" that are external to the self.

Yet how is the validity of those moral understandings established? How do these "values" come to make "claims on our conscience and behavior"? As with the psychological strategy, the *implicit* framework of moral understanding and engagement these alternative strategies convey is far more influential than any substantive lessons to which it may be applied. It is the implicit framework that teaches children enduring lessons about the reach and limits of moral imagination.

The Problem of Establishing "Objective" Morality

Consider, first, the instructive case made by Lickona himself. In his view, the objectivity of morality is no different from the objectivity of historical events. "That

Lincoln was president during the Civil War is objectively true, even if someone doesn't know it. That adultery, infanticide, torture, date rape, and cheating are morally wrong is objectively true—even if many people don't realize it."[88] But if you are one of those people who does not realize that these acts are objectively wrong, how may you come to know it? Where is the evidence or the argument to make this claim? Curiously, Lickona's argument is grounded in a rejection of subjectivism.

> The idea that there are objective moral truths is a proposition denied by the doctrine of subjectivism. About subjectivism, Boston College philosopher Peter Kreeft writes: 'Of all the symptoms of decay in our decadent civilization, subjectivism is the most disastrous of all. A mistake—be it a moral mistake or an intellectual mistake—can be discovered and corrected only if truth exists and can be known.[89]

The case, in short, is that there must be objective moral truths because without them, all we have left are subjectivism and the decadence it brings along with it. The problem, of course, is that the negative consequences of moral subjectivism do not demonstrate the existence of objective morality.

In a similar way, Lickona argues, "people must understand and be committed to the moral foundations of democracy: respect for rights of individuals, regard for the law, voluntary participation in public life, and concern for the common good."[90] But why? Because, he writes, "democratic societies have a special need" for it. Here again, the case for the existence of moral foundations to democracy is established by assertion and defended only by the argument that there are ill effects for the individual and society if they are not adhered to. While the position is defensible, it does not establish the objective character of those foundations.

So when Lickona states, for instance, that proper moral development requires that we "care about justice—be emotionally committed to it, have the capacity for appropriate guilt when I behave unjustly, and be capable of moral indignation when I see others suffer unjustly,"[91] it is not inappropriate to ask the question, why? On what grounds do we come to care about it? It is one thing to agree with the point and quite another to live by it. What are the terms that compel us to love justice? Lickona offers a few clues.

He argues, as I noted earlier, that there is a "natural moral law that prohibits injustice to others and that can be arrived at through the use of human reason."[92] Lickona is striving, of course, for nonsectarian support for the existence of an objective morality. Yet he still provides no means for explaining *how* these truths come to have a claim on our consciences. He does state that "many theologians and philosophers" hold to natural law, but we also know that just as many do not. The authority of experts, then, gets us nowhere. In the end, within the inclusive framework Lickona insists upon, there is no appeal capable of establishing the legitimacy of his assertion. Statements of value are not like statements of fact because they cannot be validated in the same way. In a context that requires inclusiveness, statements of value are just that: statements, declarations, assertions.

This general moral logic is at play in the range of pedagogies offered by character education more broadly. Objective morality is affirmed unequivocally but with thin justification at best.

Consider, for example, the Jefferson Center for Character Education curriculum, "Responsibility Skills: Success Through Accepting Responsibility." The foundation of this pedagogy is the STAR program. The acronym—*Stop, Think, Act,* and *Review*—stands for the moral reasoning used throughout the curriculum. But toward what end? The curriculum lays out twelve moral "values": "be here," "be on time," "be responsible," "be prepared," "be a tough worker," "be a good listener," "be a goal setter," "be confident," "be a risk taker," "be friendly," "be honest," and "be polite." The idea is that before deciding how to react to a situation, children should stop, think (remembering the twelve values), then act, and finally review what they have done. The assumption is that if teachers assert these values strongly and provide techniques for decision making, children will choose the right course of action.

But the pedagogy offers more content than its list of "values." It also addresses the question, lesson by lesson, of *why* it is important for children to possess all of the virtues. Though the answers they present are only intended as suggestions— meant to "prime the pump" of discussion—they are illuminating. So, for example,

> [Why] is it important to be responsible?
> If you are responsible you will have a greater chance for success.
> Why is it important to be prepared?
> So you do well in school.
> Why is it important to be a goal setter?
> It helps give you direction, helps you to become successful.
> Why is it important to be confident?
> When you are confident you have a better chance of succeeding.
> Why should you be honest?
> So others take me at my word. So I develop a good reputation. So others
>   trust me.
> Why should you be polite?
> It shows respect for others.[93]

The curriculum goes further still by explaining, in nearly every lesson, what children "get or achieve" by choosing to display each of the virtues. The lessons here are also illuminating.

What, then, do you get or achieve for being prepared?—"You feel confident. You get good grades."

What about being a goal setter?—"[You get the] things you want out of
life. Good feelings about yourself."

Confidence?—"You feel good about yourself. You take responsible risks.
You accomplish your goals."

Honesty?—"[You get] the knowledge that you have made the right decision. Respect from others. Feel good about [your]self."

Politeness?—"You feel good. You make a new friend."[94]

In short, the importance of these values—their validity to the child—is rooted
in a means-end calculation of moral reasoning in which the primary moral ends
are personal improvement and emotional satisfaction. As the curriculum sum-
marizes, a child should be responsible so he or she "can be successful and
happy."[95] The objectivity of values is affirmed decisively, but their validity is derived from the actor's personal gain and subjective fulfillment. The STAR program is not an isolated example.[96]

The same kind of problem inheres in the literary approaches to moral education. The argument, again, is that young people exposed to classic, canonical stories early in their lives will have the resources from which to draw in the
development of character. Neoclassical educators assume the objectivity and
self-evident substance of the virtues found in these stories. William Bennett, for
example, assures his readers that his "compendium of great stories, poems and
essays from the stock of human history and literature . . . embodies common
and time-honored understandings of these virtues."[97] They also assume the facility with which these virtues will be understood and appropriated. It is for this
reason that William Kilpatrick, in *Why Johnny Can't Tell Right from Wrong*, asks
that we trust "good books [to] do their own work in their own way." "It is not
necessary or wise for adults to explain the 'moral' in each story."[98] The trick, as
Allan Bloom advised readers of the classics, is to let the texts "dictate what the
questions are and the method of approaching them—not forcing them into categories we make up . . . but trying to read them as their authors wished them to
be read."[99] They are confident of the lessons this literature has to teach.

The problem is that for all the posturing about the objectivity of the virtues
and their capacity to transcend the vagaries of time and subjectivity, the neoclassical position articulated by its popularizers[100] ends up beholden to a culture of
subjectivity as well. Though they are confident that good books will "do their
own work in their own way," the problem is that when stories are lifted out of the
particularities of historical tradition, social institution, collective identity, and
normative order, their meanings are contested.

This, in many respects, is the lesson found in the very existence of such vastly different anthologies of classic stories as William Bennett's *The Book of Virtues* and Colin Greer and Herbert Kohl's *A Call to Character*. On the face of it, the books cover much the same ground, so presumably we should come away with the same understanding of the virtues they espouse. But we don't. Together they represent a deeply acrimonious division over the nature of the moral life and how it can be cultivated. And so against the objectivist position of the neoclassical educators, Greer and Kohl and kindred theorists suggest a more hermeneutical approach to understanding literature. The child is to learn to "authorize his or her own moral voice" in order to be liberated from "the social and cultural repressions" of the dominant social order.[101] To this end, they counsel readers to let the stories acquire their own meaning. "Be careful," they write,

> not to shape your conversation about literature in ways that demand definite conclusions for each session or lead to your children feeling manipulated. Trust is crucial for critical family reading. Children will use their own judgment, make up their own minds about the issues at stake, and often understand the messages of what they read in ways that are surprising to adults. The personal closeness provided by serious, non-judgmental discussion, based on shared stories, is as valuable as any specific conclusions.[102]

In this light, creativity is "the excitement of taking on something new and breaking old boundaries"; courage becomes commendable when it withstands pressure from "authority figures"; self-discipline gives children the confidence to "take chances challenging illegitimate authority"; idealism means "challenging our conventional ways of doing things." Stories of integrity can indeed lead children to conclude that this virtue is, as Greer and Kohl put it, "rooted in the comfort you feel within."[103] Needless to say, if scholars as intelligent and well-read as Bennett and Greer and Kohl don't agree on either the meaning of texts or the ways one should read them, it is not clear why we should expect that anyone else will.

But what about the justifications offered by history? To be sure, an appeal to the historical endurance of a literary canon of moral stories is perhaps the principal way in which neoclassical educators attempt to ground the validity of the virtues they espouse. But that canon remained plausible as long as it existed within a fairly stable normative culture that idealized those virtues. That stable moral culture educators now call "Judeo-Christian" has largely disintegrated. Their appeal to history may continue to convince some but in our day it will certainly convince fewer and fewer.

History is not the only appeal. All of the narrative-based pedagogies rely on empathy as well: the meaning of stories from history or the literary canon is assumed to be self-evident to anyone who can empathize with the characters portrayed. This is what makes their example inwardly compelling to the reader. But here is the rub: empathy is sentiment, and sentiments make a pulpous foundation for anything. While I will explore this matter a bit further in the next chapter, the main point here is that advocates assume that the sentiments will be shared, so that these shared sentiments are the basis for a shared interpretation. While they can hope for this, it is by no means guaranteed.[104] Indeed, at the start of the twenty-first century, this may still be possible, but it is certainly less and less probable.

And so it is that even the neoclassical educators offer no extrinsic mechanism for resisting the subjectivity they want so much to reject. In a context where the "enduring" values of great literature are finally grounded in the authority of shared sentiment, the intersubjective capacity to empathize with others in the same ways, moral "knowledge" must inevitably give way to moral interpretation. In the final analysis, the claim to objectivity is rendered weak at the least, if not meaningless.

*   *   *

In a curious way, the same kind of lesson is found in a communitarian strategy that appeals to the social consensus of shared values. Consider the case of the Community of Caring. Their goal is to create an environment in which children "grow toward adulthood with a clear sense of purpose, motivated by an understanding of community good, not self-centered individualism."[105] Here again, their statement of purpose unequivocally affirms five core values which "empower people to be responsible and caring members of a community."[106] The problem is that while strongly stated, their validity is set forth in an appeal to their personal and social consequences. Caring? "Without caring, nothing matters. That's why caring is at the heart of a decent life." Respect? "Respect for each other makes a moral community—a community of caring—possible." Trust? "Communities of people cannot exist without a certain level of trust. . . . A whole life without trust is impossible." Responsibility? "Accepting responsibility is a sign of maturity." Family? "Families . . . the 'school of character' . . . [are] essential to the health of our children and our society."

The Community of Caring is nervous about sanctioning any binding authority external to the self through which the validity of moral obligations and aspirations can be established. Indeed, "the idea is not to be an authority, but to develop an atmosphere that will allow students to engage in probing discussions and thoughtful reflection. Those who succeed in teaching values don't preach to their students; instead they nurture a disciplined and open conversation about the ways our values define our identity, shape our friendships and affect our communities."[107]

Recall too the testimony of Nancy Van Gulick of the Character Counts! Coalition before the National Commission on Civic Renewal in 1997. She unequivocally affirmed such objective and consensual values as the Golden Rule—yet almost in the same breath she insisted that teaching children to do the right thing means teaching them that "it feels good to do right." "When you help the little old lady across the street, that feels good. You know, when you do the right thing, it feels good. When you do the wrong thing, it feels bad. Teach them to be committed. Make them feel committed to doing the right thing."[108] The appeal to consensus as the ground for moral education, then, depends upon the individual's affirmation. The consensus has no authority except to the degree that the individual *chooses* to participate in that consensus and affirms that consensus as right for him or her. This point is made explicit in Etzioni's *The Spirit of Community*. Writing of the pressures that moral communities can impose upon people, he says

> But as long as these *preferred* moral expressions do not lead to discrimination against those who do not abide by them, . . . they do not amount to puritanism. Those who wish to follow other courses may join other communities—or put up with the fact that many people in a given community will avoid social contact with them. *This may sound somewhat intimidating until one realizes that one may change one's community without changing one's residence, by joining a different social club, place of worship, and so on.*[109]

Here too collective morality tends, in the end, to be self-referencing. In the end, people need not accept those values; it is their choice. Even when they do, they may interpret the meaning of those values in ways that are at odds with the consensus makers.

Virtue on the Cheap

"Character education," the president of the National Education Association proclaimed in 1997, "is not about left or right. It is about right and wrong. It is about teaching core values of honesty, respect, responsibility, and more . . . values that are essential to citizenship . . . values that virtually every American recognizes as legitimate, good, even self-evident."[110]

Are such values self-evident? If they are in our time, it is only in the realm of vague generality. What is not self-evident is the meaning of those values. Implicitly, the advocates of moral education understand this. It is easier to assert "values" as abstract universals because the moment they range into anything deeper or more practical, what is "self-evident" immediately becomes contested. And so "values" are vigorously championed by the advocates of the neoclassical and communitarian strategies but there too they end up as little more than platitudes.

Sensing the weakness of this position, character educators do try to ground core values in an appeal to universal reason. They simply insist that "there are rationally grounded, non-relative, objectively worthwhile moral values."[111] But as Alasdair MacIntyre famously observed, every notable attempt since the Enlightenment to construct a rational foundation for an objective morality has been built out of nonrational premises, premises that any rational person might reasonably deny.[112] There simply is no rational consensus, even among highly rational and sophisticated thinkers.

Thus when moral educators speak of the ideals and virtues that "reasonable people of good will" possess, what is "reasonable" cannot be established.[113] In our day there is no shared or fixed reference point for establishing the objective meaning of certain moral positions. What moral positions are proposed tend to be lifted out of the particular cultural and linguistic contexts, the social practices by which they are communally reinforced, and the historical narratives that give them weight and significance. It is no wonder that these moral positions lose the qualities by which they are made rational and coherent to people. The advocacy of virtues or consensual values then becomes little more than a mechanism for the assertion of personal preferences. Their validity depends upon little more than the sentiments of individuals who, by choice, accept them.

In the history of modern philosophy, every attempt to establish good reasons for believing that there are objective characteristics to the moral life have failed. The proponents of character education fare no better. We speak to each other as though our moral choices had a rational foundation, but that rational foundation turns out to be certain preferred and shared assumptions. Without a coherent moral philosophy, rooted in social institutions and reflected in a communally shared narrative, moral codes can only deteriorate into arbitrary personal preferences whose only sanction is the emotional weight of subjective experience.

Sentiment, to be sure, can awaken individual moral sensibilities, but to be compelling and consistent, as well as socially coherent, the moral life requires an argument—justice requires an argument; tolerance requires an argument; altruism requires an argument—based in something other than self-interest, in ways that go beyond personal choice and subjective experience. Moreover, these arguments have to be embedded in the taken for granted structures of everyday life experience.

In the final analysis, *what the advocates of the neoclassical alternative want are the forms and outcomes of traditional morality without the substance of particular religious sanctions. What the advocates of the communitarian alternative want is the moral integration of traditional community and the compact that makes that possible without the complex and often suffocating communal dependencies built into traditional community.* A morality conceptualized without basic links to a living creed and a lived community means that the morality they espouse entails few if any psychic costs; it lacks, in any case, the social and spiritual sanctions that can make morality "binding on our conscience and behavior." What is more, without the grounding of particular creeds and communities, morality in public life can be advocated only as yawning platitudes—variations of the emotivism that now prevails everywhere. Critics who point to the absolutist quality of this moral pedagogy are not far off the point. Outside the bounds of moral community, morality cannot be authoritative, only authoritarian. In the end, these alternatives do advocate virtue, but at their best, it is virtue on the cheap.

LESSONS IN SUBJECTIVISM

Moral life has always required a deep and rich subjective engagement. Culture, after all, is not merely objective but powerfully subjective as it is internalized into consciousness. It is because the moral life is internalized that it makes sense at all, compelling individuals and communities alike to grapple with moral meaning and obligation in the struggles of daily life. In this, personal experience and emotions have an important place in the dialectic of ethical reflection, character development, and moral engagement. Subjectivity has always been an essential ingredient to the moral life.

But subjectivity in our day has given way to subjectivism where the experiences, interests, and sentiments of the autonomous individual are enshrined as the standards defining the height, length, and breadth of moral hope and possibility. That this cultural transformation has taken place is rarely disputed anymore. What is particularly noteworthy is that the moral education establishments have, in various and often unintended ways, assisted and even celebrated this transformation in its work with children.

And so whether or not the pedagogies provide specific training in a range of desired behaviors, the *implicit* lessons of contemporary moral education—psychological, neoclassical, and communitarian—speak powerfully to the moral imagination. Here, the self—its appetites, preferences, and interests—is not alone on stage, but it is at center stage—and without serious rival or competition. Thus, while all strategies disparage the subjectivism and individualism of our time, none of the strategies presented are able to transcend or escape them.

—— *Part 4* ——

MORAL EDUCATION
AFTER THE DEATH OF GOD

10

Leading Children
Beyond Good and Evil

THE QUEST FOR INCLUSIVENESS

Perhaps the enduring subtext in the evolution of moral education in America, and its continuing story to the present, has been a quest for inclusiveness. While the need to provide moral instruction to young people has never been questioned, neither has the impulse to accommodate the ever-widening diversity of moral cultures. Clearly inclusion is a strategy for dealing with the problem of expanding pluralism. In the face of potentially contentious and disrupting differences, this strategy neutralizes the possibility of conflict for, in the most practical sense, inclusion means that no one's interests are neglected, no one is left out and, therefore, no one is slighted, snubbed, or offended. William Glasser captured the sum and substance of the quest for our own day as early as 1969 when he stated that "certain moral values can be taught in school *if the teaching is restricted to principles about which there is essentially no disagreement in our society.*"[1] This provision has become the unspoken imperative of all moral education—psychological, neoclassical, and communitarian.

In Theory

Among the psychologists who have dominated the field since midcentury, the framework for an inclusive moral education derives from their theories of moral agency. Simply put, if moral dispositions are innate within all human beings, then the objective of moral pedagogy is to call out these dispositions into consciousness, particularly in the formative stages of childhood development. Within this strategy, the differences one finds in pedagogical approach depend on whether one views these innate dispositions as essentially cognitive (or rational), affective (or emotional), or biological (or genetic).[2] Lawrence Kohlberg's cognitive developmentalism, so influential in the late 1970s and early 1980s, was only the most audacious attempt to elucidate within this framework the universal characteristics of moral development. A "moral principle," he argued, is "a mode of choosing which is universal, a rule of choosing which we want all people to adopt always in all situations." In particular, the principle of justice is "always the same ideal form regardless of climate and culture."[3] Only by turning justice into an abstract universal ideal could Kohlberg insist that the teaching of it was "the only constitutionally legitimate form of moral education in the schools."[4]

But he has not been alone among the psychologists in his proclivity to systematize, rationalize, and universalize morality.[5] Evolutionary psychology has, more recently, sought to do the same by demonstrating a universal basis of moral behavior in the biological constitution of the human animal. Among educational practitioners, for whom the quest to systematize anything has never had much appeal, an inclusive approach to moral education has still been the aim. But they have pursued this goal largely through affective theories of moral agency. As one educator put it, "in values education, emotive, affective techniques may be able to accomplish what debate and scientific analysis can not." That is, they can teach "core values which most Americans consider fundamental to the democratic system . . . justice, equality, fair play, consideration, and honesty."[6] What all of these approaches share in common is the assumption that what is truly "moral" or "just" is neither a matter of taste nor of dogma but rather an intrinsic feature of the human psyche. Social, cultural, racial, and institutional differences among people exist but they are largely irrelevant. What *is* relevant is that as moral agents, people possess innate dispositions, rooted in their psychological and emotional constitution, which make them morally equivalent in their potential for good or ill. In light of this fact, it is the task of moral education to "call out" these potentialities through pedagogic practices that are equally general and encompassing.[7]

The imperative for an inclusive morality into which children will be socialized is equally unquestioned among the neoclassical moral educators, except that they pursue inclusiveness not in psychology but in anthropology.[8] Thus, when these educators affirm what C. S. Lewis called "the Tao," they affirm moral principles found across all traditional cultures, principles for which there is no essential disagreement.[9] Likewise, when they speak of their commitment to the "timeless" values of "the Judeo-Christian ethic," they speak of values that are enduring across time, and, therefore, values that transcend contention. It is because there are "certain fundamental traits of character"[10] recognizable to most people that William Bennett could argue that his *Book of Virtues* would be "for everybody—all children, of all political and religious backgrounds."[11] It is because moral truth is a given of the natural order of things and reflected in all civilizations that Gary Bauer could urge Americans to "[re]discover a common body of ethical knowledge that, even if it has a religious origin, serves the purpose of maintaining and strengthening devotion to our country, to democratic institutions, to fellow citizens, to family members, and finally to an ideal of human dignity."[12]

Among communitarians (as well as many neoclassical educators) inclusiveness is explicitly sought not in psychology or anthropology but in sociology; in a social consensus that is continually rediscovered or forged anew as a social contract among various and dissimilar individuals. Needless to say, consensus values are values that are explicitly shared and affirmed and, therefore, ones that generate no friction. The emphasis varies. Where neoclassical educators tend to stress a consensus of personal virtues, communitarians emphasize the consensus of civic virtues as articulated in such documents as the U.S. Constitution, the Bill of Rights, and the Declaration of Independence. Social change compounds the need for such a consensus and also motivates people to achieve it. As Thomas Lickona put it, "Escalating moral problems in society . . . are bringing about a new consensus." "Communities are discovering that despite pluralism, they can find common moral ground." Indeed despite our diversity, "we can identify basic, shared values that allow us to engage in public moral education in a pluralistic society."[13] When this consensus is made explicit, it has the added benefit of giving confidence and authority to teachers who otherwise have been fearful of violating some law or imposing their views on others.[14]

In Practice

The chorus is repeated by the large host of educators charged with translating this mandate into practice. For instance, William Honig, the former state superintendent of schools in California, insisted that teachers instruct children in the common ethical convictions of the American people, "the ideals and standards we as a society hold to be worthy of praise and emulation."[15] The Character Counts! Coalition also insists that "there are some universal core values that can be taught—values that are not identified with any single political or religious tradition."[16]

How are these values to be identified? In April 1988, the Association for Supervision and Curriculum Development (ASCD) Panel on Moral Education suggested that "public teachers and administrators, school board members, families, higher education professionals, the media, government officials, business and industry leaders, civic, religious, ethnic, and community groups, and students . . . should be involved in planning how to infuse moral education in the curriculum.[17] This is often how it actually happens. In a survey of such efforts, the *Wall Street Journal* reported that "to decide what to teach, state education boards generally round up diverse professionals—who arrive at an acceptable list of values to be taught. Respect, responsibility, compassion, honesty and civic participation usually head the list."[18] Educators insist that "a list of civic values consciously chosen by a school system to realize the goal of developing effective citizens is the necessary first step in the teaching of civic values."[19]

In actual communities around the country, the pursuit of "consensus values" has become an undertaking of some urgency. In 1984, the 148 public schools in Baltimore County, Maryland, agreed to teach a common core of twenty-four values including compassion, courtesy, critical inquiry, due process, equality of opportunity, freedom of thought and action, honesty, human worth and dignity, integrity, justice, knowledge, loyalty, objectivity, order, patriotism, rational consent, reasoned argument, respect for others' rights, responsible citizenship, rule of law, self-respect, tolerance, and truth.[20] Nashville, Tennessee, generated a curriculum covering eighteen "universal virtues" including respect for self, doing what is right, giving service, respecting others, accepting responsibility, building community, caring, nurturing family and friends, loving learning, taking initiative, modeling democracy, forgiveness, practicing honesty, perseverance, gratitude, courage, solving problems, and respecting work.[21] The Department of Education in New Jersey likewise endorsed a set of core values to be taught in schools, including civic responsibility and respect for oneself and others.[22] In Saint Louis, the PREP program incorporated twenty-three different school districts, each of which chooses its own character traits to teach. Over fifty terms are on the lists that have been endorsed. Respect and responsibility are on nearly all of the lists, and honesty, cooperation, and self-esteem are on more than half of them.[23] A thirty-two-member task force in Raleigh, North Carolina, produced a list of eight consensus values. In Howard County, Maryland, a school board approved eighteen values for promotion in schools.[24] Not least, it was this sense of need for consensus values that motivated the Character Counts! Coalition to seek broad endorsement of its "Six Core Elements of Character." These are but a few illustrations.

The mandate to discover and cultivate "consensus values" has extended to law and public policy as well. Legislatures in Virginia, Alabama, New Hampshire, Georgia, Iowa, Indiana, Nebraska, North Dakota, Oregon, Kentucky, and Utah have created or reaffirmed laws that mandate the teaching of commonly held values in their school districts. Virginia is fairly typical in the way it articulated the requirement of inclusiveness. There, the General Assembly listed "those *core civic values and virtues* which are efficacious to civilized society and are *common to the diverse social, cultural, and religious groups* of the Commonwealth."[25] The list is typical of what other state legislatures have endorsed: "(i) trustworthiness, including honesty, integrity, reliability, and loyalty; (ii) respect, including the precepts of the Golden Rule, tolerance, and courtesy; (iii) responsibility, including accountability, diligence, perseverance, and self-control; (iv) fairness, including justice and freedom from prejudice; (v) caring, including kindness, empathy, compassion, consideration, generosity, and charity; and (vi) citizenship, including concern for the common good, respect for authority and the law, and community-mindedness."[26]

A Nonnegotiable

And so it goes. In theory and practice, in law and in administrative policies, the quest for an inclusive morality that transcends all differences is common to all moral education strategies. As we have seen, all strategies—psychological, neo-classical, and communitarian—pursue it. Their advocates all agree with William Bennett that "values can and should be taught in schools without fear of accusations of proselytizing."[27]

And there's the rub. Underlying all of these efforts is the basic fear of "violating historic traditions of secular education" or "lapsing into dogmatic indoctrination."[28] Virginia's statute mandating character education, for example, insists that the law not "be construed as requiring or authorizing the indoctrination in any particular religious or political belief."[29] The sensitivity educators have to the accusation of "indoctrination" is only partly rooted in a fear of being sued for violating the First Amendment's religion clause. They are no less fearful of violating the unwritten code of inclusion. To recognize the differences among different moral communities and take them seriously in moral education is not to risk indoctrination but to enter a difficult pluralistic quagmire in which disagreements arise, fairness is challenged, and feelings are hurt. So for understandable reasons, educators retreat from that hard and dicey work of acknowledging and working with these differences.

An inclusive morality, then, is a "safe" morality. To proclaim certain moral norms to be universal—whether it is because they are rooted in the psychological predispositions of the human person, the anthropological constitution of all human civilizations, or the social contract of a human community—means that these norms will not be controversial and they cannot be contested. The very volatile realm of life we call morality has thus been tamed. And so it is that inclusiveness is the "sacred wood" of all moral education.

And yet while this imperative is beyond dispute, it is not without cost.

THE DENIAL OF PARTICULARITY

The quest for inclusiveness in moral education can be pursued only by emptying lived morality of its particularity—those "thick" normative meanings whose seriousness and authority are embedded within the social organization of distinct communities and the collective rituals and narratives that give them continuity over time. The net effect of this denial of particularity is to engage in some extraordinary evasions.

Consider, for example, the treatment of moral exemplars in the psychological strategy. Though Kohlberg's cognitive developmentalism is unique in the psychological strategy, his treatment of Martin Luther King is typical. King is enshrined as the personification of a "just" human being. In Kohlberg's model, he exemplified "stage six" moral reasoning: autonomous, conscience-oriented morality pointing toward universal principles of justice.[30] Yet it is as though King's race, Southern heritage, generational moment, faith, and theological training—all the inconvenient particularities that bore on his leadership in the civil rights movement—were utterly incidental to his vision and his moral courage. They are simply disregarded.

Though the circumstances and issues are so different, it is certainly the same effort to evade the sticky problem of particularity that the psychological pedagogies avoid addressing the issues of abortion, gender, homosexuality, and the like. These moral matters simply cannot be addressed without getting into the particularities of moral commitment and the traditions and communities that ground those commitments. Knowledge of the cognitive and affective dimensions of moral agency just doesn't provide the resources to address these matters. And so, for all practical purposes, these issues have been defined out of existence in this framework of moral education.

The neoclassical strategy denies particularity as well but in its own way. In principle, differences of philosophical and religious tradition should be of paramount importance in this strategy, but in practice these differences are glossed over. Its advocates completely ignore the often intense disagreements between Plato and Aristotle, Kant and Mill, Jefferson and Adams, Falwell and John Paul II (and the communities for whom these are merely representatives), and no effort is given to discern the ways to sort through these differences. Of course, where these differences remain, they often do so only as fragments of more full-bodied social and moral systems. Thus when its advocates champion the "Tao" or the "Judeo-Christian ethic," they champion an ethic that never existed in reality and now only exists as an ethical abstraction or political slogan.

Communitarians also diminish particularity with the same effect. In principle, of course, an appreciation of the concrete social and normative composition of communities would seem to be essential to any adequate theory of community. In practice, these constitutive elements tend to be downplayed.[31] The reason for this may be that the dominant (and most influential) school of communitarianism tends to equate its ideal of community with the liberal welfare state. In its political structures one finds the embodiment of the common good, and in its polity of equality and redistributive justice one finds the ideal of civic life. Here, after all, is a manifestation of political consensus that permits the feeling of rootedness and connectedness but avoids most of the unpleasant realities that accompany their thick associations. As a politicized understanding of community, particular communities—whether rooted in "lifestyle" or religion—tend to be given short shrift. In their particularity, of course, community is often provincial and exclusive and messy and almost always constricting in some ways to individual freedom. The kinds of binding obligations typically rooted in the communal purposes of creedal communities, for example, make many Americans and most communitarians nervous, and so they are written off as "puritanical," authoritarian, and extreme.[32] Reluctant to affirm the underside of lived communities that often challenge received notions of liberal autonomy, it is easier to embrace a political ideal of community that does not. However one might explain this, community is championed more in theory than in reality; more as an ideal of liberal universalism than as the diverse relational structures that impose themselves upon us in everyday life.

An Awkward Silence

The denial of particularity extends as well to the way moral educators respond to the "why" questions behind moral agency, the sanctions that undergird moral action. Why should one be good? Why should one tell the truth rather than lie? Why should one shun cruelty in favor of compassion? Why should one pursue fairness for others when one's own interests are not served? Why should one care for those in need when everyone around is indifferent? These are natural questions to ask and not just by children. They point to the deep, long-standing questions at the foundations of moral philosophy. Far from abstract philosophical inquiry, these questions are implied every time we witness evil or cruelty or betrayal and we ask, Why did they commit such a horrid act? They arise just as often when we witness acts of great kindness or self-sacrifice and ask, Where did such generosity come from?

In 1951, the educational establishment recognized that these "why" questions are "of primary importance." "Children and young people," the NEA declared in *Moral and Spiritual Values in the Public Schools,* sometimes annoyingly, want to know *why*. They do not readily believe, or trust, or act upon, the instruction of those who tell them that this is no reason at all for preferring one kind of conduct over another, or that any reason at all will do equally well. Nor if it were pedagogically effective, could the doctrine of 'never-mind-why' be acceptable to any but an authoritarian state or a dictatorial school system. On neither pedagogical nor on ideological grounds can the schools ignore the problem of sanctions."[33]

Whether or not this view was widely held at midcentury, it is certainly not taken seriously in contemporary moral education. For the most part, moral educators want to believe that the virtues are self-evident goods that need no justification. As Michael Josephson of Character Counts! put it, "I suggest that it doesn't really matter how we answer the question. No one seriously questions the virtue of virtues or doubts that honesty is better than dishonesty, fairness is better than unfairness, kindness is better than cruelty, and moral courage is superior to cowardice and expediency."[34] He suggests that the challenge implicit in the "Why be ethical?" question "may arise more from a need to find an excuse for moral shortcomings than from a genuine desire to satisfy philosophical curiosity."[35]

In the rare instances when moral educators address the question as a matter of theory, their answers are consistent with the model of inclusiveness they advocate. Why should we be good? The psychologically oriented moral educator answers that moral virtue is an intrinsic need, and when we satisfy this need by being kind or compassionate, we feel good about ourselves. The neoclassical educator will appeal to the consensus of history or anthropology and say that it is "natural" for us to conform to these standards. The communitarian educator will point to the social contract and say that we are better off when we share in the will of the people. All these responses are as generalized as the morality they espouse. The aim is to offend no one and satisfy as many as possible.

At least as often, we are told that arguments for morality are unproductive and therefore unnecessary. The architects of values clarification put it this way in the 1970s: "when controversial issues or values choices are discussed, some questions are to be avoided. . . . 'Why' questions, while sometimes justified, risk pushing students who have no clear reasons for their choices into fabricating a reason."[36] Nor has established opinion changed since then. As Rheta DeVries and Betty Zan explained more recently in *Moral Classrooms, Moral Children*, "the child (and often the adult as well) is unlikely to have any idea about why he or she feels or behaves in a certain manner. Thus, we suggest that it is ineffective to ask the child, 'Why do you do this?'"[37]

The historical and empirical problem is that the reasons why one should be good are many. Their stubborn plurality signals just the kinds of irreducible differences that cannot be homogenized into an encompassing morality. In response to the question Why be good? or Why not be cruel?, a commitment to inclusiveness limits one to awkward silence.[38]

An Emptying Out

In sum, the subtext of an inclusive moral education is not the absence of morality, but rather the emptying of meaning and significance and authority from the morality that is advocated. The effort to affirm an inclusive morality reduces morality to the thinnest of platitudes, severed from the social, historical, and cultural encumbrances that make it concrete and ultimately compelling. Virtues are espoused as ungrounded generalities that can be found in various social organizations and cultural traditions but are not essentially linked to them. Deprived of anchoring in any normative community, this morality retains little authority beyond its own aesthetic appeal.

As significant, a strategy of inclusiveness means that the very vocabulary of right and wrong, good and bad, justice and injustice becomes, for all practical purposes, obsolete precisely because these words share fewer and fewer points of reference. Neologisms from the moral education establishment, like "prosocial" are only the most overt and self-conscious attempts to avoid the awkwardness of words like "good" and "evil." These words have lost resonance among professionals, particularly those operating in the psychological strategy.[39] Consider too the fate of "guilt." The power of guilt to inhibit us from doing what we believe is wrong, and to motivate us to seek to make reparation when we have done something wrong, depends upon a clear and shared understanding of what is right and wrong. But through the triumph of science and therapy, we understand the mental and social causes for behavior much better, factors that have tended to exempt or at least lessen the judgment of blame to wrongdoers. Wrongdoers need therapy not punishment.[40] And so it is that the concept of guilt and the powerful feelings that attend it have lost moral influence and plausibility. All of this is to say that words that have been central to organizing our moral frame of reference have lost so much of their power to make sense of experience. At the same time, by inventing a new vocabulary, the moral education establishment literally creates a new way of seeing reality. Altogether, *we end up epistemologically and linguistically with a moral cosmology that is beyond good and evil.*

In the same way, by rendering the self either prior to or outside of community and its culture, contemporary moral education empties the self of any concrete social and metaphysical grounding. Consider, for example, the word "character." Within professional psychology and the therapeutic establishment, the concept of character was long ago rejected in favor of the concept of personality.[41] The problem with "character" was that it bore ethical and metaphysical implications that professional psychology could not rationally explain or justify. Character, after all, is either good or bad, whereas personality is fascinating or boring, forceful or weak, attractive or unattractive. When character was disqualified as a legitimate way of thinking about the person, our concept of the self lost a measure of moral significance. Among the neoclassical and communitarian moral theorists, the ethical content of the self is precisely what they want a return to. They define themselves in principled opposition to the psychological regime on just this point. But they then go on to undermine the metaphysical, ethical, and social particularities that ground the self and make it concrete. The unwitting effect is to position moral agency within a social, historical, and cultural vacuum. Though the neoclassical and communitarian strategists would like it otherwise, they leave the self with no fixed reference points for constructing consistent moral codes. The individual is left, unwittingly, with few other resources than his or her mind and emotions, the moral justification for various actions.

In some essential way, the "decontextualized" self is reduced to little more than will, becoming what it is by exerting a will to power. The Nietzschean description of the self as essentially the will to power is neither a euphemism nor an exaggeration. From Adler to Piaget to Glasser and beyond, the psychological paradigm of moral education has made cultivating the will to power into a central pedagogic mission.[42] A discipline whose argument for morality is centered around the assumption of basic human needs literally puts forward the will to power as one of those needs and applies it to the practical problem of creating morality in schools. "Discipline problems," the argument goes, "do not occur in classrooms in which students' needs are satisfied."[43] Needless to say, young people have numerous needs—for belonging, fun, and freedom, in addition to basic survival. Yet as William Glasser sees it, "the need for power is the core—the absolute core—of almost all school problems." In his view, it is a will and exercise of power that is linked to significance and well-being, and the frustration of a will to power that is the source of feelings of inferiority.

> Even the good students don't feel all that important in school, and the students who receive poor grades certainly can't feel important from the standpoint of academic performance. So they say to themselves, 'I won't work in a place in which I have no sense of personal importance, in which I have no power, in which no one listens to me.' Literally no one in the world who isn't struggling for bare survival will do intellectual work, unless he or she has a sense of personal importance.[44]

In this, the emphasis in moral education on well-being (a.k.a. self-esteem, self-actualization, and the like) is here justified as a response to the rudimentary needs of the self—in this case, the need to find expression in the exercise of power.

Thin Sources, Shallow Selves

There have never been "generic" values. Yet this is what contemporary moral education ends up teaching children. But how is this really a problem? Why should anyone worry about the specifics—especially since we are so likely to disagree on them—as long as we're united around the overall norms?

Charles Taylor, who posed this question in his book, *The Sources of the Self*, has suggested that it is the particularities that lead us to the sources of morality, the sources that sustain our commitment to goodness and fair play. The answers to these questions speak to higher purposes that take us beyond ourselves and that, in turn, make morality compelling. It is one thing to affirm general standards of goodness, he says, and quite another to be motivated by a strong understanding "that human beings are eminently *worth* helping or treating with justice, a sense of their dignity or value."[45] High ethical standards, Taylor has argued, require strong sources. Without them, there is little imperative and no direction for moral action.

Take as an example the value of empathy. For many moral educators, it is our capacity to imagine ourselves in the situation of others that is the source of our moral sentiments. The pedagogic principle is that children learn from those with whom they are empathetic the array of values that will constitute their moral universe. In this, empathy becomes the foundation of an ethical life. But empathy has an even more specific significance. It is through our capacity to imagine the suffering of others, even those in circumstances that are utterly alien to us, that we learn compassion and mercy.

The argument cannot and should not be dismissed. Empathy indeed serves as an aid to understanding and a motive to enacting justice.[46] But when it is decontextualized—lifted out of the framework of embedded habits and moral traditions—empathy can become indiscriminate. Thus, in a materialistic and hedonistic culture, empathy may lead a child to experience nothing more significant than the anguish of another child who didn't receive all the Christmas presents she wanted or the boy whose parents actually require him to do chores on Saturday morning when all of his friends are playing.[47] Detached from the concrete habits and ideals that ground particular moral communities, empathy also would not enable a person to discriminate among competing kinds of suffering. With whom do we stand in solidarity, offering our energy and resources?[48] Somalian refugees? Upper-middle-class women who are victims of workplace discrimination? Sexually abused children? Spotted owls in endangered habitats? Gun owners who fear their rights are threatened? Holocaust survivors? Then too, how is empathy experienced in daily life? In an age saturated with media accounts of tragedy and suffering, few stories produce anything more than a fleeting emotion, often enough the relief that we were spared the misfortune ourselves. Empathy on its own simply does not lead to consistent, enduring, or discriminating moral commitments. Indeed, it can lead to just the opposite! As Bernard Williams observed, "If it is a mark of a man to have a conceptualized and fully conscious awareness of himself as one among others, aware that others have feelings like himself, this is a precondition not only of benevolence but (as Nietzsche pointed out) of cruelty as well."[49]

When moral rules and selves are abstracted from the normative traditions that give them substance and the social context that makes them concrete, "values" become little more than sentiments; moral judgments, expressions of individual preference. In such a framework, the defining moral action is the capacity of the individual to choose as he or she sees fit. The individual is capable of making commitments, of course, but these commitments need not be binding. One can engage but one always retains "the right of withdrawal."[50] When notions of the "good" or any other ideal has its basis within the self, these ideals are incapable of sustaining binding obligations precisely because the highest normative ideal, trumping all others, is the ideal of an individual free to move among multiple attachments; and the merit of those attachments is measured by the degree to which they facilitate personal well-being.[51] Unanchored as they are to anything concrete outside of the self, the "values" or virtues encouraged by the leading strategies of moral education provide meager resources at best for sustaining and supporting "our far-reaching moral commitments to benevolence and justice."

Into a Void

When moral discourse is taken out of the particularity of the moral community—the social networks and rituals that define its practice, the weltanschauung that gives it significance and coherence, and the communal narrative that forms its memory—both the self and the morality it seeks to inculcate operate in a void. Filling the void, in part, is a system of rules, laws, procedures, and entitlements designed to ensure due process among individuals and groups who are assumed to be maximizing their interests. A myriad of good intentions stand behind each federal and state regulation and behind each court order. But here too there are unintended consequences. In such an environment, the very idea of "developing values," "cultivating character," or generating "good" human beings is difficult to imagine, much less realize.

In a Broader Context: Moral Education and the Legacy of Romantic Modernism

It is worth stepping back for a moment to consider briefly the larger cultural context within which the vagaries of contemporary moral education are worked out. The structure and content of moral education, after all, have not emerged out of thin air. My contention here is that in ways that are certainly unintended, the dominant strategies of moral education today both exemplify and carry forward the distinctive elements of Romantic modernism. Why this is significant will be explored shortly.

Romantic modernism is a complex phenomenon to be sure.[52] It is a philosophy, an aesthetic, an ethic, and even a mythic ideal all at the same time. Its roots trace to certain streams of Enlightenment thought, and through the nineteenth century it found expression in such wide-ranging movements as transcendentalism, abstract impressionism, and the literature of Arnold, Whitman, Blake, Wordsworth, Coleridge, Shelley, Hawthorne, and Melville. In the twentieth century, the same impulse has found a voice in liberal religious thought, the Beat movement, and humanistic psychotherapy.

In their most basic contours, the philosophy and literature of Romantic modernism derived from traditional theology. The movement sought to sustain the inherited cultural order of Christianity but without its dogmatic understructure. The problem, of course, was that orthodox theology was no longer tenable in an age dominated by speculative rationality and progressive humanism. Among the urban, well-educated classes, traditional dogma and its assorted pieties had to be abandoned. Yet the moral ideals that Christendom had bequeathed to the late eighteenth and nineteenth century—such ideals as benevolence, civility, and justice—all retained a deep and profound existential relevance. The task, then, was to reconstitute moral philosophy to make it intellectually acceptable as well as emotionally and spiritually fitting to the times. To do this, the traditional Christian narrative and its central concepts were both demythologized and reconceived.

Particularly in the nineteenth century, Romanticism evolved into a neoplatonized Christianity in which all of the core concepts of biblical theology were transformed into ethical universals. God "the Father" was displaced by a notion of an impersonal first principle—variously understood as "mind" or "spirit." Divine perfection was equated with the notion of a natural, self-sufficient, and undifferentiated unity in the cosmos. Likewise, traditional concepts of evil, represented by rebellion against a holy deity, were transmogrified into notions of a "division" and "estrangement." In this, Romantic modernists did not so much discard the old myths as translate them into the conceptual framework of an agnostic and intuitive humanism.

Romantic Modernism and the Self

At the heart of this reconstitution of theology and moral philosophy was an attempt to relocate the source of moral value and significance. The earliest streams of Romantic modernism aspired to establish moral significance in a high view of Nature. Transcendentalists, for example, sought to ground their view in this way as have certain streams of liberal theology. Because the person was part of the natural order, they could no longer entertain the notion that the self was inherently evil. Traditional theological conceptions of human nature were turned inside out. The core of our being was not just benign: rather, each self was a "portal of the divine," a natural repository of inborn qualities, capacities, and talents, not least of which was a disposition toward good will, kind-heartedness, fair play, and so on. But for all of their efforts to establish metaphysical grounds for this view, its advocates could never move significantly beyond a persistent subjectivism.[53] As those who tell the story so well have argued, the early Romanticists eventually abandoned their metaphysical aspirations and concluded instead that the only conceivable source of value and purpose was the necessity of the individual self. In this light, neither "Nature" nor any deity was the source of value but only the occasion for humankind to project it. Culture, and the order it provided, merely symbolized those self-generated values.

It was precisely because the self was the locus of values that the Romantics believed a person could read a work of literature or encounter a work of art and recognize its moral and aesthetic significance. The good inherent in the work was validated internally through qualities the observer or reader naturally possessed. The same could be said for the ethical significance of history. It too would be validated by intrinsic structures of morality latent within the person. To cultivate good in the world it was only necessary to encourage inborn dispositions and capabilities into their full maturation. In this, of course, empathy would be of paramount importance.[54] It was the basis of any notion of shared morality.

This imperative—to draw out the latent potentialities innate to the self—has been and remains central to the moral cosmology of Romantic modernism. It is from this imperative that its ethic of self-actualization derives. This imperative also defined the terms through which Romantic modernists leveled their critique of the contemporary world.

Given their assumptions, the essence of their critique is not surprising. If the authentic self was defined largely through its autonomy from the collective standards of social propriety and aesthetic judgment, then conformity to collective expectations was a measure of the self's distortion and even corruption. In principle, anything that repressed emotion, constricted individual autonomy, or violated the individual's expressive freedom undermined the development of the self's natural endowments and capabilities. Its net effect would be to fashion a self that existed in opposition to its true and natural propensities. Repressed selves, in turn, would reproduce an oppressive social order.

Dominated as it is by the impersonal forces of bureaucratic rationality, contemporary society is especially given to the repression of personal needs and interests. The goal, then, would be to liberate the individual from all of these constraints. Institutions still exist, of course, but their legitimacy now depends upon their capacity to accommodate the expressive needs of the individual.[55] With this reorientation, not only would people be restored but society itself will be renewed in the process. In this, the ethical reconstitution of traditional moral theology in Romantic modernism is complete: because human beings are defined by their capacity to create a meaningful world, it is human beings who must, in the end, redeem that world.[56]

Cultural Affinities

Even in its diversity and conflict, contemporary moral education bears more than a passing resemblance to the cosmology of the Romantic modernism that has been so prominent in modern American and European cultural history.

In the case of the dominant regime of moral education, the fit is nearly perfect. The psychological strategy fully shares its optimistic assumptions about the inherent benevolence abiding in all people, the moral significance of the individual's expressive needs, the absolute moral priority of the unhindered and unencumbered individual over the exigencies of the group, as well as its antipathy toward social convention and traditional institutions. Whether or not its proponents are aware of it, the psychological strategy of moral education faithfully translates the assumptions and ideals of Romantic modernism into its theoretical literature and practical pedagogy. They are of a fabric.

Though there are clear points of resistance, the neoclassical and communitarian strategies share affinities with Romantic modernism as well. In practice, as we have seen, they offer no real alternative but instead operate with many of the same psychological assumptions and techniques as the dominant model. At this level, they too are of a fabric with the culture of Romantic modernism. In principle, there are significant differences between the neoclassical and communitarian strategies and the dominant psychological model, and mainly in their respective view of institutions. Whether the community, the family, the canon, or the "bag of virtues" that Kohlberg derided, neoclassical and communitarian educators all accord these traditional institutions and influences much greater legitimacy and authority in the moral development of children. In principle they would want to bring young people into conformity with their standards.

But even if their principled embrace of objective values and strong institutions were realized in practice, it would be incapacitated by their unqualified commitment to inclusiveness. In their rejection of particularity, they end up advocating a morality of abstract universals, a neoplatonic morality disengaged from history, culture, and society.

Once again, we see that the different strategies of moral education do not so much offer distinct options of moral instruction. Rather, they emphasize different themes within the same broad moral philosophy. The dominant stream, however, tends toward an antimetaphysical perspective, viewing the self as the autonomous source of order, beauty, and virtue unsupported by any social or cosmic order.

CONCLUDING IRONIES

Seeing moral education in this larger cultural context brings at least two ironies into relief. The first, of course, is that the subjectivism and emotivism of the psychological strategy—so pervasive in all models and institutions of moral instruction—reflect a moral cosmology that is not so universal after all.[57] This is to say that the quest for an inclusive morality has succeeded only in propagating a moral culture with its own distinctive set of prejudices and its own distinct method of indoctrination. It only feels inclusive to those who share its assumptions and moral horizons.

The final irony has to do with the role of moral education in the larger society. The purpose of moral education is to change people for the better and, in so doing, to improve the quality of life in society, so that, individually and collectively, we are to become better people than we might otherwise be. The difficulty is that moral education, as it is presently configured and institutionalized, is utterly captive to the society in which it exists. It embodies too well the normative assumptions that have brought the social order to its present place and that continue to maintain it. It is, in so many respects, a reflection of the moral order it seeks to transcend and then transform. In this regard it is clear that moral education, even in its diversity and its oppositions, is more a story about the legitimation of American culture than it is about its transformation. In this, we have a continuation of patterns well established in history. In every context, in every generation in America, the evolving substance of moral education has reflected the central assumptions and ideals of prevailing zeitgeist. It is no different in our present moment.

11

The Death of Character

We want to believe that the culture we live in is stable and dependable, that the moral confusion and depravity we see around us are merely aberrations of settled and established moralities, deviations from the rule of social convention in American life. We want to believe in what an ethicist once described as the "astonishing infallibility" of "the order of the heart":[1] that people still recognize the difference between right and wrong and good and evil, and that with a few troubling exceptions they are inclined to do what is right and committed to do what is good. Where problems exist, we just need to try harder.

The moral education establishment shares this view. It too presupposes a strong and stable moral culture where the sensibilities of right and wrong and good and evil (even if we don't use those words any more) remain fixed in public consciousness. It assumes that a stable, enduring culture is both our inheritance and our legacy. All we need do to better our children, our communities, and our nation is to capitalize on the vast reservoirs of good will and to refine and expand existing programs of moral instruction.

Much the same is true for the political establishment. In all of their contentious variety, political figures affirm the adage that "America is great because it is good," and that there is nothing about American society that can't be fixed precisely because of the inherent beneficence of its people. Politicians, of course, are keenly attuned to trends in social pathology and quite adept at turning them to political advantage. At the same time, the conventional wisdom is that to deal with these pathologies we just have to tinker with the system—post the Ten Commandments in classrooms, create tougher gun-control restrictions, make films less violent, require uniforms in school, impose curfews, and so on.

Even activists and ideologues in the contemporary culture war who advocate remaking certain aspects of American life tend to believe that underneath the particular issue they champion is a fairly stable foundation of moral understanding and sympathy to which they can appeal. They want to believe one may alter elements of the social landscape without really affecting the underlying moral ecology; that the essential ecosystem of moral decency remains fundamentally intact.

And yet already present in public discussion on this matter is an implicit recognition that the normative frameworks of our culture may not be so enduring after all. In his *Book of Virtues*, to take just one example, William Bennett wrote that his purpose was "to show parents, teachers, students, and children what the virtues look like, what they are in practice, how to recognize them, and how they work."[2] What is significant about his "'how to' book for moral literacy" is the tacit recognition that Americans no longer know what the virtues look like, what they are in practice, how to recognize them, and how they work; that the virtues he wants to promote may have already been lost to the living memory of the culture.[3]

Habitus and its Dissolution

"Habitus" is the technical term that scholars often use to describe the continuity and stability of culture, especially as it frames the parameters of our experience. In everyday speech we use the expression of a "fish in water" as a metaphor for something natural and oblivious to the environment it inhabits. The metaphor is simple but useful. Habitus refers to the taken-for-granted assumptions that prevail in a particular society or civilization that make our experience of the world seem commonsensical. At the most basic level of experience, habitus operates as a system of dispositions, tendencies, and inclinations that organizes our actions and defines our way of being. Socialized as children into this habitus, we live with an intuitive feeling about the nature of the world around us. Culture, in this way, becomes so deeply embedded into our subjective consciousness that the ways of the world seem "natural" to us. As with a sport in which we become proficient, we not only *implicitly* know the "rules of the game" but we also acquire a "feel for the game" as well. The way we think, speak, and act become second nature to us. It is true that all of us make choices and, therefore, participate in shaping our own destiny, but we too are limited in ways in which we are rarely conscious for we do not choose the framework of those preferences and decisions.

It is important, in this regard, to acknowledge the historical character of habitus. Rooted in neither nature nor revelation, habitus is, rather, a slow product of history. It is, as Pierre Bourdieu put it, the unconscious that has forgotten its historical origins.[4]

And here is the rub: while culture—even in the sense of "habitus"—is durable, it is by no means eternal. Archeology, anthropology, and history all teach us that cultures do not last forever. They change, are transformed, and, at some point, come to an end. So it is with the sensibilities, intuitions, dispositions, and imperatives that define a moral culture. They too change, are transformed, and in time become obsolete.

This, finally, is the point: though we all imagine that the culture we live in is stable and dependable, there are also good reasons to believe that we underestimate the degree to which there has been a dissolution in the system of dispositions that give common meaning to our moral vocabulary and coherence and purpose to our moral aspirations. How so?

American culture has always been in flux. Even so, through the better part of the nineteenth century and the first half of the twentieth, the powerful institutions and ideals of a Protestant-Republican habitus broadly defined the nation's character ideal, moral sensibilities, and civic ethos. We have inherited the moral vocabulary of this cultural epoch, yet the habitus that makes it comprehensible, consistent, and compelling has steadily dissipated.[5] What, after all, is a family? What are "family values"? How do we ideally raise children? What do we tell them about meaning in life? Where is it found? How to attain it? And what do we tell them of the rules for living an honorable life? To whom or what do they appeal when seeking direction in their lives? The confusion over these rather basic issues spills out into public controversies over gender, sexuality, the family; over the nature of art, faith, and life itself; over the meaning of justice, public welfare, tolerance, and liberty; over the purpose of schools, philanthropy, technology and markets. The effect is double-edged. While healthy in so many important ways, these debates also cumulatively signal the dissolution of more or less settled (or at least uncontested) agreements at the deepest level of culture. "The center cannot hold," the poet Yeats once wrote and, at least on this matter, he was correct. Habitus is indeed wearing thin. Where a consensus remains in our moral culture, it does so only in terms of the shallowest of platitudes.

The changes that have occurred are not just cultural. They have been accompanied by profound changes in the social environment in which children grow up. The increases in family instability, the absence of the father from children's lives, the number of hours children are left alone and unsupervised by adults, and the role of television and other electronic media of popular culture have all been well documented.

An Aside on Popular Culture

Let us consider for a moment the place of popular culture in our lives, television in particular. Though I have spent little space in this essay addressing it, popular culture has obviously filled a void left by the weakening influence of the family, faith institutions, and other communal networks. As such it operates, as never before, as an independent and even dominant source of moral pedagogy.

Those who rage over the specific content of television shows or films are certainly right about the vulgarity and the violence but they tend to miss the larger point. Very, very few people who see a rape portrayed will commit one, and very, very few who witness a murder on the screen—even thousands of them—will act it out themselves. At the end of the day, the explicit content of television and film is probably less significant than its implicit lessons. The question, then, is not so much what 27 hours per week of television watching by the average preschool child overtly teaches them, but what it does to their moral imagination. And beyond children and adolescents, how does a steady diet of these media—in the case of television, 250 billion hours of viewing per year as a nation[6]—shape our dispositions and, in turn, re-form the habitus of our culture?

The main thing about television is that it is an entertainment medium.[7] It does not intend to be destructive but only to amuse, delight, and sometimes educate, with the preeminent goal of turning a profit. The prevailing style of entertainment places a premium on glibness over gravity, chattiness over reticence, image over words, and style over substance. Nearly everything in this medium is transient, expendable, and without enduring importance. Presented in rapidly moving images and sounds, it focuses our attention on the moment, eclipsing both the past and the future as relevant categories of consciousness. In television, one is never burdened by the past and rarely oriented, morally, to the future. As much as it is an entertainment medium, it is also a marketing medium. The values that prevail are the values of the marketplace. In all situations, the viewer is placed in the position of customer. This is no less true for children who, by the time they are five or six, have been introduced to public space not as citizens but as market-tested consumers.

The net cultural effect of all of this is a flattening out of moral depth and distinction. On the surface, of course, distinctions expand with every channel and every time segment—offering news, popular music, political commentary, home shopping, televangelism, daytime drama, feature films, market information, and so on. The discontinuity that comes with the rapid juxtaposition of images and narrative—from news of a tragic accidental death to a shampoo commercial, from the scores of the NBA playoffs to an update on the Dow, from the derisive comedy of a *Seinfeld* rerun to the earnest discussion of an Oprah Winfrey talk show—tends to blur the distinction among the plethora of images and information. It is difficult to discern how any particular message carries more inherent significance than another. Packaged in a common style that tends to emphasize irony, banter, the quick repartee, the implicit moral pedagogy is that nothing is to be taken too seriously because nothing really matters much beyond its market value; no one is to be taken too seriously because no one really commands our attention beyond their ability to entertain us.

The Net Effect

One could say much more about popular culture and its significance, but I don't want to lose sight of the central point: the habitus out of which our moral vocabulary and aspirations come has disintegrated significantly, the institutional structures that sustained it have weakened, and the cultural apparatus that has filled much of the void does little to address the predicament—assuredly, just the opposite. When one couples a steady evacuation of a cultural habitus with the weakening of key socializing institutions, one has, in effect, undermined the social and cultural conditions necessary for the cultivation of good character. It will undoubtedly take generations before the full consequences are played out, but the conditions of which I write are well in place.

The Death of Character

It is in this context that we find the enterprise of moral education—in all of its apparent variety. Its objective is to generate character and the values upon which it is based. In one way the moral education establishment also recognizes the dissolution of a settled habitus and seeks to accommodate it. And so, against the tide of fragmentation and disintegration in our culture is a well-meaning effort to capitalize on what habitus remains by creating an inclusive moral vocabulary that is shared by all. But to implement this strategy, the moral education establishment obliterates the differences of particular communities and creeds and empties morality of its substance and depth. In so doing, it renders itself incapable of accomplishing the very ends it has set for itself. Intending to deepen innate moral sympathies and even build character, moral education takes shape in ways that make that impossible. It is through a strategy of inclusion, which includes the denial of all particularity, that one guarantees the death of all god-terms capable of rendering morality authoritative within communities and binding on conscience. The problem is that character cannot develop out of values "nominated" for promotion, "consciously chosen" by a committee, negotiated by a group of diverse professionals, or enacted into law by legislators. Such values have, by their very nature, lost the quality of sacredness, their commanding character, and thus their power to inspire and to shame.

The range of normative institutions that socialize the young, therefore, are unable to communicate their ideals in ways that are inwardly compelling. Needless to say, this quandary is not one that affects children alone. When *Newsweek* magazine poses the question "How Do We Restore a Sense of Right and Wrong" on its cover, it tacitly acknowledges that our "sense of right and wrong" is less and less present to the living memory of our entire culture.[8] It has been said before, and rightly, that "morality is by no means self-evident"—except in a powerful and deeply compelling system of culture.[9] It is this system of culture or habitus that has begun to dissolve and thus why it is that the matter of "right and wrong," not to mention the entire range of questions dealing with morality and ethics, is less and less obvious.

So much of what we think of as "innate" in our moral sensibilities, then, derives mainly from cultural resources that are dwindling. What is more, the justice and benevolence (however we define them) we all want to see prevail in our private and public life cannot be sustained on the grounds available to us. Law and consensus and psychology and literature and technology and all of America's extraordinary wealth—individually or combined—cannot replenish them. Neither can the political thunderings of the Christian Right. There is nothing here, then, that can rebut the challenge of nihilism. Whether psychological pragmatism, general social consensus, anthropological universals, or legislation mandating character education—none of these can answer the claims of nothingness.

Of good intentions there is no end. The commitment to do well by our children is serious and unflagging. In the end, however, while we desperately want the flower of morality to bloom and multiply, we have, at the same time, pulled the plant up out from the soil that sustains it. We so urgently desire the cultivation of moral qualities, but under conditions (we insist upon) that finally render those qualities unattainable.[10]

CHARACTER AS STORY

Implicit in the word "character" is a story. It is a story about living for a purpose that is greater than the self. Though this purpose resides deeply within, its origins are outside the self and so it beckons one forward, channeling one's passions to mostly quiet acts of devotion, heroism, sacrifice, and achievement.

These purposes, and the narrative in which they are embedded, translate character into destiny. In so doing they also establish the horizons of the moral imagination—the expanse of the good that can be envisioned. The moral excellences of character, then, are not the end toward which one strives but rather a means. At the same time, the moral disciplines within which one is habitualized *are* enactments of the purposes to which one is called, embodiments of the vision to which one is committed.

The vision itself is imbued with a quality of sacredness. The standards by which one lives and the purposes to which one aspires have a coherence and an inviolability about them and they beckon ever forward . . . but never alone. The story implicit within the word "character" is one that is shared, it is never just for the isolated individual. The narrative integrates the self within communal purposes binding dissimilar others to common ends. Character outside of a lived community, the entanglements of complex social relationships, and their shared story, is impossible.

The nostalgia for those grand, encompassing stories is high in our day and yet nearly everything in our culture undermines their credibility. It is not just the skepticism of intellectuals or the inadequacies of moral education but the structural and cultural realities of our society in this historical moment that make us doubt any kind of transcending narrative. There is no reversal of history or simple recovery of older virtues. American culture is defined more and more by an absence, and in that absence, we provide children with no moral horizons beyond the self and its well-being. In spite of good intentions, our best efforts lead children uncomfortably close to Nietzsche's "last men" who have little aspiration beyond "pitiable comfort."

This is not to say that we have seen the last of character or the moral qualities of which it is made. It will be found, here and there, in pockets of social life— within families and communities that still, somehow, embody a moral vision. Needless to say, it will manifest itself culturally in various and particular ways. In such settings people will not merely acquire techniques of moral improvement but rather find themselves encompassed within a story that defines their own purposes within a shared destiny, one that points toward aims that are higher and greater than themselves. For parents and other adults the task of "saving our children" means, in large part, telling children what they are being saved for. The task of educating children means teaching them the larger designs that could give form and focus to their individual aspirations, so that they come to understand not only how to be good but why. And though it is made explicit from time to time, this moral vision is communicated and reinforced mainly through the enactments of the particular lives, traditions, and institutions that constitute the living memory of our communities.

Democracy and
Moral Education

It would be a concession to despair to say that there is no possibility of cultivating good character in children and the moral excellences of which it is comprised; that human agency is futile in the face of present circumstances. Even the most pessimistic would not be willing to make such a concession. Still, the historical realities of our moment seem rather overwhelming—whatever possibilities exist at our time seem rather meager. It is difficult to think of another age when the key socializing institutions for the cultivation of normative ideals and virtuous habit have been so reluctant to communicate to children their standards and the god-terms that give them sanction. It is difficult to remember another time when these same institutions have been so overwhelmed by the influence of other powerful forces in society. Indeed, it is difficult to think of another context where the individual has been so disconnected, both socially and metaphysically, from stable communities—spectacularly free to determine one's own fate to be sure, yet at the same time, restless with few if any fixed bearings for the journey.

Against this formidable array of historical and sociological circumstances, our political establishment offers a range of trite palliatives—"just say no" slogans, the posting of the Ten Commandments, metal detectors in schools and stricter gun-control measures, studies of the entertainment industry's effect on teenage violence, laws mandating virtue-of-the-month programs, and so on—as though these, individually or cumulatively, could substantively address the present situation or respond to the need. At the end of the day these proposals probably don't hurt anyone but, on the other hand, they should be seen for what they are: gestures of a symbolic nature that generate at least as much cynicism as good will.

So what is there to do?

As I have argued repeatedly, my concern with moral education is not borne out of any direct relationship it has with the development of good character. Rather, in this book the enterprise of moral education is a prism through which we observe a larger and changing moral culture.

What does it reveal? Among other things, it reveals that the habitus within which inherited moral vocabularies made sense and were compelling has all but disintegrated; that a new *paradigm* of moral understanding and interpretation has been firmly established within which we formally and informally socialize our children. I use the word paradigm in the sense that Thomas Kuhn intended in his theory of normal science and scientific change.[11] A paradigm is an accepted model of understanding and inquiry defined by common assumptions, rules, and social practices. For all of the variation and contradiction we see in contemporary American society and moral pedagogy in particular, there are definable patterns and tendencies at work that comprise an underlying consensus, one strong enough to suppress innovation when innovation is subversive to the basic commitments of the paradigm. And so it is that the reigning paradigm of moral understanding, therapeutic to the core, envelops virtually every effort to socialize the young, even those efforts that, in principle, oppose it.

The question, then, is not about how to reform moral education in order to make it work better, for moral education is inextricably bound to the moral culture within which it is found. Rather, the question is about how moral cultures change and what, if anything, people might do to influence that change in ways that secure benevolence and justice.

Even this question sounds far-fetched. Ours is a society no longer capable of generating creeds and the god-terms that make those creeds sacred. This incapacity is especially apparent in our collective life; except, of course, in such fringe groups as survivalist communities and reactionary religious orders. The sacred, as we understand it historically, is not something that can be willed into existence and, once it does exist, it is particularly resistant to social engineering. Even so, one would have to admit the possibility of a slow revolution in the moral order that will challenge the established paradigm, perhaps in a way analogous to Kuhn's scientific revolutions. Max Weber, of course, intimated such things in his reflections on "charisma"; those periodic ruptures in the flow of history generated by epiphany and its directed obediences. Are we not ripe for such a revolution?

In the meantime, perhaps the most we can do is create greater space in our social life (and not just in private life) for what remains of our wide-ranging and diverse moral communities to be renewed and to renew. As I noted in Chapter 8, it is in precisely these kinds of social worlds, defined by a clear and intelligible understanding of public and private good mediated consistently through integrated social networks of adult authority, that moral instruction has its most enduring effects on young people. Such space is not a given in American democratic practice. It presently exists primarily in the rather besieged private realm of family and local voluntary organizations. To push the boundaries outward to embrace other civic institutions (most notably public education) will require new ways of thinking about the relationship between democracy and the diversity it putatively embraces.

Democracy and the Dilemma of Difference

In our public rhetoric, we say that diversity is not just a social reality but a political ideal; a given of social life and an aspiration of public justice in a democratic polity. Nowhere has the rhetoric of diversity been more enthusiastically received than in the realm of education. It is not without effect either: public education has been fairly responsive in acknowledging and addressing racial differences, ethnic differences, gender differences.

And yet when it comes to the moral life, our educational philosophies and policies aggressively contradict the ideals and policies promoting diversity. We actually fear diversity of this deeply normative kind, and therefore do all in our power to domesticate the troubling particularities of moral commitment and community.

It is in this light that we need to consider again the Enlightenment commitment to create a universal and inclusive moral vocabulary capable of satisfying everyone. Its consequences, as we have seen, are not salutary for moral education and they are dubious for democracy.[12] Thus, if one is to create greater space in our public culture for differences in moral communities to exist, it is essential to abandon the high priority we give to this commitment. To do so does not mean the sacrifice of a common public life defined by commonly held moral ideals.[13] But instead of forcing commonality in our moral discourse at the expense of particularity, one *discovers* commonality *through* particularity. Certainly the humanist, the Jew, and the Christian who join in condemnation of racism will differ over whether humanist, Jewish, and Christian conviction provide the most trustworthy reasons for their agreement, yet each provides thick moral arguments that preserve the most important commitments of the other.[14] We will most certainly discover other moral agreements about integrity, fairness, altruism, responsibility, respect, valor—agreements too numerous to mention. But these agreements will be found *within* moral diversity not in spite of it. Where disagreements remain, they can be addressed through a substantive engagement that enhances rather than undermines democracy.[15]

Here, of course, I raise issues that are too complicated to elaborate in a brief postscript to this book. My main point is that democratic alternatives exist already that recognize differences in moral culture and commitment as a matter of polity and this recognition neither weakens nor violates democratic principles of nondiscrimination and nonrepression.[16] Creating space in this way for different moral communities to flourish in public and private life might very well lead to conditions that are conducive to the growth of people of good character—conditions spawning a more grounded experience of subjective autonomy (than is presently found in the psychological strategy), a more robust encounter with the authority of communities (than is presently found in the communitarian strategy[17]), and a deeper understanding of virtuous habit formation (than is presently found in the neoclassical strategy).

As immense a task as this may seem, an even bigger challenge will be simply overcoming our fear of each other.

NOTES

Postmortem

1. Philip Rieff, "The New Noises of War in the Second Culture Camp: Notes on Professor Burt's Legal Fictions," *Yale Journal of Law and the Humanities* 3, no. 2 (Summer 1991), pp. 315–388.

Chapter One

1. Proverbs 29:2, New English Bible.
2. Deuteronomy 11:26–28, New International Version. The catalog of blessings and curses listed in Deuteronomy 28, for example, is incredibly elaborate:

Blessings for Obedience

If you fully obey the Lord your God and carefully follow all his commands I give you today, the Lord your God will set you high above all the nations on earth. All these blessings will come upon you and accompany you if you obey the Lord your God:
    You will be blessed in the city and blessed in the country.
    The fruit of your womb will be blessed, and the crops of your land and the
    Young of your livestock—the calves of your herds and the lambs of your flocks.
    Your basket and your kneading trough will be blessed.
    You will be blessed when you come in and blessed when you go out.
    The Lord will grant that the enemies who rise up against you will be defeated before you. They will come at you from one direction but flee from you in seven. The Lord will send a blessing on your barns and on everything you put your hands to. The Lord your God will bless you in the land he is giving you. The Lord will establish you as his holy people, as he promised you on oath, if you keep the commands of the Lord your God and walk in his ways. Then all the peoples on earth will see that you are called by the name of the Lord, and they will fear you. The Lord will grant you abundant prosperity—in the fruit of your womb, the young of your livestock and the crops of your ground—in the land he swore to your forefathers to give you.
    The Lord will open the heavens, the storehouse of his bounty, to send rain on your land in season and to bless all the work of your hands. You will lend to many nations but will borrow from none. The Lord will make you the head, not the tail. If you pay attention to the commands of the Lord your God that I give you this day

and carefully follow them, you will always be at the top, never at the bottom. Do not turn aside from any of the commands I give you today, to the right or to the left, following other gods and serving them.

Curses for Disobedience

However, if you do not obey the Lord your God and do not carefully follow all his commands and decrees I am giving you today, all these curses will come upon you and overtake you:
You will be cursed in the city and cursed in the country.
Your basket and your kneading trough will be cursed.
The fruit of your womb will be cursed, and the crops of your land, and the calves of your herds and the lambs of your flocks.
You will be cursed when you come in and cursed when you go out.
The Lord will send on you curses, confusion and rebuke in everything you put your hand to, until you are destroyed and come to sudden ruin because of the evil you have done in forsaking him. The Lord will plague you with diseases until he has destroyed you from the land you are entering to possess. The Lord will strike you with wasting disease, with fever and inflammation, with scorching heat and drought, with blight and mildew, which will plague you until you perish. The sky over your head will be bronze, the ground beneath you iron. The Lord will turn the rain of your country into dust and powder; it will come down from the skies until you are destroyed.
The Lord will cause you to be defeated before your enemies. You will come at them from one direction but flee from them in seven, and you will become a thing of horror to all the kingdoms on earth. Your carcasses will be food for all the birds of the air and the beasts of the earth, and there will be no one to frighten them away. The Lord will afflict you with the boils of Egypt and with tumors, festering sores and the itch, from which you cannot be cured. The Lord will afflict you with madness, blindness and confusion of mind. At midday you will grope about like a blind man in the dark. You will be unsuccessful in everything you do; day after day you will be oppressed and robbed, with no one to rescue you.
You will be pledged to be married to a woman, but another will take her and ravish her. You will build a house, but you will not live in it. You will plant a vineyard, but you will not even begin to enjoy its fruit. Your ox will be slaughtered before your eyes, but you will eat none of it. Your donkey will be forcibly taken from you and will not be returned. Your sheep will be given to your enemies, and no one will rescue them. Your sons and daughters will be given to another nation, and you will wear out your eyes watching for them day after day, powerless to lift a hand. A people that you do not know will eat what your land and labor produce, and you will have nothing but cruel oppression all your days. The sights you see will drive you mad. The Lord will afflict your knees and legs with painful boils that cannot be cured, spreading from the soles of your feet to the top of your head.
The Lord will drive you and the king you set over you to a nation unknown to you or your fathers. There you will worship other gods, gods of wood and stone. You will become a thing of horror and an object of scorn and ridicule to all the nations where the Lord will drive you.

You will sow much seed in the field but you will harvest little, because locusts will devour it. You will plant vineyards and cultivate them but you will not drink the wine or gather the grapes, because worms will eat them. You will have olive trees throughout your country but you will not use the oil, because the olives will drop off. You will have sons and daughters but you will not keep them, because they will go into captivity. Swarms of locusts will take over all your trees and the crops of your land.

The alien who lives among you will rise above you higher and higher, but you will sink lower and lower. He will lend to you, but you will not lend to him. He will be the head, but you will be the tail.

All these curses will come upon you. They will pursue you and overtake you until you are destroyed, because you did not obey the Lord your God and observe the commands and decrees he gave you. They will be a sign and a wonder to you and your descendants forever. Because you did not serve the Lord your God joyfully and gladly in the time of prosperity, therefore in hunger and thirst, in nakedness and dire poverty, you will serve the enemies the Lord sends against you. He will put an iron yoke on your neck until he has destroyed you.

The Lord will bring a nation against you from far away, from the ends of the earth, like an eagle swooping down, a nation whose language you will not understand, a fierce-looking nation without respect for the old or pity for the young. They will devour the young of your livestock and the crops of your land until you are destroyed. They will leave you no grain, new wine or oil, nor any calves of your herds or lambs of your flocks until you are ruined. They will lay siege to all the cities throughout your land until the high fortified walls in which you trust fall down. They will besiege all the cities throughout the land the Lord your God is giving you.

Because of the suffering that your enemy will inflict on you during the siege, you will eat of the fruit of the womb, the flesh of the sons and daughters the Lord your God has given you. Even the most gentle and sensitive man among you will have no compassion on his own brother of the wife he loves of his surviving children, and he will not give to one of them any of the flesh of his children that he is eating. It will be all he has left because of the suffering your enemy will inflict on you during the siege of all your cities. The most gentle and sensitive woman among you—so sensitive and gentle that she would not venture to touch the ground with the sole of her foot—will begrudge the husband she loves and her own son or daughter the afterbirth from her womb and the children she bears. For she intends to eat them secretly during the siege and in the distress that your enemy will inflict on you in your cities.

If you do not carefully follow all the words of this law, which are written in this book, and do not revere this glorious and awesome name—the Lord your God—the Lord will send fearful plagues on you and your descendents, harsh and prolonged disasters, and severe and lingering illnesses. He will bring upon you all the diseases of Egypt that you dreaded, and they will cling to you. The Lord will also bring upon you every kind of sickness and disaster not recorded in this Book of Law, until you are destroyed. You who were as numerous as the stars in the sky will be left but few in number, because you did not obey the Lord your God. Just as it pleased the Lord to make you prosper and increase in number, so it will please him to ruin and destroy you. You will be uprooted from the land you are entering to possess.

Then the Lord will scatter you among all the nations, from one end of the earth to the other. There you will worship other gods—gods of wood and stone, which neither you nor your fathers have known. Among those nations you will find no repose, no resting place for the sole of your foot. There the Lord will give you an anxious mind, eyes weary with longing, and a despairing heart. You will live in constant suspense, filled with dread both night and day, never sure of your life. In the morning you will say, "If only it were evening!" and in the evening "If only it were morning!"—because of the terror that will fill your hearts and the sights that your eyes will see. The Lord will send you back in ships to Egypt on a journey I said you should never make again. There you will offer yourselves for sale to your enemies as male and female slaves, but no one will buy you.

Clearly, the God of the Jews meant business.

3. Plato, *The Republic,* trans. Desmond Lee (London: Penguin, 1987), pp. 119, 127.

4. Montesquieu, *The Spirit of the Laws,* bk. 8, trans. Anne M. Cohler, Basia C. Miller, and Harold Stone (Cambridge: Cambridge University Press, 1989), p. 112.

5. Ibid, pp. 22, 23.

6. Quoted in *The Real Thomas Jefferson,* Andrew M. Allison, M. Richard Maxfield, K. DeLynn Cook, and W. Cleon Skousen (Washington D.C.: National Center for Constitutional Studies, 1983), p. 363.

7. Thomas Jefferson, *Notes on Virginia,* quoted ibid., p. 653.

8. James Madison, "The Virginia Convention Debates, Friday, 20 June 1788," in *The Documentary History of the Ratification of the Constitution: Virginia,* vol. 10, edited by John P. Kaminski and Gaspare J. Saladino (Madison, Wis.: State Historical Society of Wisconsin, 1993), p. 1417.

9. Thomas Jefferson, quoted in Allison et al., *The Real Thomas Jefferson,* p. 653.

10. Alexis de Tocqueville, *Democracy in America,* vol. 1 (New York: Anchor-Doubleday, 1969), p. 292. Tocqueville was adamant about this, arguing that this was the "central point in the range of observations, and the common termination of all [his] inquiries."

11. Ibid., p. 294.

12. See James Q. Wilson, "The Rediscovery of Character: Private Virtue and Public Policy," *The Public Interest,* no. 81 (Fall 1985), pp. 3–16.

13. I draw extensively here from Warren I. Sussman, "'Personality' and the Making of Twentieth-Century Culture," in *New Directions in American History,* edited by John Higham and Paul K. Conkin (Baltimore: Johns Hopkins University Press, 1979), pp. 212–226.

Chapter Two

1. For documentation of the expansion of the professions of contemporary psychology, see John Steadman Rice, *A Disease of One's Own* (New Brunswick, N.J.: Transaction, 1996), pp. 25–28.

2. As Durkheim put it, "Morality is a comprehensive system of prohibitions. That is to say, its objective is to limit the range within which individual behavior should and must

normally occur" (Emile Durkheim, *Moral Education: A Study in the Theory and Application of the Sociology of Education* [New York: Free Press, 1961], p. 42).

3. See Craig Dykstra, "Moral Virtue or Social Reasoning," *Religious Education* 75, no. 2 (March-April 1980), p. 126.

4. Durkheim speaks of discipline as the fundamental element of morality.

5. "To act morally," Durkheim once said, "is to act in terms of the collective interest"(Durkheim, *Moral Education*, p. 85).

6. The person without character, by contrast, does not feel the reality or constraints of any moral imperatives. All normative forces are of the same order. There is no regularity and there is no authority regulating behavior. A person with character is one who resists the temptation to violate the imperatives within. Without discipline and restraint vis-à-vis the social order, there can be no character. In this way, character and culture are inseparable.

7. Ralph Waldo Emerson, *Character* (Philadelphia: Henry Altemus, 1896), pp. 10–11.

8. Plato, *The Republic*, trans. Desmond Lee (London: Penguin, 1987), pp. 119, 120, 121.

9. "There is in every moral force that we feel as above or beyond ourselves something that bends our wills. . . . There is no rule, properly speaking, which does not have this imperative character in some degree, because . . . every rule commands. It is this that makes us feel that we are not free to do as we wish" (Durkheim, *Moral Education*, p. 29).

10. Robert Oxton Bolt, *A Man For All Seasons* (New York: Vintage Books, 1966), p. 81.

11. Ibid.

12. The earliest printed version added the words: "Here I stand, I cannot do otherwise." As Roland Bainton points out in his biography of Luther, "the words, though not recorded on the spot, may nevertheless be genuine, because the listeners at the moment may have been too moved to write" (Roland Bainton, *Here I Stand: A Life of Martin Luther* [New York: Abingdon Press, 1950], p. 188).

13. Plato, "Apology of Socrates," in *Four Texts on Socrates*, trans. T. West and G. S. West (Ithaca: Cornell University Press, 1998), p. 81.

14. Writing in *The Present Age*, Kierkegaard observes: "Morality is character, character is that which is engraved; but the sand and the sea have no character and neither has abstract intelligence" (trans. Alexander Dru [New York: Harper and Row, 1962], p. 43). The etymology is traced in the *Oxford English Dictionary*, 2d ed., s.v. "character." The first meaning given in Samuel Johnson's *Dictionary* is "a mark, a stamp, a representation." Elsewhere the words "sharpen," "furrow," "scratch," "engrave" are used to define the term.

15. One such "Ethical Fitness Seminar" was offered by the Institute for Global Ethics in Washington, D.C. on April 24–25, 1997. Its motto: "Ethical Fitness is like physical fitness: important to have, not always easy to maintain, but essential to survival." The seminar boasts of being able to "provide you with the tools and confidence required to resolve the ethical dilemmas you face every day, at work and at home."

Another illustration of this is found in the program offered by Nightingale Conant, "The World Leader in Personal Development." The program is entitled, "Cultivating An Unshakable Character: How to Walk Your Talk All the Way to the Top." According to its advertising literature:

When you have strong character, you're a person of substance . . . and you truly deserve the personal and professional success you'll naturally attain. If you want to achieve a greater degree of excellence and build the kind of unshakable character that forms the basis for real leadership ability . . . this dynamic new program will serve as your motivational guide. . . . In this emotionally riveting program, [your instructor uncovers] the 12 pillars of character that form the indestructible foundation for personal and professional success.

Character, we learn, "is a conscious process of design . . . a work of art created from your own individual identity." As with the "ethical fitness seminar," one learns "an easily applied model" of how to acquire these attributes.

16. The social equivalent would have been excommunication. As Philip Rieff explains, in excommunication one was regarded as "dead to the truth in which the credal community found its life." See his brilliant essay, "The New Noises of War in the Second Culture Camp: Notes on Professor Burt's Legal Fictions," *Yale Journal of Law and the Humanities* 3, no. 2 (Summer 1991), pp. 315–388.

17. Plutarch, *The Lives of the Noble Grecians and Romans*, trans. John Dryden (New York: Modern Library, 1864). Consider, for example, the story of Alexander the Great's drunken murder of Clitus. As Plutarch recounts the events that took place, the iconoclastic philosopher Anaxarchus counseled Alexander in such a way as to allay "the king's grief, but [he also] withal corrupted his character, rendering him more audacious and lawless than he had been before" (p. 839). As Anaxarchus put it, "Is this the Alexander whom the world looks to, lying here weeping like a slave, for fear of the censure and reproach of men, to whom he himself ought to be a law and measure of equity, if he would use the right his conquests have given him as supreme lord and governor of all, and not be the victim of a vain and idle opinion? Do not you know," he said, "that Jupiter is represented to have Justice and Law on each hand of him, to signify that all the actions of a conqueror are lawful and just?"

18. I draw again from Rieff, "The New Noises of War in the Second Culture Camp," pp. 343–344.

19. Every ethic construes the world in a particular way.

20. Aristotle's *Nichomachean Ethics* might well have been translated as "Matters to do with Character." On the notion of prohairesis, see Nancy Sherman, "The Choices of a Character," chap. 3 in *The Fabric of Character: Aristotle's Theory of Virtue* (Oxford: Clarendon Press, 1989).

21. Plato, *The Republic,* pp. 119, 121.

22. Though Aristotle finally rejected the basic metaphysical theory of his master, Plato, they shared a basic agreement about the centrality of moral purpose to the nature of good character. See, for example, the discussion of this theme by Whitney Oates, *Aristotle and the Problem of Value* (Princeton: Princeton University Press, 1963).

23. Leviticus 11:44, New International Version.

24. 1 Samuel 16:7, New International Version.

25. Matthew 12:35, New International Version.

26. Otherwise, morality is not authoritative, only authoritarian.

27. My views here owe much to Arnold Gehlen. See, for example, Arnold Gehlen, *Man: His Nature and Place in the World*, trans. Clare McMillan and Karl Pillemer (New York: Columbia University Press, 1988).

28. Society, thus, provides us the moral codes, world views, and ideals; society provides normative boundaries for our thinking and behaving. These patterns or boundaries are what we typically call institutions. Indeed, the power of institutions is that they provide for us what instincts provide for other species—a relatively stable world. Morality, in this light, is the sense of obligation, even duty, we have to abide by the rules of our society, whatever those rules may be. As Durkheim put it, the domain of morality is the domain of duty. See Durkheim, *Moral Education*, pp. 21–30.

29. In this light, culture can be thought of, in Ann Swidler's helpful term, as a "tool kit," a set of resources by which we negotiate the world around us, not least of which is our identity-in-the-world. Culture provides a repertoire of skills, habits, disposition, as well as symbols, stories, ritual practices, and even relationships out of which we devise strategies for acting in the world. Culture, then, not only makes sense of ourselves and our environment, but makes it possible to actively engage the world in ways that are consistent with our self-understanding and our understanding of the world around us. See Ann Swidler, "Culture in Action: Symbols and Strategies," *American Sociological Review* 51 (April 1986), pp. 273–286.

30. Ernest L. Boyer, "The Third Wave of School Reform," *Christianity Today*, 22 September 1989, pp. 14–19.

31. Remarks made by Robert Chase, National Educational Association president, at the Fourth Annual Character Counts! Coalition Meeting, Washington, D.C., 11 April 1997, NEA home page, 3 January 1999, http://www.nea.org.

32. William Kilpatrick, *Why Johnny Can't Tell Right from Wrong* (New York: Simon and Schuster, 1992), p. 226. The leadership of the Jefferson Center for Character Education put it this way: "Schools must reevaluate or rededicate themselves to systematic character education. . . . This alone can help break the cycle of violence, apathy, abuse and lack of a work ethic" (B. David Brooks and Frank Goble, *The Case for Character Education*, [Northridge: Studio 4 Productions, 1997], p. 63).

33. Amitai Etzioni, *The Spirit of Community* (New York: Crown, 1993), p. 89.

34. Amitai Etzioni, *The New Golden Rule: Community and Morality in a Democratic Society* (New York: Basic Books, 1996), p. 186. Consider as well the case made by Kevin Ryan in this regard: schools should "reassert their moral function [in order to] help young people escape from materialistic self-preoccupation." "The education profession must make moral education and character development high priorities—part of the profession's core responsibilities" (Kevin Ryan, "The New Moral Education," *Phi Delta Kappan* 68, no. 2 [October 1986], p. 170).

35. Mark B. Tappan and Lyn Mikel Brown, "Stories Told and Lessons Learned: Toward a Narrative Approach to Moral Development and Moral Education," *Harvard Educational Review* 59, no. 2 (May 1989), p. 204.

36. Philip Rieff, *The Feeling Intellect*, edited by Jonathan Imber (Chicago: University of Chicago Press, 1990), p. 234. On this point, consider the very typical sentiment of William Glasser: "Unless we can provide schools where children, through a reasonable use of their

capacities, can succeed, we will do little to solve the major problems of our country" (William Glasser, *Schools Without Failure* [New York: Harper and Row, 1969], p. 6).

Chapter Three

1. Cotton Mather, quoted in William B. Lauderdale, "Moral Intentions in the History of American Education," *Theory Into Practice* 14, no. 4 (1975), p. 265.

2. Mary Cable, *The Little Darlings: A History of Child Rearing in America* (New York: Scribner, 1975), p. 51.

3. Benjamin Wadsworth, "The Well-Ordered Family," in *The Colonial American Family: Collected Essays* (New York: Arno Press, 1972), p. 71.

4. Ibid., p. 74.

5. Ibid., pp. 59, 60, 62.

6. John Locke, *Some Thoughts Concerning Education* (Cambridge: Cambridge University Press, 1880), p. 116. In the earlier selection set off in the text, emphasis was added.

7. Ibid., pp. 134–135.

8. See Eleazar Moody, "The School of Good Manners," in *The Colonial American Family* (New York: Arno Press, 1972), pp. 33–34; 45ff.

9. Locke, *Some Thoughts Concerning Education*, p. 143.

10. Ibid., pp. 81–82.

11. Ibid., p. 82.

12. Wadsworth, "The Well-Ordered Family," pp. 90–102. Cable writes that "the most important message that adults wished to convey to children was that they must be good and mind their parents" (Cable, *The Little Darlings*, p. 51).

13. Wadsworth, "The Well-Ordered Family," pp. 90–102.

14. Moody, "The School of Good Manners," pp. 8–23.

15. John Demos, "Developmental Perspectives on the History of Childhood," in *The Family in History*, edited by Theodore K. Rabb and Robert I. Rotberg (New York: Harper and Row, 1973), pp. 132–133.

16. Puritan John Ward in Cotton Mather, *Magnalia Christi Americana*, vol. 1 (Hartford, Conn.: Silas Andrus and Son, 1853), p. 522.

17. Cotton Mather, "Some Special Points, Relating to the Education of My Children," in *The Puritans*, vol. 2, edited by Perry Miller and Thomas H. Johnson (New York: Harper and Row, 1963), pp. 724–727.

18. Locke, *Some Thoughts Concerning Education*, p. 57.

19. Ibid., p. 21.

20. Ibid., p. 25.

21. Wadsworth, "The Well-Ordered Family," p. 49. In his advice to schoolmasters, Locke suggests that they set such tasks "to be done in such a Time as may allow him [the student] no Opportunity to be idle" (Locke, *Some Thoughts Concerning Education*, p. 109).

22. Moody, "The School of Good Manners," p. 35.

23. Quoted in Cable, *The Little Darlings*, p. 7.

24. Dennis H. Karpowitz, "A Conceptualization of the American Family," in *Handbook on Parent Education*, edited by Marvin J. Fine (New York: Academic Press, 1980), p. 27. Life in agrarian and mercantile America also allowed for the sharing of parental duties between father and mother. Unlike the bourgeois views of the industrial era that the mother is the primary caregiver, in colonial times the father was significantly involved in the process of childrearing. This was due in large measure to the occupational proximity of the father, who worked together with his children on the farm. Puritan leader John Robinson went so far as to say that fathers were better suited than mothers for disciplining children. "A mother's role was to bear, suckle, and care for infants, but after the first few months, fathers should take over and 'by their severity' correct 'the fruits of their mother's indulgence'" (Cable, *The Little Darlings*, pp. 3–4). Whether or not the primacy of paternal authority was so pronounced, it is evident that fathers played an important role in the rearing of children. For example, Jonathan Edwards, though he was often away from home, "oversaw every phase of his children's development." This letter to his wife is evidence of such concerted engagement with the lives of his children: "I hope thou wilt take special care of Jonathan yt he don't Learn to be rude and naughty etc. of which thee and I have lately discoursed. I wouldn't have thee venture him to ride out into ye woods with Tim. I hope God will help thee to be very carefull yt no harm happen to ye little Children by Scalding wort, whey, water, or by standing too nigh to Tim when he is cutting wood . . . And let Esther and Betty Take their powders as Soon as the Dog Days are Over, and if they don't help Esther, talk further with ye Doctr about her for I wouldn't have her be neglected. Something else Should be done for Anne who as thou knowest is weakly. Take Care of thy Self and Dont Suckle little Jerusha too long" (Cable, *The Little Darlings*, p. 48).

25. Wadsworth, "The Well-Ordered Family," p. 60.

26. Steven L. Schlossman, "Before Home Start: Notes toward a History of Parent Education in America, 1897–1929," *Harvard Educational Review* 46 (1976), p. 443.

27. As Hamner and Turner note, "church and the state actually worked together to manage child behavior according to the strict interpretation of the Bible." In this context, "parents believed it was important for children to conform to religious doctrine" (Tommie Hamner and Pauline Turner, *Parenting in Contemporary Society*, 2d ed. [Englewood Cliffs, N.J.: Prentice Hall, 1990], pp. 24, 10).

28. John B. Dillon, *Oddities of Colonial Legislation in America, As Applied to the Public Lands, Primitive Education, Religion, Morals, Indians, Etc., With Authentic Records of the Origin and Growth of Pioneer Settlements. Embracing Also a Condensed History of the States and Territories, with a Summary of the Territorial Expansion, Civil Progress and Development of the Nation* (Indianapolis: Robert Douglas Publishers, 1879), pp. 106–107.

29. Ibid., pp. 111–112.

30. Ibid., p. 114.

31. This insight was Carl Kaestle's, who is quoted in Mustafa Kemal Emirbayer, "Moral Education in America, 1830–1990: A Contribution to the Sociology of Moral Education" (Ph.D. diss., Cambridge, Mass.: Harvard University, October 1989 [University Microfilms International, Dissertation Information Services, Ann Arbor, 1990], p. 104).

32. Carl Kaestle quoted in Richard H. Hersh, John P. Miller, and Glen D. Fielding, *Models of Moral Education* (New York: Longman Inc., 1980), p. 16.

33. For discussions of the *New England Primer* see Carl Kaestle, "Moral Education and Common Schools in America: A Historian's View," *The Journal of Moral Education* 13, no. 2 (May 1984), pp. 101–102; Emirbayer, "Moral Education in America, 1830–1990," pp. 103–104; and Lawrence Cremin, *American Education: The Colonial Experience 1607–1783* (New York: Harper and Row, 1970), p. 394.

34. Enos Weed, *The Educational Directory* (Morristown, N. J.: Peter A. Johnson's bookbinder, 1803), pp. 23–24.

35. George R. Merrill, "Robert Raikes and the Eighteenth Century," in *The Development of the Sunday-School 1780–1905* (Boston: The Fort Hill Press, 1905), p. 3; Frank Lankard, *A History of the American Sunday School Curriculum* (New York: The Abingdon Press, 1927), p. 64; Anne Boylan, *Sunday School: The Formation of an American Institution, 1790–1880* (New Haven: Yale University Press, 1988), pp. 6, 7.

36. Boylan, *Sunday School*, p. 6.

37. Lankard, *A History of the American Sunday School Curriculum*, p. 55.

38. Ibid., p. 56.

39. Ibid.

40. Boylan, *Sunday School*, p. 7.

41. Lankard, *A History of the American Sunday School Curriculum*, p. 62.

42. Ibid., p. 61; Boylan, *Sunday School*, pp. 7–8.

43. Robert W. Lynn and Elliot Wright, *The Big Little School: Sunday Child of American Protestantism* (New York: Harper and Row, 1971), p. 3.

44. Boylan, *Sunday School*, p. 10.

45. According to Joseph Kett, "Sunday schools were now portrayed as divinely appointed instruments for the regeneration of the nation" (Joseph F. Kett, *Rites of Passage: Adolescence in America 1790 to the Present* [New York: Basic Books], p. 117).

46. Lankard, *A History of the American Sunday School Curriculum*, p. 97.

47. Charles Trumbell, "The Nineteenth Century Sunday School," in *The Development of the Sunday-School 1780–1905* (Boston: The Fort Hill Press, 1905), p. 10.

48. "The years 1823 and following, mark the beginning of the use of lesson material directly from the Bible, which rapidly crowded the catechisms out of its long-established place." See Lankard, *A History of the American Sunday School Curriculum*, p. 98.

49. Trumbell, "The Nineteenth Century Sunday School," p. 9.

50. Lynn and Wright, *The Big Little School*, p. 14.

51. Boylan, *Sunday School*, p. 7; Kett, *Rites of Passage*, pp. 117–118; Jack Seymour, *From Sunday School to Church School: Continuities in Protestant Church Education in the United States, 1860–1929* (Washington, D.C.: University Press of America, 1982), p. viii.

52. Robert Church, "Moral Education in the Schools," in *Morality Examined*, edited by Lindley J. Stiles and Bruce D. Johnson (Princeton: Princeton Book Company, 1977), p. 57.

53. See David Tyack, "The Kingdom of God and the Common School: Protestant Ministers and the Educational Awakening in the West," *Harvard Educational Review* 36 (Fall 1966), pp. 447–469. See also Timothy Smith, "Protestant Schooling and American Nationality, 1800–1850," *Journal of American History* 53, no. 4 (1967), pp. 679–695.

54. Cited in R. Freeman Butts, *Public Education in the United States: From Revolution to Reform* (New York: Holt, Rinehart and Winston, 1978), p. 29.

55. Bryce Christenson, "Against the Wall," *Persuasion at Work* 9, no. 2 (February 1986), p. 2.

56. Ibid.

57. Cited in John S. Baker, Jr., "Parent-centered Education," *Notre Dame Journal of Law, Ethics, and Public Policy* (Summer 1988), p. 539.

58. As in most of the colonies, piety was defined as religious orthodoxy. See Cremin, *American Education: The Colonial Experience, 1607–1783*, p. 187.

59. See Maris A. Vinovskis, "Family and Schooling in Colonial and Nineteenth-Century America," in *Family History at the Crossroads*, edited by Tamara Hareven and Andrejs Plakans (Princeton: Princeton University Press, 1987), pp. 19–38.

60. New York, *Laws of the State of New York . . . 28 Sess.* (1805) in *Children and Youth in America: A Documentary History*, vol. 2, edited by Robert H. Bremner (Cambridge, Mass.: Harvard University Press, 1970), pp. 515–522.

61. From a teacher's "Manual" published by the Public School Society (1830) quoted in *Children and Youth in America: A Documentary History*, vol. 1, edited by Robert H. Bremner (Cambridge, Mass.: Harvard University Press, 1970), pp. 259–60.

62. Smith, "Protestant Schooling and American Nationality, 1800–1850," p. 691.

63. Theron Baldwin, quoted ibid. One state superintendent of schools viewed public schools as "the noblest legacy bequeathed by Christian learning to the nation and the age" (Newton Batemen, quoted ibid., p. 694).

64. Seymour, *From Sunday School to Church School*, p. ix.

65. Lynn and Wright, *The Big Little School*, p. 69.

66. Ibid.

67. Ibid., pp. 82–83.

68. Ibid., p. 63.

69. Ibid., p. 64.

70. Lankard, *A History of the American Sunday School Curriculum*, pp. 201, 270.

71. Ibid., p. 263.

72. Karpowitz, "A Conceptualization of the American Family," p. 30.

73. Cable, *The Little Darlings*, p. 90.

74. John S. C. Abbott, *The Mother at Home* (New York: American Tract Society, 1833), p. 25.

75. Ibid., pp. 27f.

76. Ibid., p. 39.

77. Ibid., p. 40

78. Ibid., p. 61.

79. Ibid., p. 62.

80. Theodore Dwight, Jr., *The Father's Book, or, Suggestions for the Government and Instruction of Young Children, on Principles Appropriate to a Christian Country* (Springfield, Mass.: G & C Merriam, 1834), p. 31.

81. Ibid., pp. 117–118.

82. Tipping his hat to the fashions of the day, he states that "every judicious parent will endeavor to render punishment of any kind unnecessary; but yet will not shrink from administering it when duty imperiously requires. . . . The child must be his own chief

disciplinarian through life, and the art of self-government must be taught him, as a regular part of his education, and that both by precept and example. Not a hasty expression, not a step, nor a motion, nor a look, ought ever to be seen in the parent, indicative of passion. The constant study of a model of self-possession in a father, or a mother, will do more to control the temper of a child, than any series of punishments" (ibid., p. 112).

83. Cable, *The Little Darlings*, p. 98.

84. Ibid., p. 99.

85. Hammer and Turner, *Parenting in Contemporary Society*, p. 25.

86. As Joseph Kett noted in his discussion of Bushnell and Beecher, "These genres began to pay far more attention than previously to the conditioning role of family environment and to the humble and ordinary events of childhood as shaping forces of development" (Kett, *Rites of Passage*, p. 116).

87. Quoted in Cable, *The Little Darlings*, p. 101.

88. Quoted ibid., p. 102.

89. Ibid., p. 100.

90. Smith, "Protestant Schooling and American Nationality, 1800–1850," p. 687.

91. A 1929 *Saturday Evening Post* article once described the tremendous influence of McGuffey's Readers: "For seventy-five years his [McGuffey's] system and his books guided the minds of four-fifths of the school children of the nation in their taste for literature, in their morality, in their social development and next to the Bible in their religion." (John H. Westerhoff, *McGuffey and His Readers: Piety, Morality and Education in Nineteenth Century America* [Nashville: Abingdon, 1978], p. 15.)

92. Ibid., p. 76.

93. W. H. McGuffey, *The Eclectic First Reader* (1836, reprint, Milford, Mich.: Mott Media, 1982), pp. 118–120.

94. Westerhoff, *McGuffey and His Readers*, p. 15.

95. Ibid., p. 20.

96. As Westerhoff notes, "the theistic Calvinist world view so dominant in the first editions had disappeared, and the prominent values of salvation, righteousness, and piety were entirely missing. All that remained were lessons affirming the morality and life-style of the emerging middle class and those cultural beliefs, attitudes, and values that undergird American civil religion" (ibid., p. 15).

97. David Tyack, Thomas James, and Aaron Benavot, *Law and the Shaping of Public Education, 1785–1954* (Madison: University of Wisconsin Press, 1987), pp. 100–102.

98. Horace Mann, *The Twelfth Annual Report to the Massachusetts Board of Education* (Boston, 1848).

99. Neil McCluskey, *Public Schools in Moral Education* (New York: Columbia University Press, 1958), pp. 145–146.

100. Horace Mann, *Tenth Annual Report to the Massachusetts Board of Education* (1847) cited in Bremner, ed., *Children and Youth in America*, vol. 1, p. 456.

101. Emirbayer, "Moral Education in America, 1930–1990," p. 100.

102. See Jesse Flanders, *Legislative Control of the Elementary Curriculum* (New York: Bureau of Publications, Teachers College, Columbia University, 1925).

103. Ibid., p. 153.

104. Ibid.

105. Ibid., p. 159.

106. Ibid., p. 160.

107. See David Tyack, "Onward Christian Soldiers: Religion and the American Common School," in *History and Education*, edited by Paul Nash (New York: Random House, 1970), pp. 221–226, 241–242.

108. McCluskey, *Public Schools in Moral Education*, p. 29.

109. See Carl F. Kaestle, *Pillars of the Republic: Common Schools and American Society, 1780–1860* (New York: Hill and Wang, 1983), p. 104. This Boston minister was not by any means alone. A county commissioner of schools in Massachusetts wrote in his annual report in 1861 that "in our fear of sectarianism we are in danger of pushing all religious and even moral culture, out of our schools, thus leaving the children, so far as the school is concerned, without any fixed principles to guide them."

110. Boylan, *Sunday School*, pp. 54–57.

111. Boston Schoolmasters, *Remarks on the Seventh Annual Report of the Honorable Horace Mann* (Boston, 1844), pp. 128–131. Emphasis in the original.

112. Emirbayer, "Moral Education in America, 1930–1990," p. 102.

Chapter Four

1. D. Starke, *Character: How to Strengthen It* (New York: Funk and Wagnalls Company, 1916), p. 14.

2. Ralph Waldo Emerson, "Character," in *Essays* (New York: Houghton, Mifflin and Company, 1904), pp. 89–115.

3. James Russell Miller, *The Building of Character* (New York: Thomas Y. Crowell Company, 1894). Selections quoted are from pages 1–7. This active religious humanism was also expressed in Booker T. Washington's Sunday evening addresses at Tuskegee Institute published under the title of *Character Building* (New York: Doubleday, Page and Company, 1902).

4. See, for example, Starke, *Character: How to Strengthen It*, p. 14. This booklet was part of a line of publications Funk and Wagnalls published called the "Mental Efficiency Series."

5. Edward O. Sisson, *The Essentials of Character: A Practical Study of the Aim of Moral Education* (New York: Macmillan, 1910), p. 3.

6. Starke, *Character: How to Strengthen It*, p. 15. Emphasis added.

7. Ibid., p. 19.

8. William J. Hutchins, "The Children's Morality Code," *Journal of the National Educational Association* 13 (1924), p. 292.

9. Howard Hopkins, *History of the Y.M.C.A. in North America* (New York: Association Press, 1951), p. 5; Laurence Doggett, *History of the Young Men's Christian Association* (New York: International Committee of the Young Men's Christian Association, 1896), p. 47.

10. This was a summary statement from *U.S. Department of the Interior, Bureau of Education Report*, 1923, pp. 21, 26. The report states further that "the association seeks,

through its training system and the summer conferences, to help women and girls to a better understanding of how to use the Bible, and to apply its teachings to personal, social, and international life today" (p. 21).

11. Sir Robert Baden-Powell, founder of the Scouting movement, observed a number of "chinks" in a young person's education that school and home did not adequately address. These were character, physical health, service to others, and the learning of a handicraft for making a career. See Judith Erickson, "Non-formal Education in Organizations for American Youth," *Children Today*, January-February 1986, pp. 17–25.

12. Michael Rosenthall, *The Character Factory* (New York: Pantheon Books, 1986), p. 2.

13. From *The Training of a Working Boy*, 1914, quoted ibid. Writing of adult society's "duty to children" in 1908, Judge Ben Lindsey, Judge of the Juvenile Court of Denver, Colorado, expressed a similar sentiment even more boldly: "In the bosom of the American home is the little child, and there also is the State; for the child is the State, and the State is the child. Preserve the child and indeed you shall preserve the State, for the citizenship of tomorrow will take care of itself" (B. B. Lindsey, "How We are Injuring Our Children," *Ladies Home Journal*, October 1908, p. 28).

14. David I. Macleod, *Building Character in the American Boy: The Boy Scouts, YMCA, and their Forerunners, 1870–1920* (Madison: University of Wisconsin Press, 1983), p. 29.

15. Quoted in Rosenthal, *The Character Factory*, p. 6.

16. W. J. Hoxie, *How Girls Can Help Their Country* (New York: Knickerbocker Press, 1913), p. v.

17. Juliette Low, "Girl Scouts as an Educational Force," *U.S. Department of the Interior, Bureau of Education Bulletin*, no. 33 (1919), p. 3.

18. Hoxie, *How Girls Can Help Their Country*, p. 12. Emphasis in the original.

19. All of these quotes are taken from ibid., pp. 13–14.

20. In *Building Character in the American Boy*, MacLeod highlights this essentially Protestant concern in the development of American youth organizations founded at the beginning of the twentieth century. Even the Boys' Clubs of America whose main purpose was more geared toward keeping poor urban boys off the streets had intertwined "Christian and philanthropic motives." Though building character was not their main objective at least some of the early clubs evangelized openly. According to Macleod, "changes in the 1900s and 1910s brought them closer to the character builders" (p. 69). However, it appears as though "keeping boys busy" with recreational activities and alternatives to the vices of street life has remained the main objective of the Boys' Club movement.

21. Norman E. Richardson and Ormond E. Loomis, *The Boy Scout Movement Applied by the Church* (New York: Charles Scribner's Sons, 1915).

22. David Macleod, "Act Your Age," *Journal of Social History* 16, no. 2 (Winter 1982), p. 7.

23. All of these quotes are taken from Hoxie, *How Girls Can Help Their Country*, pp. 117–118.

24. Luther Halsey Gulick, "The Camp Fire Girls and the New Relation of Women to the World," *National Education Association, General Session* (1912), p. 327.

25. Kaestle's discussion was very helpful here. See Carl Kaestle, "Moral Education and Common Schools in America: A Historian's View," *The Journal of Moral Education* 13, no. 2 (May 1984), p. 103.

26. See, for example, Dewey's "Credo," *Forum* 83 (March 1930), pp. 176–182. Neil McCluskey's *Public Schools and Moral Education* (New York: Columbia University Press, 1958) was enormously helpful in framing this discussion.

27. Dewey, "Credo," p. 176. Emphasis added.

28. John Dewey, *The Study of Ethics: A Syllabus* (Ann Arbor: Register Publishing Co., 1894), pp. 280–281.

29. John Dewey, *Human Nature and Conduct* (New York: Modern Library, 1922), p. 37.

30. John Dewey, *Democracy and Education* (New York: Macmillan, 1916), p. 143.

31. The intelligent control of these experiences is what he called a reflective or scientific ethics. For Dewey, "ethical competence is achieved by reflecting on one's actual, concrete experience" (Richard H. Hersh, John P. Miller, and Glen D. Fielding, *Models of Moral Education* [New York: Longman, 1980], p. 21). By extension, the central element of Dewey's concept of moral education was his emphasis on experience.

32. McCluskey makes this point. See *Public Schools and Moral Education*, p. 266.

33. John Dewey, *The School and Society* (Chicago: University of Chicago Press, 1900), pp. 3–4.

34. John Dewey, "Teaching Ethics in the High School," *Educational Review* 7 (November 1893), p. 315.

35. Robert Church, "Moral Education in the Schools," in *Morality Examined*, edited by Lindley J. Stiles and Bruce D. Johnson (Princeton: Princeton Book Company, 1977), p. 72.

36. Ibid., p. 75.

37. Hersh, Miller, and Fielding, *Models of Moral Education*, p. 20.

38. John Dewey and Evelyn Dewey, *Schools of Tomorrow*, pp. 303–316, reprinted in Robert H. Bremner, ed., *Children and Youth in America*, vol. 2 (Cambridge, Mass.: Harvard University Press, 1970), p. 1129.

39. This was the point of an article by Boyd H. Bode, "The New Education Ten Years After," *New Republic* 63 (1930). See p. 63.

40. All quotations in this paragraph are taken from National Education Association, Educational Policies Commission, *Moral and Spiritual Values in the Public Schools* (Washington, D.C.: National Education Association, 1951), pp. 4, 6, 12, 18–19, 33, 34, 52.

41. As the text reads, "The basic moral and spiritual value in American life is the supreme importance of the individual personality. . . . It implies that each human being should have every possible opportunity to achieve by his own efforts a feeling of security and competence in dealing with the problems arising in daily life. It implies also that self-realization cannot be fully achieved without social relationships based on moral and spiritual values" (ibid., p. 18).

42. Ibid., p. 19.

43. Ibid., p. 38. Emphasis in the original.

44. Ibid., p. 48.

45. Kate Wiggin, *Children's Rights: A Book of Nursery Logic* (Boston: Houghton Mifflin and, 1892), p. 19.

46. Ibid., pp. 118, 122, 150, 152.

47. Ibid., pp. 18–19.

48. Ibid., pp. 10, 15, 18–19.

49. Ibid., pp. 46, 118, 122, 162. Emphasis added.

50. Ibid., p. 120.

51. The concept is most exhaustively developed in his two volume set, *Adolescence*, first published in 1905 (New York: D. Appleton and Company).

52. Ibid, p. 301.

53. Steven L. Schlossman, "Before Home Start: Notes toward a History of Parent Education in America, 1897–1929," *Harvard Educational Review* 46 (1976), p. 443.

54. Hersh, Miller, and Fielding, *Models of Moral Education*, p. 19.

55. Emirbayer describes the unintended consequences of the common school movement in this way: "Crusaders for common schooling had set out with the goal of creating a 'sacred counter-center' of society; paradoxically, however, their efforts culminated in the teaching of moral and civic virtues quite different from any which they might originally have aspired to cultivate" (Mustafa Kemal Emirbayer, "Moral Education in America, 1830–1990: A Contribution to the Sociology of Moral Education" [Ph.D. diss., Cambridge, Mass.: Harvard University, October 1989 (University Microfilms International, Dissertation Information Services, Ann Arbor, 1990)], p. 102).

56. Robert W. Lynn and Elliot Wright, *The Big Little School: Sunday Child of American Protestantism* (New York: Harper and Row, 1971), pp. 84–85.

57. Ibid., p. 85.

58. George A. Coe, "What is Pragmatism?" *The Methodist Quarterly Review* 57 (April 1908), p. 218.

59. Ibid., p. 217.

60. Heather A. Warren, "Character, Public Schooling, and Religious Education, 1920–1934," *Religion and American Culture* 7, no. 1 (Winter 1997), p. 65.

61. Walter Athearn, *Character Building in a Democracy* (New York: Macmillan Company, 1924), p. 123, quoted ibid. Emphasis in the original.

62. See Mary Cable, *The Little Darlings: A History of Child Rearing in America* (New York: Scribner, 1975), p. 164.

63. Differing markedly in his opinion and advice was the famous psychologist John B. Watson. Watson felt parents gave children too much love and coddling, and encouraged a more behavioral approach to the training of children. For Watson, too much coddling results in harmful consequences in adult life. "Nearly all of us have suffered from over-coddling in our infancy. How does it show? It shows in individualism" (John B. Watson, *Psychological Care of Infant and Child* [New York: W. W. Norton and Company, Inc., 1928], p. 76). He goes so far as to say, "never hug and kiss [your children], never let them sit in your lap. . . . Shake hands with them in the morning . . . put [the child] in the backyard a large part of the day" (p. 81). He sums up his admonition against loving motherly care by encouraging parents to remember that "mother love is a dangerous instrument. . . . An instrument which may inflict a never healing wound, a wound which may make infancy unhappy, adolescence a nightmare, an instrument which may wreck your adult son or daughter's vocational future and their chances for marital happiness." According to

Cable, Watson's ideas were widely disseminated, and were greeted with enthusiasm by parents and child-care professionals. See Cable, *The Little Darlings*, pp. 176–177.

64. Ruth Wendell Washburn, *Children Have Their Reasons* (New York: Appleton-Century, 1942), p. 13.

65. Dorothy Baruch Miller, "New vs. Old Ways in Discipline," *Parents Magazine*, March 1949, p. 119.

66. Sara Lewis, "If Your Youngster Lies, Cheats, Steals . . . " *Better Homes and Gardens*, May 1950, pp. 271, 272, 273.

67. Miriam P. Dunham, "Is Punishment Really Necessary?" *Parents Magazine*, September 1950, p. 84.

68. Morris W. Brody, "Teaching a Child to Behave," *Parents Magazine*, September 1949, p. 112.

69. Rhoda Bacmeister, "What Builds Character?" *Parents Magazine*, February 1950, p. 49.

70. Gladys G. Jenkins, "Character Begins at Home: Old Ideas of Character Building Have Given Place to New Ones that Parents Need to Understand," *Parents Magazine*, February 1949, pp. 36, 83.

71. Bacmeister, "What Builds Character?" p. 104.

72. Brody, "Teaching a Child to Behave," p. 35.

73. Marie Coleman, "Loving Children Wisely and Well," *Parents Magazine*, December 1950, p. 143.

74. Gladys Toler Burris, "Children Want and Need Rules," *Parents Magazine*, June 1949, p. 85.

75. As Betty Sichel noted, when comparing the two editions of Dewey and Tuft's *Ethics*, published in 1908 and revised in 1932, the concept of character does not retain the same role and importance in both editions. "It almost seems that Dewey gradually eliminated the notion 'character' and wholly relies instead on habit, reflective thinking, and intelligence" (Betty Sichel, *Moral Education: Character, Community, and Ideals* [Philadelphia: Temple University Press, 1988], p. 60).

76. For instance, in the early 1920s, the National Education Association commissioned a six-year inquiry into the effectiveness of character-education programs. See the U.S. Department of the Interior, Bureau of Education, "Character: Report of the Committee on Character Education of the NEA," *U.S. Department of the Interior, Bureau of Education Bulletin* no. 7 (1926), pp. 23–27.

77. See Hugh Hartshorne and Mark May, *Studies in the Nature of Character*, vol. 1, *Studies in Deceit* (New York: Macmillan, 1928); Hugh Hartshorne and Mark May, *Studies in the Nature of Character*, vol. 2, *Studies in Service and Self-Control* (New York: Macmillan, 1929); and Hugh Hartshorne and Mark May, *Studies in the Nature of Character*, vol. 3, *Studies in the Organization of Character* (New York: Macmillan, 1930).

78. Gordon W. Allport, *Personality: A Psychological Interpretation* (New York: Henry Holt and Company, 1937), p. 52.

79. G. Stanley Hall, *Adolescence*, vol. 2, p. 301. My colleague, Joseph F. Kett, explores the connection between religious experience and developmental psychology at some length in his essay, "Adolescence and Youth in Nineteenth-Century America," in *The*

Family in History, edited by Theodore K. Rabb and Robert I. Rotberg (New York: Harper and Row, 1973), p. 95.

80. Erik Erikson, *Identity and the Life Cycle* (New York: W. W. Norton, 1980), pp. 67–77.

81. Rudolf Dreikurs, *Children: The Challenge* (New York: E. P. Dutton, 1964), p. 292.

82. Ibid., p. 291.

83. Ibid.

84. Erickson, "Non-formal Education in Organizations for American Youth," p. 21.

85. The Laws according to the 1920 *Girl Scout Handbook* were as follows: 1. A Girl Scout's honor is to be trusted. 2. A Girl Scout is loyal. 3. A Girl Scout's duty is to be useful and to help others. 4. A Girl Scout is a friend to all, and a sister to every other Girl Scout. 5. A Girl Scout is courteous. 6. A Girl Scout is a friend to animals. 7. A Girl Scout obeys orders. 8. A Girl Scout is cheerful. 9. A Girl Scout is thrifty. 10. A Girl Scout is clean in thought, word, and deed (Girl Scouts of the USA, *Girl Scouts Handbook* [New York: Girls Scouts of the USA, 1920], pp. 3, 12).

86. Girl Scouts of the USA, *Girl Scout Handbook*, 2d. ed. (New York: Girl Scouts of the USA, 1948), p. 8. Emphasis added.

87. Girl Scouts of the USA, *National Council Meeting Workbook/Guide* (New York: Girl Scouts of the USA, 1972), p. 24.

88. Girl Scouts of the USA, *Girl Scout Handbook* (New York: Girl Scouts of the USA, 1929), p. 268.

89. Girl Scouts of the USA, *Girl Scout Handbook*, 2d. ed., p. 10.

90. Girl Scouts of the USA, *National Council Meeting Workbook/Guide*, p. 24.

91. Ibid., p. 23.

92. Eisenhower quoted in Kaestle, "Moral Education and Common Schools in America," p. 107.

93. Hersh, Miller, and Fielding, *Models of Moral Education*, p. 23.

94. H. Warren Button and Eugene E. Provenzo, *History of Education and Culture in America* (New York: Allyn and Bacon, 1989), p. 313.

95. See *Engel v. Vitale*, 370 U.S. 421 (1962) and *School District of Abington Township, Pa. v. Schemp/Murray v. Curlett*, 374 U.S. 203 (1963).

96. See M. A. McGheney, "Control of the Curriculum," in *The Courts and Education*, edited by Clifford P. Hooker (Chicago: University of Chicago Press, 1978).

97. Idaho State Law (1919), § 944.

98. Idaho State Law (1963), § 33–1224. See James L. Nolan, *The Therapeutic State* (New York: New York University Press, 1998), pp. 146–147.

99. Theodore R. Sizer and Nancy F. Sizer, eds., *Moral Education: Five Lectures* (Cambridge, Mass.: Harvard University Press, 1970).

100. The compatibility is at several levels—they share assumptions about the authority of the autonomous self, the prime importance of rationality in making moral decisions, and the priority of processes over content in determining values among other matters. I explore this further in the next two chapters.

101. Louis Raths, Merrill Harmin, and Sidney Simon, *Values and Teaching* (Columbus, Ohio: C. E. Merrill Publishing Co., 1966).

102. In emphasizing values rooted in and determined by the individual and his experience and rational reflection, as well as the importance of democratic settings, one can see the clear influence of Dewey and the early twentieth-century progressives. Indeed, the authors explicitly draw from Dewey's essay, "Theory of Valuation" and his *Moral Principles in Education* in their work. The influence of Carl Rodgers is seen in the authors' emphasis on the need to help people become more positive and self-directed, and to create an "accepting" and "encouraging" environment where the facilitator values the person's ideas and feelings, won't give advice, and above all shuns moralizing. Here too the authors explicitly cite Rodgers's *On Becoming a Person* as a complementary source. See Louis Raths, Merrill Harmin, and Sidney Simon, *Values and Teaching,* 2d. ed. (Columbus, Ohio: C. E. Merrill Publishing Co., 1978), p. 11. Alan Lockwood goes so far as to argue that "the similarities between client-centered therapy and values clarification are significant enough to conclude that values clarification is, in essence, a form of client-centered therapy" (A. L. Lockwood, "A Critical View of Values Clarification," in *Moral Education,* edited by David Urpel and Kevin Ryan [Berkeley, Calif.: McCutchan Publishing Corporation, 1976], p. 164).

103. Merrill Harmin, Howard Kirschenbaum, and Sidney Simon, *Clarifying Values Through Subject Matter* (Minneapolis: Winston Press, Inc., 1973), p. 31.

104. Raths, Harmin, and Simon, *Values and Teaching,* p. 4.

105. Sidney Simon, Leland W. Howe, and Howard Kirschenbaum, *Values Clarification,* rev. ed. (New York: Hart, 1978), back cover.

106. Harmin, Kirschenbaum, and Simon, *Clarifying Values Through Subject Matter,* pp. 34–35.

107. Simon, Howe, and Kirschenbaum, *Values Clarification,* back cover; see also pp. 18–22. Emphasis in the original.

108. Howard Kirschenbaum, *Advanced Value Clarification* (La Jolla, Calif.: University Associates, 1977), p. 21.

109. Raths, Harmin, and Simon, *Values and Teaching,* pp. 27–28.

110. Gordon M. Hart, *Values Clarification for Counselors* (Springfield, Ill.: Charles C. Thomas, 1978), p. 24.

111. Ibid.

112. Harmin, Kirschenbaum, and Simon, *Clarifying Values Through Subject Matter,* p. 33.

113. Hart, *Values Clarification for Counselors,* p. 23.

114. Ibid., p. 24.

115. Maury Smith, *A Practical Guide to Value Clarification* (La Jolla: University Associates, 1977), p. 5.

116. Raths, Harmin, and Simon, *Values and Teaching,* p. 41.

117. Ibid., p. 12.

118. Ibid., p. 81.

119. Ibid., p. 26.

120. Ibid., p. 4.

121. Ibid., pp. 48–49.

122. Quoted in *The Boston Recorder,* 14 January 1847.

123. The statement is made by Mathew Hale Smith in a sermon collected in his book, *The Bible, the Rod, and Religion in Common Schools* (Boston: Redding and Co., 1847), pp. 48–49.

124. Robert S. Michaelsen quoted in Kaestle, "Moral Education and Common Schools in America," p. 106.

Chapter Five

1. With the important exception of the work of Gareth Matthews, who has shown us how earnestly even young children, hardly old enough to attend school, search for moral truths. See Gareth Matthews, *The Philosophy of Childhood* (Cambridge: Harvard University Press, 1994); *Dialogues with Children* (Cambridge: Harvard University Press, 1984); *Philosophy and the Young Child* (Cambridge: Harvard University Press, 1980).

2. See Phillipe Aries in his *Centuries of Childhood* (New York: Vintage, 1962).

3. Jean Piaget, *The Moral Judgment of the Child* (New York: Free Press, 1969), p. 122.

4. Lawrence Kohlberg, "Education for Justice: A Modern Statement of the Platonic View," in *Moral Education: Five Lectures*, edited by Theodore R. Sizer and Nancy F. Sizer (Cambridge, Mass.: Harvard University Press, 1970), p. 58.

5. Ibid.

6. In formulating his developmental scheme, Kohlberg and his colleagues posed a number of hypothetical moral dilemmas to youngsters, in order to see how they would respond. The most famous of these quandaries involved a man named Heinz whose wife was dying of cancer. A pharmacist in town had discovered the drug that would cure this cancer, but was charging an exorbitant fee for it. Heinz not only could not afford the cost but was not able to borrow the money from friends and acquaintances. He begged the pharmacist to sell the drug for less but the druggist refused. In his desperation, Heinz stole the drug. Kohlberg then asked, Did Heinz do the right thing—and if so, why? See F. Clark Power, Ann Higgins, and Lawrence Kohlberg, *Lawrence Kohlberg's Approach to Moral Education* (New York: Columbia University Press, 1989), pp. 243–244.

7. As Richard Shweder put it in his review of Kohlberg's *The Philosophy of Moral Development*, "what Kohlberg seeks is a conceptualization of what is moral derived from premises that no rational person could possibly deny by means that no rational person could possibly avoid—preferably deductive logic" (Richard Shweder, "Liberalism as Destiny," *Contemporary Psychology* 27, no. 6 [1982], p. 422).

8. More recent research has focused upon the cognitive dimensions of emotion, particularly in the neurophysiological aspects of emotions (e.g., the biochemical reactions in the brain when one feels, say, anger or elation), and in the peculiar behavioral expressions of emotions (such as knitting one's brow when one is worried or breaking into a smile when one is happy). Indeed, they view emotions as a kind of cognitive process, a "hot cognition" as some call it. See Jerome Kagan's essay, "The Idea of Emotion in Human Development," in *Emotions, Cognitions and Behavior*, edited by Carroll E. Izard, Jerome Kagan, and Robert B. Zajonc (Cambridge: Cambridge University Press, 1984), p. 69. This volume provides the most comprehensive treatment of the subject.

9. Bettie B. Youngs, "Self-Esteem in the School," *NAASP Bulletin*, January 1993, p. 59.

10. Ibid., pp. 59–60.

11. Ibid., pp. 65–66. So too, Virginia Noiles, the early childhood coordinator at the E. B. Newton School in Winthrop, Massachusetts, states that "it's a documented fact that a child with high intelligence but low self-esteem will not achieve as well as a child with average ability and high self-esteem . . . Children with higher self-esteems are more likely to be risk takers" (Marie C. Franklin, "Building Self-Esteem: Educators Say Good Self-image Boosts Performance," *Boston Globe*, 8 November 1992, p. 43). Still another advocate discussing how to prevent students from dropping out of school writes, "often children are not promoted because they lack the needed reading skills. Therefore, this problem must be addressed in the early years. In addition to carefully selecting the instructional strategy, the teacher must concentrate on building the child's self-esteem" (Ann F. Reitzammer, "Dropout Prevention: The Early Years," *Reading Improvement* 28, no. 4 [Winter 1991], p. 255).

12. Merrie Harrison, seventh-grade teacher, quoted in Romesh Ratnesar, "Teaching Feelings 101," *Time*, 29 September 1997, p. 62.

13. Designed by Don Dinkmeyer and published by American Guidance Service (AGS) based in Circle Pines, Minnesota.

14. Don Dinkmeyer, Sr., and Don Dinkmeyer, Jr., *DUSO–1*, teacher's guide, rev. ed. (Circle Pines, Minn.: American Guidance Service, 1982), p. 7.

15. Don Dinkmeyer, Sr., and Don Dinkmeyer, Jr., "Tell Me About DUSO," informational pamphlet (Circle Pines, Minn.: American Guidance Service, 1991).

16. See Dinkmeyer, Sr., and Dinkmeyer, Jr., "Unit 1: Developing Understanding of Self," in *DUSO–1*, pp. 43–124.

17. Dinkmeyer, Sr., and Dinkmeyer, Jr., "Tell Me About DUSO."

18. Dinkmeyer, Sr., and Dinkmeyer, Jr., *DUSO–1*, p. 12.

19. See Dinkmeyer, Sr., and Dinkmeyer, Jr., "Unit 1: Developing Understanding of Self," in *DUSO–1*, pp. 65–84.

20. See Dinkmeyer, Sr., and Dinkmeyer, Jr., "Unit 3: Developing Understanding of Choices," in *DUSO–1*, pp. 228–247.

21. Dinkmeyer, Sr., and Dinkmeyer, Jr., *DUSO–1*, p. 66.

22. Dinkmeyer, Sr., and Dinkmeyer, Jr., "Tell Me About DUSO."

23. This is a nonprofit educational organization founded in 1975 with resources from the W. K. Kellogg Foundation. In 1984, Lions Clubs International, the largest service organization in the world, made the Lions-Quest (SFA) program for middle schools the primary component of its international drug prevention efforts. See Quest International, "Frequently Asked Questions," undated, p. 1.

24. Initial information came from Quest International, "Summary of Evaluation Results," undated. This was updated in a telephone interview, 14 July 1999.

25. Ibid., p. 4.

26. Quest International, *Skills for Adolescence* (Granville, Ohio: Quest International, 1988), section III–11.

27. Ibid., section III–3.

28. Ibid., section III–8.

29. Ibid., section II–9. Why is self-confidence in this curriculum so important? "People who feel good about themselves tend to: *Be aware of their positive traits; *Stand up for what they believe; *Say "No" when pressured to do things they think are dangerous, unhealthy, or not in their best interest; *Keep themselves healthy; *Work hard to achieve goals; *Respect themselves and others; *Accept responsibility for their actions" (section II–13).

30. Ibid., section II–9.

31. Ibid., section III–5.

32. James L. Nolan, Jr., "Public Education," chap. 5 in *The Therapeutic State* (New York: New York University Press, 1998).

33. The Commission's thirty-five members represent a broad range of educational, political, religious, and business interests as well as concerned parents. The Commission met from September 1987 to 1988.

34. Commission of Values-Centered Goals for the District of Columbia Public Schools, *Final Report of the Commission of Values-Centered Goals for the District of Columbia Public Schools*, 1988, pp. 3, 4.

35. Ibid.

36. Ibid., p. 16.

37. Quoted in John Leo, "Sex in Schools," *Time*, 24 November 1986, p. 55.

38. See, for example, the publication of the U.S. Department of Health, Education, and Welfare, "Implementing DHEW Policy on Family Planning" (Washington, D.C.: GPO, 1966).

39. These guidelines were updated in 1996.

40. "Sex Education: Too Little, Too Late," *New York Times*, 22 May 1989, p. A16.

41. These curriculum guidelines were revised by the state's Department of Education in 1983 and again in 1988.

42. Virginia Department of Education, *Family Life Education: Curriculum Guidelines*, rev. ed. (Richmond, Virginia: Commonwealth of Virginia, Department of Education, 1983), p. 1.

43. Ibid., p. 9.

44. Ibid., p. 19.

45. Ibid., pp. 19–20.

46. Ibid., p. 27.

47. Ibid., pp. 32–33.

48. Teen-Aid, *Me, My World, My Future* (Spokane, Wash.: Teen-Aide, Inc.), p. 128. This curriculum is used in all fifty states by more than 100,000 parents and teenagers.

49. CHEF, "Here's Looking at You, 2000," promotional brochure (Seattle, Wash.: CHEF, 1990).

50. Natural Helpers, "Overview of the *Natural Helpers* Program," information sheet, undated, pp. 1–2.

51. Richard R. Clayton et al., "DARE (Drug Abuse Resistance Education): Very Popular But Not Very Effective," in *Intervening with Drug-Involved Youth*, edited by Clyde B. McCoy, Lisa R. Metsch, and James A. Inciardi (Thousand Oaks, Calif.: SAGE Publications, 1996), pp. 101–102.

52. See, for example, Haim Ginott, "Parent Education Groups in a Child Guidance Clinic," *Mental Hygiene* 41 (1957), pp. 82–86; Haim Ginott, *Group Psychotherapy with Children* (New York: McGraw-Hill, 1961); Haim Ginott, *Between Parent and Child: New Solutions to Old Problems* (New York: McGraw-Hill, 1965); Thomas Gordon, *Parent Effectiveness Training: The 'No-lose' Program for Raising Responsible Children* (New York: P. H. Wyden, 1970); Thomas Gordon, "The Case of Disciplining Children at Home or in School," *Person-Centered-Review* 3, no. 1 (February 1988), pp. 59–85.

53. See Lee and Marlene Canter, *Assertive Discipline: Competency-Based Resource Materials and Guidelines* (Santa Monica, Calif.: Lee Canter and Associates, Inc., 1979); Lee Canter, "Competency-Based Approach to Discipline—It's Assertive," *Thrust for Educational Leadership* 8, no. 3 (January 1979), pp. 11–13; Lee Canter, "You Can Do It! Discipline," *Instructor* 89, no. 2 (September 1979), pp. 106–108, 110, 112; Lee Canter, "Assertive Discipline," *Phi Delta Kappan* 71, no. 1 (September 1989), pp. 57–61.

54. The assertive-discipline approach remained part of the mix for two decades but not without considerable criticism. See, for example, Marilyn Watson, "Classroom Control: To What Ends? At What Price?" *California Journal of Teacher Education* 9, no. 4 (Fall 1982), pp. 75–95 and Vincent Crockenberg, "Assertive Discipline: A Dissent," *California Journal of Teacher Education* 9, no. 4 (Fall 1982), pp. 59–74.

55. "I have been haunted," she wrote in the Preface to the American edition of *For Your Own Good*, "by the question of what could make a person conceive the plan of gassing millions of human beings to death and of how it could then be possible for millions of others to acclaim him and assist in carrying out this plan" (Alice Miller, *For Your Own Good*, trans. Hildegarde and Hunter Hannun [New York: Farrar, Straus and Giroux, 1983], p. vii).

56. Ibid.

57. Ibid., p. 67.

58. Ibid., p. 187.

59. Ibid., p. 90.

60. Ibid., pp. 65f.

61. Ibid., p. 146.

62. Alice Miller, *Thou Shalt Not Be Aware: Society's Betrayal of the Child*, trans. Hildegarde and Hunter Hannun (New York: Farrar, Straus and Giroux, 1998), p. 18.

63. She borrows this term from Morton Schatzman, *Soul Murder: Persecution in the Family* (New York: Random House, 1973).

64. As Miller writes, "The reader will have noticed long before now that all pedagogy is pervaded by the precepts of 'poisonous pedagogy,' no matter how well they may be concealed today. . . . My antipedagogic position is not directed against a specific type of pedagogical ideology but against all pedagogical ideology per se, even if it is of an anti-authoritarian nature" (Miller, *For Your Own Good*, p. 96).

65. Here I draw upon the relationship explored in summary fashion by Dana Mack, "Are Parents Bad for Children?" *Commentary* 97, no., 3 (March 1994), pp. 30–35.

66. Ibid., p. 33.

67. Don Dinkmeyer, Sr., Gary McKay, and Don Dinkmeyer, Jr., STEP *Leader's Resource Guide* (Circle Pines, Minn.: American Guidance Services, 1997), p. 5.

68. Inga Weberg, American Guidance Services, interview by author, Circle Pines, Minn., 15 July 1997.

69. Dinkmeyer, McKay, and Dinkmeyer, STEP *Leader's Resource Guide*, p. 14.

70. Don Dinkmeyer, Sr., Gary D. McKay, and Don Dinkmeyer, Jr. *The Parent's Handbook: Systematic Training for Effective Parenting* (Circle Pines, Minn.: American Guidance Services, 1997), p. 37. Emphasis in the original.

71. Ibid., p. 68. Emphasis in the original.

72. Ibid., pp. 52–53.

73. Ibid.

74. Ibid., pp. 104–107.

75. Don Dinkmeyer and Gary McKay, *Raising a Responsible Child: Practical Steps to Successful Family Relationships*, rev. ed. (New York: Fireside, 1996).

76. Fitzhugh Dodson, "6 Easy Ways to Get Kids to Behave," *Redbook*, July 1987, p. 136.

77. Fred Rogers, "You Can Be a More Sensitive Parent," *Redbook*, April 1987, p. 88.

78. Ibid. Emphasis in the original.

79. Ron Levant, Associate Professor of Counseling Psychology at Boston University, quoted in Sheila Weller, "How to Help Your Husband be a Better Dad," *Redbook*, January 1988, p. 87.

80. Rogers, "You Can Be a More Sensitive Parent," p. 89. Emphasis in the original.

81. Don Dinkmeyer and Gary McKay, *Raising a Responsible Child: Practical Steps to Successful Family Relationships* (New York: Simon and Schuster, 1973), p. 91.

82. Stephanie Marston, "Feeling Good: Five Ways to Help Build Your Child's Self-Esteem," *Sesame Street Parents' Guide*, October 1990, pp. 28–33.

83. Letitia Baldrige, *More than Manners: Raising Today's Kids to Have Kind Manners and Good Hearts* (New York: Simon and Schuster, 1997), pp. 25–26. These five statements were italicized in the original, presumably for emphasis.

84. Judith B. Erickson, "Non-Formal Education in Organizations for American Youth," *Children Today*, January-February 1986, p. 18.

85. "Multicultural Awareness for First-Grade Brownie Girl Scouts," *Girl Scout Leader*, Summer 1980, p. 5.

86. Quoted in "YMCA of the United States," YMCA program materials (New York: YMCA, 1980).

87. YMCA, "YMCA Youth Sports" (New York: YMCA, undated).

88. Quoted in Jill Tabbutt, "Empowering Teens: The National YWCA's PACT Program," *Siecus Report* 16, no. 2 (November/December 1987), pp. 8–9. It is worth noting that with the Boys Club as well, its "nearly 150,000 volunteers and 9,000 career professionals and staff help young people gain self-esteem and develop the motivation to become productive citizens and leaders (Boys Clubs of America, *Testimony to Boys Clubs: A Report to the Leaders of America compiled by Boys Clubs of America* [New York: Boys Clubs of America, undated], p. 12).

89. Sharon Hussey, Director of Programs for the Girl Scouts. Interview by James L. Nolan, New York, 13 March 1991.

90. Juliette Gordon Low, "How Girls Can Help Their Country," in *Girl Scout Handbook* (New York: Girl Scouts of the USA, 1916), pp. 9–10. Emphasis in the original.

91. Girl Scouts of the USA, "You Make the Difference" in *The Handbook for Cadette and Senior Girl Scouts* (New York: Girl Scouts of the USA, 1980), p. 33.

92. Girl Scouts of the USA, "Spotlight on You" in *Options—A Resource for Senior Scouts* (New York: Girl Scouts of the USA, 1974).

93. Girl Scouts of the USA, "You Make the Difference," pp. 9f. Later in the decade, this goal of "self-awareness" was reworded as "developing self-potential."

94. Girl Scouts of the USA, "Program," Girl Scouts of the USA home page, 22 February 1999, http://www.gsusa.org.

95. All of these quotes are from Girl Scouts of the USA, *The Handbook for Cadette and Senior Girl Scouts* (New York: Girl Scouts of the USA, 1987), pp. 5, 19–23.

96. Girl Scouts of the USA, *The Guide for Cadette and Senior Girl Scout Leaders* (New York: Girl Scouts of the USA, 1995), p. 2. On the off chance that anyone conclude that the concern for self-esteem was losing its appeal, it should be noted that self-esteem remained "the focal point" of this edition of the *Guide*. The reason, according to the manual, is "because of the role self-esteem plays in shaping girls into mature, independent thinkers. The goal is for girls to value themselves and to *act accordingly*" (ibid., p. 29. Emphasis added). The assumptions laden within such a statement are significant. (See Chapter 9.)

97. Such ideals, they explain, have always been implicit in the "traditional" values of service, patriotism, and "spirituality" but "by expressing these values more directly and comprehensively . . . , the girl gains even more insight into who she is and why she is special" (Girl Scouts of the USA, Notes on the "Rewording of the Law," 1996, p. 33).

98. Girl Scouts of the USA, *Girl Scout Handbook* (n.p.: Girl Scouts of the USA, 1913), pp. 5–6.

99. Girl Scouts of the USA, *Girl Scout Handbook* (New York: Girl Scouts of the USA, 1920), p. 9.

100. Edna M. Black, "The Founder and the Laws: The Eighth Law: A Girl Scout is Cheerful," *Girl Scout Leader* 33, no. 8 (Nov. 1956), p. 28.

101. Girl Scouts of the USA, Notes on the "Rewording of the Law," p. 31.

102. Girl Scouts of the USA, "The World of Well-Being" in *The Brownie and Junior Girl Scout Handbook* (New York: Girl Scouts of the USA , 1977), pp. 88–89.

103. Girl Scouts of the USA, *Junior Girl Scout Handbook* (New York: Girl Scouts of the USA, 1986), p. 31.

104. See, for example, Girl Scouts of the USA, *Cadette Girl Scout Handbook* (New York: Girl Scouts of the USA, 1995), pp. 56–57, where in a section entitled, "Your Values," girls are given a chart listing a range of interests from "doing well in school," "caring for the environment," "being active politically," and "volunteering in my community," to "having a boyfriend," "wearing expensive clothes," "earning money," and "being popular." The exercise is to write in "How I feel Now" and how I feel "six months later."

105. Girl Scouts of the USA, *Options: A Resource for Senior Scouts*, p. 19.

106. Ibid.

107. Girl Scouts of the USA, *The Handbook for Cadette and Senior Girl Scouts*, pp. 35, 38, 63.

108. These programmatic goals are found in many of the documents of the organization. Here they are taken from the Girl Scouts of the USA home page, 22 February 1999, http://www.gsusa.org.

109. See, for example, Girl Scouts of the USA, *The Handbook for Cadette and Senior Girl Scouts,* p. 74.

110. The search was through Amazon.com home page, 23 January, 1999, http://www.amazon.com.

Chapter Six

1. Christina Hoff Sommers, "Teaching the Virtues," *The Public Interest* 111 (Spring 1993), pp. 10–11.

2. Edward Wynne and Paul Vitz call this convergence of moral teaching, "the great tradition." For an elaboration of this model, see Edward Wynne and Paul Vitz, "The Major Models of Moral Education: An Evaluation," section 2: part 2, National Institute of Education, *Equity in Values Education,* final report (Washington, D.C.: National Institute of Education, Department of Education, July 1985).

3. Lewis describes the Tao as "the doctrine of objective value," something one gets when one "lumps together . . . the traditional moralities of East and West, the Christian, the pagan, and the Jew." He also equates the Tao with "Natural Law" or "First Principles of Practical Reason." See C. S. Lewis, *The Abolition of Man* (New York: Macmillan, 1947), pp. 29, 56–57.

4. Kevin Ryan, "Character and Coffee Mugs," *Education Week,* 17 May 1995, p. 48.

5. Aristotle, *Nicomachean Ethics,* quoted in Nancy Sherman, *The Fabric of Character: Aristotle's Theory of Virtue* (Oxford: Clarendon Press, 1989), p. 177.

6. Thomas Lickona, *Educating for Character: How Our Schools Can Teach Respect and Responsibility* (New York: Bantam, 1992), p. 51.

7. James Q. Wilson, *On Character* (Washington, D.C.: AEI Press, 1991), p. 108.

8. William Kilpatrick, *Why Johnny Can't Tell Right from Wrong* (New York: Simon and Schuster, 1992), p. 231.

9. Aristotle, *Nicomachean Ethics,* quoted in Sherman, *The Fabric of Character,* pp. 179–180.

10. Mary Riser, "Uncovering the Hidden Curriculum," *Perspectives* (Charlottesville, Va.: St. Anne's-Belfield, May 1996), p. 13.

11. Denis P. Doyle, "Education and Character," *Phi Delta Kappan* 78 (February 1997), p. 442.

12. In the same genre is *Books That Build Character: A Guide to Teaching Your Child Moral Values Through Stories,* edited by William Kilpatrick, Gregory Wolfe, and Suzanne Wolfe (New York: Simon and Schuster, 1994).

13. William J. Bennett, *American Education: Making It Work* excerpted in *Focus on the Family Citizen* 2, no. 9 (September 1988), p. 16. See too, Lynne Cheney, in "The Importance of Stories," *Academic Questions* 4 (Spring 1991).

14. Gary Bauer, "The Moral of the Story: How to Teach Values in the Nation's Classrooms," *Heritage Foundation Policy Review* 38 (Fall 1986), p. 26.

15. Sommers, "Teaching the Virtues," p. 13.

16. Kilpatrick, *Why Johnny Can't Tell Right from Wrong*, p. 197. Kilpatrick has gone so far as to say that "schools can learn a lot from the army," and to acknowledge, with approval, the ways in which schools in the past were "unapologetically authoritarian" (p. 228).

17. Sommers, "Teaching the Virtues," p. 13.

18. William J. Bennett, "Moral Literacy and the Formation of Character," *USA Today* 117, no. 2518 (July 1988), p. 86. Indeed, moral educator Kevin Ryan of Boston University put the matter explicitly when he stated that "our history and our literature contain our moral wisdom and serve as the moral compass that is passed from one generation to the next" (Kevin Ryan, "The New Moral Education," *Phi Delta Kappan* 68, no. 2 [October 1986], p. 170).

19. Bill Honig, *Last Chance for Our Children: How You Can Help Save Our Schools* (Reading, Mass.: Addison-Wesley, 1985).

20. Colin Greer and Herbert Kohl, eds., *A Call to Character* (New York: HarperCollins, 1995); Steven Barboza, ed., *The African-American Book of Values: Classic Moral Stories* (New York: Doubleday, 1998).

21. Amitai Etzioni, *The Spirit of Community* (New York: Crown, 1993), pp. 99–100.

22. Ibid., p. 25.

23. Sherman, *The Fabric of Character*, p. 192.

24. The National Commission on Youth, *The Transition of Youth to Adulthood: A Bridge Too Long* (Boulder, Colo.: Westview, 1980), p. 35. This was a revision of the Panel on Youth for the President's Science Advisory Committee, *Youth: Transition to Adulthood* (Chicago: University of Chicago Press, 1972).

25. See Ernest Boyer, *High School* (New York: Harper and Row, 1983); Charles H. Harrison, *Student Service* (Princeton: Carnegie Foundation for the Advancement of Teaching, 1987); Frank Newman, *Higher Education and the American Resurgence* (Princeton: Carnegie Foundation for the Advancement of Teaching, 1985); and Ernest Boyer, *College* (New York: Harper and Row, 1987). In Newman's words, "If there is a crisis in education in the United States today, it is less that test scores have declined than it is that we have failed to provide the education for citizenship that is still the most significant responsibility of the nation's schools and colleges" (p. 31).

26. Etzioni states elsewhere that "While narratives and dialogues have their place, the way to educate is to shape the experiences children have at home, at school, and in the community" (Amitai Etzioni, "Building A Better Child," *The Washington Post Book World*, 29 December 1996, p. 1).

27. Etzioni, *The Spirit of Community*, pp. 103–104.

28. Ibid., p. 108.

29. Ibid., p. 113.

30. Benjamin R. Barber, "Public Talk and Civic Action: Educating for Participation in a Strong Democracy," *Social Education* 53 (October 1989), pp. 355–370.

31. Charles Moskos, *A Call to Civic Service: National Service for Country and Community* (New York: Free Press, 1988), p. 9.

32. Tom Lickona, Eric Schaps, and Catherine Lewis, "Principles of Effective Character Education," Character Education Partnership, pamphlet, undated, p. 1.

33. Lickona, *Educating for Character*, p. 67. Emphasis added.

34. Lickona, Schaps, and Lewis, "Principles of Effective Character Education," p. 1. Emphasis added.

35. Lickona, *Educating for Character*, p. 230; Thomas Lickona, "The Case for Character Education," *Tikkun* 12, no. 1 (January/February 1997), p. 23.

36. Lickona, *Educating for Character*, pp. 42–43.

37. Lickona, Schaps, and Lewis, "Principles of Effective Character Education," p. 1.

38. All of these quotations are taken from Lickona, Schaps, and Lewis, "Principles of Effective Character Education," pp. 2–4.

39. Utah, North Dakota, Nebraska, Oregon, Iowa, Indiana, Georgia, and New Hampshire all created or revised existing laws dealing with character education between 1988 and 1999.

40. Character Counts!, "Character Counts! Information," Character Counts! home page, 1 April 1997, http://www.charactercounts.org.

41. For instance, the National Education Association, YMCA of the USA, National Association of Professional Educators, American Association of School Administrators, American Federation of Teachers, 4-H, Future Homemakers of America, National Association of Secondary School Principals, National Federation for Catholic Youth Ministry, Boys and Girls Clubs of America, Big Brothers Big Sisters of America, Camp Fire Boys and Girls, American Youth Soccer Organization, National Catholic Educational Association, United Way of America, USA Police Athletic League, and the Jefferson Center for Character Education.

42. This statement is made on an information sheet attached to the "1998 Report Card on the Ethics of American Youth" (Marina del Rey, Calif.: Josephson Institute of Ethics, 1998), p. 47.

43. These quotations are taken from the Character Counts! Coalition home page, 19 February 1999, http://www.charactercounts.org.

44. Character Education Partnership, "Mission Statement," *Character Educator* 6, no. 2 (Spring 1998), p. 3.

45. Its members include the National Education Association, the American Association of School Administrators, the American Federation of Teachers, the Association for Supervision and Curriculum Development, the National PTA, the National School Boards Association, as well as an individual membership made up of teachers, principals, counselors, parents, and psychologists.

46. Character Education Partnership, "Character-Based Sex Education in Public Schools: A Position Statement," Character Education Partnership home page, 19 February 1999, http://www.character.org.

47. Tom Lickona, Eric Schaps, and Catherine Lewis, "Eleven Principles of Effective Character Education," Character Education Partnership home page, 19 February 1999, http://www.character.org.

48. The Character Education Partnership home page, 19 February 1999, http://www.character.org.

49. Maureen Kyprioanos, "Service Learning at Work," *Student Assistance Journal* (November/December 1996), p. 19.

50. Jefferson Center for Character Education, "Let Us Show You How to Teach Responsibility Skills," informational brochure, undated.

51. Robert Jamieson and Rex Dalby, *Responsibility Skills* (Pasadena, Calif.: Jefferson Center for Character Education, 1997).

52. Jefferson Center for Character Education, *How to Be Successful in Less than Ten Minutes a Day* (Monrovia, Calif.: Jefferson Center for Character Education, 1991).

53. Jefferson Center for Character Education, *How to be Successful In Less than Ten Minutes a Day*, principal's handbook (Monrovia, Calif.: Jefferson Center for Character Education, 1991), p. 3.

54. Ibid., p. 2.

55. The organization was founded in 1942 under the name of the American Institute for Character Education. By the end of 1998, the resources of the Character Education Institute were transferred to the Learning for Life organization. The Institute's curricula would be used primarily for the home schooling component of the Learning for Life business.

56. Character Education Institute, brochure, undated.

57. According to Institute documents, it also has an adult-education program of parents, educators, and other youth-serving professionals.

58. The Teel Institute, "Moral Classrooms: The Development of Character and Integrity in the Elementary School," research report, undated.

59. The Heartwood Institute home page, 19 February 1999, http://www.enviroweb.org/heartwood.

60. Learning for Life home page, 19 February 1999, http://www.learning-for-life.org.

61. Adopted on September 20, 1996, according to material on the Character Education Partnership home page, 19 February 1999, http://www.character.org.

62. Ibid.

63. Ibid.

64. Another worth mentioning is the Illinois-based curriculum "Sex Respect," adopted in several thousand schools nationwide. Its theme is that if young people are given the right information and motivation, they will practice and maintain abstinence. The course has ten lessons that basically make up ten arguments against premarital intercourse. Class activities include listing ways humans are different from animals, discussions about alternatives to sex when on dates (playing Monopoly, bicycling, dinner parties), role-playing, information on sexually transmitted diseases, and the failure rate of condoms and other birth control devices. What it lacks in sophistication, it makes up in boldness. Lessons are laced with cheeky sloganeering (i.e., "Control your urgin', be a virgin," "Pet your dog, not your date," "Don't be a louse, Wait for your spouse," and so on).

65. In this program the curriculum is based on seven "universal" ethical principles: "worth and potential, rights and responsibilities, fairness and justice, care and consideration, effort and excellence, personal integrity, and social responsibility" (Teen-Aid home page, 19 February 1999, http://www.teen-aid.org).

66. Teen-Aid claims that this curriculum is used in all fifty states by more than 100,000 parents and teenagers.

67. Teen-Aid home page, 19 February 1999, http://www.teen-aid.org.

68. Michael Horowitz of the Manhattan Institute quoted in Howard Fineman, "The Virtuecrats," *Newsweek*, 13 June 1994, p. 36.

69. Community of Caring, "What is the Community of Caring?" (Washington, D.C.: Community of Caring, 1990), p. 1.

70. Frances Schoonmaker Bolin, *Growing Up Caring: Exploring Values and Decision Making* (Lake Forest, Ill.: Glencoe, Macmillan/McGraw-Hill, 1990), p. 109.

71. Ibid., p. 117.

72. Ibid., p. 116.

73. Ibid., p. 123.

74. Ibid.

75. Jack Canfield and Frank Siccone, *101 Ways to Develop Student Self-Esteem and Responsibility* (Needham Heights, Mass.: Allyn and Bacon, Inc., 1992).

76. Bolin, *Growing Up Caring*, p. 34.

77. Ibid., p. 51.

78. Character Education Institute, "Questions and Answers," information pamphlet on the Character Education Curriculum (San Antonio, Texas: Character Education Institute, undated), p. 9.

79. Character Education Institute, "Character Education and the Teacher," pp. 1–2.

80. Ibid., p. 2.

81. Character Education Institute, brochure, undated, p. 14.

82. Young Jay Mulkey, "Why Character Education? An Editorial" (San Antonio, Texas: Character Education Institute, undated).

83. "Research," Mulkey's institute explains, "has shown that the degree of students' self-esteem is directly related to their academic performance as well as instrumental in determining how well they are able to work and play with others" (Character Education Institute, "Character Education and the Teacher," p. 2).

84. Character Education Institute, "Character Education and the Teacher," p. 1. In his editorial entitled "Why Character Education?" Y. J. Mulkey provides a concise statement of the moral reasoning they inculcate within children: "to develop responsible citizens by raising students' self-esteem, showing them the benefits of determining the consequences of their behavior to themselves and to others before acting upon their decisions to solve their problems."

85. Character Education Institute, "Character Education and the Teacher," p. 2.

86. Y. J. Mulkey, Director of the Character Education Institute, interview with author, 11 April 1991, San Antonio, Texas.

87. Designed to give children a "better understanding of themselves" and raise their self-esteem, the activity involves cutting out magazine pictures that symbolize their own individual character traits and paste these on construction paper cut to form the word ME. *Character Education Curriculum News* 3, no. 1 (February 1991), p. 1.

88. Thomas Jefferson Center, *The Year in Review: Annual Report 1989* (Pasadena, Calif.: Thomas Jefferson Center, 1989), p. i.

89. Jefferson Center for Character Education, "Year I, Unit I," in *How to Be Successful in Less than Ten Minutes a Day*, p. 2.

90. Thomas Jefferson Center, *Responsibility Skills: Lessons for Success*, elementary school curriculum (Pasadena, Calif.: Jefferson Center for Character Education, 1987), p. 1.

91. Jefferson Center for Character Education, "Year I, Unit VI" in *How to Be Successful in Less than Ten Minutes a Day*, p. 3.

92. Ibid., p. 12.

93. B. David Brooks and Robert C. Paull, *How to Be Successful in Less than Ten Minutes a Day* (Pasadena, Calif.: Thomas Jefferson Center, 1986), pp. 9, 14.

94. Teen-Aid, *Me, My World, My Future* (Spokane, Wash.: Teen-Aid, Inc.), p. 128.

95. Ibid., pp. 165–166.

96. Ibid., p. 91.

97. Ibid.

98. Ibid., p. 18. At the center of the self are the sentiments. It is for this reason that the text encourages "Coming to a better understanding and appreciation of ourselves [by] look[ing] at our emotions or feelings." "Identifying feelings, dealing with them and acting appropriately is," as they say, "very helpful in building self-awareness" (ibid., p. 11).

99. Ibid., p. 19.

100. Ibid., p. 21.

101. The Teel Institute, "Moral Classrooms: The Development of Character and Integrity in the Elementary School," research report, undated.

102. Sue Teel quoted ibid.

103. Sue Teel quoted ibid. Emphasis added.

104. Ibid. Emphasis added.

105. Learning for Life, Sample Lesson Plans: Grade 6, "Code of Ethics," Learning for Life Home Page, 19 February 1999, http://www.learning-for-life.org.

106. The National Commission on Civic Renewal, transcript of the second plenary session, Washington, D.C., 19 May, 1997, p. 23.

107. Michael Josephson, "Ethics: Easier Said Than Done," precourse reading materials, Character Counts Seminars (Marina del Rey, Calif.: Josephson Institute, 1997), p. 212.

108. Bill Moyers, "Our Changing American Values: An Interview with Michael Josephson," in *A World of Ideas: Conversations with Thoughtful Men and Women About Life Today and the Ideas Shaping Our Future*, edited by Betty Sue Flowers (New York: Doubleday, 1989), p. 18.

109. See, for example, Don Eberly, *America's Promise: Civil Society and the Renewal of American Culture* (Lanham, Md.: Rowman and Littlefield, 1998). In Chapter Eight, Eberly speaks of the character-education movement as "one of the most dynamic movements to strengthen civil society in the United States" (p. 125). See as well the deliberations of the National Commission on Civic Renewal.

110. The ambivalence between the behavioral and the therapeutic paradigms of moral education is even hinted at in the work of Thomas Lickona. A committed Catholic who dedicates his *Educating for Character* to God, he is as articulate and forthright an advocate of traditional character education as one will find. At the same time his doctorate is in developmental psychology. The melding of competing paradigms is, perhaps, inevitable. As we have seen, Lickona emphasizes the objectivity of moral values, arguing forcefully that there is a "natural moral law" that "is consistent with revealed religious

principles" and this moral law "prohibits injustice to others"; even "demand[s] that we treat as *morally wrong* any action by any individual, group, or state that violates these moral values" (Lickona, *Educating for Character*, p. 42. Emphasis in original). At the same time he has stated that "morality *begins* with valuing one's own person" (Lickona, "Four Strategies for Fostering Character Development in Children," *Phi Delta Kappan* 69 [February 1988], p. 421. Emphasis added). Consider, in this light, his reflections on the moral significance of community. "A sense of community," he argues, "is important because it contributes to self-esteem, partly by creating a norm of mutual respect that inhibits putdowns and partly by helping children to feel known and positively valued by their peers" (ibid.). "A sense of community also supplies a vital affective dimension to moral education, a flow of good feeling that makes it easier for children to be good, easier for them to cross the bridge from knowing what is right to doing it. Teachers who take the trouble to build positive 'group feeling' know (at least intuitively) that developing virtue is as much an affair of the emotions as of the mind." What is morally significant is not community, but rather the sense of community. The theme of self-esteem, so important to the psychologistic model of moral education is further elaborated upon in Thomas Lickona, "Moral Development in the Elementary School Classroom," in *Handbook of Moral Behavior and Development*, vol. 3, edited by William Kurtines and Jacob Gewirtz (Hillsdale, N.J.: Lawrence Erlbaum Associates, 1991), pp. 143–161.

Chapter Seven

1. Through the better part of the twentieth century, mainstream religious education remained fairly contested terrain. In addition to the divisions between traditionalists and progressives, a neo-orthodox approach to religious education emerged in the 1930s that emphasized the content of faith traditions and the influence of the ecclesiastical institutions themselves as agents of religious formation. Since that time, the fragmentation in religious education has only increased—especially within Protestantism. As Robert Lynn observed, by the closing decades of the twentieth century one could find the range of Sunday school designs, each reflecting a different stage of the movement's development. See Robert Lynn and Elliot Wright, *The Big Little School: Sunday Child of American Protestantism* (New York: Harper and Row, 1971), p. 96. Yet the variety does not reflect so much a healthy pluralism within competing religious traditions as much as a dissipation of energy and a confusion of purposes within this once formidable institution.

2. In the case of Protestantism, Sunday school enrollments in the United States dropped about a third, from 40.5 million to 26.6 million from 1970 to 1986, a level that remained fairly stable through the 1990s. Consistent with this, Gallup polls have shown that the number of adults reporting no Sunday school training during their childhood rose from 10 percent in 1970 to 27 percent in 1986. See Joe Maxwell, "Will Sunday School Survive?" *Christianity Today*, 9 December 1988, p. 63. The number of willing, reliable, and trained volunteers has always been a challenge but, in this demographic context, it is a challenge that has only increased. Add to this a general drop-off in denominational support for religious education and the cumulative evidence suggests that the institution is

facing problems from which it may not recover. See Daniel J. Lehman, "Whatever Happened to Sunday School?" *Christian Century*, 19 April 1989, p. 404.

3. Though faith-based professional associations have joined the Character Counts! Coalition, by 1999, no churches, synagogues, or denominations were members of the Coalition.

4. James Dobson, *Preparing for Adolescence* (Ventura, Calif.: Regal Books, 1989), p. 139.

5. Ibid., p. 80.

6. Kenneth A. Erickson, *Helping Your Children Feel Good About Themselves: A Guide to Building Self-Esteem in the Christian Family* (Minneapolis, Minn.: Augsburg, 1994).

7. Ibid., p. 8. He is citing James Dobson, *Hide or Seek* (Old Tappan, N.J.: Fleming H. Revell, 1974), pp. 20–21.

8. Ibid., p. 12.

9. Ibid., pp. 30, 53, 63, 70–71, 103, 131.

10. Charles Gerber, *Christ-Centered Self-Esteem: Seeing Ourselves Through God's Eyes* (Joplin, Mo.: College Press Publishing Company, 1996).

11. All the quotations in this paragraph, ibid., pp. 12, 18, 19, 144, 148, 157–159.

12. Nell W. Mohney, *Don't Put a Period Where God Put a Comma: Self-Esteem for Christians* (Nashville: Dimensions for Living, 1993).

13. Ibid., p. 31.

14. Ibid., pp. 19–20.

15. Ibid., pp. 32, 51, 65, 81, 92, 99.

16. Ibid., p. 21.

17. See, for example, National Council of Churches in Christ in the United States, *The Church's Educational Ministry: A Curriculum Plan* (St. Louis: Bethany Press, 1966), published by the National Council of Churches Division of Christian Education in cooperation with sixteen denominations. Quotations are take from pp. xv, xvi, 54.

18. Herman C. Ahrens, *Feeling Good About Yourself: Helping Young People Build Self-Esteem* (New York: Pilgrim Press, 1983), p. 3.

19. Ibid., pp. 3, 4, 8, 9.

20. Lisa Walker, "Believing in Yourself," *Devo'zine*, March-April 1997, p. 38.

21. Ibid.

22. Randall Murphee, "TV Values," *Devo'zine*, May-June 1998, p. 28.

23. Steve Smith, "Say Yes to Jesus," *Devo'zine*, May-June 1997, p. 27.

24. Faye Burdick, ed., "Living with Choices" (Louisville, Ky.: Presbyterian Publishing House, 1995), p. 3.

25. Mary Lee Talbot, ed., *God's Gift of Sexuality*, leaders ed. (Louisville, Ky.: Witherspoon Press, 1998), p. 9.

26. In their view, it "is a mistake" because it is "hazardous to a teenager's health of body, mind, and spirit" (ibid., p. 43).

27. Ibid., p. 92.

28. See ibid., p. 97.

29. For younger adolescents, the Presbyterian Church USA (PCUSA) offers the drug education curriculum, "Just Say Yes!" (Faye Burdick, ed., [Louisville, Ky.: Presbyterian

Publishing House, 1994]). Here too biblical guidance is woven together with the moral concerns of emotional and physical well-being. Straight off, young people are presented with thirty-one "price tags" of drug abuse, only one of which bears on the spiritual consequences. The rest emphasize cancer and other serious physical illnesses along with suicidal depression, embarrassment, and other emotional and psychological problems. Session two is on self-esteem. Session three focuses upon "personal power," to make tough autonomous decisions. The final session addresses "freedom"—mainly from bad habits, but also freedom to choose positive goals.

30. Judith Caine Ekman, *Together: Growing Up Drug Free* (Louisville, Ky.: Bridge Resources, 1998), p. 6.

31. Ibid., p. 33.

32. Ibid., p. 63.

33. Manternach Janaan and Carl J. Pfeifer, *This is Our Faith*, teacher ed. (Morristown, N.J.: Silver Burdett, 1987). I also consulted the 1999 edition for Grade 3.

34. Janaan and Pfeifer, *This is Our Faith*, 1987, p. T18.

35. Thomas Groome, John Barry, John Nelson, and Catherine Nelson, *Growing with the Commandments* (New York: Sadlier, 1988), pp. 1–7.

36. These are: (1) that each person is created unique in the image of God; (2) despite original sin, all human life in its physical, psychological, and spiritual dimensions is fundamentally good; (3) each person is created to be loved and to love, as Christ loved by the Father, loves us; (4) human relationships are expressed in a way that is enfleshed and sexed; (5) human sexuality carries the responsibility to work toward Christian sexual maturity; (6) mature Christian sexuality, in whatever state of life, demands a life-enriching commitment to other persons and the community; and (7) conjugal sexuality is an expression of the faithful, life-enriching love of husband and wife and is ordained toward the loving procreation of new life. See Patricia Miller, "Parent to Parent" (Los Angeles: Franciscan Communications, 1988), p. 18.

37. Ibid., p. 29.

38. These are: (1) They should be aware that this decision is a serious matter; (2) They should know and understand fully the Church's teachings on that matter; (3) They should read and discuss with a Church authority the gravity of such a decision; and (4) They should pray and give serious consideration to the consequences of their decision. Ibid.

39. Arthur C. Blecher, *Stories From Our Living Past* (New York: Behrman House, Inc., 1974).

40. Ibid., introduction.

41. Louis Newman, *A Child's Introduction to Torah* (New York: Behrman House, Inc., 1972), p. iv.

42. Seymour Rossel, *When a Jew Seeks Wisdom: The Sayings of the Fathers* (New York: Behrman House, Inc., 1975). A "textbook of Jewish values" comprising five books in the Mishnah, the *Pirke Avot* contains the teachings of about sixty rabbis who taught between 300 B.C.E. and 200 C.E.. This book is organized around the three famous questions of Hillel found in *Pirke Avot*: "If I am not for myself, who will be for me? And if I am only for myself, what am I? And if not now, when?"

43. Ibid., pp. 19, 40, 42, 211, 219.

44. Roland Gittelsohn, *How Do I Decide?: A Contemporary Jewish Approach to What's Right and What's Wrong* (West Orange, N.J.: Behrman House, Inc., 1989).

45. Ibid., p. 4.

46. Ibid., p. 6.

47. Principal, Holy Spirit Catholic Church School, interview by author, San Antonio, Texas, 11 April 1991.

48. Youth Minister, Fourth Presbyterian Church, interview by author, Chicago, Illinois, 11 July 1991.

49. Director of Education, Central Synagogue, interview by author, New York, 16 April 1991.

50. Youth Minister, Fourth Presbyterian Church, interview.

51. Youth leader, First Baptist Church, interview by author, Dallas, Texas, 10 April 1991.

52. Principal, Holy Spirirt Catholic Church School, interview.

53. Director of Education, Central Synagogue, interview.

54. The rabbi described the situation this way: "Should that child drop out, we go back to the parent and we say 'What message did you just deliver to your kid? They were your witness as you were their witness when they were eight, nine, ten, eleven, twelve, thirteen years old that you said 'We're into this, we're going to do it, we believe it, and we're going to support you. We're even going to do this even against the child's will.' And now you've just destroyed all credibility with your child. So when your kid says, 'Hey, Mommy, look, commitments don't mean anything. You broke a commitment with a synagogue.' There are further ramifications in your kid's life and you're going to see those problems later on.' It scares the life out of these parents, but it works."

55. Director of Education, Central Synagogue, interview.

56. Youth Leader, First Baptist Church, interview.

57. Ibid.

58. Youth leader, Precious Blood Catholic Church, Chicago, Illinois, 22 April 1991.

59. See, for example, Philip Rieff, "The American Transference: From Calvin to Freud" in *The Feeling Intellect*, edited by Jonathan Imber (Chicago: University of Chicago Press, 1990), pp. 10–15.

Chapter Eight

1. Michael Josephson of the Character Counts! Coalition spoke of the "hole in the moral ozone" in the introduction to the 1998 Josephson Institute Survey of Youth Ethics. This was reported in the Institute's newsletter, "Ethics in Action," October-December 1998, p. 1.

2. See, for example, Barbara L. McCombs, "The Role of the Self-System in Self-Regulated Learning," *Contemporary Educational Psychology* 11, no. 4 (October 1986), p. 315.

3. Alfie Kohn, "Caring Kids: The Role of the Schools," *Phi Delta Kappan* 72 (March 1991), p. 501.

4. The question is an empirical one and has been tested by an army of social scientists who make up the guild of educational policy analysis. To be sure, the scholarly literature that has accumulated since the early 1970s is voluminous. One estimate places the number of scientific studies evaluating this general strategy of moral instruction at over 10,000. See Jerry Adler, "Hey, I'm Terrific!" *Newsweek*, 17 February 1992, pp. 46–51.

The test setting, of course, is the school itself, for the simple reason that the agenda is institutionally explicit, and the money and energy set aside to make this agenda work is so concentrated. At the same time, these efforts have been evaluated with considerable care over the decades by social scientists who make up the guild of educational policy. Though the therapeutic strategy of moral understanding infuses all institutions of moral instruction to one degree or another, its formal establishment in the school has made that institution something of a laboratory. If the therapeutic strategy of moral education has had a positive influence on children, then it will be clearest here.

The question can be sharpened. As we have seen, the reigning idea of the moral education establishment since the mid-1960s has been that psychological well-being is the foundation for positive social behavior and moral conduct. The basic idea has been packaged and presented in a wide variety of models and programs—some concerned with general self-improvement, others focusing on specific areas of moral concern such as sexuality, drug use, and interpersonal conflict. Yet as varied as these programs have been, they nevertheless share this same basic supposition—that any capacity to become a better person, any capacity to resist "wrongdoing," depends upon an empowerment of the inner self through the cultivation of knowledge and appropriation of skills. These are the mechanisms by which young people will be able to answer the hard questions of life for themselves.

But does the strategy deliver what it promises?

Some of the earliest clues came in the early 1970s, when values clarification was being broadly promoted and widely studied. (Earlier still was the judgment of J. C. Diggory who, in 1966, spoke of "the utter bankruptcy of it all." See J. C. Diggory, *Self-Evaluation: Concepts and Studies* [New York: Wiley, 1966], p. 66.) In one review of the empirical studies conducted in the first half of that decade, the conclusion could not have been more clear: Values clarification accomplished very little if anything at all. Values clarification had no positive impact on students' self-esteem, their self-concept, their personal adjustment, or their interpersonal relationships. Moreover, there was no evidence that this technique had any demonstrable effect on the students' values. This was a review of thirteen studies, all conducted in the first half of the 1970s. See Alan L. Lockwood, "The Effects of Values Clarification and Moral Development Curricula on School-Age Subjects: A Critical Review of Recent Research," *Review of Educational Research* 48 (1978), pp. 325–364. A few years later, another more comprehensive review of studies evaluating values-clarification programs was conducted and the conclusion was much the same. See James S. Leming, "Curricular Effectiveness in Moral Values Education: A Review of the Research," *Journal of Moral Education* 10 (1981), pp. 147–184. In this instance, the author counted seventy tests of significance measuring the relationship between values clarification and a host of desired opinions and behaviors. Eighty percent of these tests showed that values clarification either had no significant effect or else significant negative effects on these outcomes. Values clarification simply did not generate the ends either predicted or desired.

Since the 1970s the evidence has only mounted. At the end of the 1970s, Ruth Wylie published an updated edition of her massive corpus, *The Self-Concept.* See Ruth C. Wylie, *The Self-Concept,* vol. 2 (Lincoln: University of Nebraska Press, 1979). In this work she reviewed nearly every serious piece of research conducted to that time on the question of self-regard and "positive" behavior. Though modestly stated, her conclusion was rather arresting: "*the most impressive thing which emerges from an overview of this book is that null or weak findings have been obtained many times in each of a number of areas in which theory and conventional wisdom very confidently predicted strong trends*" (p. 690; emphasis added). Translation: most studies of the impact of self-regard on a whole range of areas of life fail to turn up a statistically meaningful relationship, even when researchers hoped or expected to find them. The foundation of the psychologistic model of moral education has proven either thin or nonexistent; the very premise upon which the entire strategy of moral education has been based was proven wrong.

These findings were not anomalous either. By the time "self-esteem" had become the watchword within the moral education establishment, studies had merely confirmed the weakness of any strategy of moral education based upon psychologistic premises. Here again the adequacy of the basic ideas, concepts, and associations were under dispute. In 1983, for example, a review out of Cornell University concluded that, "despite 1500 articles on adolescent self-esteem published since 1967, we know relatively little of its correlates, determinants, or predictors. The majority of research presents a view of self-esteem that is too limited to be of much consequence either for developing a theory of adolescence or for those concerned with adolescent development" (Ritch C. Savin-Williams and David Demo, "Conceiving or Misconceiving the Self: Issues in Adolescent Self-Esteem," *Journal of Early Adolescence* 3, nos. 1–2 [1983], p. 131). Despite all of the effort, the connection between psychological well-being and positive moral conduct simply could not be made.

The accumulating evidence neither dissuaded nor dampened the enthusiasm for the strategy among its advocates. Perhaps its boldest initiative came in 1986 in California. There, state assemblyman John Vasconcellos established a task force to study the social impact of self-esteem and self-esteem programs. The agenda of this "State Task Force to Promote Self-Esteem and Personal and Social Responsibility" was ambitious. As Neil Smelser, one of the principal investigators of the project, put it,

> The more particular proposition that informs our enterprise here is that many, if not most, of the major problems plaguing society have roots in the low self-esteem of many of the people who make up society. It is supposed that those citizens who appreciate themselves and have a sense of personal empowerment will cultivate their own personal responsibility and will attend to the tasks that are necessary for the welfare of the community and the society. It is further supposed that those in society who are burdened with the conviction that they are not worthy will take refuge in behaviors that are unproductive, costly, deviant, and dangerous to society and will, by that measure, contribute disproportionately to serious social problems. That is the agenda of the California Task Force to Promote Self-Esteem, and that is

the agenda that we in this special volume on self-esteem and social problems are putting to the best critical test in light of the best social scientific literature available to us. (Neil J. Smelser, "Self-Esteem and Social Problems: An Introduction," in *The Social Importance of Self-Esteem*, edited by Andrew M. Mecca, Neil J. Smelser, and John Vasconcellos [Berkeley: University of California Press, 1989], p. 1.)

For Vasconcellos himself, "self-esteem [would be] the likeliest candidate for a *social vaccine*, something that empowers us to live responsibly and that inoculates us against the lures of crime, violence, substance abuse, teen pregnancy, child abuse, chronic welfare dependency and educational failure." Quoted in Adler, "Hey, I'm Terrific!" p. 51. If the benefits of self-esteem could be established here, its implementation in various moral educational programs in the state would be fully justified.

After three years of intensive study, the task force came to its conclusions. Published as *The Social Importance of Self-Esteem*, the results were disappointing to say the least, particularly for those who placed such hope in this idea. See, for example, Jerry Adler, "Hey, I'm Terrific!" and Chester Finn, Jr., "Narcissus Goes to School," *Commentary* 8–9 (June 1990), pp. 46–51.

On the association between self-esteem and child mistreatment, "there is insufficient evidence to support the belief in a direct relationship between low self-esteem and child abuse" (Bonnie Bhatti, David Derezotes, Seung-Ock Kim, and Harry Specht, "The Association Between Child Maltreatment and Self-Esteem," in *The Social Importance of Self-Esteem*, edited by Andrew M. Mecca, Neil J. Smelser, and John Vasconcellos [Berkeley: University of California Press, 1989], p. 61).

On self-esteem and failure in school, "the most disquieting feature of these studies is the generally low magnitude of association found between self-esteem and achievement. . . . The demonstrated relationship between self-esteem and academic performance [is] so uniformly low." What association there is is "little more than circumstantial value in making a case for causation or for the direction of any causal relationship" (Martin V. Covington, "Self-Esteem and Failure in School: Analysis and Policy Implications," in *The Social Importance of Self-Esteem*, edited by Andrew M. Mecca, Neil J. Smelser, and John Vasconcellos [Berkeley: University of California Press, 1989], p. 79).

On self-esteem and teenage pregnancy, "these studies do not support an association between self-esteem and sexual intercourse during adolescence" (Susan B. Crockenberg and Barbara A. Soby, "Self-Esteem and Teenage Pregnancy," in *The Social Importance of Self-Esteem*, edited by Andrew M. Mecca, Neil J. Smelser, and John Vasconcellos [Berkeley: University of California Press, 1989], p. 139). "There simply is no compelling evidence on which to base a claim that increasing self-esteem will reduce the number of teenagers who engage in premarital sex" (ibid., p. 150). At the same time, two studies in the report even linked high self-esteem with increased sexual activity by teens.

On self-esteem and crime and violence, "Self-esteem may be positively or negatively correlated with aggression" (cited in Adler, "Hey, I'm Terrific!" p. 48).

On self-esteem and chronic welfare dependency, "cross-sectional evidence for a relationship between self-esteem and welfare dependence is inconclusive. . . . Although cross-sectional studies might lean toward positing a relationship between low self-esteem and dependency, the longitudinal data generally negate the observed finding. . . . As yet, no finding ties persistent welfare dependence to a generalized loss of self-esteem" (Leonard Schneiderman, Walter M. Furman, and Joseph Weber, "Self-Esteem and Chronic Welfare Dependency," in *The Social Importance of Self-Esteem*, edited by Andrew M. Mecca, Neil J. Smelser, and John Vasconcellos [Berkeley: University of California Press, 1989], pp. 226, 233, 235).

On self-esteem and alcohol and drug use, "self-esteem [is] not directly linked to substance abuse in most research to date" (Harry H. L. Kitano, "Alcohol and Drug Use and Self-Esteem: A Sociocultural Perspective," in *The Social Importance of Self-Esteem*, edited by Andrew M. Mecca, Neil J. Smelser, and John Vasconcellos [Berkeley: University of California Press, 1989], p. 319).

In summing up the work of the task force, Smelser stated that, "*if the association between self-esteem and behavior is so often reported to be weak, even less can be said for the causal relationship between the two*" (Smelser, "Self-Esteem and Social Problems: An Introduction," p. 17. Emphasis added). Put another way, Smelser notes that "the scientific efforts to establish those connections that we are able to acknowledge and generate from an intuitive point of view do not reproduce those relations" (ibid., p. 18). Smelser echoed what other researchers have found over the years: even when sympathetic to the intentions of this agenda, one must acknowledge the absence of any significant findings. The evidence has continued to accumulate and it has continued to point in the same direction.

5. "In sum, high self-esteem appears to offer no guarantee of inclining people toward prosocial behavior—or even of steering them away from antisocial behavior" (Alfie Kohn, "The Truth About Self-Esteem," *Phi Delta Kappan* 76 [December 1994], pp. 272–283). This point is made as well by Thomas J. Scheff, Suzanne M. Retzinger, and Michael T. Ryan, in their essay, "Crime, Violence, and Self-Esteem: Review and Proposals," in *The Social Importance of Self-Esteem*, edited by Andrew M. Mecca, Neil J. Smelser, and John Vasconcellos (Berkeley: University of California Press, 1989), p. 176.

6. With regard to school-based, therapeutically oriented drug prevention programs, the story is the same. The case of DARE (Drug Abuse Resistance Education) is especially remarkable because the program has become so large—the most expansive drug education program in America. Study after study has shown that the level of drug use among teenagers who have gone through the DARE program is virtually identical to those who have not gone through it. See Earl Wysong and David Wright, "A Decade of DARE: Efficacy, Politics and Drug Education," *Sociological Focus*, 28, no. 3 (August 1995), p. 306. As Clayton et al., put it, "Overall, measurable effects of the intervention on students' drug use and other outcomes were modest and not sustained over the full measurement interval" (Richard R. Clayton, Anne Cattarello, and Bryan M. Johnstone, "The Effectiveness of Drug Abuse Resistance Education: 5-Year Follow-Up Results," *Preventive Medicine* 25 [1996], pp. 307–318). See also Earl Wyson, Richard Aniskiewicz, and David Wright, "Truth and DARE: Tracking Drug Education to Graduation and as Symbolic Politics," *Social Problems* 41, no. 3 (August 1994), pp. 448–468; Richard Clayton, C. G. Leukefeld, Nancy Harrington, and Anne Cattarello, "DARE: Very Popular but Not Very Effective," in *Intervening with Drug-Involved Youth*, edited by Clyde McCoy (Thousand Oaks, Calif.: Sage, 1996), pp. 101–109; and finally, "Doubtful DARE," *Harvard Mental Health Letter* 11, no. 9 (March 1995), p. 1. Students themselves have judged the program as having no lasting influence on their drug-related attitudes or behaviors. As one student put it,

If your friends say 'Let's go out and get drunk,' you don't say 'Oh my gosh, well DARE teaches me not to.' You don't stop and think about it. You just go and do what your friends do. Does DARE help you deal with peer pressure? No! You're just going to follow your friends.' (Quoted in Wysong, Aniskiewicz, and Wright, "Truth and DARE: Tracking Drug Education to Graduation and as Symbolic Politics," p. 457.)

None of this has given pause to those who hold some stake in the program. Around the country, school administrators, teachers, local police, and, most of all, the national DARE administrators defend the program to the end. And yet all of the training it provides in building self-esteem and resisting peer-pressure results in "no long-term effects" in either preventing or reducing adolescent drug use.

7. As to comprehensive sex-education techniques, the key review of the literature was commissioned by the Division of Adolescent and School Health within the Centers for Disease Control and Prevention. See Douglas Kirby, Lynn Short, Janet Collins, Deborah Rugg, Lloyd Kolbe, Marion Howard, Brent Miller, Freya Sonenstein, and Laurie Zabin, "School-based Programs to Reduce Sexual Risk Behaviors: A Review of Effectiveness," *Public Health Reports* 109, no. 3 (May-June 1994), pp. 339–361. See also Douglas Kirby, "Sex and HIV/AIDS Education in Schools: Have a Modest but Important Impact on Sexual Behaviour," *British Medical Journal* 311, no. 7002 (12 August 1995), p. 403; Douglas Kirby, "School-Based Programs to Reduce Sexual Risk-Taking Behaviors," *Journal of School Health* 62, no. 7 (September 1992), pp. 280–287; Douglas Kirby, "Sex Miseducation," *Mother Jones* 20, no. 1 (Jan-Feb 1995), p. 48. Do such programs help young people make moral decisions about sexuality? There is no answer to this question because most of these programs focus on the cognitive and behavioral dimensions of sexuality. On the cognitive side of this equation, children exposed to these pedagogies do know more than other children about the mechanics of human sexuality—they seem to know about such matters as menstruation, intercourse, pregnancy, and sexually transmitted diseases. Studies also show that young people are also less shy than others about talking about sex. On the behavioral side, current programs neither hasten the onset of intercourse nor increase its frequency. Maximally they modestly increase the use of contraception. A few of these programs might help delay the onset of intercourse and even reduce the number of sexual partners. Yet over all, these programs and techniques have been shown to have little effect on teenagers' actual decisions to engage in sex. In particular, knowledge-based sex-education programs have not demonstrated any significant capacity to reduce teenage pregnancy, sexually transmitted diseases, or HIV infection. At the same time values-clarification programs and programs designed to teach communication and decisionmaking skills have little measurable effect in making young people more sexually responsible, much less morally reflective about such matters. Moreover, the number of years children are exposed to these strategies seems to have little impact on making children sexually responsible.

8. Most of the research conducted over the decades has been published in refereed journals or in doctoral dissertations. To accept the explanation is to indict the entire field of educational policy. Perhaps the indictment is merited, but not likely.

9. Studies from the 1970s on the effectiveness of Kohlbergian techniques of moral development were turning up much the same finding. Often enough the interventions had no positive or predicted effect on children at all. In the instances where an influence on

children could be observed, the developmental effect toward "moral maturity" was usually just one-third of a stage (out of five full stages), and these, typically, were at the lower stages of psychological development. In Leming's review, the mean change was "due to a movement in only a little over half of the subjects. Between 30 and 50 percent of the students will be unaffected by the treatment" (Leming, "Curricular Effectiveness in Moral Values Education," pp. 147–164). See also R. Enright and M. Levy, "Moral Education Strategies," in *Cognitive Strategy Research: Educational Applications*, edited by M. Pressley and I. Levin (New York: Springer-Verlag, 1983); J. A. Lawrence, "Moral Judgment Intervention Studies Using the Defining Issues Test," *Journal of Moral Education* 9 (1980), pp. 178–191; A. Schlaefli, J. Rest, and S. J. Thoma, "Does Moral Education Improve Moral Judgment? A Meta-analysis of Intervention Studies Using the Defining Issues Test," *Review of Educational Research* 5 (1985), pp. 319–352. Even here, though, it was impossible to have much confidence in the developmental effects of these programs. As Lockwood put it, "the exploratory nature of the studies, their subsequent design weaknesses, and the multifaceted treatments employed make it difficult to claim developmental effects with confidence and impossible to determine what features of treatment contribute to obtained effects" (Lockwood, "The Effects of Values Clarification and Moral Development Curricula on School-Age Subjects," p. 358). For one, up to half of the students were completely unaffected by the intervention. For another, the researchers could never identify what it was about the intervention that was contributing to the change.

10. Kohlberg's experimental Cluster School in Cambridge, Massachusetts, sought to create a world for adolescents in a school where justice was "a living matter." It was not to be a utopia imposed by adults upon the young but a "shared democratic process of community building." The reason, for Kohlberg, was his belief that democracy was the highest manifestation of a just society; a social order where the relations of equal participation and respect for individual rights prevailed.

According to Joseph Reimer and Clark Power, four norms emerged during its existence as of central concern: regular attendance; respect for the property rights of others; integration among racial, ethnic, and class groups; and no drug or alcohol use in school or at school functions. In the first two years, theft and unexcused absence were rampant among students. Theft declined after the first year and remained fairly stable thereafter, although it wasn't until after the second year that cutting class came under some control. Integration improved only slightly over the years—for the most part, students remained in exclusive racial and class cliques. As to drug (which was mainly marijuana) and alcohol use, it only got worse over the years. See Joseph Reimer and Clark Power, "Educating for Democratic Community: Some Unresolved Dilemmas," in *Moral Education: A First Generation of Research and Development*, edited by Ralph L. Mosher (New York: Praeger, 1980), pp. 303–320. Following Reimer and Powers' observations, consider what happened in the school's fourth-year retreat.

> When it came time at the end of the fourth year to plan the retreat the faculty grew more adamant about wanting assurances that there would be no use of drugs. Reluctant assurances were given, but the teacher who the previous year had challenged the students stated frankly that he did not believe them and would refuse to attend the retreat.

The retreat took place without that teacher but was a disaster. Students made little attempt to hide their use of drugs and alcohol, and a number, in the words of one, 'got totally wasted.' The staff called a meeting and the students promised greater discretion. When it became known that two white students had drawn up a list of students who had broken the agreement by using drugs, some of the black students got very angry and confronted the two. A fight ensued, after which there was an unprecedented degree of tension between the white and black students. The staff felt powerless to act. Sensing that there was no community to draw upon, they thought it futile to call another meeting. Although upon returning home many of the students expressed shock and genuine regret for what had happened, and wanted, even desperately, to make amends, the events on the retreat had torn at the school's social fabric. Thereafter it proved increasingly difficult to sustain a strong sense of community in Cluster. (ibid., pp. 314–315)

Reimer and Power noted that, "what made it hard for students to give up drugs was that smoking marijuana played an important prosocial function within Cluster's adolescent community" (ibid., p. 315). They also recounted a very telling exchange between a student and teacher about the relation between drugs and integration:

Black student: . . . The only time people get together in a group is on a retreat when we are high.

Consultant: I don't think that we can say we can't work on it at a community meeting and go off on a retreat and get high. We've got to work it through to some extent here.

Teacher: I can see why getting high on a retreat makes it a lot easier to relate to some other people in the community. But I am also being pulled the other way in saying we have to learn to confront one another's innermost thoughts and communicate without the help of a drink or a reefer. There ought to be other ways of doing that during the school day. (Ibid., p. 316)

It is extraordinary that integration primarily took place when they were "partying when the social barriers could recede, partially through the use of drugs. Retreats were viewed as a type of partying for they allowed for free mixing, partially through the use of drugs" (ibid., p. 317). Reimer and Power conclude that "while these teachers continued to appeal to the student's better judgment—to what they ought to do for the sake of the community, that appeal and advocacy only functioned as the application of pressure to the point of explosion. The teachers acted in accordance with the just community approach as outlined by Kohlberg (Chapter 2) but did not get the just results they anticipated" (ibid., p. 318).

11. Hugh Hartshorne and Mark May, *Studies in the Nature of Character,* vol. 1, *Studies in Deceit* (New York: Macmillan, 1928), p. vi.

12. Ibid., p. 413.

13. Hugh Hartshorne and Mark May, *Studies in the Nature of Character,* vol. 2, *Studies in Service and Self-Control* (New York: Macmillan, 1929), p. 273.

14. Ibid., p. 453.

15. Hugh Hartshorne and Mark May, *Studies in the Nature of Character,* vol. 1, *Studies in Deceit,* p. 413. This conclusion was reaffirmed in their third volume: "Prevailing ways

of teaching ideals and standards probably do little good and may do harm when the ideals set before the pupils contradict the practical demands of the very situations in which the ideals are taught" (Hugh Hartshorne and Mark May, *Studies in the Nature of Character*, vol. 3, *Studies in the Organization of Character* [New York: Macmillan, 1930] p. 377).

16. As of 1993, there had been no studies of the effectiveness of literature-based programs and the evidence provided by the Character Education Institute (in San Antonio, Texas) and the Jefferson Center for Character Education (in Los Angeles) is only informal. Claims of their success are supported primarily by testimonials of teachers and principals. See James S. Leming, "In Search of Effective Character Education," *Educational Leadership* 51 (November 1993), pp. 63–71.

17. D. Solomon, E. Schaps, M. Watson, and V. Battistich, "Promoting Prosocial Behavior in Schools: A Second Interim Report on a Five-Year Longitudinal Project" (paper presented at the annual meeting of the American Educational Research Association, Washington, D.C., March 1987), cited in Leming, "In Search of Effective Character Education," pp. 63–71.

18. Empirical studies fairly consistently point to the dubious effects that extrinsic incentives have on the intrinsic interest, motivation, and creativity of children. See Richard Fabes et al., "Effects of Rewards on Children's Prosocial Motivation," *Developmental Psychology* 25 (1989), pp. 509–515; Edward Deci and Richard Ryan, *Intrinsic Motivation and Self-Determination in Human Behavior* (New York: Plenum Press, 1985); Mark Morgan, "Reward-Induced Decrements and Increments in Intrinsic Motivation," *Review of Educational Research* 54 (1984), pp. 5–30; Joan E. Gusec and Theodore Dix, "The Socialization of Prosocial Behavior: Theory and Reality," in *Altruism and Aggression: Biological and Social Origins*, edited by Carolyn Zahn-Waxler, E. Mark Cummings, and Ronald Iannottie (Cambridge: Cambridge University Press, 1986); Mark Lepper and David Green, eds., *The Hidden Costs of Reward* (Hillsdale, N.J.: Erlbaum, 1978); C. Daniel Batson et al., "Buying Kindness: Effect of an Extrinsic Incentive for Helping on Perceived Altruism," *Personality and Social Psychology Bulletin* 4 (1978), pp. 86–91; Robert J. Sternberg, "Prototypes of Competence and Incompetence," in *Competence Considered*, edited by R. J. Sternberg and J. Kolligian, Jr. (New Haven, Conn.: Yale University Press, 1990), p. 144.

19. See Kirby, "School-Based Programs to Reduce Sexual Risk-Taking Behaviors," p. 282. See also, Mark Roosa and F. Scott Christopher, "Evaluation of an Abstinence-Only Adolescent Pregnancy Prevention Program: A Replication," *Family Relations* 39, no. 4 (1990), pp. 363–367. Roosa and Christopher conclude that "there is no scientifically credible information to suggest that any of the abstinence-only programs have successfully reduced adolescent pregnancy rates" (p. 366). This research team reviewed similar literature and found that knowledge and attitudes supportive of abstinence do change for the short term but dissipate after three months. Further, these programs brought about no change in sexual activity. F. Scott Christopher and Mark Roosa, "An Evaluation of An Adolescent Pregnancy Prevention Program: Is 'Just Say No' Enough?," *Family Relations* 39, no. 1 (1990), pp. 68–72. A study that included evaluations of Teen-Aid and Sex Respect showed some *short-term* changes in attitudes and values but nothing about be-

havioral changes. See Stan Weed and Larry Jensen, "A Second Year Evaluation of Three Abstinence Sex Education Programs," *Journal of Research and Development in Education* 26, no. 2 (1993), pp. 92–96. The identical finding for Teen-Aid was reported in J. de Gaston et al., "Teacher Philosophy and Program Implementation and the Impact on Sex Education Outcomes," *Journal of Research and Development in Education* 27, no. 4 (1994), pp. 265–270. In one of the most widely reported success stories—that the Teen-Aid program lowered the rate of pregnancy at a San Marcos, California high school from 147 to only 20 in two years—the San Diego *Union* looked into it and found that while the 147 figure was well documented, the number 20 had apparently been fabricated. See Philip Elmer-Dewitt, "Making the Case for Abstinence," *Time*, 24 May 1993, p. 65.

20. See R. Rutter and F. Newmann, "The Potential of Community Service to Enhance Civic Responsibility," *Social Education* 53 (1989), pp. 371–374, especially p. 372. See also Leming, "In Search of Effective Character Education," p. 67; and A. Holland and T. Andre, "Participation in Extracurricular Activities in Secondary School: What is Known, What Needs to Be Known," *Review of Educational Research* 57 (1987), pp. 437–466.

21. Indeed, the standards of evaluation are fairly low. So many of the studies showing positive short-term effects of any particular program are often based on nothing more than before and after self-assessment questionnaires.

22. In this regard, Gerald Grant speaks of an "education [that] is inseparable from the concept of what constitutes a good life and good community." See G. Grant, *The World We Created at Hamilton High* (Cambridge, Mass.: Harvard University Press, 1986), pp. 173–174; G. Grant, "The Character of Education and the Education of Character," *Daedalus* 110 (Summer 1981), pp. 135–149; G. Grant, "Schools That Make an Imprint: Creating a Strong Positive Ethos," in *Challenge to American Schools: The Case for Standards and Values*, edited by J. Hunzel (New York: Oxford University Press, 1985), pp. 127–146. The literature I refer to here includes the important work by Michael Rutter, Barbara Maughan, Peter Mortimore, and Janet Ouston, *Fifteen Thousand Hours* (Cambridge, Mass.: Harvard University Press, 1979). Consider too Paul T. Hill, Gail E. Foster, and Tamar Gendler, *High Schools with Character* (Santa Monica: The Rand Corporation, 1990); Anthony Bryk, "Musings on the Moral Life of Schools," *American Journal of Education* 96, no. 2 (1988), pp. 256–290; Anthony Bryk, Valerie Lee, and Peter Holland, *Catholic Schools and the Common Good* (Cambridge, Mass.: Harvard University Press, 1993); and James Coleman and Thomas Hoffer, *Public and Private High Schools: The Impact of Communities* (New York: Basic Books, 1987). As to sex education, Douglas Kirby's exhaustive evaluation research concludes as well that the most successful programs are multidimensional in nature: grounded in social learning theories; focused narrowly upon reducing specific sexual risk-taking behaviors; learned through experiential activities; instructed in social influence; and reinforced by social pressures from enforced group norms. See, for example, Douglas Kirby et al., "School-based Programs to Reduce Sexual Risk Behaviors: A Review of Effectiveness," pp. 339–361. Here again, what seems to work best are programs that imitate totalizing learning environments.

23. The individual's moral orientation was determined by their response to the following question: If you were unsure of what was right or wrong in a particular situation, how would you decide what to do? In general, would you:

Do what would make you happy
Do what would improve your situation or get you ahead
Follow the advice of an authority, such as a parent, teacher or youth leader
Do what would be best for everyone involved
Do what God or scriptures tell you is right

Each of the responses to this question, as you can see, relates to one of the moral cultures described in the text. There were other similar questions we asked that drew out much the same information. For example, we asked, "In your view, the most important reason for helping people in your community is that:

It makes you feel good personally
It might help you get ahead
Everyone has a responsibility to help others
Your religious and philosophical beliefs encourage you to
Some other reason

We also asked, "What, in your opinion, is the most believable authority in matters of truth?

Your own personal experience
What you learn from television, newspapers and magazines
The teachings of scripture
What science teaches
What your parents or other adults teach you
What church leaders say
Other

24. See Robert Bellah et al., *Habits of the Heart: Individualism and Commitment in American Life* (Berkeley: University of California Press, 1985).

25. Alasdair MacIntyre, *After Virtue* (Notre Dame, Ind.: University of Notre Dame Press, 1984), p. 2.

26. When social scientists see variation in how people respond to questions, their chief concern is to explain the sources of that variation. Once they know the factors influencing variation, they can then speculate about the "whys." This is all well and good in itself but there are problems in how this typically is worked out. A moment's diversion into the somewhat arcane world of sociological method in order to explain this is appropriate, for it will help to demonstrate just how novel these findings are.

The long-standing practice among social scientists is to look for the sources of variation in the observable features of people's lives—that is, how wealthy or poor people are, whether they are white, black, or Hispanic, whether they live in the suburbs, the city, or the country, whether they are male or female, whether they live in a one-parent or two-parent family, and so on. It is these social and demographic characteristics of the population that scholars always look to for the reasons people have different attitudes and beliefs.

But more than a convention of social-scientific research, it also represents the methodological and conceptual bias of a "sociological materialism." The prejudice implied is that the only factors that *really* count in people's lives are the material conditions of their existence—class, race and ethnicity, gender, family composition, and so on and all of these as they determine their location in and relation to the existing power structures of society. The opinions people have about different issues, then, are merely a reflection of those sociological "givens" over which the individual has little or no control. The social sciences have offered a variety of theories which attempt to explain why children think and act the way that they do. Investigations into the etiology of variant patterns among youth have explored a host of social/environmental, psychological, and in some cases physiological variables, the latter revived most recently with the hereditary explanations of Wilson and Herrnstein (James Q. Wilson and Richard J. Herrnstein, *Crime and Human Nature* [New York: Simon and Schuster, 1985]).

The psychological and social/environmental explanations clearly resonate more palatably with policymakers. As we have seen, the developmental models of Piaget and Kohlberg are the major pedagogical staples of contemporary moral education in the U.S.; the Rodgersian derived notion of self-esteem has become the central value that educators, politicians, and social workers wish to inculcate into America's youth. Though psychological variables are increasingly used to understand the attitudinal and behavioral patterns of children, it is the social/environmental factors that are seen to be the major determinants of the conduct of their lives. In this regard, sociologists have considered the impact of income and class (Albert K. Cohen, *Delinquent Boys: The Culture of the Gang* [New York: Free Press, 1955]; Christopher Jencks and Paul E. Peterson, *The Urban Underclass* [Washington, D.C.: Brookings Institute, 1991]), family structure and education (Nan M. Astone and Sara S. McLanahan, "Family Structure, Parental Rights and High School Completion," *American Sociological Review* 51 [1991], pp. 403–412), race (Susan E. Mayer, "How Much Does a High School's Racial and Socioeconomic Mix Affect Graduation and Teenage Fertility Rates?" in *The Urban Underclass*, edited by Christopher Jencks and Paul E. Peterson [Washington, D.C.: Brookings Institute, 1991]; Douglas S. Massey, Andrew B. Gross, and Mitchell L. Eggers, "Segregation, the Concentration of Poverty, and the Life Chances of Individuals," *Social Science Research* 20, no. 4 [1992], pp. 397–420), subcultural associations (Walter Miller, "Lower-class Culture as a Generating Milieu of Gang Delinquency," in *The Sociology of Crime and Delinquency*, edited by Marvin E. Wolfgang, Leonard Savitz, and Norman Johnston [New York: Wiley, 1970]), and neighborhoods (Christopher Jencks and Susan E. Meyer, "The Social Consequences of Growing Up in a Poor Neighborhood," in *Inner-city Poverty in the United States*, edited by Laurence E. Lynn, Jr. and Michael G. H. McGeary [Washington, D.C.: National Academy, 1990]; Jeanne Brooks-Gunn et al., "Do Neighborhoods Influence Child and Adolescent Development?" *American Journal of Sociology* 99, no. 2 [Sept. 1993], pp. 353–395) on a child's ability or inability to operate and achieve within the normative expectations of society. These factors have all been invoked to explain such outcomes as juvenile delinquency, teenage pregnancy, high school drop-out rates, drug and alcohol use, and so on.

This prejudice is not only shared by most social scientists, but by the public policy establishment as well. The idea is that if attitudes, opinions, and behaviors are a reflection of the material conditions of their lives, then in order to change those attitudes, opinions, and behaviors, one must change the sociological conditions. As it pertains to the problems children face, public policy tends to be oriented toward changing the conditions of their lives that predispose children to do things that are not good for them or for society. Make changes in the structures of society and the drug-taking, stealing, lying, irresponsible sexual behavior, fatalism, and so on, will come to an end.

The evidence of these surveys suggests that there is much more to the story.

27. There is more than one element of common sense here. As children (or even as adults) we rarely anticipate nor work out beforehand what we would or should do when we confront a predicament or face a difficult choice. Implicitly though, we look to our deepest beliefs about right and wrong, good and bad, and so on for the principles for making "the right" decision. In this way, moral culture, internalized, acts like a compass, giving consistency and predictability to a person's decisions.

28. In this survey the elementary age children in 4th through 6th grades were not presented with this question or other questions about sexuality.

29. This explanation was initially described in the simple statistical analysis found in *The Survey on the Beliefs and Moral Values of America's Children*, but it was confirmed through high level statistical techniques of discriminant analysis to measure the relative importance of factors thought to impact the behavioral dispositions of children.

My colleague Daniel Johnson and I generated twelve separate indicators of moral judgment and opinion that were used as dependent variables in the analysis. The first two simply recorded whether students agreed or disagreed with the following statements: (1) "Abortion is all right, if having a baby will change your life plans in a way you will find hard to live with," and (2) "Homosexual relations are OK, if that is the person's choice." The last ten all came out of the series of questions wherein students were presented with real-life scenarios and asked what they would do in each case. The series as a whole has already been introduced in the text, but there are a couple of specific variables that have yet to be described in detail. They dealt with issues of stealing and of relating with known homosexuals and were worded as follows:

You really want some money to go out with your friends, and you don't have any of your own. Yet there is money belonging to your parents in the kitchen drawer which they have told you not to use. Your parents are not home. In this situation, you would probably . . .

Do without the money
Try to reach your parents for their permission
Take the money without asking, hoping they won't notice

You discover to your surprise that a good friend of your own sex is involved in a homosexual relationship. In this situation . . .

Your friendship would continue and not change at all
Your friendship would continue but not as close as before
Your friendship would probably come to an end

All the rest of the variables have already been described at length in the text. They gauged students' dispositions toward such behaviors as cheating on a test, lying about an act of vandalism, drinking alcohol, "petting," engaging in premarital sex, having an abortion, or helping a homeless person or ailing classmate.

Given the mature themes raised by some of these questions, many were only asked of older students. To be more specific, the items dealing with abortion, sexual activity and homosexuality, and underage drinking were only asked of those in grades 7 through 12. Meanwhile, the items on stealing, cheating, lying, helping a homeless person, and helping an ailing classmate were asked of the entire sample.

Note that while the two agree/disagree variables are dichotomous in nature, all ten of the situation-based variables have three or four valid response categories. Discriminant analysis is a flexible enough procedure to handle these more complex variables, and in our own explorations we did go ahead and run a series of analyses with them as they were originally coded. The results offer an intriguing picture of how various moral commitments "map" onto a host of subtly different behaviors. Yet because our focus for the present analysis is much simpler, we opted to streamline the presentation and interpretation of the discriminant function coefficients by dichotomizing all of the dependent variables.

The decision we made in collapsing categories of the situation-based variables was generally straightforward. In the few cases where the choice of a cutting point seemed somewhat arbitrary (e.g., with the items on lying to the school principal, helping an ailing classmate, or having sex), we experimented with several different options. In no case did the choice of cutting point make an appreciable impact on the results observed. In the end, we decided to break the variables down as follows:

Those who would copy a neighbor's exam or glance occasionally *vs.* Those who would answer an exam on their own

Those who would go without money or get parents' permission to take some *vs.* Those who would take the money without asking

Those who would steadfastly lie about a friend's act of vandalism *vs.* Those who would tell what they knew (be it anonymously or in person)

Those who would ignore or speak harshly to a homeless person *vs.* Those who would give either money or time/kind words

Those who would refuse to help an ailing classmate or help only if convenient *vs.* Those who would help without reservation

Those who would refuse a glass of alcohol or take it and not drink *vs.* Those who would take the glass and drink

Those who would be willing to go beyond kissing *vs.* Those who would not go beyond kissing

Those who would unreservedly have sex or would *try* to hold off if possible *vs.* Those who would refuse to have sex or insist on waiting until marriage

Those who would advise their friend to get an abortion *vs.* Those who would advise her to have the baby

Those who would remain friends with a known homosexual *vs.* Those who would cut off their friendship

This set of dichotomies certainly glosses over the nuances of the original set of variables, but when it comes to gauging the relative impact of moral compass on behavioral dispositions, the two sets lead to essentially the same conclusion.

The independent variables for the analysis included a range of demographic factors as well as our moral compass variable. The student's sex, race, and religious upbringing were all expressed as single dummy-coded variables, with values of "1" for male, white (as opposed to nonwhite), and Protestant (as opposed to Catholic, Jewish, other, or none). The broad array of family types was also reduced to two and expressed in a dummy-coded variable—a "1" indicated that the child lived with both mother and father, while a "0" indicated some other living arrangement. Grade in school and income were both left as interval variables in their natural metrics, although the derivation of the income variable was not exactly straightforward. Since young people are not generally in a position to provide accurate family income information, the students in each school were just assigned the median income for the primary zip code area served by the school (as identified by their principal). Place of residence (urban, suburban, or rural) was expressed in a series of three dummy variables; for all estimations of discriminant functions, "urban" served as the omitted variable. Similarly, the moral compass variable was recoded into a series of five dummy variables (expressivist, utilitarian, civic humanist, conventionalist, and theist), with "expressivist" serving as the reference category for all analyses.

Consider the results from discriminant analyses conducted on each of our dependent variables. The first two dependent variables listed are the simple agree-disagree items asking about abortion and homosexuality; the remaining ten are the set of (dichotomized) situation-based variables. While the signs of discriminant function coefficients are generally arbitrarily assigned, they have been modified here such that positive coefficients indicate a push toward agreement with a statement or toward willingness to commit a given act. A positive discriminant function coefficient in the column labeled "cheating," for example, denotes an increased chance of a student's reporting that she would probably cheat on the exam. A negative coefficient, of course, denotes a decreased chance of her saying as much.

In every single one of the analyses, the moral compass variables are among the most important variables in the equation (and this is so regardless of whether we focus on the coefficients themselves or on the item-function correlations). In four of them, the largest coefficients (and correlations) are those associated with the moral compass variables. Especially important are the distinctions between theists and expressivists (a difference captured in the coefficient for theist itself) and between theists and utilitarians. Indeed, in nearly half of the cases, utilitarians are even more distant from theists than are expressivists (i.e., the difference between the coefficients for theists and utilitarians is greater than the theist coefficient alone).

The only variable that routinely rivals (or even eclipses) the moral compass variables in terms of magnitude of effect is that for students' grade in school. This is to be expected, given all that we know about moral development and the normal progression of ethical thought over the course of childhood. All other things being equal, older children are simply more likely to engage in activities that go against the conventional grain.

The only other variable that deserves mentioning in this analysis is gender. Males, we find, are much more likely than are females to report that they would engage in sexual activity. Indeed, gender proves to be the strongest determinant of behavioral disposition when it comes to questions about petting or premarital sex. This does not come as a surprise. What may be a little surprising, however, is the fact that gender is also the strongest determinant when it comes to the question about staying friends with someone who is known as gay. For all the license males are willing to give themselves in the area of personal sexual activity, they are clearly more uncomfortable with the thought of relating with gays than are females.

30. I am not suggesting that this is the end of the story. Future research efforts could provide a more specific sociodemographic profile of children, and how those factors relate to moral orientation. For example, it would be highly useful to acquire more detailed information regarding the characteristics of children's families (e.g., the number of siblings, the structure of child supervision, and the education level of parents) and their role in the development and maintenance of moral commitment. In addition, given the distinctiveness of the theistic orientation, it would be useful to learn of the specific ways in which different theological traditions (e.g., Protestant, Catholic, Jewish, Mormon) shape moral compasses.

31. The survey was "The 1996 Survey of American Public Culture," conducted by The Post-Modernity Project at the University of Virginia in conjunction with the Gallup Organization. Carl Bowman of Bridgewater College and I were the principal investigators designing the survey, analyzing the data, and writing the report. In determining moral compass, the same question used in the 1989 Girl Scout Survey was used in this survey as well. (See note 24.)

32. Just 56 percent of those operating with an expressivist worldview and 60 percent of those operating with a utilitarian moral commitment embraced the golden rule.

33. The distribution was as follows: expressivist (38 percent), utilitarian (50 percent), civic humanist (26 percent), conventionalist (29 percent), and theist (13 percent).

34. On the matter of responsibility toward the local community, the distribution was as follows: expressivist (60 percent), utilitarian (59 percent), civic humanist (73 percent), conventionalist (82 percent), and theist (87 percent); toward friends and coworkers, the sense of responsibility was much less though the pattern of distribution was similar: expressivist (19 percent), utilitarian (23 percent), civic humanist (17 percent), conventionalist (26 percent), and theist (47 percent).

35. The data reads as follows: to the dictum, "live for today" as contrasted with "prepare for tomorrow" the distribution was: expressivist (55 percent), utilitarian (52 percent), civic humanists (38 percent), conventionalist (7 percent), and theist (20 percent); to the dictum, "money is the key to life's satisfactions," the pattern of distribution was very similar: expressivist (63 percent), utilitarian (44 percent), civic humanist (31 percent), conventionalist (42 percent), and theist (25 percent); finally, to the dictum, "eat, drink, and be merry," we again see a familiar pattern of distribution: expressivist (40 percent), utilitarian (34 percent), civic humanist (37 percent), conventionalist (27 percent), and theist (9 percent).

36. A higher median income is significantly but weakly associated with an increased probability of saying one would (1) cheat, (2) drink, and (3) be nonaltruistic toward an injured peer. Income is also positively associated with acceptance of abortion and homosexuality. Even among children, the wealthier, the more tolerant.

37. For example, regardless of their moral compass, minorities tend to be slightly less inclined to engage in petting and sexual intercourse. Being white also increases the probability of saying one would (1) cheat, (2) drink, and (3) disregard the plight of a homeless man.

38. The work of Carol Gilligan, a colleague of Kohlberg's at Harvard, deserves special mention as an effort to recognize the embodiment of morality. According to Gilligan, Kohlberg's research overlooked the important differences in moral judgment that are rooted in one's gender. Women, she contends, speak in "a different voice" than men. Boys and men frame moral decisions in terms of individual rights, liberties, and duties, whereas women embrace a language and logic of interpersonal responsibility and caring. In response to the Heinz dilemma (see Chapter 5, note 6), for example, an adolescent boy would typically be concerned with property rights and individual fairness, but an adolescent girl would typically express concern that the relationship between Heinz and his wife does not suffer as a result of the theft. In Kohlberg's schema, the young girl would be ranked lower in moral development than the boy, whereas, Gilligan argued, they simply embrace different ways of making moral decisions.

In these data we see this dynamic played out in the way girls regard others in need, for example, in the case of the homeless person or the case of a fellow classmate who needs help. It is also seen in the way girls tend to judge what will make a future job satisfying to them. On this, girls are much more inclined to view service in a job as that which will make them happy. Boys, by contrast, tend to be significantly more "instrumental" in the way they approach these matters. As one might guess, junior and senior high school boys are more inclined than girls to have favorable attitudes toward petting, premarital sex, and even abortion. They are also more likely to cheat or at least try to cheat. Boys too were more inclined to engage in underage drinking. Being male significantly increases the probability of saying one would (1) cheat, (2) lie (refuse to reveal information to the school principal), (3) drink alcohol, and (4) have sex, this latter outcome being a sizable effect of 41 percentage points. In addition, being male is positively associated with a lack of altruism toward a homeless man and an injured student. Males also show greater tolerance for abortion and less tolerance for homosexuality.

39. On the variable "family type," I decided to distinguish between those students who said they lived with both their mother and father (67 percent of the sample) and those students who indicated any of the other living arrangements. This coding scheme is likely to introduce some error in measurement, given that not all students may be aware that their father, for example, is actually their stepfather. An alternative coding scheme would be one that distinguishes between single- and two-parent households. This results in a considerably lopsided distribution that attenuates statistical significance; however, substantive conclusions remain similar across both versions of the variable.

40. Ideally, one would have longitudinal data to argue this point most strongly. *The Survey on the Beliefs and Moral Values of American Children* was fielded just once. So, as is common in studies of this nature, I have made certain inferences about the process of growing up from comparisons among children of various age and grade levels. On these terms, the evidence is fairly clear. The older students have higher probabilities of saying they would (1) cheat, (2) lie, (3) drink, (4) have sex, and (5) favor abortion if having a baby is inconvenient. A higher grade level is also associated with greater altruism toward a homeless man but less altruism toward an injured peer.

41. This is true for students attending all schools, especially public schools. But it is also the case for students attending religious schools. The tendency is more dramatic in

the Catholic parochial schools than the Evangelical schools but even in the latter the same pattern is evident.

Chapter Nine

1. John Dewey, *Reconstruction in Philosophy* (New York: Henry Holt and Co., 1920), p. 164.

2. John Dewey, "Teaching Ethics in the High School," *Educational Review* 6 (November 1893), pp. 313–321.

3. Quoted in Louis Raths, Merrill Harmin, and Sidney Simon, *Values and Teaching*, 2d. ed. (Columbus, Ohio: Merrill Publishing, 1978), p. 290.

4. See John Dewey, *Problems of Men* (New York: Philosophical Library, 1946), p. 156.

5. Carl Rodgers, "Becoming a Person: The Nellie Heldt Lectures," Oberlin College, 1954, p. 42.

6. Carl Rodgers, *On Becoming a Person* (Boston: Houghton-Mifflin, 1961), p. 122.

7. In his own words, the "overall implication for education would be that the task of the teacher is to create a facilitating classroom climate in which significant learning can take place" (ibid., p. 287).

8. Ibid., pp. 287–289.

9. Ibid., p. 291.

10. William Glasser, *Schools Without Failure* (New York: Harper and Row, 1969), p. 186.

11. Ibid., p. 22.

12. Ibid., p. 186. In this light, he says, the class becomes "a social problem-solving group."

13. Sidney Simon, Leland Howe, and Howard Kirshenbaum. *Values Clarification*, rev. ed. (New York: Hart, 1978), pp. 15–16. Disciples of the approach echoed the opinion, calling content-based moral pedagogies nothing more than a form of "moralism." See Maury Smith, *A Practical Guide to Values Clarification* (La Jolla, Calif.: University Associates, 1977), p. 191.

14. Howard Kirschenbaum, *Advanced Value Clarification* (La Jolla, Calif.: University Associates, 1977), p. 149.

15. Ibid., p. 63.

16. See Lawrence Kohlberg, "Education for Justice: A Modern Statement of the Platonic View," in *Moral Education: Five Lectures*, edited by Theodore R. Sizer and Nancy F. Sizer (Cambridge, Mass.: Harvard University Press, 1970).

17. See, for example, C. K. Kamii, *Young Children Reinvent Arithmetic: Implications of Piaget's Theory* (New York: Teachers College Press, 1985), and E. Duckworth, "*The Having of Wonderful Ideas*" *and Other Essays on Teaching and Learning* (New York: Teachers College Press, 1987).

18. Rheta DeVries and Betty Zan, *Moral Classrooms, Moral Children: Creating a Constructivist Atmosphere in Early Education* (New York: Teachers College Press, 1994), p. 28.

19. DeVries and Zan put it just this way: "Do not dictate rules to children. The teacher may lead children toward rules but should not specifically suggest them. As long as deci-

sions are made by others, children will experience these decisions as being imposed from somewhere outside themselves" (ibid., pp. 132–133).

20. Ibid., p. 78. One is not likely to miss the theme, for it is amplified throughout their volume. Consider, for example, the admonition that "the teacher establishes an atmosphere in which children feel that the teacher cares for them, enjoys being with them, and respects them by taking their feelings, interests, and ideas into account" (p. 179).

21. Hunter Lewis, *A Question of Values: Six Ways We Make the Personal Choices That Shape Our Lives* (San Francisco: Harper and Row, 1990). Lewis states that the book is about the six ways in which we choose values.

22. Kohn derides the "drill and skill" approach of teaching moral content, an approach that essentially "conk[s] students on the head with their morals," saying it "is tantamount to indoctrination," an imposition of "conservative ideology." See Alfie Kohn, "How Not to Teach Values," *Phi Delta Kappan* 78 (February 1997), pp. 429–443.

23. Rodgers, "Becoming a Person: The Nellie Heldt Lectures," pp. 5–6. See his elaboration of this argument in Rodgers, *On Becoming a Person*, p. 122.

24. Glasser, *Schools Without Failure*, pp. 21–22.

25. Merrill Harmin, Howard Kirschenbaum, and Sidney Simon, *Clarifying Values Through Subject Matter: Application for the Classroom* (Minneapolis, Minn.: Winston Press, 1974), pp. 34–35.

26. "Too much praise can lead to the opposite results." This is why "encouragement is a better choice than praise" (Don Dinkmeyer, Sr., Gary D. McKay, and Don Dinkmeyer, Jr., *The Parent's Handbook* [Circle Pines, Minnesota: American Guidance Service, Inc., 1997], pp. 52–53).

27. Dorothy Corkille Briggs, *Your Child's Self-Esteem: The Key to His Life* (New York: Doubleday, 1970), pp. 312, 313.

28. These terms are taken from William Glasser in an interview with Pauline B. Gough, "The Key to Improving Schools: An Interview with William Glasser," *Phi Delta Kappan* 68 (May 1987), p. 661.

29. Piaget is quoted by Clark Power, "Democratic Schools and the Problem of Moral Authority," in *Handbook of Moral Behavior and Development*, vol. 3, edited by William Kurtines and Jacob Gewirtz (Hillsdale, N.J.: Lawrence Erlbaum Associates, 1991), p. 319.

30. Ibid.

31. F. Clark Power, Ann Higgins, and Lawrence Kohlberg, *Lawrence Kohlberg's Approach to Moral Education* (New York: Columbia University Press, 1989), p. 62. See also Clark Power, "The Just Community to Moral Education," *Journal of Moral Education* 179, no. 3 (Oct. 1988), pp. 195–208.

32. Don Dinkmeyer, Sr., Gary D. McKay, and Don Dinkmeyer, Jr., *STEP Leader's Resource Guide* (Circle Pines, Minnesota: American Guidance Service, Inc., 1997), p. 5.

33. Alfie Kohn, "Choices for Children: Why and How to Let Students Decide," *Phi Delta Kappan* 75 (September 1993), p. 16. See also Alfie Kohn, "Discipline is the Problem—Not the Solution," *Learning* 24 (October/November 1995), p. 34.

34. See James Beane, *Affect in the Curriculum: Toward Democracy, Dignity, and Diversity* (New York: Teachers College Press, 1990), p. 53.

35. Dewey, *Reconstruction in Philosophy*, p. 177.

36. It was not only Rodgers and Maslow but Erich Fromm as well who was explicit about this. See his book, *Escape from Freedom* (New York: Holt, 1941). This view was popularized more recently by the televangelist, Robert Schuler, whose theology seems far more influenced by Rodgers than by Calvin (of the Reformed tradition of which he is a part). See Robert Schuler, *Self-Esteem: The New Reformation* (Waco: Word Books, 1982).

37. Harmin, Kirschenbaum, and Simon, *Clarifying Values Through Subject Matter*, pp. 34–35. "[The teacher] may offer his own viewpoint, but he is careful to describe it as his opinion, not as the final answer." As they put it elsewhere, "To us one value does not seem as good as another" (Raths, Harmin, and Simon, *Values and Teaching*, p. 290).

38. DeVries and Zan, *Moral Classrooms, Moral Children*, p. 133.

39. The most important source on this word and its meaning is Ervin Staub, *Positive Social Behavior and Morality*, vols. 1 & 2 (New York: Academic Press, 1978).

40. Quest International, *Skills for Adolescence* (Granville, Ohio: Quest International), Section III–8.

41. Dinkmeyer, Sr., McKay, and Dinkmeyer, Jr., *STEP Leader's Resource Guide*, p. 13.

42. Rodgers, "Becoming a Person: The Nellie Heldt Lectures," p. 38. Emphasis in the original. This was reaffirmed in his book by the same title, *On Becoming a Person*, p. 119.

43. See Kohn, "How Not to Teach Values," pp. 429–443.

44. DeVries and Zan, *Moral Classrooms, Moral Children*, p. 46.

45. Raths, Harmin, and Simon, *Values and Teaching*, p. 41.

46. Ibid., p. 47.

47. See Kohn, "How Not to Teach Values," p. 435.

48. Dinkmeyer, Sr., McKay, and Dinkmeyer, Jr., *The Parent's Handbook*, p. 7.

49. The phrase is Albert Camus's.

50. This is seen in the person

moving away from the compelling image of what he 'ought to be.' Some individuals have absorbed so deeply from their parents the concept 'I ought to be good,' or 'I have to be good,' that it is only with the greatest of inward struggle that they find themselves moving away from this goal. . . . Over against these pressures for conformity, . . . when [people] are free to be any way they wish, they tend to resent and to question the tendency of the organization, the college or the culture to mould them to any given form (Rodgers, *On Becoming a Person*, pp. 167–170).

51. DeVries and Zan, *Moral Classrooms, Moral Children*, p. 26. The similarities between schools that require discipline and authority and prisons are that "liberty is suppressed," "inmates and children are excluded from power in decision-making," "rewards are manipulated as exchange for compliance with authorities," and "punishments are decided bureaucratically, sometimes for minor infractions of petty rules" (p. 26).

52. Ibid., p. 253.

53. John Rice enlarges on this point in a study of the co-dependency movement. See John Steadman Rice, *A Disease of One's Own* (New Brunswick: Transaction Press, 1996).

54. Michael Sandel, *Liberalism and the Limits of Justice* (Cambridge: Cambridge University Press, 1982), p. 62. Though referring to John Rawls, I believe his criticism fairly de-

scribes the moral cosmology latent in this pedagogy—what Sandel calls, "deontological liberalism."

55. Erik Erikson, *Life History and the Historical Moment* (New York: Norton, 1975), p. 207.

56. James W. Fowler, *Stages of Faith: The Psychology of Human Development and the Quest for Meaning* (San Francisco: Harper and Row, 1981).

57. Kirschenbaum, *Advanced Value Clarification*, pp. 12–13.

58. See Alfie Kohn, "The Truth About Self-Esteem," *Phi Delta Kappan* 75 (December 1994), pp. 272–283.

59. Abraham Maslow, *The Psychology of Science* (New York: Harper and Row, 1966), p. 133.

60. The exception here is Kohlberg who viewed himself as a neoplatonist.

61. In Piaget's influential view, the basic moral sensibilities were "feelings of liking or disliking."

62. Rodgers, "Becoming a Person: The Nellie Heldt Lectures," p. 9.

63. Ibid.

64. Abraham Maslow, "Some Basic Propositions of a Growth and Self-actualization Psychology," in *Theories of Personality: Primary Sources and Research*, edited by G. Lindzey and C. S. Hall (New York: John Wiley and Sons, 1965), p. 309.

65. Abraham Maslow, "Psychological Data and Value Theory," in *New Knowledge in Human Values*, edited by Abraham Maslow and Pitrim Sorokin (New York: Harper and Row, 1959), p. 130.

66. Ibid.

67. Dinkmeyer, Sr., McKay, and Dinkmeyer, Jr., *The Parent's Handbook*, pp. 27–34.

68. Ibid., p. 28.

69. Ibid., p. 33.

70. Recall, as an illustration, the Washington D.C. Commission of Values-Centered Goals mentioned in Chapter 5. Among other things, it sought to encourage students to learn "*responsibility to self and others*—to help students revere the gift of healthy bodies and minds, appreciate the interdependence of all things, behave compassionately toward others and learn by example and experience *that unselfish service is a key component of self-gratification.* In another text, the purposes of friendship are framed in terms of self-gratification. "Your best choice of a friend is someone who wants you to take care of your health, do well in school, be responsible, and obey your parents or guardian. This is what is meant by 'A friend is a gift you give yourself.' The gift of friendship can improve the quality of your life" (Linda Meeks and Philip Heit, *Health Focus on You*, grade 7 [Columbus, Ohio: Merrill Publishing Company, 1990], p. 43–44).

71. William Glasser, *The Quality School Teacher* (New York: Harper, 1993), p. 25.

72. Alfie Kohn, *Beyond Discipline: From Compliance to Community* (Alexandria: Association for Supervision and Curriculum Development, 1996), p. 10. The Child Development Project based in Oakland, California, has based its entire moral education program on the premise that "by meeting children's needs, we increase the likelihood that they will care about others." Alfie Kohn, "How Not to Teach Values," p. 437.

73. Ron Brandt, "Punished by Rewards? A Conversation with Alfie Kohn," *Educational Leadership* 53 (September 1995), pp. 13–16.

74. For example, when Kohlberg and his colleagues spoke of community commitment, it is framed individualistically and psychologically; as a commitment that derives from the reference point of the self and its needs and its values. In predictable style the nature of communal commitment—in the case of students in their schools—is described in five stages: Level 0 – Individuals do not value the school; Level 1 – Instrumental value (school helps individuals meet their needs); Level 2 – Enthusiastic identification (school valued at special moments such as when a team wins a sporting event); Level 3 – Spontaneous community (school valued for closeness of members); and Level 4 – Normative community (school valued for its own sake and membership involves a social contract to respect the norms and ideals of the community). Kohlberg and his colleagues elucidate their view in Power, Higgins, and Kohlberg, *Lawrence Kohlberg's Approach to Moral Education*.

75. Milton Meyerhoff, *On Caring* (New York: HarperPerennial, 1990), p. 40.

76. Her ethical theory is addressed in Nel Noddings, *Caring: A Feminine Approach to Ethics* (Berkeley: University of California Press, 1984) and her approach to moral education is put forward in Nel Noddings, *The Challenge to Care in Schools* (New York: Teachers College Press, 1992), p. xi.

77. Noddings, *The Challenge to Care in Schools*, p. 15.

78. Noddings, *Caring*, pp. 28–29.

79. Sandel, *Liberalism and the Limits of Justice*, pp. 23–24.

80. As Sandel points out, this view of the moral life and the moral agent goes far beyond either Locke or Kant for it rejects the transcendental deductions that both insisted upon. See *Liberalism and the Limits of Justice*, p. 24.

81. See Gough, "The Key to Improving Schools: An Interview with William Glasser," p. 660.

82. John Dewey, *Freedom and Culture* (New York: G. P. Putnam, 1939), p. 125.

83. John Dewey, *Democracy and Education* (New York: Macmillan, 1916), p. 143.

84. John Dewey, "Ethical Principles Underlying Education," in National Herbart Society, *Third Yearbook* (Chicago: University of Chicago Press, 1897), p. 12.

85. Quoted in Tim Stafford, "Helping Johnny be Good," *Christianity Today*, 11 September 1995, p. 39.

86. Thomas Lickona, "The Case for Character Education," *Tikkun* 12, no. 1 (January-February 1997), p. 23.

87. Thomas Lickona, *Educating for Character: How Our Schools Can Teach Respect and Responsibility* (New York: Bantam, 1992), p. 42. Here he writes, "There are rationally grounded, nonrelative, objectively worthwhile moral values: respect for human life, liberty, the inherent value of every individual person, and the consequent responsibility to care for each other and carry out our basic obligations" (p. 230).

88. Lickona, "The Case for Character Education," p. 23.

89. Ibid.

90. Ibid., p. 24.

91. Ibid., p. 23. See also Lickona, *Educating for Character*, pp. 56–61.

92. Lickona, *Educating for Character*, p. 42.

93. Robert Jamieson and Rex Dalby, *Responsibility Skills: Success Through Accepting Responsibility* (Pasadena, Calif.: Jefferson Center for Character Education, 1997), pp. 13, 17, 29, 33, 45, 49. In the text, the virtues are capitalized for emphasis.

94. Ibid., pp. 17, 29, 33, 45, 49.

95. Ibid., p. 14.

96. In some of the material advocated, even these justifications are absent. Consider, in this regard, material from the Character Counts! Coalition. On honesty: "DO: tell the truth; be sincere. DON'T: betray a trust, deceive, mislead, cheat, or steal; don't be devious or tricky."

On integrity: "DO: stand up for your beliefs; be your best self; walk your talk. DON'T: do anything you think is wrong."

On respect for others: "DO: judge all people on their merits; be courteous and polite, tolerant, appreciative and accepting of individual differences. DON'T: abuse, demand, or mistreat anyone; don't use, manipulate, exploit or take advantage of others."

On fairness: "DO: treat all people fairly; be open-minded; listen to others; try to understand what they are saying and feeling; make decisions which affect others only after appropriate consideration. DON'T: take advantage of others' mistakes or take more than your fair share."

On caring: "DO: show you care about others through kindness, caring, sharing and compassion, live by the Golden Rule and help others. DON'T: be selfish, mean, cruel or insensitive to others' feelings."

And so on. Character Counts! Coalition, promotional information, quoted in B. David Brooks and Frank Goble, *The Case for Character Education* (Northridge: Studio 4 Productions, 1997), pp. 69–71.

97. William J. Bennett, *The Book of Virtues: A Treasury of Great Moral Stories* (New York: Simon and Schuster, 1994), p. 13.

98. William Kilpatrick, *Why Johnny Can't Tell Right from Wrong* (New York: Simon and Schuster, 1992), p. 268.

99. Allan Bloom, *The Closing of the American Mind* (New York: Simon and Schuster, 1987), p. 344.

100. This is an important qualification. The neo-classical position can be formulated in a way that is grounded in specific traditions.

101. See, for example, Mark B. Tappan and Lyn Mikel Brown, "Stories Told and Lessons Learned: Toward a Narrative Approach to Moral Development and Moral Education," *Harvard Educational Review* 59, no. 2 (May 1989), pp. 182–205.

102. Colin Greer and Herbert Kohl, eds., *A Call to Character* (New York: Harper-Collins, 1995), p. 8.

103. Ibid., pp. 14, 15, 45, 68, 293.

104. Bernard Williams, *Morality: An Introduction to Ethics* (New York: Harper and Row, 1972), p. 66.

105. Community of Caring, "Our Children Can Not Succeed As Students, Professionals, Parents or Community Leaders Until They First Succeed as Human Beings" (Washington, D.C.: Community of Caring, undated).

106. Ibid.

107. Community of Caring, "How to Create a Community of Caring School" (Washington, D.C.: The Joseph P. Kennedy Foundation, 1993/1994), p. 38.

108. The National Commission on Civic Renewal, transcript of the second plenary session, Washington, D.C., 19 May 1997, p. 23.

109. Amitai Etzioni, *The Spirit of Community* (New York: Crown Books, 1993), pp. 43–44. Emphasis added.

110. Remarks made by Robert Chase, National Educational Association president, at the Fourth Annual Character Counts! Coalition Meeting, Washington, D.C., 11 April 1997, NEA home page, 3 January 1999, http://www.nea.org.

111. These include: "respect for human life, liberty, the inherent value of every individual person, and the consequent responsibility to care for each other and carry out our basic obligations" (Lickona, *Educating for Character*, p. 230).

112. Alasdair MacIntyre, *After Virtue* (Notre Dame, Ind.: University of Notre Dame Press, 1984), pp. 52–54. MacIntyre made this point earlier in his book, *A Short History of Ethics* (New York: Macmillan, 1966) in his discussion of Kierkegaard's work.

Suppose that one believes that one's moral position can be rationally justified, that it is a conclusion which can be validly derived from certain premises. Then these premises in turn must be vindicated, and if their vindication consists in deriving them from conclusions based on more fundamental premises, the same problem will arise. But the chain of reasons must have an ending, and we must reach a point where we simply choose to stand by certain premises. At this point decision has replaced argument; and in all arguments on human existence there will be some such point (p. 216).

113. William J. Bennett and Edwin Delattre, "A Moral Education," *American Educator* 3, no. 4 (Winter 1979), p. 7.

Chapter Ten

1. William Glasser, *Schools Without Failure* (New York: Harper and Row, 1969), p. 186. Emphasis added.

2. See, for example, Edward O. Wilson, *Sociobiology: The New Synthesis* (Cambridge, Mass.: Belknap Press of Harvard University Press, 1975); Edward O. Wilson, *On Human Nature* (Cambridge, Mass.: Harvard University Press, 1978).

3. See Lawrence Kohlberg, "Education for Justice: A Modern Statement of the Platonic View," in *Moral Education: Five Lectures,* edited by Theodore R. Sizer and Nancy F. Sizer (Cambridge, Mass.: Harvard University Press, 1970), p. 58. "Justice," he argues, "is a matter of equal and universal human rights" (p. 69). To accentuate the point, he refers to his interviews with children and adults in the U.S., Britain, Turkey, Taiwan, and Yucatan (p. 70). In a curious elaboration of his ideas, he argues that the universality of his model was further established by the analogous development of political and social history itself: different political regimes reflect different stages of moral development, and thus history slowly inches us toward higher and higher stages of moral development. The establish-

ment of liberal democracy (a higher stage of political development) from the rubble of authoritarian regimes (a lower stage) is a sign of this tendency in history.

4. Ibid., p. 67.

5. In the cognitive tradition, Milton Rokeach's project in the 1970s to identify within human experience a set of "instrumental" and "terminal" values was akin to this aspiration. Rokeach identified eighteen "terminal" or end-oriented values that included a sense of accomplishment, self-respect, wisdom, and freedom, and eighteen "instrumental" or means-oriented values, that included responsibility, capability, broadmindedness, and intellectuality. See Milton Rokeach, *The Nature of Human Values* (New York: Free Press, 1973).

6. Irene S. Pyskowski, "Moral Values and the School—Is There a Way Out of the Maze?" *Education* 107, no. 1 (Fall 1986), p. 46.

7. This is the language that Kohlberg uses to describe the pedagogic task. See Kohlberg, "Education for Justice," p. 58.

8. The anthropological case is made explicitly by Henrietta Schwartz and Edward Wynne, "Transmitting Values to the Young: A Cross-Cultural Perspective," in *Equity in Values Education: Do the Values Education Aspects of Public School Curricula Deal Fairly with Diverse Belief Systems?* final report prepared for the U.S. Department of Education (Washington, D.C.: Department of Education, 1985). Schwartz and Wynne identify eight cultural universals found in all classrooms, essential ingredients in the socialization of children.

9. One of the more enthusiastic endorsements of this view is Don Eberly, *The Content of America's Character: Recovering Civic Virtue* (Lanham: Madison Books, 1995), pp. 20–21. These, he says, "not only transcend cultures, they predate the Victorian Age and terms like 'bourgeois' values by thousands of years" (p. 21).

10. William J. Bennett, "Moral Literacy and the Formation of Character," *USA Today* 117, no. 2518 (July 1988), p. 86.

11. William J. Bennett, *The Book of Virtues: A Treasury of Great Moral Stories* (New York: Simon and Schuster, 1994).

12. Gary Bauer, "The Moral of the Story: How to Teach Values in the Nation's Classrooms," *Policy Review* (Fall 1986), p. 26.

13. Thomas Lickona, "Educating the Moral Child," *Principal* 68 (November 1988), pp. 8, 20.

14. See Kevin Ryan, "The Moral Education of Teachers," in *Character Development in Schools and Beyond,* edited by Kevin Ryan and G. McLeon (New York: Praeger, 1987).

15. Bill Honig, *Last Chance for Our Children: How You Can Help Save Our Schools* (Reading, Mass.: Addison-Wesley, 1985).

16. The National Commission on Civic Renewal, transcript of the second plenary session, Washington, D.C., 19 May 1997, p. 23.

17. ASCD Panel on Moral Education, "Moral Education in the Life of the School" (Alexandria, Va.: Association for Supervision and Curriculum Development, 1988), pp. 37–38. This organization also insisted that American democracy required a consensus on the values that should be taught in public schools.

18. Sonia Nazario, "Schoolteachers Say It's Wrongheaded To Try to Teach Students What's Right," *Wall Street Journal*, 6 April 1990, pp. 1, 6.

19. E. Dale Davis, "Should the Public Schools Teach Values?" *Phi Delta Kappan* 65 (January 1984), p. 360.

20. M. E. Saterlie, "Developing a Community Consensus for Teaching Values," *Educational Leadership* 45, no. 8 (May 1988), pp. 44–47.

21. Project: Solution, Character Education Partnership home page, 15 February 1999, http://www.character.org.

22. Suzanne Daley, "The Pendulum is Swinging," *New York Times*, 12 December 1990, sec. B, p. 14f.

23. Tim Stafford, "Helping Johnny Be Good," *Christianity Today*, 11 September 1995, pp. 35–39.

24. Nazario, "Schoolteachers Say It's Wrongheaded To Try to Teach Students What's Right," pp. 1, 6.

25. Virginia General Assembly, *Elementary School Character Education Programs*, Senate Bill No. 817, adopted 4 April 1999. Emphasis added. In New Hampshire, the legal mandate was for the State Board of Education to "assist local districts in the identification of . . . basic values of character and citizenship" (New Hampshire State Board of Education, *Policy Statement on Character and Citizen Education*, 30 November 1988). In Georgia, the State Board of Education adopted a "core list of values" for implementation in the public schools (Georgia State Board of Education, *List of Core Values*, March 1991). In Oregon, it is also to help "students develop and practice the core ethical values that our diverse society shares and holds important" (Oregon State Board of Education, Oregon Administrative Rule 581–21–200, July 1993).

26. Virginia General Assembly, S.B. No. 817.

27. William Bennett quoted in Michael Cromartie, "Virtue Man," *Christianity Today*, 13 September 1993, p. 33.

28. Josephson Institute for the Advancement of Ethics, *Ethics: Easier Said Than Done* 1, no. 1 (Winter 1988), p. 7.

29. Virginia General Assemby, S.B. No. 817. This fear is not new. It was at the heart of the 1951 statement of the National Education Association, *Moral and Spiritual Values in the Public Schools*. Their conclusion was that only sanctions of a secular or naturalistic nature could be legitimately invoked in the schools, noting that religious sanctions "may not be explicitly invoked in the public school classroom," even while recognizing that they may play a powerful role in the moral and spiritual instruction of home and church. *Moral and Spiritual Values in the Public Schools* (Washington, D.C.: National Education Association, 1951), p. 3. According to David Brooks and Frank Goble, indoctrination would not only be legally problematic but "unethical as well" (*The Case for Character Education* [Northridge: Studio 4 Productions, 1997], pp. 19, 43).

30. See Kohlberg, "Education for Justice," pp. 68–69.

31. It is significant, for example, that in Amitai Etzioni's important articulation of the communitarian agenda, religion is mentioned but once. Amitai Etzioni, *The Spirit of Community* (New York: Crown Publishers, 1993), p. 43.

32. Ibid., pp. 38–53.

33. *Moral and Spiritual Values in the Public Schools.*, Washington, D.C.: The National Education Association, 1951, p. 38. Emphasis in the original.

34. Michael Josephson, "'Why Be Ethical?' The Role of Principle, God and Self-Interest," precourse reading materials, Character Counts! Character Development Seminars (Marina Del Rey, Calif.: Josephson Institute, 1997), p. 212.

35. Ibid.

36. Merrill Harmin, Howard Kirshenbaum, and Sidney B. Simon, *Clarifying Values Through Subject Matter* (Minneapolis, Minn.: Winston Press, 1974), pp. 36f.

37. Rheta DeVries and Betty Zan, *Moral Classrooms, Moral Children: Creating a Constructivist Atmosphere in Early Education* (New York: Teachers College Press, 1994), p. 268.

38. The irony, of course, is not just that the question is a natural one that ought to be answered when children ask it, it is that children are capable of much greater sophistication of moral reasoning than we often give them credit for. What is more, the story of the Excursus is that the different assumptions children hold about the foundations of moral truth—whether expressivist, utilitarian, civic humanist, conventionalist, or theistic—act as "moral compasses," guiding children in the often difficult decisions they make, in the futures they choose, and in the kinds of citizenship they anticipate. In short, the answers to the "why" questions not only matter to moral outcomes, they matter decisively.

39. As Adam Phillips observed, psychoanalysis has always been "phobic about the word" evil. See Adam Phillips, *On Flirtation: Psychoanalytic Essays on the Uncommitted Life* (Cambridge, Mass.: Harvard University Press, 1994), especially Chapter 5, "Besides Good and Evil," pp. 59–64.

40. See, in this regard, the insightful essay by Herbert Morris, "The Decline of Guilt," *Ethics* 99, 1 (October 1988), pp. 62–76.

41. As noted in Chapter 4, it was in the 1930s that Gordon Allport concluded that character was "an ethical concept," and because of this, "the psychologist does not need the term at all; personality alone will serve." "Character," he said, "is personality evaluated, and personality is character devalued" (Gordon W. Allport, *Personality: a Psychological Interpretation* [New York: Henry Holt and Company, 1937], p. 52).

42. See, for example, Alfred Adler, *The Practice and Theory of Individual Psychology*, 2d ed. (New York: Harcourt Brace Jovanovich, 1927), pp. 348–349. See also Jean Piaget, "Intelligence and Affectivity: Their Relation During Child Development" (Palo Alto, Calif.: Annual Reviews, 1981), pp. 61–65. These works are cited approvingly by DeVries and Zan in *Moral Classrooms, Moral Children*.

43. Pauline B. Gough, "The Key to Improving Schools: An Interview with William Glasser," *Phi Delta Kappan* 68 (May 1987), p. 658.

44. Ibid.

45. Charles Taylor, *The Sources of the Self: The Making of Modern Identity* (Cambridge, Mass.: Harvard University Press, 1989), p. 515.

46. See M. L. Hoffman, "Empathy, Its Limitations, and Its Role in a Comprehensive Moral Theory," in *Morality, Moral Behavior, and Moral Development*, edited by William Kurtines and Jacob Gewirtz (New York: Wiley, 1984), pp. 283–302, and M. L. Hoffman, "The Contributions of Empathy to Justice and Moral Development," in *Empathy and its Development*, edited by N. Eisenberg and J. Strayer (New York: Cambridge University Press, 1987), pp. 47–80.

47. Amitai Etzioni made this point in his essay, "Building A Better Child," *Washington Post Book World*, 29 December 1996, p. 9.

48. Hoffman observes that "to make moral judgments in complex situations may require moral principles that go beyond considering others and against which anyone's behavior can be assessed with minimal bias. Such moral principles would enable one to decide with more objectivity than empathy alone which moral claims deserve priority" (Hoffman, "Empathy, Its Limitations, and Its Role in a Comprehensive Moral Theory," p. 297). "Empathy and existential guilt," he says, cannot explain how one acquires the justice principle, but mainly "they may provide a motive base for being receptive to it and for guiding one's actions in accordance with it" (p. 300). Elsewhere, he reiterates the point saying in effect that empathy is not "an adequate substitute for moral principle" (Hoffman, "The Contributions of Empathy to Justice and Moral Development," p. 76).

49. Bernard Williams, *Morality: An Introduction to Ethics* (New York: Harper and Row, 1972), p. 64.

50. The term is from Kenneth Gergen, *The Saturated Self* (New York: Basic Books, 1991), p. 196.

51. I draw here from the incisive argument made by John Steadman Rice in his working paper, "The Triumph of Romantic Modernism: The Therapeutic Ethic and Post-Modern Theory," unpublished paper, University of North Carolina, Wilmington, 1998, pp. 39ff.

52. Morse Peckham, *The Triumph of Romanticism* (Columbia, S.C.: University of South Carolina Press, 1970).

53. Even when transcendentalism maintains all sorts of metaphysical pretensions, George Santayana called it "systematic subjectivism" (George Santayana, *Atoms of Thought: An Anthology of Thoughts from George Santayana*, edited by Ira D. Cardiff [New York: Philosophical Library, 1950], p. 119).

54. Empathy, here, speaks to the nature of value as well as the means of its development. If one consists of self and a personality, then so do other human beings; if one experiences a range of emotions, then so would others.

55. The idea that institutions, and schools in particular, need to be altered to draw out the potential of individuals is a common theme, especially among the advocates of the psychological strategy. As Alfie Kohn summarized the point, "In short, if we want to help children grow into compassionate and responsible people, we have to change the way the classroom works and feels, not just the way each separate member of that class acts." The environment must serve the potential of individuals. Alfie Kohn, "How Not to Teach Values: A Critical Look at Character Education," *Phi Delta Kappan* 78 (February 1997), p. 437.

56. Morse Peckham, "Toward a Theory of Romanticism: II. Reconsiderations," in *Studies in Romanticism* 1, no. 1 (Autumn 1961), p. 5.

57. This is not the first time this observation has been made. See Richard A. Baer, Jr. "The Supreme Court's Discriminatory Use of the Term Sectarian," *Journal of Law and Politics* 6, no. 3 (Spring 1990), pp. 449–468. In his review of Kohlberg's *Philosophy of Moral Development*, Michael Levin minced no words concluding that the program is nothing more than an "instrument of propaganda" (M. Levin, "The Stages of Man?" *Commentary* 73 [January 1982], pp. 84–86).

Chapter Eleven

1. See Nicolai Hartmann, *Ethics*, vol. 2, *Moral Values* (London: Allen and Unwin, 1932), p. 189.

2. William J. Bennett, *The Book of Virtues: A Treasury of Great Moral Stories* (New York: Simon and Schuster, 1994), p. 11.

3. It is but one illustration. Consider Gary Bauer's suggestion that Americans "*attempt to discover* a common body of ethical knowledge." In this, he tacitly acknowledges that no such body of ethical knowledge really exists except as a reconstruction of moralities of the past.

4. Pierre Bourdieu, *Outline of a Theory of Practice*, trans. Richard Nice (Cambridge: Cambridge University Press, 1977), p. 78.

5. David Tyack and Elizabeth Hansot, *Managers of Virtue: Public School Leadership in America, 1820–1980* (New York: Basic Books, 1982).

6. Douglas Gomery, "As the Dial Turns," *Wilson Quarterly* 17 (Autumn 1993), pp. 41–46.

7. I offer nothing new in these observations but rather draw on the insightful work of many others. See, for example, Todd Gitlin, "Flat and Happy," *Wilson Quarterly* 17 (Autumn 1993), pp. 47–55.

8. "Shame: How Do We Bring Back A Sense of Right and Wrong?" *Newsweek*, 6 February 1995. Consider too this remarkable statement from the Community of Caring: "The teaching of values, then, is inescapable. The question is not simply, 'Why teach values?' but, more importantly, 'What values do I embody as a teacher, coach, academic adviser, confidant or member of the school's staff? What kind of model am I? What do I stand for? What values am I conveying in my verbal and nonverbal interactions?'" (Community of Caring, "How to Create a Community of Caring School" [Washington, D.C.: The Joseph P. Kennedy Foundation, 1993/1994], p. 38). Here again, when a society has to pose such questions, the sacred and binding quality of moral life has disintegrated perhaps beyond repair. Rational deliberation over "what values" one stands for cannot repair it.

9. The quote is from Nietzsche, *Twilight of the Idols*, in *The Portable Nietzsche*, edited by Walter Kaufmann (New York: Penguin, 1982), p. 515. Philip Rieff, following Freud himself, observed the same in *The Triumph of the Therapeutic* (Chicago: University of Chicago Press, 1987), p. 261.

10. As C. S. Lewis put it, "We castrate and bid the geldings be fruitful" (C. S. Lewis, *The Abolition of Man* [New York: Macmillan, 1947], p. 35).

11. Thomas S. Kuhn, *The Structure of Scientific Revolutions* (Chicago: University of Chicago Press, 1962).

12. The problem in democratic theory is that it leads to indefensible propositions about the neutrality of the state. The distinction most regularly made is between "neutral" secularity and "partisan" sectarianism. Though some continue to press this distinction, ever since Polanyi, it has been less and less tenable. The specific dilemma it now poses in education has been sharply articulated by Stephen Arons.

> The state provides 'free' public education to all children of appropriate age and qualifications through its system of public schools. But the state may not condition

the provision of this education—whether it be a right or a privilege—upon the sacrifice by parents of their first Amendment rights. Yet this is precisely the effect of a school system that requires a child to attend a school controlled by a majority of the public in order to receive a "free" education. The public school will represent and attempt to inculcate values that a particular family may find abhorrent to its own basic beliefs and way of life. The family is then faced with the choice of (1) abandoning its beliefs in order to gain the benefit of a state-subsidized education, or (2) forfeiting the proffered government benefit in order to preserve the family belief structure from government interference. (Stephen Arons, "The Separation of School and State: *Pierce* Reconsidered," *Harvard Educational Review* 46 [1976], p. 100)

This structure is inequitable precisely because it violates the democratic principles of nondiscrimination and nonrepression.

13. The most commonly heard fear is that moral diversity will get out of hand; that this would provide terms by which, say, neo-Nazi schools would be permitted. The experiences of other nations that recognize cultural diversity suggest that this fear is way overdrawn. In these settings, democratic purposes are ensured by policies of nondiscrimination on the grounds of race, income, or intelligence; high standards of academic achievement in specified areas of inquiry; standard structures and equitable procedures of governance. See, for example, John Coons and Stephen Sugarman, *Education by Choice: The Case for Family Control* (Berkeley: University of California Press, 1978), pp. 133–189.

14. I draw directly from Robin Lovin, "The School and the Articulation of Values," *American Journal of Education* 96 (February 1988), p. 150.

15. I suggest a way these knotty problems might be addressed in my book, *Before the Shooting Begins: Searching for Democracy in America's Culture War* (New York: Free Press, 1994).

16. There is something to learn, in this regard, from the Dutch, the Belgians, and the Swiss, particularly in the realm of public education. See, for example, Charles Glenn, *Choice of Schools in Six Nations* (Washington, D.C.: U.S. Department of Education, 1989).

17. Amitai Etzioni provides a helpful discussion of these tensions for communitarianism in the last chapter of his book, *The New Golden Rule: Community and Morality in a Democratic Society* (New York: Basic Books, 1996).

SELECTED
BIBLIOGRAPHY

Abbott, John S. *The Mother at Home.* New York: American Tract Society, 1833.

Adler, Alfred. *The Practice and Theory of Individual Psychology,* 2d ed. New York: Harcourt Brace Jovanovich, 1927.

Arbuthnot, Jack Braeden, and David Faust. *Teaching Moral Reasoning: Theory and Practice.* New York: Harper and Row, 1981.

Aries, Phillipe. *Centuries of Childhood.* New York: Vintage, 1962.

Astone, Nan M., and Sara S. McLanahan. "Family Structure, Parental Rights and High School Completion." *American Sociological Review* 51 (1991).

Athearn, Walter. *Character Building in a Democracy.* New York: Macmillan, 1924.

Bainton, Roland. *Here I Stand: A Life of Martin Luther.* New York: Abingdon Press, 1950.

Baker, John S., Jr. "Parent-centered Education." *Notre Dame Journal of Law, Ethics, and Public Policy* (Summer 1988).

Barber, Benjamin R. "Public Talk and Civic Action: Educating for Participation in a Strong Democracy." *Social Education* 53 (October 1989).

Barboza, Steven, ed. *The African-American Book of Values: Classic Moral Stories.* New York: Doubleday, 1998.

Bauer, Gary. "The Moral of the Story: How to Teach Values in the Nation's Classrooms." *Policy Review* (Fall 1986).

Beck, C. M., B. S. Crittenden, and E. V. Sullivan, eds. *Moral Education.* Toronto, Ont.: University of Toronto Press, 1971.

Bellah, Robert N., Richard Madsen, William M. Sullivan, Ann Swindler, and Steven M. Tipton. *Habits of the Heart: Individualism and Commitment in American Life.* Berkeley: University of California Press, 1985.

Bennett, William J. "Moral Literacy and the Formation of Character." *USA Today* 117, no. 2518 (July 1988).

———. *The Book of Virtues: A Treasury of Great Moral Stories.* New York: Simon and Schuster, 1993.

Bennett, William J., and Edwin J. Delattre. "Moral Education in the Schools." *Public Interest* 50 (1978).

Berger, Peter, Brigitte Berger, and Hansfried Kellner. *The Homeless Mind.* New York: Vintage Books, 1974.

Bode, Boyd H. "The New Education Ten Years After." *New Republic* 63 (1930).

Bok, Derek. "Can Higher Education Foster Higher Morals?" *Business and Society Review,* no. 66 (Summer 1988).

Boylan, Anne M. *Sunday School: The Formation of An American Institution, 1790–1880.* New Haven: Yale University Press, 1988.

Bremner, Robert H. *Children and Youth in America: A Documentary History.* 2 vols. Cambridge, Mass.: Harvard University Press, 1970–71.

Brooks-Gunn, Jeanne, Greg J. Duncan, Pamela Kato Klebanov, Naomi Sealand. "Do Neighborhoods Influence Child and Adolescent Development?" *American Journal of Sociology* 99, no. 2 (September 1993).

Brown, Marianna. *Sunday-School Movements in America.* New York: Fleming Revell Company, 1901.

Burton, Roger V. "Generality of Honesty Reconsidered." *Psychological Review* 70, no. 6 (November 1963).

Butts, R. Freeman. *Public Education in the United States, From Revolution to Reform.* New York: Holt, Rinehart and Winston, 1978.

Butts, R. Freeman, Donald H. Peckenpaugh, and Howard Kirschenbaum. *The School's Role as Moral Authority.* Washington, D.C.: Association for Supervision and Curriculum Development, 1977.

Cable, Mary. *The Little Darlings: A History of Child Rearing in America.* New York: Scribner, 1975.

California Department of Education. *Toward a State of Esteem: The Final Report of the California Task Force to Promote Self-esteem and Personal and Social Responsibility.* Sacramento, Calif.: California Department of Education, 1991.

Carbone, Peter F., Jr., ed. *Value Theory and Education.* Malabar, Fla.: Robert E. Krieger Publishing Company, 1987.

Carter, Robert E. *Dimensions of Moral Education.* Toronto, Ont.: University of Toronto Press, 1984.

Chazan, Barry. *Contemporary Approaches to Moral Education.* New York: Teachers College Press, 1985.

Chess, Wayne A., and Julia M. Norlin. *Human Behavior and the Social Environment: A Social Systems Model.* 2d ed. Needham Heights, Mass.: Allyn and Bacon, 1991.

Choate, Anne Hyde, and Helen Ferris. *Juliette Low and the Girl Scouts: The Story of an American Woman 1860–1927.* New York: Girl Scouts of the U.S.A., 1928.

Church, Robert L. "Moral Education in the Schools." In *Morality Examined.* Edited by Lindley J. Stiles and Bruce D. Johnson. Princeton: Princeton Book Company, 1977.

Church, Robert L., and Michael W. Sedlak. *Education in the United States, An Interpretive History.* New York: Free Press, 1976.

Churchill, Larry. "The Teaching of Ethics and Moral Values in Teaching." *Journal of Higher Education* 53, no. 3 (1982).

Coe, George A. "What is Pragmatism?" *The Methodist Quarterly Review* 57 (April 1908).

Cohen, Albert K. *Delinquent Boys: The Culture of the Gang.* New York: Free Press, 1955.

Colby, Anne. "Evolution of a Moral-Developmental Theory." *New Directions for Child Development* 2 (1978).

Colby, Anne, and Lawrence Kohlberg. *The Measurement of Moral Judgment.* 2 vols. Cambridge: Cambridge University Press, 1987.

Cremin, Lawrence. *American Education: The Colonial Experience 1607–1783.* New York: Harper and Row, 1970.

Cunnyngham, W.G.E. *The Sunday School.* Nashville: Publishing House of the M. E. Church, South, 1902.

Damon, William. *The Moral Child.* New York: Free Press, 1988.

Damon, William, ed. *Moral Development,* no. 2. San Francisco: Jossey-Bass, 1978.

_____. *Child Development Today and Tomorrow.* San Francisco: Jossey-Bass, 1989.

David, Miriam. "Teaching Family Matters." *British Journal of Sociology Education* 7, no. 1 (1986).

Davis, E. Dale. "Should the Public Schools Teach Values?" *Phi Delta Kappan* 65 (January 1984).

Demos, John. "Developmental Perspectives on the History of Childhood." In *The Family in History,* edited by Theodore K. Rabb and Robert I. Rotberg. New York: Harper and Row, 1973.

DePalma, David J., and Jeanne M. Foley, eds. *Moral Development, Current Theory and Research.* Hillsdale, N.J.: Lawrence Erlbaum Associates, Inc., 1975.

Derlega, Valerian J., and Janusz Grzelak, eds. *Cooperation and Helping Behavior.* New York: Academic Press, 1982.

DeVries, Rheta, and Betty Zan. *Moral Classrooms, Moral Children: Creating a Constructivist Atmosphere in Early Education.* New York: Teachers College Press, 1994.

Dewey, John. "Teaching Ethics in the High School." *Educational Review* 7 (November 1893).

_____. *The Study of Ethics: A Syllabus.* Ann Arbor: Register Publishing Co., 1894.

_____. *The School and Society.* Chicago: University of Chicago Press, 1900.

_____. *Democracy and Education.* New York: Macmillan, 1916.

_____. *Reconstruction in Philosophy.* New York: Henry Holt and Co., 1920.

_____. *Human Nature and Conduct.* New York: Modern Library, 1922.

_____. "Credo." *Forum* 83 (March 1930).

_____. *Problems of Men.* New York: Philosophical Library, 1946.

_____. *Theory of the Moral Life.* New York: Holt, Rinehart and Winston, 1960.

_____. *Moral Principles in Education.* Carbondale: Southern Illinois University Press, 1975.

Dillon, John B. *Oddities of Colonial Legislation in America, As Applied to the Public Lands, Primitive Education, Religion, Morals, Indians, Etc., With Authentic Records of the Origin and Growth of Pioneer Settlements. Embracing Also a Condensed History of the States and Territories, with a Summary of the Territorial Expansion, Civil Progress and Development of the Nation.* Indianapolis: Robert Douglas Publishers, 1879.

Dogget, Laurence. *History of the Young Men's Christian Association.* New York: International Committee of Young Men's Christian Association, 1896.

Doyle, Denis P. "Education and Character." *Phi Delta Kappan* 78 (February 1997).

Dreikurs, Rudolf. *Children: The Challenge.* New York: E. P. Dutton, 1964.

Durkheim, Emile. *The Division of Labor in Society.* New York: Free Press, 1984.

_____. *Moral Education: A Study in the Theory and Application of the Sociology of Education.* New York: Free Press, 1961.

Duska, Ronald, and Mariellen Whelan. *Moral Development*. New York: Paulist Press, 1975.

Dwight, Theodore, Jr., *The Father's Book, or, Suggestions for the Government and Instruction of Young Children, on Principles Appropriate to a Christian Country*. Springfield: G & C Merriam, 1834.

Eisenberg, N., and J. Strayer, eds. *Empathy and its Development*. New York: Cambridge University Press, 1987.

Emerson, Ralph Waldo. *Character*. Philadelphia: Henry Altemus, 1896.

———. *Essays*. New York: Houghton, Mifflin and Company, 1904.

Emirbayer, Mustafa Kemal. "Moral Education in America, 1830–1990: A Contribution to the Sociology of Moral Education." Ph.D. diss., Harvard University, 1989. Ann Arbor: University of Michigan Dissertation Services.

Erickson, Judith B. "Non-Formal Education in Organizations for American Youth." *Children Today* (January-February 1986).

Etzioni, Amitai. *The Moral Dimension: Toward a New Economics*. New York: Free Press, 1988.

———. "Money, Power and Fame." *Newsweek*, 18 September 1989.

———. *The Spirit of Community*. New York: Crown, 1993.

———. *The New Golden Rule: Community and Morality in a Democratic Society*. New York: Basic Books, 1996.

Evans, Richard I. *Jean Piaget, The Man and His Ideas*. New York: E. P. Dutton, 1973.

Finn, Chester E., Jr. "Narcissus Goes to School." *Commentary* 89, no. 6 (June 1990).

Gergen, Kenneth. *The Saturated Self*. New York: Basic Books, 1991.

Gilligan, Carol. "In a Different Voice: Women's Conceptions of Self and of Morality." *Harvard Educational Review* 47, no. 4 (November 1977).

———. "The Contribution of Women's Thought to Developmental Theory: The Elimination of Sex Bias in Moral Development Research and Education." NIE-G-80-0086, Washington, D.C.: National Institute of Education.

———. *In a Different Voice*. Cambridge, Mass.: Harvard University Press, 1982.

Gilligan, Carol, Janie Victoria Ward, and Jill McLean Taylor, eds. with Betty Bardige. *Mapping the Moral Domain: A Contribution of Women's Thinking to Psychological Theory and Education*. Cambridge, Mass.: Harvard University Press, 1988.

Glasser, William. *Schools Without Failure*. New York: Harper and Row, 1969.

Goodlad, John. "Studying the Education of Educators: Values-Driven Inquiry." *Phi Delta Kappan* 70 (October 1990).

Gough, Pauline B. "The Key to Improving Schools: An Interview with William Glasser." *Phi Delta Kappan* 68 (May 1987).

Gow, Kathleen M. *Yes Virginia, There is Right and Wrong!* Toronto, Ont.: John Wiley and Sons Canada Ltd., 1980.

Green, Thomas F. "The Formation of Conscience in an Age of Technology." *American Journal of Education* 94 (November 1985).

Greer, Colin, and Herbert Kohl, eds. *A Call to Character*. New York: HarperCollins, 1995.

Gross, David M., and Sophfronia Scott. "Proceeding with Caution." *Time*, 16 July 1990.

Gulick, Luther Halsey. "The Camp Fire Girls and the New Relation of Women to the World." National Education Association, General Session, 1912.

Haan, Norma. "Processes of Moral Development: Cognitive or Social Disequilibrium?" *Developmental Psychology* 21, no. 6 (1985).

Haan, Norma, Eliane Aerts, and Bruce A. B. Cooper. *On Moral Grounds.* New York: New York University Press, 1985.

Haan, Norma, Robert N. Bellah, Paul Rabinow, and William M. Sullivan, eds. *Social Science as Moral Inquiry.* New York: Columbia University Press, 1983.

Hall, G. Stanley. *Adolescence.* 2 vols. New York: D. Appleton and Company, 1905.

Hall, Robert T., and John U. Davis. *Moral Education in Theory and Practice.* Buffalo, N.Y.: Prometheus Books, 1975.

Hamilton, Alexander, James Madison, and John Jay. *The Federalist Papers.* New York: New American Library of World Literature, 1961.

Hamner, Tommie J., and Pauline Hamner. *Parenting in Contemporary Society.* 2d ed. Englewood Cliffs, N.J.: Prentice Hall, 1990.

Hanushek, Eric A., and John E. Jackson. *Statistical Methods for Social Scientists.* New York: Academic Press, 1977.

Hargreaves, David H. "A Sociological Critique of Individualism in Education." *British Journal of Educational Studies* 28, no. 3 (June 1980).

Harmin, Merrill, Howard Kirschenbaum, and Sidney B. Simon. *Clarifying Values Through Subject Matter, Applications for the Classroom.* Minneapolis, Minn.: Winston Press, 1974.

Hart, Gordon M. *Values Clarification for Counselors.* Springfield, Ill.: Charles C. Thomas, 1978.

Hartshorne, Hugh, and Mark A. May. *Studies in the Nature of Character.* 3 vols. New York: Macmillan, 1928–30.

Hauerwas, Stanley. *A Community of Character.* Notre Dame, Ind.: University of Notre Dame Press, 1981.

Hersh, Richard H., John P. Miller, and Glen D. Fielding. *Models of Moral Education.* New York: Longman, 1980.

Hey, Robert P. "Experts Concerned Over US Ethics." *The Christian Science Monitor,* 19 June 1989.

Hirsch, E. D. *Cultural Literacy: What Every American Needs to Know.* Boston: Houghton Mifflin, 1987.

Hirst, Paul H. *Moral Education in a Secular Society.* London: University of London Press, 1974.

Honig, Bill. *Last Chance for Our Children: How You Can Help Save Our Schools.* Reading, Mass.: Addison-Wesley, 1985.

Hopkins, Howard. *History of the Y.M.C.A. in North America.* New York: Association Press, 1951.

Howe, Leland W., and Mary Martha Howe. *Personalizing Education.* New York: Hart Publishing Company, 1975.

Hunt, Thomas C., and Marilyn M. Maxson. *Religion and Morality in American Schooling.* Washington, D.C.: University Press of America, 1981.

Hunter, James Davison. *Evangelicalism: The Coming Generation.* Chicago: University of Chicago Press, 1988.

_____. *Girl Scouts Survey on the Beliefs and Moral Values of America's Children.* New York: Girls Scouts of the United States of America, 1989.

_____.*Culture Wars: The Struggle to Define America.* New York: Basic Books, 1991.

_____.*Before the Shooting Begins: Searching for Democracy in America's Culture War.* New York: Free Press, 1994.

Hutchins, William J. "The Children's Morality Code." *Journal of the National Educational Association* 13 (1924).

International Sunday School Association. *The Development of the Sunday-School 1780–1905. The Official Report of the Eleventh International Sunday-School Convention, Toronto, Canada, June 23–27, 1905.* Boston: The Executive Committee of the International Sunday-School Association, 1905.

Izard, Carroll E., Jerome Kagan, and Robert B. Zajonc, eds. *Emotions, Cognitions and Behavior.* Cambridge: Cambridge University Press, 1984.

Jeal, Tim. *Baden-Powell.* London: Hutchinson, 1989.

Jencks, Christopher, and Susan E. Meyer. "The Social Consequences of Growing Up in a Poor Neighborhood." In *Inner-city Poverty in the United States,* edited by Laurence E. Lynn, Jr. and Michael G. H. McGeary. Washington, D.C.: National Academy, 1990.

Jencks, Christopher, and Paul E. Peterson. *The Urban Underclass.* Washington, D.C.: Brookings Institute, 1991.

Kaestle, Carl F. *Pillars of the Republic: Common Schools and American Society, 1780–1860.* New York: Hill and Wang, 1983.

Kagan, Jerome, and Sharon Lamb, eds. *The Emergence of Morality in Young Children.* Chicago: University of Chicago Press, 1987.

Kay, William. *Moral Development.* London: George Allen and Unwin, 1970.

Kett, Joseph F. "Adolescence and Youth in Nineteenth-Century America." In *The Family in History,* edited by Theodore K. Rabb and Robert I. Rotberg. New York: Harper and Row, 1973.

_____. *Rites of Passage: Adolescence in America 1790 to the Present.* New York: Basic Books, 1977.

Kierkegaard, Søren. *The Present Age.* Translated by Alexander Dru. New York: Harper and Row, 1962.

Kilpatrick, William. *Why Johnny Can't Tell Right from Wrong.* New York: Simon and Schuster, 1992.

Kilpatrick, William, Gregory Wolfe, and Suzanne Wolfe, eds. *Books That Build Character: A Guide to Teaching Your Child Moral Values Through Stories.* New York: Simon and Schuster, 1994.

Kirk, Russell. *Decadence and Renewal in the Higher Learning.* South Bend, Ind.: Gateway Editions, 1978.

_____. "Virtue: Can It Be Taught?" *Modern Age* 26 (Summer/Fall 1982).

Kirschenbaum, Howard. *Advanced Value Clarification.* La Jolla, Calif. University Associates, 1977.

Kohlberg, Lawrence. "Revisions in the Theory and Practice of Moral Development." *New Directions for Child Development,* 2 (1978).

_____. *Essays on Moral Development.* Vol. 2, *The Psychology of Moral Development.* San Francisco: Harper and Row, 1981.

Kohn, Alfie. "Caring Kids: The Role of the Schools." *Phi Delta Kappan* 72 (March 1991).

_____. "Choices for Children: Why and How to Let Students Decide." *Phi Delta Kappan* 75 (September 1993).

_____. "The Truth About Self-Esteem." *Phi Delta Kappan* 76 (December 1994).

_____. "Discipline is the Problem—Not the Solution." *Learning* 24 (October/November 1995).

_____. *Beyond Discipline: From Compliance to Community.* Alexandria: Association for Supervision and Curriculum Development, 1996.

_____. "How Not to Teach Values: A Critical Look at Character Education." *Phi Delta Kappan* 78 (February 1997).

Krauthammer, Charles. "Education: Doing Bad and Feeling Good." *Time,* 5 February 1990.

Kuhmerker, Lisa, Marcia Mentkowski, and V. Lois Erickson, eds. *Evaluating Moral Development and Evaluating Educational Programs That Have a Value Dimension.* Schenectady, N.Y.: Character Research Press, 1980.

Kuhn, Thomas S. *The Structure of Scientific Revolutions.* Chicago: University of Chicago Press, 1962.

Kurtines, William M., and Jacob L. Gewirtz, eds. *Morality, Moral Behavior, and Moral Development.* New York: John Wiley and Sons, 1984.

Lankard, Frank Glenn. *A History of the American Sunday School Curriculum.* New York: Abingdon Press, 1927.

Lauderdale, William B. "Moral Intentions in the History of American Education." *Theory into Practice* 14, no. 4 (1975).

Lehman, Daniel J. "Whatever Happened to Sunday School?" *Christian Century,* 19 April 1989.

Leming, James S. *Contemporary Approaches to Moral Education: An Annotated Bibliography and Guide to Research.* New York: Garland Publishing, 1983.

_____. *Foundations of Moral Education: An Annotated Bibliography.* Westport, Conn.: Greenwood Press, 1983.

Lester, Julius. "Morality and Education." *Democracy* 2 (April 1982).

Levin, Michael. "The Stages of Man?" *Commentary* 73 (January 1982).

Lickona, Thomas. "Educating the Moral Child." *Principal* 68 (November 1988).

_____. "Four Strategies for Fostering Character Development in Children." *Phi Delta Kappan* 69 (February 1988).

_____. "Moral Development in the Elementary School Classroom." In *Handbook of Moral Behavior and Development.* Vol. 3. Edited by William Kurtines and Jacob Gewirtz. Hillsdale, N.J.: Lawrence Erlbaum Associates, 1991.

_____. *Educating for Character: How Our Schools Can Teach Respect and Responsibility.* New York: Bantam, 1992.

Locke, John. *Some Thoughts Concerning Education.* Cambridge: Cambridge University Press, 1880.

Lovin, Robin W. "The School and the Articulation of Values." *American Journal of Education* 96 (February 1988).

Low, Juliette. "Girl Scouts as an Educational Force." *U.S. Department of the Interior, Bureau of Education Bulletin*, no. 33, 1919.

Lund, Leonard, and Cathleen Wild. *Ten Years After "A Nation at Risk."* New York: Conference Board, 1993.

Lynn, Robert, and Elliot Wright. *The Big Little School: Sunday Child of American Protestantism.* New York: Harper and Row, 1971.

Macaulay, J., and L. Berkowitz. *Altruism and Helping Behavior.* New York: Academic Press, 1970.

MacIntyre, Alasdair. *After Virtue.* Notre Dame, Ind.: University of Notre Dame Press, 1984.

Macleod, David I. "Act Your Age: Boyhood, Adolescence, and the Rise of the Boy Scouts of America." *Journal of Social History* 16, no. 2 (Winter 1982).

———. *Building Character in the American Boy: The Boy Scouts, YMCA, and their Forerunners, 1870–1920.* Madison, Wis.: University of Wisconsin Press, 1983.

Marquand, Robert. "Moral Education, Has 'Values Neutrality' Left Students Adrift?" *Christian Science Monitor*, 30 January 1987.

Mather, Cotton. *Magnala Christi Americana.* Vol. 1. Hartford: Silas Andrus and Son, 1853.

Maxwell, Joe. "Will Sunday School Survive?" *Christianity Today*, 9 December 1988.

May, Philip R. *Moral Education in School.* London: Methuen Educational, 1971.

Mayer, Susan E. "How Much Does a High School's Racial and Socioeconomic Mix Affect Graduation and Teenage Fertility Rates?" In *The Urban Underclass*, edited by Christopher Jencks and Paul E. Peterson. Washington, D.C.: Brookings Institute, 1991.

McCluskey, Neil Gerard. *Public Schools and Moral Education.* New York: Columbia University Press, 1958.

McGuffey, W. H. *The Eclectic First Reader.* 1836. Reprint, Milford, Mich.: Mott Media, 1982.

Meilaender, Gilbert C. *The Theory and Practice of Virtue.* Notre Dame, Ind.: University of Notre Dame Press, 1984.

Merrill, George R. "Robert Raikes and the Eighteenth Century." In *The Development of the Sunday-School 1780–1905.* Boston: Fort Hill Press, 1905.

Miller, Alice. *For Your Own Good: Hidden Cruelty in Child-rearing.* Translated by Hildegarde and Hunter Hannun. New York: Farrar, Straus and Giroux, 1983.

———. *Thou Shalt Not Be Aware: Society's Betrayal of the Child.* Translated by Hildegarde and Hunter Hannun. New York: Farrar, Straus and Giroux, 1998.

Miller, James Russell. *The Building of Character.* New York: Thomas Y. Crowell Company, 1894.

Miller, Perry, and Thomas H. Johnson, eds. *The Puritans.* Vol. 2. New York: Harper and Row, 1963.

Miller, Walter. "Lower-class Culture as a Generating Milieu of Gang Delinquency." In *The Sociology of Crime and Delinquency*, edited by Marvin E. Wolfgang, Leonard Savitz, and Norman Johnston. New York: Wiley, 1970.

Mischel, Theodore, ed. *Cognitive Development and Epistemology.* New York: Academic Press, 1971.

Montesquieu, Charles de Secondat. *The Spirit of the Laws*. Translated by Anne M. Cohler, Basia C. Miller, and Harold Stone. Cambridge: Cambridge University Press, 1989.

Moody, Eleazar. "The School of Good Manners." In *The Colonial American Family: Collected Essays*. New York: Arno Press, 1972.

Mosher, Ralph, ed. *Moral Education, A First Generation of Research and Development*. New York: Praeger Publishers, 1980.

Moskos, Charles. *A Call to Civic Service: National Service for Country and Community*. New York: Free Press, 1988.

National Board of Y.W.C.A. Education and Research Division. "Educational Work of the Young Women's Christian Association." *U.S. Department of the Interior, Bureau of Education Bulletin*, no. 26, 1923.

National Commission on Excellence in Education. "A Nation at Risk: The Imperative for Educational Reform: A Report to the Nation and the Secretary of Education, U.S. Department of Education." Washington, D.C.: GPO, 1983.

National Council of Churches in Christ in the United States. *The Church's Educational Ministry: A Curriculum Plan*. St. Louis: Bethany Press, 1966.

National Education Association. *Moral and Spiritual Values in the Public Schools*. Washington, D.C.: National Education Association, 1951.

Newman, Anne, and Dinah Richard. *Healthy Sex Education in Your Schools: A Parents' Handbook*. Pomona, Calif.: Focus on the Family Publishing, 1990.

Nolan, James L., Jr. *The Therapeutic State*. New York: New York University Press, 1998.

Oates, Whitney. *Aristotle and the Problem of Value*. Princeton: Princeton University Press, 1963.

Peckham, Morse. "Toward a Theory of Romanticism II: Reconsiderations." *Studies in Romanticism* 1, no. 1 (Autumn 1961).

_____. *The Triumph of Romanticism*. Columbia, S.C.: University of South Carolina Press, 1970.

Phillips, Adam. *On Flirtation: Psychoanalytic Essays on the Uncommitted Life*. Cambridge, Mass.: Harvard University Press, 1994.

Piaget, Jean. *The Moral Judgment of the Child*. New York: Free Press, 1969.

_____. "Intelligence and Affectivity: Their Relation During Child Development." Palo Alto, Calif.: Annual Reviews, 1981.

Plutarch. *The Lives of the Noble Grecians and Romans*. Translated by John Dryden. New York: Modern Library, 1864.

Power, F. Clark, Ann Higgins, and Lawrence Kohlberg. *Lawrence Kohlberg's Approach to Moral Education*. New York: Columbia University Press, 1989.

Pritchard, Ivor. "Character Education: Research Prospects and Problems." *American Journal of Education* 96 (August 1988).

Purpel, David, and Kevin Ryan, eds. *Moral Education . . . It Comes With the Territory*. Berkeley: McCutchan Publishing Corporation, 1976.

Pyskowski, Irene S. "Moral Values and the Schools—Is There a Way Out of the Maze?" *Education* 107, no. 1 (Fall 1986): 41–48.

Rabb, Theodore K., and Robert I. Rotberg, eds. *The Family in History*. New York: Harper and Row, 1973.

Reichley, A. James. *Religion in American Public Life*. Washington, D.C.: The Brookings Institute, 1985.

Reimer, Joseph, Diana Pritchard Paolitto, and Richard H. Hersh. *Promoting Moral Growth from Piaget to Kohlberg*. 2d ed. New York: Longman, 1983.

Rich, John Martin, and Joseph L. DeVitis. *Theories of Moral Development*. Springfield, Ill.: Charles C. Thomas, 1985.

Richardson, Norman E., and Ormond E. Loomis. *The Boy Scout Movement Applied by the Church*. New York: Charles Scribner's Sons, 1915.

Rieff, Philip. *The Triumph of the Therapeutic*. Chicago: University of Chicago Press, 1987.

_____. *The Feeling Intellect*. Edited by Jonathan B. Imber. Chicago: University of Chicago Press, 1990.

Roche, George. *A World Without Heroes*. Hillsdale, Mich.: Hillsdale College Press, 1987.

Rodgers, Carl. "Becoming a Person: The Nellie Heldt Lectures." Oberlin College, 1954.

_____. *On Becoming a Person*. Boston: Houghton-Mifflin, 1961.

Rosen, Hugh. *The Development of Sociomoral Knowledge*. New York: Columbia University Press, 1980.

Rosenthall, Michael. *The Character Factory*. New York: Pantheon Books, 1986.

Rothstein, Stanley William. "The Sociology of Schooling." *Urban Education* 21, no. 3 (October 1986).

Ryan, Kevin. "Character and Coffee Mugs." *Education Week*, 17 May 1995.

Ryan, Kevin, and G. McLeon, eds. *Character Development in Schools and Beyond*. New York: Praeger, 1987.

Sampson, Edward E. "Cognitive Psychology as Ideology." *American Psychologist* 36, no. 7 (July 1981).

Scharf, Peter, ed. *Readings in Moral Education*. Minneapolis: Winston Press, 1978.

Schlossman, Steven L. "Before Home Start: Notes toward a History of Parent Education in America, 1879–1929." *Harvard Educational Review* 46 (1976).

Schwartz, Henrietta, and Edward A. Wynne. "Transmitting Values to the Young: A Cross-Cultural Perspective." In *Equity in Values Education: Do the Values Education Aspects of Public School Curricula Deal Fairly with Diverse Belief Systems?* Final report prepared for the U.S. Department of Education. Washington, D.C.: National Institute of Education, 1985.

Sebbelov, Gerda. "Camp Fire Girls." National Education Association, General Session, 1912.

Seymour, Jack L. *From Sunday School to Church School: Continuities in Protestant Church Education in the United States: 1860–1929*. Washington, D.C.: University Press of America, 1982.

Sherman, Nancy. *The Fabric of Character: Aristotle's Theory of Virtue*. Oxford: Clarendon Press, 1989.

Shires, Paul R. "How Do You Keep the Children Moral After School?" *Social Education* 51 (March 1987).

Shultz, Gladys Denny, and Daisy Gordon Lawrence. *Lady From Savannah: The Life of Juliette Low*. New York: J. B. Lippincott Company, 1958.

Sichel, Betty. *Moral Education: Character, Community, and Ideals*. Philadelphia: Temple University Press, 1988.

Simon, Sidney, Leland Howe, and Howard Kirshenbaum. *Values Clarification*. Rev. ed. New York: Hart, 1978.

Simpson, Elizabeth Leonie. "Moral Development Research: A Case Study of Scientific Cultural Bias." *Human Development* 17, no. 2 (1974).

Sisson, Edward O. *The Essentials of Character: A Practical Study of the Aim of Moral Education*. New York: Macmillan, 1910.

Sizer, Theodore R., and Nancy F. Sizer, eds. *Moral Education: Five Lectures*. Cambridge, Mass.: Harvard University Press, 1970.

Smith, Mathew Hale. *The Bible, the Rod, and Religion in Common Schools*. Boston: Redding and Co., 1847.

Smith, Maury. *A Practical Guide to Value Clarification*. La Jolla, Calif.: University Associates, Inc., 1977.

Sommers, Christina Hoff. "Ethics Without Virtue, Moral Education in America." *American Scholar* 53 (Summer 1984).

_____. "Teaching the Virtues." *Public Interest* 111 (Spring 1993).

Spicer, Michael W., and Edward W. Hill. "Evaluating Parental Choice in Public Education: Policy Beyond Monopoly Model." *American Journal of Education* 98 (February 1990).

Sprinthall, Norman A., and Ralph L. Mosher. *Value Development . . . As the Aim of Education*. Schenectady, N. Y.: Character Research Press, 1978.

Stafford, Tim. "This Little Light of Mine." *Christianity Today*, 8 October 1990.

_____. "Helping Johnny Be Good." *Christianity Today*, 11 September 1995.

Starke, D. *Character: How to Strengthen It*. New York: Funk and Wagnalls Company, 1916.

Stiles, Lindley J., and Bruce D. Johnson, eds. *Morality Examined: Guidelines for Teachers*. Princeton: Princeton Book Co., Publishers, 1977.

Strommen, Merton. "The Future of Sunday School: A Researcher's Reflection." *Religious Education* 78 (Summer 1983).

Sullivan, Edmund V. "A Study of Kohlberg's Structural Theory of Moral Development: A Critique of Liberal Social Science Ideology." *Human Development* 20 (1977).

Swidler, Ann. "Culture in Action: Symbols and Strategies." *American Sociological Review* 51 (April 1986).

Tappan, Mark B., and Lyn Mikel Brown. "Stories Told and Lessons Learned: Toward a Narrative Approach to Moral Development and Moral Education." *Harvard Educational Review* 59, no. 2 (1989).

Taylor, Charles. *The Sources of the Self: The Making of Modern Identity*. Cambridge, Mass.: Harvard University Press, 1989.

Tocqueville, Alexis de. *Democracy in America*. Vol. 1. New York: Anchor-Doubleday, 1969.

Trumbell, Charles. "The Nineteenth Century Sunday School." In *The Development of the Sunday-School 1780–1905*. Boston: Fort Hill Press, 1905.

Tyack, David. "The Kingdom of God and the Common School: Protestant Ministers and the Educational Awakening in the West." *Harvard Educational Review* 36 (Fall 1966).

Vitz, Paul C. "The Use of Stories in Moral Development." *American Psychologist* 45, no. 6 (June 1990).

Wadsworth, Benjamin. "The Well-Ordered Family." In *The Colonial American Family: Collected Essays*. New York: Arno Press, 1972.

Wagner, Melinda Bollar. *God's Schools: Choice and Compromise in American Society*. New Brunswick, N.J.: Rutgers University Press, 1990.

Wallace, James D. *Virtues and Vices*. Ithaca, N.Y.: Cornell University Press, 1978.

Warren, Heather A. "Character, Public Schooling, and Religious Education, 1920–1934." *Religion and American Culture* 7, no. 1 (Winter 1997).

Warwick, Dennis, and John Williams. "History and the Sociology of Education." *British Journal of Sociology of Education* 1, no. 3 (1980).

Washburn, Ruth Wendell. *Children Have Their Reasons*. New York: Appleton-Century, 1942.

Washington, Booker T. *Character Building*. New York: Doubleday, Page and Company, 1902.

Watson, John B. *Psychological Care of Infant and Child*. New York: W. W. Norton and Company, Inc., 1928.

Weed, Enos. *The Educational Directory*. Morristown, N.J.: Peter A. Johnson's Book-binder, 1803.

Westerhoff, John H., III. *McGuffey and His Readers: Piety, Morality and Education in Nineteenth Century America*. Nashville, Tenn.: Abingdon, 1978.

Wiggin, Kate. *Children's Rights: A Book of Nursery Logic*. Boston: Houghton Mifflin, 1892.

Wilson, James Q. "The Rediscovery of Character: Private Virtue and Public Policy." *The Public Interest*, no. 81 (Fall 1985).

_____. *On Character*. Washington, D.C.: AEI Press, 1991.

Wilson, James Q., and Richard J. Herrnstein. *Crime and Human Nature*. New York: Simon and Schuster, 1985.

Wynne, Edward A. "The Great Tradition in Education: Transmitting Moral Values," *Educational Leadership* 43, no. 4 (1985).

Wynne, Edward A., and Paul C. Vitz. "The Major Models of Moral Education: An Evaluation." In National Institute of Education. *Equity in Values Education*. Final report. Washington, D.C.: National Institute of Education, Department of Education, July 1985.

Wynne, Edward A., and Herbert J. Walberg. "The Complementary Goals of Character Development and Academic Excellence," *Educational Leadership* 43, no. 4 (1985).

Wynne, Edward A., and Mary Hess. "Long-Term Trends in Youth Conduct and the Revival of Traditional Value Patterns," *Educational Evaluation and Policy Analysis* 8, no. 3 (Fall 1986).

INDEX

Production vs Consumption
- goals / career / priorities / quality/reward
life

872 - 1910 International Uniform Lessons
7 years worth of lessons for
any age.

If a child or person is going to utilize my
finances or time or other resources
to further his/her education, then they
should choose to do so under my
ideology, or else go elsewhere for an
education?

LaVergne, TN USA
06 October 2010

199873LV00001B/7/A

9 780465 031771